Ritual and Economy in a
Pre-Columbian Chiefdom

Ritual and Economy in a Pre-Columbian Chiefdom

THE EL CAJÓN REGION OF HONDURAS

Kenneth Hirth
Susan Hirth
George Hasemann
Gloria Lara-Pinto

UNIVERSITY PRESS OF COLORADO
Denver

Published by University Press of Colorado
1580 North Logan Street, Suite 660
PMB 39883
Denver, Colorado 80203-1942

The University Press of Colorado is a proud member of the Association of University Presses.

The University Press of Colorado is a cooperative publishing enterprise supported, in part, by Adams State University, Colorado State University, Fort Lewis College, Metropolitan State University of Denver, University of Alaska Fairbanks, University of Colorado, University of Denver, University of Northern Colorado, University of Wyoming, Utah State University, and Western Colorado University.

∞ This paper meets the requirements of the ANSI/NISO Z39.48-1992 (Permanence of Paper).

ISBN: 978-1-64642-474-0 (hardcover)
ISBN: 978-1-64642-475-7 (ebook)
https://doi.org/10.5876/9781646424757

Library of Congress Cataloging-in-Publication Data

Names: Hirth, Kenn, author. | Hirth, Susan Grant, author. | Hasemann, George, author. | Lara
    Pinto, Gloria, 1952– author.
Title: Ritual and economy in a pre-Columbian chiefdom : the El Cajón region of Honduras /
    Kenneth Hirth, Susan Hirth, George Hassemann, Gloria Lara-Pinto.
Other titles: El Cajón region of Honduras
Description: Denver : University Press of Colorado, [2023] | Includes bibliographical refer-
    ences and index.
Identifiers: LCCN 2023014121 (print) | LCCN 2023014122 (ebook) | ISBN 9781646424740
    (hardcover) | ISBN 9781646424757 (ebook)
Subjects: LCSH: Chiefdoms—Honduras—Cajón Reservoir—Antiquities. | Rites and ceremo-
    nies—Honduras—Cajón Reservoir—Antiquities. | Excavations (Archaeology)—Honduras. |
    Cajón Reservoir (Honduras)—Antiquities. | Honduras—Antiquities.
Classification: LCC F1505.1.C35 H57 2023 (print) | LCC F1505.1.C35 (ebook) | DDC
    972.83/01—dc23/eng/20230425
LC record available at https://lccn.loc.gov/2023014121
LC ebook record available at https://lccn.loc.gov/2023014122

Subvention funds provided by Penn State University.

Cover photographs courtesy of the authors.

To George Hasemann
(1944–1998)
Friend, scholar, spouse, father, and a great field archaeologist

Contents

Figures

In 1978 the Empresa Nacional de Energia Electrica of Honduras initiated planning with the Motor-Columbus Engineers of Baden, Switzerland, for construction of the El Cajón dam and hydroelectric power facility directly below the intersection of the Sulaco and Humuya Rivers (ENEE 1978). Cultural and environmental impact studies were carried out in 1979, and the Proyecto Arqueológico El Cajón (PAEC) was initiated by the Instituto Hondureño de Antropología e Historia (IHAH) to study the prehistoric remains to be destroyed by flooding in the reservoir impact zone. Drs. Hirth (director), Lara-Pinto (co-director), and Hasemann (field director) were contracted by the IHAH to design and oversee the salvage investigations. This was the IHAH's first large-scale regional project in a non-Maya area of west-central Honduras. An archaeological survey was initiated and completed in 1980 that assessed the type and scale of prehispanic resources to be destroyed once the hydroelectric facility was completed. Additional archaeological explorations were conducted from 1981 to 1984 that intensively excavated the four largest centers in the region, tested twenty-four sites of intermediary and small size, and conducted a second survey of the El Cajón highlands outside the reservoir impact zone to understand the broad scope of prehispanic adaptation in the region. This publication provides an overview of the main contributions of the El Cajón research to our understanding of prehistoric adaptation in west-central Honduras.

https://doi.org/10.5876/9781646424757.c000a

The Proyecto Arquelógico El Cajón (PAEC) was conducted over the ten-year period between 1980 and 1989. As a national project, the IHAH took charge of the publication and dissemination of research results in Spanish from the investigation (Hirth, Lara-Pinto, and Hasemann 1989, 1990). Unfortunately, budget cuts and limited financial resources never led to the publication of subsequent research findings (e.g., Hirth, Lara-Pinto, and Hasemann n.d.). With permission of the IHAH, this English volume provides a summary of some of the project's major research findings in the hope that funds can be found to translate and publish it and other volumes that present the results in Spanish in Honduras.

The PAEC project adopted an explicit ecological approach to carry out the research. Several investigators had characterized many of the pre-Columbian societies of west-central Honduras as part of Mesoamerica's eastern frontier—in short, as part of the Mesoamerican periphery and an area of lesser cultural development than was found in the Maya sites of Copán and Quirigua further to the west. The approach taken here was to study the El Cajón region on its own terms rather than automatically place it on the Mesoamerican periphery. The study did not assume that an understanding of Mesoamerican society provided an adequate model for interpreting all its pre-hispanic remains. There were cultural similarities to be sure in the construction of platform mounds, ritual plazas, and an agricultural regime based on maize agriculture. But there were also differences that included a lack of evidence for hereditary rulers, the presence of smaller polities, the absence of writing, and what appeared to be a heavier emphasis on feasting as a central feature of ritual activity. The questions that intrigued us were how inhabitants exploited their environment, how their society was organized and integrated, and whether people in El Cajón interacted with groups in lower Central America.

The El Cajon region was chosen by the national government for the construction of the hydroelectric power facility because of its topographic suitability and low resident population, which meant that flooding the reservoir impact zone would displace only a small number of families. In logistical terms, the area was remote and presented myriad problems for archaeological research. No road entered the reservoir impact zone until we built one into Salitrón Viejo, which served as the project base camp. The initial survey was done by pedestrian survey, stopping and camping at vega pockets along the Sulaco and Humuya Rivers to record and map sites. Excavation teams working along the more than 120 km of river frontage had to be provisioned by mule team, which was a slow process. Archaeologists had to walk in and out of the zone; it usually took two to three days to travel back to Tegucigalpa to get provisions, obtain funds to meet worker payrolls, or take a break from fieldwork once every two to three weeks. There was no electricity, refrigeration, communications, and running water (except in the rivers). Archaeologists lived in tents and in the process enjoyed the majestic nights that were unencumbered by modern noise and electric lights. Everyone participating in the project made many personal sacrifices to conduct this research and grew enormously, both professionally and personally, in the process. All of the project's logistic challenges—from packing mules and dealing with local labor to building laboratory and dormitory equipment—were solved by George Hasemann, the project's field director, whose incredibly diverse skill set and ingenuity solved every imaginable problem the project encountered. A full discussion of project challenges can be found in Hirth (2023).

This research would not have been possible without the extensive support of the IHAH, its administrative personnel and archaeological support team, and members of the restauration unit, as well as the former Museo Nacional de Antropología. We are especially indebted to all the archaeologists who worked in the field and conducted a range of important laboratory analyses. The names of project personnel are listed next in this volume. We are deeply grateful to directors and administrators of the IHAH who made this research possible. Foremost among these are Adan Cueva, Vito Veliz, Ricardo Agurcia, Víctor Cruz, and José María Casco.

We are also indebted to all the national and international agencies that have provided support and funding for the research. National institutions that supported this research include ENEE, IHAH, and the Honduran National Congress. Many international agencies and universities supported this research, including the National Science Foundation (BSN-8606432), the American Philosophical Society, the Sigma Xi Foundation, the John Heinz III Charitable Trust, and the Fulbright-Hayes Research Program (CIES). A wide range of support was provided by the Universities of Kentucky, Alabama, Colorado, Minnesota, Pittsburgh, Penn State, and SUNY-Albany. Finally, we are grateful for contributions by several private corporations that included the United Fruit Company and engineers of the El Cajon Consortium (CELCA).

The success of any archaeology project is dependent on collaborative team research. We will always be indebted to all the individuals who worked with us to bring the research to a successful conclusion. A special mention goes to Ildefonso Orellana and his wife, Zoila; to our faithful field cook, Doña María Rivera; and to all the fieldworkers from Montañuelas and the other nearby communities, which are now under water.

DIRECTORS

Kenneth Hirth, Director (1979 to date)

George Hasemann, Field Director (1979 to 1998)

Gloria Lara-Pinto, Sub-director (1981 to date)

Vito Veliz, Sub-director (1980)

ARCHAEOLOGISTS

Diane Ballinger, Human Osteology

Brian Bauer, Survey

Julie Benyo, Excavation Supervisor

Boyd Dixon, Excavation

Randy Fouts, Survey, Laboratory Supervisor

Thomas Fouts, Laboratory

John Hansen, Survey

Susan Grant Hirth, Excavation, Flotation

George Hasemann, Survey and Excavation
    Supervisor

Jorge Herrera, Excavation Supervisor

Kenneth Hirth, Excavation Supervisor

Gloria Lara-Pinto, Excavation Supervisor

William Loker, Excavation Supervisor

Lewis Messenger, Excavation Supervisor

Phyllis Messenger, Laboratory Supervisor

Mike Mucio, Laboratory

https://doi.org/10.5876/9781646424757.c000b

Kazuo Okamura, Excavation

Scott O'Mack, Excavation

Ildefonso Orellana, Excavation, Lab Analysis

John Picklesimer, Laboratory

Jonathan Pollack, Excavation

Kenneth Robinson, Excavation Supervisor

Alex Rush, Excavation, Topography

Edward Schortman, Survey

Russel Sheptak, Excavation

Jorge Silva, Excavation

Vaughn Skidmore, Excavation

Sandy Stevens, Survey

Mark Tucker, Excavation

Patricia Urban, Survey

Jeff Walker, Excavation

Paul Webb, Excavation

John Yonk, Survey, Excavation

James Young, Excavation

ARCHAEOLOGICAL ASSISTANTS

Emilio Aguilar, Excavation

Isabel Fugón, Laboratory

Sid Hisle, Laboratory

Rigoberto Lanza, Excavation

Sally Loker, Flotation

Albina Mendoza, Laboratory

Zoila Rodríguez, Laboratory

SPECIALIZED ANALYSES

Rani Alexander, Fauna

Marilyn Beaudry, Material Sourcing

Julie Benyo, Ceramics, Mortuary Analysis

Ronald Bishop, Material Sourcing
Gina Buckley, Human Osteology
Ana Mara Carías de López, Ceramic Reconstruction
Maynard Cliff, Ceramics
Michael Collins, Geoarchaeology
Dennis Coskren, Geology
Brendan Culleton, AMS Dating
Anne Dowd, Technical Illustration (Jade)
Larry Feldman, Malacology
Steve Ferguson, Material Sourcing
Eric Fernandez, Fauna
Alejandro Figueroa, Obsidian Sourcing
George Hasemann, Obsidian Hydration
Kacey Hirth, Statistics
Kenneth Hirth, Ceramics, Jade, Lithics
Susan Hirth, Ceramics, Jade
Emily Kate, Mortuary Analysis, Illustration
Nedenia Kennedy, Ceramics, Laboratory Supervisor
Gloria Lara-Pinto, Ethnohistory
David Lentz, Ethnobotany
Taylor Lenz Cliff, Technical Illustration
William Loker, Modern Land Use
Russel Meigs, Botanical Taxonomy
Charles Norville, Geoarchaeology
Cynthia Ott, Technical Illustration (Jade)
Alex Rush, Topography
Jerrel Sorenson, Lithics: Flaked Stone
Mary Spink, Lithics: Ground Stone
Malinda Stafford, Ethnoarchaeology
Rebecca Storey, Human Osteology
Daniel Wolfman, Obsidian Hydration
Steve Wurzback, Topography

Ritual and Economy in a
Pre-Columbian Chiefdom

1

Understanding the organization and development of intermediate-level societies known as chiefdoms is one of the most fascinating and challenging areas of archaeological research. Chiefdoms[1] are important in developmental terms because they represent a level of organization beyond the kin-based village. They were regional socio-political entities with leaders who were able to coordinate and integrate populations of thousands to tens of thousands of individuals (Earle 2021:1; Kirch 1989). Chiefdom societies across Central America are fascinating because of the diversity of sumptuous goods they procured, produced, and used in different ways to reinforce social positions and belief systems.[2] But they are challenging because of the diversity of their population size, the different ways they were organized, and the way they cycled through episodes of growth and decline. A good deal of the variability in chiefdoms reflects the different organizational pathways they followed in shaping forms of regional integration. Recent research has identified three intertwined sources of power leaders used to shape these polities: religious ideology, warrior might, and control of individual and social wealth (Earle 1991).

Much of what is known about the organization of chiefdom societies has come from excellent ethnographic and ethnohistoric studies conducted over several centuries of European and American colonial expansion. Nevertheless, a comparative study of chiefdoms in the Americas concluded that these two

Introducing Ritual Economy

https://doi.org/10.5876/9781646424757.c001

traditional sources will not by themselves further our understanding of their development. What is needed are long-term studies of single societies using archaeological information from which processes of cultural development can be identified (Drennan and Uribe 1987:viii–ix).

This study examines the long-term development of a single, small chiefdom society in the El Cajón region of west-central Honduras (figure 1.1). West-central Honduras covers the five Honduran departments of Atlántida, Yoro, Cortés, Comayagua, and Santa Bárbara. It covers the roughly triangular area from the mouth of the Ulúa River south into the Comayagua valley and the site of Yarumela, then northwest through the sites of Gualjoquito and El Coyote to the Guatemala border (see figure 2.1). Pre-Columbian societies throughout this region are characterized as chiefdoms because communities were small and regional integration appears to have been based on ritual practices. When conditions are evaluated for the development of complex societies in west-central Honduras, little evidence is found for inter-societal conflict. Archaeological sites are generally in undefended locales; lack palisades, terraces, or other defensive features; and show little evidence of warfare-related trauma in burial populations. Likewise, while there is evidence for some wealth inequality in the early stages of cultural development, the control of wealth goods was not an important source of elite power and appears to decrease over time.[3] Ritual celebrations, feasting, and the power associated with them were the primary way regional networks were established and maintained in these societies.

Cultural development in the El Cajón region conforms to the expectations of a chiefdom society in several ways. The largest community in the El Cajón region was the site of Salitrón Viejo, with a population of 1,000–1,600 residents. Salitrón also was the center of ritual activity, which provided the means for building linkages with other communities throughout the region. Ritual-focused leadership involved the sponsorship of community feasts as part of public ceremonies and the mobilization of corvée labor for corporate work projects (e.g., Dietler and Hayden 2001; Dietler and Herbich 2001; Durrenberger 2008). The importance of community feasting has been documented for the historic Lenca of Honduras (Chapman 1985:87, 109–122; Herrera y Tordesillas 1944–1947:6:23; Lara-Pinto 1991b) and has been identified at numerous archaeological sites across southeastern Mesoamerica (Brown 2001; Hendon 2003; LeCount 2001; Wells 2007:38–51; Wells and Davis-Salazar 2008:200). An important feature of ritual activity in the El Cajón region was the construction of civic-ceremonial architecture at Salitrón Viejo and other

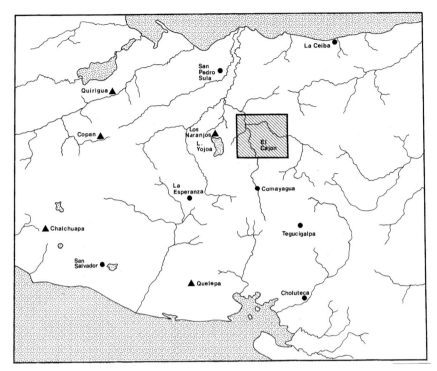

FIGURE 1.1. *Location of the El Cajón region in Central America*

sites along the Sulaco and Humuya Rivers. At Salitrón Viejo, large offerings of jade and other wealth goods were incorporated into civic-ceremonial constructions to sanctify their ritual use-life. The context and scale of these offerings also served to reinforce the social position of the leaders who supervised their ritual use.

This study explores the growth and decline of a regional chiefdom centered on the community of Salitrón Viejo over a 1,400-year period between 400 BC and AD 1000. It does so through the lens of ritual economy, which provides a means of assessing the importance and effectiveness of ritual celebrations as an integrative mechanism for the growth and maintenance of chiefdom societies. The goal of this volume is to present both the evidence for past ritual behavior and an analytic framework for interpreting it. The discussion that follows begins by exploring what is meant by the term *ritual economy* and how it can be applied to the study of small-scale pre-Columbian societies located across Honduras.

RITUAL AND ECONOMY IN PRE-COLUMBIAN SOCIETY

Archaeologists have had a long-standing interest in reconstructing both ritual and economic behavior in past societies (Friedman 1975). But as a rule, ritual and economy are topics examined separately by investigators using different types of data that are interpreted from distinct theoretical perspectives. Here they are discussed together using the perspective of ritual economy. Recent discussions have defined ritual economy as the process through which worldview and social ideology are materialized through the production, provisioning, and consumption of economic resources (Barber and Joyce 2007:237; McAnany and Wells 2008:1; Stanish 2017; Wells and Davis-Salazar 2007:2). Ritual from this perspective involves the communication of information through both verbal and non-verbal means (Rappaport 1971:26). It is not confined to religious messages but includes the broad range of behaviors that reinforce culturally meaningful ideologies that shape social, economic, and political behavior (Davis-Salazar 2007:198–202; Rappaport 1999:24; Wells 2006:278–279; Wells and Davis-Salazar 2007:4–5). This view of ritual is strongly economic in nature because it is through the production, transfer, and use of material goods in ritual contexts that social ideologies are established and reinforced.

Patricia McAnany (2010:3) has argued that economic practice is difficult to examine apart from the political, social, and cosmological frameworks in which it is practiced. From this perspective, economic activities in the pre-Columbian world were so entangled with socio-political interactions and individual identity that it is hard to determine what aspects of economic provisioning lie within the realm of ritual economy and which do not. Separating the task of provisioning from how pre-Columbian actors viewed the world in which they carried it out is a difficult task for archaeologists. Nevertheless, John Watanabe (2007) has proposed a partial solution. He argues that investigators can explore the topic of ritual economy from two distinct perspectives: as the *economics of ritual* and, less directly, as the *ritual of economy*. The "economics of ritual" perspective explores the costs of producing and carrying out ritual performances, with all the calculation, politicking, and profiting implied for those who organize and conduct them. It includes an evaluation of both the material goods and the types of behaviors involved in shaping and reinforcing social and political ideologies. The economics of ritual approach is more amenable to archaeological analysis, and that is the perspective adopted here. The "ritual of economy" perspective is different. It is concerned with identifying how mundane acts of provisioning and exchange are ritualized in cultural or symbolic ways that can run contrary to a strict neoclassical perspective involving the allocation of scarce resources to alternative ends (Watanabe 2007:301). While also important to consider, it is more elusive to identify but needs to be recognized as an ever-present aspect of economic behavior. Given the distinctiveness of these two perspectives, it is useful to examine how ritual and economic practices work together in society as a first step in understanding how archaeological investigation can explore the ritual economy.

UNDERSTANDING RITUAL ECONOMY

The ritual economy helps develop a shared ideology among group participants as resources are produced and consumed collectively in culturally meaningful ways. Ritual behaviors reinforce a belief ideology, with social and sacred propositions that give it unquestionable validity (Rappaport 1971). Likewise, the demands of ritual economy create important provisioning needs that stimulate production for the feasts and offerings consumed in private and public events. Furthermore, it is in the context of public ceremony that rituals provide the framework for community and regional political integration while at the same time providing the individuals who lead them with opportunities to enhance their personal recognition and social authority. Each of these facets of ritual behavior is important to consider when the structure of ritual economy is examined in individual societies.

Ideologies are the shared beliefs and values that groups have in common. They are the structuring assumptions about how things operate that range from beliefs about the cosmos to the organization of the family, work, or entire socio-political systems. Shared ideologies build community and common identity (Durrenberger 2008:74; Goldschmidt 2006:40). They are an integral component of human interaction as well as the basis for individual power strategies. The information fundamental to shaping ideologies is conveyed, in part, through the material paraphernalia employed in ritual performances. It is the material and symbolic components of rituals that convey and transform ideas, values, stories, and myths into systems of collective belief and action. The use of material items in ritual celebrations provides some constancy to the messages communicated as well as linking past ritual outcomes to the present, at the same time that they provide continuity into the future. Because ideology is expressed through material media, ritual enactments normally involve the consumption of food, labor, and other resources. This creates a situation where leaders can control ritual performances and shape ideology as they direct the production, assembly, and use of the material goods employed within them. This provides a degree of ritual power within societies in the same way individual control of wealth goods can become a power strategy within emergent complex societies (DeMarrais, Castillo, and Earle 1996:17; Hirth 1996b).

Ideology is an effective integrative device as long as individuals adhere to its principles and do not question its validity. Ideologies are commonly reinforced in two ways: by increasing the level of social buy-in within the participating groups or by making ideological principles inviolate by imbuing then with the sacred. Social buy-in involves the physical investment of time and resources in feasting celebrations, pilgrimages, and the construction of special facilities (e.g., plazas and ceremonial complexes) where rituals are conducted. Katherine Spielmann (2008:46) notes that civic-ceremonial buildings are especially important in this regard because their construction involves a public investment that leads to community cohesion and identity. Developing the sacred is another matter and involves linking ideologies to spiritual forces that cannot be questioned. Sacred propositions are neither verifiable nor falsifiable. According to Roy Rappaport (1971:36), imbuing social conventions with sanctity hides their arbitrary premises in a cloak of unquestionable necessity. Ritual is the vehicle that helps establish sacred propositions, especially when it creates a spiritual experience or altered consciousness brought on by group emotion, alcohol, or imbibing hallucinogenic substances.

All ritual in Mesoamerica was embedded in a pantheism worldview. In pantheism, the universe is the deity and everything in the world is imbued with its spirit (Maffie 2014:79; Sandstrom 2008:98). The earth was believed to be a living creature; human activities such as planting, hunting, and resource collection disturbed the balance of relationships within it. The imbalance produced by these activities was restored through rituals directed by specialists involving sacrifices made to the spirit world (Sandstrom and Sandstrom 1986:78, 2017:109). It is in this context that spectacular or unusual features of the landscape such as caves, springs, mountaintops, and cosmological features (i.e., sun, moon, stars) often became the conduits for special ritual offerings (Hasemann-Lara and Lara-Pinto 2014, 2019). Offerings in these contexts were often a response to repaying debts to the world of spirits.

The ritual economy consumes resources in feasting, mortuary or ceremonial offerings, and the labor to construct special facilities where rituals are conducted (Davis-Salazar 2007:197). These needs place demands on participating households to allocate labor to the production of resources that do not contribute to domestic support or household reproduction (Watanabe 2007:305). Eric Wolf (1966:10–11) placed these domestic obligations in what he called the household ceremonial fund, whether resources were extracted directly from the coffers of household production or were produced outside the household in contexts dedicated to that purpose.[4] The manufacture of items specifically for ritual use has been called the ritual mode of production[5] and has been found in a wide range of societies, from tribal groups to archaic states (Berdan 2007; Hirth 2016:44–46; Rappaport 1968, 1979; Spielmann 2002:203, 2008:64–68). The demand for food used in feasts increased subsistence production in society, which could have served as a safeguard during periods of resource shortfall (Halstead 1989; Halstead and O'Shea 1989). Likewise, the need for socially valued goods for special offerings could have increased the level of craft production or fostered the long-distance acquisition of luxury goods (Wells and Davis-Salazar 2007:1). Levies of corvée labor for special work projects were part of the extra effort the ritual economy could have imposed on participating communities.

Feasts and other celebrations within and between communities do not occur spontaneously but require planning and organization. Ritual economy materializes meaning through economic action and provides an opportunity for increased social differentiation. The leader or sponsor of a celebration[6] can use it as an avenue to enhance their personal status or to build social authority at the community or regional level. It is here that the ideology of the sacred can be used to create hierarchical differences and social categories that are beyond dispute and allow individual-centered positions of leadership to emerge (McAnany 2008:219). The creation of a regionally centralized authority created new demands on populations as more people were incorporated into larger social formations, whether they were individual-centered or organized through more collective means (Barber and Joyce 2007:230; Blanton et al. 1996; Carballo 2013). Christian Wells (2007:29) frames these demands within the concept of *ritual finance* where labor and resources were mobilized from supporting populations to validate the social, political, and cosmic order. Appealing to ritual needs makes the demands for labor or resources unquestionable (Foias 2007:171–172). It also provides leaders of celebrations with the ability to control resource disposition and to use resources as an important source of personal power.

ADDRESSING THE ECONOMICS IN RITUAL ECONOMY

The topic of ritual economy cannot be addressed without clarifying what view of the economy is brought to the discussion. The economy is perceived of here as "a socially mediated form of material provisioning and interaction involving the production and allocation of resources among alternative ends" (Hirth 2020:4). Ritual economy is examined from the perspective of behavioral economics, which does not accept all the tenets of neoclassical economics (Cartwright 2018; Thaler 2015, 2016). Instead, it considers the effects cultural, social, emotional, and cognitive factors have on the decisions individuals, groups, and institutions make with regard to economic provisioning. While it acknowledges that individuals and groups make economic choices, behavioral economics assumes that the criteria that govern those choices are learned and dictated by the social principles of the societies in which people live. Behavioral economics is not neoclassical economics in a new wrapper. Instead, it is a socially and ethnographically informed descriptive perspective on how people *actually* behave rather than assuming actions based on unemotional, perfectly rational principles of maximization.[7]

The field of behavioral economics is used to develop a framework for understanding ritual economy and to explore both the economics of conducting rituals and some of the cultural and emotional factors behind their operation. In broad terms, behavioral economics is the psychology of economic decision making. It recognizes the existence of altruism in human decision making and that individuals often make choices that benefit the group instead of maximizing self-interest. Behavioral economics views individuals as rational actors who frequently "misbehave" because of the systematic biases that affect their decisions (Thaler 2015). This is especially important when evaluating economic behavior oriented toward addressing unseen spiritual forces. While behavioral economists often use choice tests to identify the principles behind decision making, archaeologists must infer those principles from the outcomes of their decisions and the material remains they produced. A place to begin interpretation is with observed behavioral regularities found in ethnographically documented societies as test propositions for how they might reflect past ritual behavior.

The pantheistic Mesoamerican worldview placed humans in an animated landscape that required reciprocatory offerings for the resources removed and consumed in everyday life. These offerings were intended to reestablish spiritual balance for both past and future resource withdrawals. From an economic perspective, they can be viewed as a type of spiritual business transaction. Among the ancient Nahua, sacrifices to the gods were called *nextlahualiztli*, which translates as an act of repayment (López Austin 1988:74). This same transactional logic has been observed in contemporary Nahua and Otomí rituals (Lupo 1995; Sandstrom 2008; Sandstrom and Sandstrom 2017). Timothy Knowlton (2021), in a recent study of K'iche texts from highland Guatemala, observes that reciprocal obligations defined the relations between human beings and the broader cosmos in which they lived and served as the foundation for their moral and ritual economy. If ritual can be seen in transactional terms, how can insights from behavioral economics productively inform us?

Archaeologists, ethnographers, and ethnohistorians have been fascinated by the scale of labor invested in civic-ceremonial structures and the places where rituals were conducted (Knapp 2009; McMahon 2013; Trigger 1990). Behavioral economics models this behavior in terms of its *transactional utility*, that is, its relative value vis-à-vis the setting and the expected return from the rituals performed. In short, the more expensive or elaborate the setting where rituals are conducted, the greater the expectation that it will lead to successful outcomes and reduced risk. This differs from the notion of *acquisitional utility* based on standard neoclassical principles, where the benefit from an offering or ritual performance should be the same regardless of the location where it was consumed or witnessed (Thaler 2015:59–60). Ritual settings are important because they affect the perceived value and return from the ritual enactments and offerings involved.

A second behavioral principle is that the expected returns from activities are often directly proportional to the amount of previous participation or investment in them. This is the *sunk cost* caveat, which contradicts neoclassical thinking that all previous expenditures (or sunk costs) are irrelevant in economic decision making.[8] Recognition that previous expenditures affect current behavior helps explain why some of the most important sacred locales are also the oldest ritual places in societies. Investments in the labor and material to construct temples, platforms, plazas, and shrines are sunk costs that anchor important places and communal ideology in the minds of the people who use then. Sunk costs help make sacred constructions durable. Likewise, the time invested in pilgrimages or rituals at natural places such as caves or mountaintops can reinforce a tradition of repeated visitation to these locales (Hasemann-Lara and Lara-Pinto 2014, 2019).

Another facet of human behavior is *hindsight bias*. This aspect of human perception leads people to believe they knew an event would come to pass after it has occurred (Thaler 2015:21). This bias works for events that turn out good as well as bad, but on the whole, there is a tendency to remember successes over failures. This is especially the case for successful ritual outcomes, which maintains a tradition of relying on them for future results. It invokes the idea that what worked in the past will work again.

The combination of sunk costs and hindsight bias help explain what is often referred to as the *endowment effect*. This principle holds that the items people own or that are already part of their cultural toolkit (their endowment) are held to be more valuable and reliable than things that are not. This explains the commitment to tradition at all levels of society, from resistance to adopting new foods or technology (Anderson, Chabot, and Van Gijn 2004; Kurin 1983) to adhering to established stylistic traditions[9] and religious practices (McAnany 2010:199–252). The mantra of hindsight bias and the endowment effect professes that traditional remedies provide the best solutions to new problems. When long-standing practices are overturned, it often takes place in the context of a dramatic rejection of the old in favor of the new, as can be seen in revitalization movements and some of the rapid conversions to charismatic Christianity in Guatemala in the 1970s (Duncan 1992; Wallace 1956).

One confounding variable behavioral economics identifies is that of *intertemporal choice*. This concept recognizes that many individuals place a higher value on consumption in the present than on consumption in the future. This is a confounding variable for explaining ritual behavior because offerings are often made against the hope of future returns. This is exactly the process involved when rituals are conducted in agricultural fields to foster healthy plant growth and a good harvest. This practice contradicts the higher value placed on consumption in the present *unless* ritual offerings are seen as something like an investment, where the value of goods offered today is multiplied several-fold into future returns—much like the effect of compound interest or organic growth.

This is precisely what Alan and Pamela Effrein Sandstrom (2017) have observed with pilgrimage ritual among contemporary Nahua groups in northern Veracruz, Mexico. The Nahua see rituals as a form of sacred exchange. They invest in goods, time, and labor to repay spirits for health, rain, prosperity and to fulfill current needs and reduce future risk (Sandstrom 2008:102–103). People target offerings to specific spirits based on individual needs within a collective community context.[10] This enables individuals to measure the cost of the ritual in terms of the specific result they seek (e.g., curing, harvest, marriage, children). While this individualized view of ritual participation differs from the way archaeologists often perceive community ritual (e.g., Berdan 2007), it underscores how the concept of reciprocity can structure relationships with ritual just as it did in other socioeconomic relationships (Mauss 1990). Community ritual provided the glue that held larger socio-political units together, and their success in doing so was reinforced by parallel rituals carried out at the household level.

Behavioral economics seeks to develop descriptive models that accurately reflect human economic behavior. In this way, it deviates sharply from the normative models of human behavior employed by neoclassical economics.

As a theoretical perspective, it permits the examination of three important dimensions of ritual economy. First, it permits an approximation of what the *economy of ritual* consisted of in terms of the human effort required to organize and carry it out. Second, it facilitates an assessment of how rituals were organized and what their relationship was to leadership in society. Third and finally, it allows a more intuitive interpretation of the ritual worldview and beliefs of participants. All three of these behavioral dimensions will be examined using information from the El Cajón region and the site of Salitrón Viejo. The manner in which the presentation is organized is discussed below. The approach used is telescopic in nature. It begins at the broadest level, with an overview of chiefdom development in west-central Honduras, and gradually focuses down on ritual activity in the Salitrón community and what it informs about the development in the El Cajón region.

PRE-COLUMBIAN LIFE AND RITUAL IN
WEST-CENTRAL HONDURAS

The El Cajón region is a mountainous area along the middle reaches of the Ulúa River (see figure 1.1). It includes both lowland and upland regions of the Sulaco and Humuya River valleys, and it is along the Sulaco River that the site of Salitrón Viejo is located. The pre-Columbian cultures of northwestern and west-central Honduras were non-Maya groups identified as Lenca speakers who occupied the area up through the Spanish Conquest (Chapman 1978; Gómez Zúñiga 2021; Lara-Pinto 1991a, 2021). The second chapter in this volume begins by asking what a chiefdom is and how it is represented in the archaeological record. It then presents an overview of cultural development found along the middle Ulúa River and its tributaries during the Formative and Classic periods (1600 BC–AD 1000). This discussion provides the background for the appearance of population in the El Cajón region and the development of the Salitrón community between 400 BC and AD 1000. This discussion is not a comprehensive culture history of all Honduras but instead identifies the salient features of community and ritual life that provide a comparative framework for developments at Salitrón Viejo. As such, the discussion is selective in the sites and regional surveys examined.

Chapter 3 examines the El Cajón region and cultural developments that occurred from its initial settlement around 400 BC to its final abandonment 1,400 years later. It begins with a general discussion of the regional geography and natural landscape pioneer agriculturalists encountered as they settled along the Sulaco and Humuya Rivers. The regional chronology is presented along with resource availabilities and environmental differences between upland areas and valley bottoms. The discussion then shifts to the site of Salitrón Viejo and other communities in the El Cajón region. Salitrón was the earliest, largest, and longest-occupied community in the Sulaco valley, so its history chronicles the development of political complexity in the region. Its unique architectural layout is summarized, which includes two residential groups with elite architecture and two distinct civic-ceremonial precincts. These four zones are discussed in terms of what they indicate about community organization and ritual activity at the site and regional levels. The chapter concludes with a discussion of how Salitrón Viejo's position in the El Cajón region changed over time.

The next three chapters examine the evidence for ritual activities at Salitrón Viejo in specific detail. They present the archaeological information available for reconstructing the economy of ritual in the El Cajón region. Two ritual areas were constructed at Salitrón Viejo: the Iglesia Precinct and the North Precinct. The Iglesia Precinct was the most important civic-ceremonial area in the region. The most prominent feature in this precinct was the Acropolis platform that was 2 m high and covered 0.75 ha. It was on this platform that other important structures were constructed and community celebrations were performed. Chapter 4 describes the main architectural features of the Iglesia Precinct, reconstructs its sequence of construction, and dates its different episodes of building, modification, and use. The pace of construction is discussed and the scale of architectural construction at Salitrón Viejo is compared to the broader region, along with how civic-ceremonial construction changed over time.

An important feature of ritual activity at Salitrón Viejo was the incorporation of a large quantity of jade and other high-value wealth goods as dedicatory offerings in civic-ceremonial constructions. Chapter 5 examines and describes the jade, marble, and other artifacts recovered from both ritual and non-ritual contexts. Over 3,000 pieces of lapidary regalia and other offerings were recovered in the El Cajón region, the vast majority of which were from Salitrón Viejo and date to the Late Yunque phase (AD 0–400). These materials are unique in two regards. First, the El Cajón materials are the largest in situ assemblages of finished jade and marble artifacts ever recovered from carefully excavated and dated contexts in eastern Mesoamerica. Second, this collection is associated with a non-Maya culture and provides insight into what the symbolically valued images were in a society where hereditary kingship was not the mainstay of centralized authority. These wealth goods and the different raw materials they were manufactured from are described and illustrated to capture their diversity. This collection is important from both an archaeological and an art historical perspective because it provides new information on the diverse array of lapidary traditions operating in eastern Mesoamerica during the Early Classic period. (In addition to the illustrations provided here, a photographic catalog of key pieces from the collection is also available in Hirth and colleagues 2023.)

The types of offerings and their spatial locations represent two manifestations archaeologists employ to study ritual behavior. Chapter 6 brings the artifacts and their contextual associations together. It is one thing to look at the stylistic aspects of individual artifacts; it is another to look at how different artifact types (e.g., beads, pendants, earspools, unworked raw material) were used to form offering groups in the areas where they were deposited. This discussion explores the synergism between types of artifacts and how they were used in ritual contexts. Patterns of color, breakage, and simultaneous ritual use and deposition are examined in relation to construction episodes in the Iglesia Precinct and across Salitrón Viejo. Wealth goods and high-value ornamental regalia are often associated with the burial of high-ranking individuals in Maya sites to the west. This was not the case in the El Cajón region, which suggests that leadership followed a different, more group-oriented strategy that did not require the individual accumulation of wealth by elite to forge personal networks of power.

Chapter 7 returns to the topic of the economy and ritual. The discussion revisits the evidence for ritual activity at contemporaneous sites in northwest and west-central Honduras and compares it to evidence at Salitrón Viejo. The importance of feasting is discussed and the architectural sequence for the Iglesia Precinct is reexamined to generate an energetic estimate of the time and labor needed to construct it. Ritual spaces and their associated buildings required more than stone and mortar; they also required dedication behaviors so they could fulfill their civic and ceremonial functions. Because high-value jade artifacts were used in these dedications, an energetic estimate is also presented for the cost of obtaining a portion of the ritual assemblage. Three procurement models are then evaluated for how ritual offerings were obtained: on-site production, procurement through down-the-line exchange, and direct procurement trade.

The final chapter summarizes what the materials at Salitrón Viejo contribute to the understanding of indigenous belief systems, ritual economy, and the role that economy played in the development of its regional chiefdom. The chapter examines the imagery identified on lapidary items as a way to explore the structure of its underlying belief system. The abundance of zoomorphic imagery suggests a strong animistic worldview. The location and treatment of ritual offerings in the Iglesia Precinct suggest that items were broken to animate civic-ceremonial structures and to provide strong spiritual protection throughout its future use-life. The broader role of ritual offerings in the natural landscape at caves and springs is also discussed as part of the broader animistic worldview. Hunched or hunchback figures are a particularly important iconographic element in the El Cajón collection, and their meaning is explored in Honduras and Mesoamerica. The diversity and stylistic richness of the collection are examined in terms of what they imply about the nature of lapidary carving traditions in eastern Mesoamerica. Finally, the discussion concludes with an evaluation of what information from the El Cajón region can contribute to a broader understanding of pre-Columbian chiefdom development in west-central Honduras.

Ritual and its associated religious beliefs and practices are difficult dimensions of pre-Columbian behavior to reconstruct solely using archaeological approaches. Nevertheless, it is through the careful analysis of empirical data that archaeological investigations can explore the ritual economy and the role it played in the organization of mid-range chiefdom societies across eastern Mesoamerica. It is hoped that the research presented here provides valuable insights into how the economy of ritual was organized and operated in the El Cajón region of west-central Honduras.

One of the primary pursuits in archaeology over the past century has been to understand the development of complex society. While a great deal of attention has been placed on the emergence of state-level society, chiefdoms represent a prominent and important middle range of complexity that is found the world over at different points in time. They were the key political formations in Africa, in most of the Americas, and throughout Oceania at the time of European colonization. Recent scholarship has recognized the diversity and varied manifestations of chiefdoms and has acknowledged that many of the political entities researchers have labeled as kingdoms and state-level societies actually represent a form of indirect rule over uneasy confederacies of chiefdoms. In a recent treatment of this topic, Peter Skalník (2004) argues that chiefdoms are a universal form of political organization that is suitable for describing a good many forms of organization, not only in the past but also in the modern world.[1]

Pre-Columbian societies across Honduras have been characterized as chiefdoms organized at various scales of complexity and integrated through a combination of ideological, economic, and martial means (Baudez 1986; Begley 1999; Dixon 1989b; Gómez Zúñiga 2021; Hasemann 1985; Healy 1992; Hirth 1996a; Joyce 2021, n.d.; Lara-Pinto 1991b, 2020, 2021; Weeks, Black, and Speaker 1987). The term *chiefdom* (or *cacicazgo*) is used throughout this discussion as a matter of convenience.

Chiefdom Societies in West-Central Honduras

https://doi.org/10.5876/9781646424757.c002

In so doing, we recognize that some archaeologists object to the term because it lacks precision and refers to societies that vary greatly in size and organization (Feinman and Neitzel 1984; Steponaitis 1981:320–321; Upham 1987). These criticisms notwithstanding, the term has utility because it is widely employed by scholars studying and describing the range of small prehispanic societies found throughout Honduras and lower Central America.[2] The term *chiefdom* is employed for its descriptive and comparative value without any of the evolutionary assumptions often attached to it (Abrutyn and Lawrence 2010; Service 1962).

This chapter provides an overview of the development of chiefdom societies across northwestern and west-central Honduras between 1600 BC and AD 1000. It begins by examining the term *chiefdom* and the characteristics used to identify societies in the archaeological record, then moves to a discussion of cultural complexity in Honduras. The scale of integration, level of inequality, and nature of decision making are examined for societies during the Formative and Classic periods and how they changed over time. This discussion provides a backdrop for understanding what chiefdom societies represent in Honduran prehistory and how their development compares to processes at work in the El Cajón region that are examined in subsequent chapters.

CHARACTERIZING CHIEFDOM SOCIETY

So, what is meant by the term *chiefdom*? According to Skalník (2004:78), most anthropologists would characterize chiefdoms "as small-scale societies organized according to kinship and other face-to-face ties, led by a hereditary or elected chief." They are multiscalar organizations where families embedded in local communities are linked to others in a broader regional polity. These societies often had multiple authority hierarchies and competing social and economic interests that came in conflict with one another (Brumfiel 1992; Feinman and Neitzel 1984).

What chiefdom societies are not are self-regulating monolithic systems that can be defined in typological terms using a list of traits. Their diversity is too great for that. While the linkages that hold these societies together are systemic in nature, they also rest on the personal abilities and charisma of individual leaders to reinforce common values and motivate participation in collective activities. In this sense, chiefdoms are best studied in terms of the centralizing processes and leadership activities that hold them together (Earle 2021:47). Colin Renfrew (1974) made this point when he identified the difference between individualizing and corporate chiefdoms. Individualizing chiefdoms are marked by leaders who aggrandize their personal position in the social hierarchy through the control of wealth, as is reflected in elite mortuary assemblages and their personal residences (Friedman and Rowlands 1978; Hayden 2001b; Sheehy 1996). Corporate chiefdoms, in contrast, lack the personalized accumulation and use of wealth in shaping social systems (Brumfiel and Earle 1987b); in these systems, leaders may be invisible or difficult to distinguish from the broader population (Blanton and Fargher 2008; Blanton et al. 1996; DeMarrais, Castillo, and Earle 1996).

Archaeologists have used a range of different criteria to identify chiefdoms, including small population size, settlement hierarchy, warfare, economic inequality, and the presence of civic-ceremonial architecture (Drennan and Uribe 1987; Duffy 2015; Earle 1991; Feinman 1996; Flannery and Marcus 2012; Gilman 1995). Timothy Earle (1987:279) identifies the salient features of chiefdom societies as follows: "Chiefdoms are intermediate-level societies, providing an evolutionary bridge between acephalous societies and bureaucratic states. As the term is presently used, most view chiefdoms as political entities that organize regional populations in the thousands or tens of thousands. This organization is provided by a centralized hierarchy of leaders set off from the rest of the population."

Chiefdoms lie within that middle range of complexity between egalitarian societies and stratified states (e.g., Feinman and Neitzel 1984). While their form of organization can vary, several characteristics are important when discussing their archaeological manifestations: their scale of integration, centrality and nature of decision making, and the level of stratification and inequality they display.

Scale of integration refers to the size of a society and how effectively it coordinates activities within and between communities. In a very general sense, this refers to the capacity of a society's social mechanisms to control and coordinate behaviors between individuals. Elman Service (1978) noted that one of the best measures of a society's integrative mechanisms was its ability to mediate the internal social disputes and pressures that arise in residential communities. When pressures can be mediated, populations stay together. When they cannot, communities tend to fission and bud off new settlements into the surrounding region (Kopytoff 1987). Resource availabilities mediate this process, as does the presence or absence of endemic warfare and the need for protection. But the idea is that communities can only grow in size when they have the mechanisms to mediate internal frictions and create an ordered and collective community in which all individuals maintain their rightful place of membership.

Community size, therefore, can be an important indicator of integration and cultural complexity (Drennan 1987:309). The largest communities are usually where effective local leaders and mediators reside. The most influential communities often have the longest sequences of occupation and are the oldest communities in a region. While size is a product of successful and prolonged interaction, integration refers to how communities were linked in coordinated activities within a region. It is in this context that chiefdoms can range from several hundred to tens of thousands of individuals (Earle 2021:3). Measuring social and economic integration using archaeological material is a challenging task. The most direct way is through the level of shared material culture found between communities (i.e., ceramics, architecture, textiles, lithics, and a variety of trade goods) that reflect shared ideas of form, function, and decorative design (Lara-Pinto 2019). The practice of craft specialization and the movement of finished goods from producers to consumers can document the extent of linkages within or between regions (Berrey, Drennan, and Peterson 2021; Goralski 2008; Helms 1979) and the form of distribution through which goods moved (Hirth 1998, 2010; Hirth and Cyphers 2020; Renfrew 1975).

The *centrality and nature of decision making* refers to the emergence of leaders and the roles they play in society. Leaders don't exist in a vacuum. They fulfill specific needs and provide services within society that range from the cosmological and economic to the political and juridical. These services are their raison d'être and the basis for their influence in society. For that reason, leadership is often cast in political terms (Spencer 1987:369), even when the basis for integration is ritualistic or economic in nature (Earle 1997; Hirth 1996b:221–226, 2020). What is important is that central decision makers were a necessary feature of chiefdom societies, and it is from their ubiquitous presence that the title of chief is derived. Kent Flannery (1972:403) believes leadership is a fundamental feature of chiefdom society where "the office of 'chief' exists apart from the man who occupies it, and on his death the office must be filled by one of equally noble descent." The ubiquity of leaders is a function of their roles—whether in the realm of religion, warfare, communal labor mobilization, intensification of production, risk reduction, or external trade (Creamer and Haas 1985:740). In this sense, differentiation of social status is a critical feature of chiefdom organization.

Archaeologists have identified levels of centralized decision making in a variety of ways. Differentiation in site size and community function is often used. Since chiefdoms are regional entities, the presence of a multi-level settlement hierarchy is often interpreted as reflecting the hierarchy of leaders in society, with the most influential individuals residing in the largest communities

(Lightfoot 1987; Spencer 1987:371–372). The scale and functional differences in architecture also help define levels within the site hierarchy, since the labor invested in monumental construction can be used as a measure of both labor mobilization and centralized planning (Earle 1987:290; Webster 1990). While the identification of site hierarchies is useful, the hierarchies do not necessarily reflect the levels of integrated social control archaeologists often assign to them. Moreover, recent discussions of Honduran settlement systems have recognized more heterarchical forms of organization in which multiple factors of political, economic, and religious interaction shaped settlement patterns in different ways (Joyce 2021, n.d.; Schortman and Urban 2021:317).

Chiefdoms also display degrees of *stratification and inequality* between members. This is due in part to the roles leaders fulfill (e.g., for rituals, feasts, sponsorships), which often require mobilizing resources beyond those supplied from their own households. These resources may be produced communally or mobilized from households through a variety of voluntary and involuntary donations. Leaders manage and mobilize social resources and in the process benefit from the way they are dispersed (Hirth 1996b). Similarly, the development of social institutions can require the construction and maintenance of special facilities (e.g., temples, plaza areas for assembly) that mobilize labor and expend resources at different levels. In lieu of special facilities, leaders may run society-wide activities out of their own households. This can result in the expansion in the number of household residents, an increase in the size of their domiciles, or the creation of special purpose activity areas in the domiciles. James Sheehy (1996) has examined how chiefly residences expanded with the number of activities leaders undertook. In this sense, chiefly residences are an embryonic form of the palaces found in state-level societies.

Stratification and inequality can be measured in several ways in archaeology. One of the most common is through mortuary treatments, with high-ranking individuals identified from more elaborate or unusual burial architecture (e.g., tombs) (Schele and Mathews 1999), monuments (mounds, kerns) (DeMarrais, Castillo, and Earle 1996:20; Spielmann 2008), and associated offerings (Clark and Blake 1994; Goldstein 1981). Leaders may also be separated from followers by differences in domestic assemblages and the presence of the wealth goods they consume in their official and daily lives. These can be non-local exotic trade goods or goods imbued with special power or meaning (Earle 1987:299; Friedman and Rowlands 1978; Helms 1987, 1988; Plourde 2009). A third way inequality and social difference can be expressed is in the power of leaders to mobilize labor. This can be reflected in forms of landesque capital that range from ritual and mortuary monuments to infrastructure features such as defensive structures, irrigation systems, and terrace constructions (Håkansson and Widgren 2007, 2014). Finally, chiefly status can be marked by large, elaborate domestic structures that can carry more overt symboling regarding the elevated status of their occupants relative to commoner residences (Feinman and Neitzel 1984; Sheehy 1996).

CULTURAL COMPLEXITY IN HONDURAN CHIEFDOMS

Scale of integration, centrality of decision making, and the level of inequality provide useful measures for describing chiefdom societies at different levels of socio-political complexity. While they don't provide specific information about the societies' forms of economic or ideological organization, they supply valuable clues that can be used to reconstruct their internal organization and the trajectory of cultural development. Characteristics of scale, degree of centralization, and economic inequality are used here to describe the similarities and differences between chiefdom-level societies found in west-central Honduras.

One characteristic of chiefdom societies is the diversity of forms they take. The available archaeological, ethnographic, and ethnohistoric information indicates that some chiefdoms invested much more heavily than others in the construction of public and ritual architecture. Similarly, some display sharp divisions of economic inequality between elites and non-elites in residential architecture, burial constructions, and mortuary assemblages while others do not. Likewise, the form and expression of hierarchical differences can vary greatly (Drennan and Uribe 1987:xi). The importance of long-distance trade in obtaining exotics is often associated with underwriting elite social identities, building social networks, and establishing alliance relations within and between societies (Brumfiel and Earle 1987a; Clark and Blake 1994; Dalton 1977; Friedman and Rowlands 1978; Junker 1993). But this too is highly variable, with some societies actively seeking external goods and others relying on mobilizing local products to build social networks. All of these features recombine in different ways as societies adapt internal kinship and social systems to local natural and cultural conditions.

Researchers have dichotomized the different effects these variables have on the development of complex societies in distinct contexts (Blanton et al. 1996; Friedman and Rowlands 1978). Particularly important has been the contrast of collective feasting and control over food resources (Friedman 1982; Friedman and Rowlands 1978; Hayden 2001a, 2001b, 2014; Hayden and Dietler 2001), with the effect of elite control over the procurement and use of high-value prestige goods (Brumfiel and Earle 1987a, 1987b; Frankenstein and Rowlands

1978; Gilissen 2003). Another dimension of this discussion has been how collective versus strongly hierarchical forms of social control developed and affected the form of organizational leadership (Blanton et al. 1996; Carballo 2013; DeMarrais, Castillo, and Earle 1996).

Regional variation is evident in the organization and development of chiefdoms in west-central Honduras. Information from several regions[3] is used here to develop a composite picture of society during the Formative through Late Classic periods (1600 BC–AD 1000). While information varies from region to region, two general trends can be observed over time. First, some of the greatest differences in the expression of elite power and authority occurred during the Formative period. Second, although population reached its highest levels during the Middle and Late Classic periods, this did not result in the appearance of sites with larger civic-ceremonial architecture than what occurred earlier. Throughout both periods, community ritual and feasting were important integrative mechanisms for the formation and maintenance of Honduran chiefdoms. The basic chronological sequences for western Honduras are presented in table 2.1 and provide a framework for discussing differences in the type and scale of these prehispanic chiefdoms.

THE FORMATIVE PERIOD (1600 BC–AD 250)

Settled agricultural communities and the first chiefdom societies appeared in west-central Honduras during the *Early Formative period* (1600–800 BC). One of the earliest communities during this period is the site of Puerto Escondido (figure 2.1), where Olmec traits reflecting emerging social differences were incorporated into local ceramic assemblages between 1260 and 900 cal BC. Wealth differences within this community are evident in the presence of fancy ceramic service ware, shell ornaments for personal adornment, and plain marble vessels (Joyce and Henderson 2010:193; Luke et al. 2003). Marble vessels during the Formative periods are plain and should not be confused with the elaborately carved marble vessels manufactured during the Late Classic (see Luke et al. 2003). Cacao was present and was most likely consumed as a beverage in celebrations in the community (Joyce and Henderson 2007:643). The long tradition of depositing cache offerings in civic-ceremonial constructions was initiated at this time with the incorporation of obsidian and shell artifacts under the construction of a civic-ceremonial platform (Joyce and Henderson 2002:12).

The Middle Formative (800–400 BC) and Late Formative (400 BC–AD 250) periods witnessed the acceleration of social differentiation and the

TABLE 2.1. Chronological sequences in western Honduras

	Period	El Cajón	Lake Yojoa	Comayagua	Ulúa Valley	Copán
1200	Late Postclassic				Naco	
1000	Early Postclassic		Rio Blanco	Las Vegas	Botija	Ejar
	Terminal Classic	Late Sulaco		Tenampua	Santiago	Coner/Ejar
800	Late Classic	Middle Sulaco	Yojoa	Comayagua	Late Ulúa	Coner
600		Early Sulaco				Acbi
400	Early Classic			Maradiaga	Early Ulúa	
AD 250		Late Yunque	Eden II		Late Chamelecón	Bijac
0	Late Formative			Miravelle	Middle Chamelecón	Chabij
200 BC		Early Yunque	Eden I		Early Chamelecón	
				Rinconada		
400	Middle Formative		Jaral	Chilal	Playa	Uir
600						
800						Gordon
1000	Early Formative			Yarumela	Puerto Escondido	Rayo
1200						
1400						

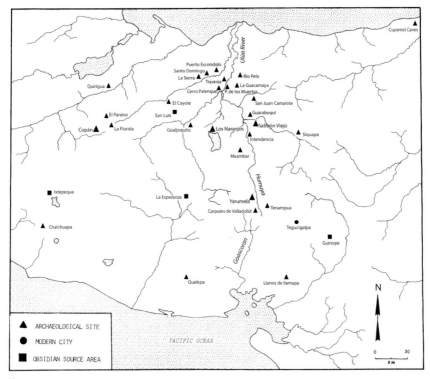

FIGURE 2.1. *Location of important archaeological sites in Honduras*

construction of large-scale civic-ceremonial architecture. Differential social status began to be expressed in mortuary assemblages at the transition between the Early and Middle Formative periods. Social differentiation is evident in mortuary offerings in the Cuyamel caves along the Rio Aguan (Healy 1974) and at Copán in southwestern Honduras (Fash 2001; Gordon 1898a). Burial VIII-27 at Copán dates to 1000–850 BC and is particularly interesting because of the richness of its associated offerings. Four ceramic vessels, 9 greenstone celts, and over 300 drilled and polished jade objects accompanied a male buried with 2 child skulls and a decapitated individual (Fash 2001:70; Fash and Davis-Salazar 2008:143–144). The ability of this individual to acquire an exceptional level of wealth together with the authority to take others with him into the afterlife suggests that a high level of social differentiation existed at Copán at this time. In the Ulúa valley, social differentiation was evident in Middle Formative mortuary assemblages at Playa de los Muertos (Popenoe 1934). Here, some burials lacked offerings while others had jade and shell beads, jade and ceramic earspools, jade and shell pendents, and ceramic vessels, seals, and figurines (Joyce, Hendon, and Sheptak 2008:cuadro 4; Popenoe 1934).

Several important burials occur for the first time in public architecture. The earliest association of burials with architecture occurs at Copán where forty-nine burials, including Burial VIII-27, were interred in a cobble platform. The tradition of burying important individuals in civic-ceremonial constructions continued throughout the Middle Formative period. At Puerto Escondido, two burials with ceramic vessels, pigment, and one jade ornament were associated with the construction of a stepped earthen platform (Joyce and Henderson 2001). An elaborate Jaral phase burial at Los Naranjos (table 2.1) was recovered from Structure IV. This individual had an elaborate offering that included a pair of jade earspools, a jade necklace, and a belt made of multiple strands of beads (Baudez and Becquelin 1973:91, figure 145a–d). The presence of burials in public architecture reflects the broad authority these individuals had in their communities (Joyce 1999:15).

Important centers appeared and grew in prominence during the Formative as they constructed large civic-ceremonial platform mounds in and around public plazas (table 2.2). Unfortunately, little information is available on the population size of these sites because their residential areas have been obliterated or their associated house mounds recycled into the construction fill of later architectural structures. Overall, however, many of these sites appear small despite the size of their civic-ceremonial structures. In the Ulúa valley, the population of the large center of La Guacamaya is estimated at 773 residents (Robinson 1989:137), while Río Pelo only had eleven residential structures around its central platform, which was 6 m high (Wonderley 1985:2). Only the site of Yarumela in the Comayagua valley has good information on the distribution of Middle and Late Formative domestic debris, which covers an area of 30 ha around its civic-ceremonial core.[4] It appears that many ritual centers were supported by dispersed regional populations that were integrated through periodic celebrations and associated construction events. It is paradoxical that Formative period elites were able to mobilize a significant amount of labor to construct large civic-ceremonial structures at sites with small resident populations.

Chiefdoms during the Formative period engaged in a level of civic-ceremonial activity that is distinctively different in two ways from what is found during the subsequent Classic period. First, it was during the Formative period when most of the largest civic-ceremonial architecture was constructed across west-central Honduras. These constructions defined ritual precincts of lasting regional importance well into the Early Classic period. Second, many of these precincts contained stone carvings that were created to enhance the ritual experience and

TABLE 2.2. Large Late Formative mound structures in Honduras

Site	Region	Structure	Size (m)	Height (m)	Reference
El Guayabal	El Paraíso	N/A		8.0–10.0	Canuto and Bell 2013; Reyes Mazzoni 1976
Baide	Santa Bárbara	—	35–50	4.0–6.0	Schortman et al. 1986
Los Naranjos	Lake Yojoa	Jaral-Str. IV	75 × 100	6.0	Baudez and Becquelin 1973:75
Los Naranjos	Lake Yojoa	Jaral-Fosse 1	1,300 m long	6.5 m deep	Baudez and Becquelin 1973:51–53
Los Naranjos	Lake Yojoa	Eden-Str. I	80 × 85	18.5	Baudez and Becquelin 1973:75
Los Naranjos	Lake Yojoa	Jaral-Fosse 2	3,000 m long	—	Baudez and Becquelin 1973:66–69
Río Pelo	Ulúa valley	Md 1	22.6 × 22.6	6.0	Wonderley and Caputi 1984:figure 5
La Guacamaya	Ulúa valley	Md 1	N/A	5.0	Robinson 1989:103
Salitrón Viejo	El Cajón	Str. 3	16 × 15	5.35	Hirth 1987a
Salitrón Viejo	El Cajón	Str. 1	17 × 14	4.4	Hirth 1987a
Santa Domingo	Naco valley	—	N/A	6.0	Henderson et al. 1979:187
Lo de Vaca	Comayagua	—	35 × 30	10	Baudez 1966
Yarumela	Comayagua	Str. 101	115 × 70	20	Dixon 1989b:261
Yarumela	Comayagua	Str. 102	25 × 35	9.0	Dixon et al. 1994:74
Yarumela	Comayagua	Str. 103	20 × 30	6.0	Dixon et al. 1994:74
Yarumela	Comayagua	Str. 104	20 × 25	6.0	Dixon et al. 1994:75
Las Liconas (CM-11)	Comayagua	—	33 × 43	6.0	Dixon 1989a:68
Quebracho Sur (CM-26)	Comayagua	—	41 × 41	9.0	Dixon 1989a:78
Tambla (CM-45)	Comayagua	Acropolis	34 × 54	5.5	Dixon 1989a:87
Manzanilla (CM-69)	Comayagua	—	42 × 42	9.0	Dixon 1989a:94
Llanos de Ilamapa	Francisco Morazán	—	N/A	6.0–8.0	Reyes Mazzoni 1976

N/A: Not available

reinforce mythical beliefs shared by the participating population. These stone carvings include both bas-relief carvings and free-standing stone sculptures that were displayed on platform mounds and their adjoining spaces. The association of carved stone monuments with large civic-ceremonial structures replicates the pattern of ritual activity found across Mesoamerica during the Middle and Late Formative periods in the Gulf Coast, Chiapas, and Guatemala.

Archaeologists working in Honduras are accustomed to classifying any mound or platform over 2 m tall as a monumental structure because they contrast sharply with the smaller platforms on which perishable domestic structures were built (Dixon et al. 1994:77; Hasemann 1987:90). While the 2-m designation is useful for distinguishing functional differences in platform usage, it shrouds the variation in construction scale found during the Formative and Classic periods. In many cases, the largest structures recorded for a region date to the Formative period. Table 2.2 records a number of large architectural constructions that date to the Middle and/or Late Formative periods. Their final dimensions, of course, were the result of their durability as ritual centers and the multiple building episodes that added to their height incrementally over time.

Two sites with especially large monumental constructions are Los Naranjos at Lake Yojoa and Yarumela in the Comayagua valley. Two very substantial structures were constructed at Los Naranjos. Structure I is 18.5 m tall and was the tallest mound at Los Naranjos, while Structure IV is a broad acropolis platform that is 6 m high. In addition to these mounds, two extensive defensive ditches[5] were constructed during the Formative to protect or enclose the site's main civic-ceremonial areas.

The site of Yarumela contains the largest Formative civic-ceremonial architecture in Honduras. Structure 101 was initiated during the Middle Formative and reached its maximum dimensions of 110 m long (E–W), 70 m wide (N–S), and 20 m high[6] by the end of the phase (Canby 1949; Dixon 2008b; Dixon et al. 1994). Four other platform mounds over 3 m in height also were constructed at Yarumela. Structure 102 was located on the east side of the main plaza across from Structure 101 and reached a height of 9 m during the Late Formative period (Dixon et al. 1994:81). An empty burial chamber with ceramic offerings but no mortuary interment was identified in Structure 102 that dates to the end of the Formative period.

Regional survey in the Comayagua valley provides good information on the regional population and how it was linked to Yarumela. Twenty-seven Late Formative sites were identified, sixteen of which had architectural constructions while eleven did not, suggesting that some domestic structures were constructed directly on ground surface. Yarumela was at the center of a three-tier settlement

TABLE 2.3. Largest Late Formative mounds at sites in the Comayagua valley

Site Name	Site Number	Site Size (ha)	Platform Mound (m)	Superstructure Mound (m)	Total Height of Mound (m)
Casa Blanca	CM-13	5	4	—	4
El Batallón	CM-17	2	3	—	3
El Chilcal	LP-6	1	3	—	3
Las Liconas	CM-11	2.5	4.5	1.5	6
Las Pitallas	CM-24	2.5	4	1	5
Manzanilla	CM-69	4	6	3	9
Monte Negro	CM-5	5	2.5	1.5	4
Quebracho Sur	CM-26	1	6	3	9
San Jose	CM-39	2	1.5	2	3.5
Tambla	CM-45	6	2	3.5	5.5
Yarumela	LP-1	30	20	1	20
Zanjón Grande/ Ajuterique	CM-27	3.5	4	1	5

hierarchy, with all sites located within half a day's walk from its dominant ceremonial architecture (Dixon 1989a:figure 2). The scale of monumental construction at the regional level is greater than anywhere else in Honduras. Eleven of the fifteen secondary centers in the valley (Dixon 1989a, 1989b) had one mound at least 3 m high, while two others (Manzanilla, Quebracho Sur) had a mound that was 9 m tall. Table 2.3 identifies the sites in the Comayagua valley that have a civic-ceremonial platform 3 m or more in height. The distinction between Yarumela and secondary centers in the valley is clear in both the size of the sites and the height of their civic-ceremonial constructions (tables 2.2 and 2.3).

The second important aspect of ritual activity during the Formative period was the presence of carved stone monuments in ritual centers (figure 2.2). These monuments range in form from relief carvings to full-round and pedestal sculptures. The imagery on these sculptures includes both anthropomorphic and zoomorphic forms, with the former predominating over the later. While sculpture is difficult to date when it is not recovered from usage contexts, table 2.4 summarizes some of the carved stone monuments dated to Formative and Classic period sites in west-central Honduras. The two sites in which carved monuments are best represented are Los Naranjos and Yarumela.

TABLE 2.4. Formative and Classic period monuments in west-central Honduras

Site	Region	Monument	Monument	Imagery	Reference
FORMATIVE PERIOD MONUMENTS					
Baide	Santa Bárbara	Unnumbered	Low relief	Anthropomorphic	Benyo and Melchionne 1987:60
Copán	Copán valley	Foundation, stela 4	Low relief	Anthropomorphic	Lothrop 1921:figure 70d; Richardson 1977:figure 37
Copán	Copán valley	Foundation, stela 5	Pedestal, low relief	Anthropomorphic	Lothrop 1921:figure 70d
La Florida	La Florida	Unnumbered	Full-figure sculpture	Seated human, animal on back	Lothrop 1921:figure 69b; Richardson 1977:figure 35c
La Guacamaya	Ulúa valley		Column sculpture, low relief	Anthropomorphic	Gordon 1898b:figure 4; Lothrop 1921:figure 68a; Henderson, pers. comm.
La Islita	Lake Yojoa	Monument 5	Tenon sculpture	Serpent head	Yde 1938:figure 17
La Islita	Lake Yojoa	11	Column sculpture	Anthropomorphic	Baudez and Becquelin 1973:83
Los Naranjos	Lake Yojoa	Monument 1	Full-figure sculpture	Anthropomorphic	Baudez and Becquelin 1973:82
Los Naranjos	Lake Yojoa	Monument 2	Tenon sculpture	Serpent head	Baudez and Becquelin 1973:82
Los Naranjos	Lake Yojoa	Monument 3	Column sculpture	Anthropomorphic	Baudez and Becquelin 1973:82; Joyce and Henderson 2002:figura 10
Los Naranjos	Lake Yojoa	Monument 4	Full-figure sculpture	Anthropomorphic	Baudez and Becquelin 1973:82, figure 65; Joyce and Henderson 2002:figure 11
Los Naranjos	Lake Yojoa	11 column sections	Circular columns	Plain	Baudez and Becquelin 1973:83–84
Los Naranjos	Lake Yojoa	Monument 1	Tenon sculpture	Serpent head	Joyce and Henderson 2002:figura 8
Los Naranjos	Lake Yojoa	Monument 2	Sculpture	Anthropomorphic	Joyce and Henderson 2002:figurura 9

Mogotillo	Tegucigalpa		Peg-based	Sculpture	Stone 1957:95
Ocotepeque	Ocotepeque	Unnumbered	Peg-based	Sukia figure	Richardson 1977:406
Puerto Escondido	Naco valley	Monument 1	Sculpture	Anthropomorphic	Joyce and Henderson 2002:figura 7
Yarumela	Comayagua	Monument 1	Stela, bas-relief	Serpent and designs	Stone 1957:plate 41
Yarumela	Comayagua	Monument 3	Bas-relief	—	Boyd Dixon, pers. comm.
Yarumela	Comayagua	2 column sections	Circular columns	Plain	Boyd Dixon, pers. comm.
Yarumela	Comayagua	—	—	Cupulate	Boyd Dixon, pers. comm.
YR-124	Sula valley	Monument	Plain column	Cylindrical	Robinson 1989:319
Playa de los Muertos	Ulúa valley	—	—	—	Seated stone figure?
CLASSIC PERIOD MONUMENTS					
Travesia	Ulúa valley	Monument 1	Shaped stela	Google-eye grotesque	Stone 1941:figure 49c, 1977a:8
Travesia	Ulúa valley	Monument 2	Shaped stela	Google-eye grotesque	Stone 1941:figure 49b
Travesia	Ulúa valley	Monument 3	Shaped stela	Google-eye grotesque	Stone 1941:figures 49a, 50
Travesia	Ulúa valley	Monument 4	Bas-relief fragment	Circle eyes	Stone 1941:figure 60
Travesia	Ulúa valley	Monument 5	Plain stone slab	Triple triangular design	Stone 1941:figure 59
Cerro Palenque	Ulúa valley	Slab sculpture	Notched stone slab	Grotesque-triple triangular design	Hendon, Joyce, and Lopiparo 2013:figure 6.9
El Cedral (PC205)	Meambar	Engraved slab	Flat rock stela	Google-eye grotesque	Hirth, Lara-Pinto, and Hasemann 1990:42

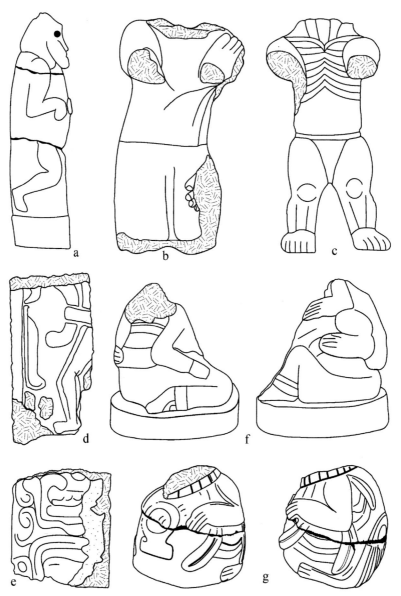

FIGURE 2.2. *Formative period sculptured monuments from west-central Honduras: (a) column sculpture from La Guacamaya, (b) monument 3 from Los Naranjos, (c) monument 4 from Los Naranjos, (d–e) bas-relief carvings from Yarumela, (f) sculpture from La Florida, (g) sculpture from Copán. Illustration by Emily Kate and Kenneth Hirth.*

Los Naranjos has the largest number of sculpted monuments recovered to date. They include six basalt carvings and eleven plain basalt column sections. Four of these six sculptures display anthropomorphic figures, while the other two are serpent images.[7] Rosemary Joyce and John Henderson (2002, n.d.) link the anthropomorphic figures (figures 2.2b–c) to leadership themes and the high-ranking elite individual buried in Structure IV. The serpent images, in contrast, may be linked to rituals involving mythology, corporate identity, and cosmology rather than rulership (Joyce and Henderson n.d.:17). The basalt columns were recovered in the plaza between Structures I and IV and could have been used to bound the ceremonial zone in much the same way they were at the Olmec site La Venta (14). Two bas-relief carvings reminiscent of monuments at Kaminaljuyú have been recovered at Yarumela (figure 2.2d–e), in addition to two stone column fragments and a cupulate monument. The two column fragments were recovered in the plaza area between Structures 101 and 102; like those at Los Naranjos, they may have been used to designate important ritual space.

Formative period monuments have been reported elsewhere in Honduras, at Puerto Escondido, Copán, and La Florida. Monument 1 at Puerto Escondido is a fragment of a human figure seated in a cross-legged position that was recovered from a stone cist grave that was opened and refilled in antiquity, a practice already noted for Yarumela. An anthropomorphic column sculpture (figure 2.2a) was identified at the site of La Guacamaya in the Ulúa valley (Lothrop 1921:figure 68a). Two squat anthropomorphic sculptures were also recovered at Copán from the foundation platforms of later stelae.[8] Their incorporation into platform fill suggests that earlier sculptures (e.g., figure 2.2g) were no longer venerated by the Copán ruling elite (Lothrop 1921:figure 70d). Another stylistically early sculpture has been reported from La Florida, located 25 km northeast of Copán. Here, a sculpture (figure 2.2f) was recorded of a seated human with a bird image on his back, reminiscent of sculptures recovered from Nicaragua (Lothrop 1921:figure 69b). These images point to an early tradition of stone sculpture use in Honduras that declined during the Classic period (table 2.4).

An important component of ritual life across Mesoamerica was the use of feasting as a mechanism to draw people together and foster integration at both the community and regional levels. Feasting was used to mobilize work parties (Monaghan 1996; Vogt 1969:147) for a range of community activities, including the construction of civic-ceremonial architecture. It was a prominent way labor was mobilized within Lenca chiefdoms during the sixteenth century, where considerable quantities of fermented beverages were consumed in communal celebrations (Herrera y Tordesillas 1944–1947:6:16, 23; Wells 2007:35–38).

The earliest evidence for feasting dates to the Early Formative period, where the consumption of fermented and non-fermented cacao beverages was identified at Puerto Escondido as early as 1150 BC (Joyce and Henderson 2007:642, 649). Special vessels in the burials at the Cuyamel caves reflect food sharing and feasting that united the deceased with their survivors (Joyce 1999:18). Deposits reflecting feasting activity were recovered underneath the Late Formative ballcourt at the site of San Juan Camalote (figure 2.1), which may be the product of a feast carried out to initiate its construction (Joyce, Hendon, and Sheptak 2008:294). Another large concentration of Late Formative feasting refuse was recovered at the site of Río Pelo alongside Mound I and under Mounds II and IV (Joyce, Hendon, and Sheptak 2008:304; Wonderley 1985:4, 9).

Exotic goods were important in some chiefdom societies as a way elite built individualized social networks (Brumfiel and Earle 1987a; Friedman 1982) or established alliances with their neighbors (Dalton 1977). One way to obtain these goods was to sponsor their manufacture in direct or indirect ways (Clark 1987; Clark and Parry 1990). Nevertheless, control over the production of wealth goods does not appear to have been an important pathway to power in Honduran chiefdoms. A small amount of production debris from jade, marine shell, and marble objects was recovered from Middle Formative deposits at Puerto Escondido (Joyce and Henderson 2001:13, 2002:5). Marble vessels were also important wealth items in Honduran societies, most of which were likely manufactured in the Ulúa valley where the highest-quality raw material is located (Luke and Tykot 2007). Unfortunately, no marble vessel workshops have been identified, so it remains unclear whether elites were involved in promoting the production of these wealth goods. Elsewhere in Honduras there is little evidence for production of craft goods for exchange during the Formative period beyond the manufacture of ceramics and some obsidian blades.

Trade was another means to obtain wealth goods in chiefdom societies (Creamer and Haas 1985:739–749; Drennan and Uribe 1987:xi; Rathje 1972). Understanding the type of goods that moved through interregional exchange (e.g., exotic or utilitarian) and how they were used in society is critical for identifying their role in early chiefdoms. Interregional trade networks were established early in prehistory, with small quantities of jade, shell, and marble artifacts moving across Honduras as early as 1100 BC.[9] As noted above, all three classes of these exotics occur in special contexts during the Formative at Puerto Escondido (Joyce and Henderson 2002:5), Playa de los Muertos (Kennedy 1986; Popenoe 1934), La Guacamaya (Robinson 1989:189), Río Pelo (Wonderley 1985:5), Los Naranjos (Baudez and Becquelin 1973), Salitrón Viejo (Hirth

1988; Hirth and Hirth 1993), central Santa Bárbara (Ashmore 1987:34),[10] and Yarumela (Dixon et al. 1994:74; Urban, Schortman, and Ausic 2002:147). Marble vessels were important elite items that were manufactured and traded into the Maya region during the Classic period, even reaching lower Central America (Luke and Tykot 2007:322). The recovery of twenty-seven plain marble vessel fragments at Yarumela indicates that these items were traded across Honduras beginning in the Early Formative period (Joesink-Mandeville 1987:204).

But trade was not limited to wealth goods. Utilitarian items, including ceramics and obsidian, also moved over considerable distances. In this regard, obsidian provides precise information on the structure of interregional exchange networks (e.g., Golitko and Feinman 2015; Golitko et al. 2012). Obsidian was exchanged across Mesoamerica during the Archaic period and was an important component of provisioning networks in many areas from 1800 cal BC onward (Hirth et al. 2013; Stark et al. 2016). Obsidian is present in the preceramic levels at Puerto Escondido and moved through trade networks as roughly shaped cobbles used for percussion flaking[11] during the Early Formative period (Hirth and Cyphers 2020). Obsidian blades made by craft specialists appear at sites after 1000 BC and increased in frequency over time in relation to percussion flakes produced from nodules.[12]

Some of the most complete information on obsidian usage and trade comes from Yarumela.[13] Pressure blades were recovered from all levels during the Early Formative period, which were manufactured from three important obsidian sources: La Esperanza, Honduras, and El Chayal and San Martin Jilotepeque in Guatemala (Dixon 1989b; Joyce et al. 2004:tabla 1; Joyce, Hendon, and Sheptak 2008:290; Wonderley 1985:15). Despite the presence of blades, there is no clear evidence that they were produced locally in the sites where they occur (Urban, Schortman, and Ausic 2002:148), although some obsidian blade core fragments were recovered from Yarumela (Elder 1984:table 3). It is likely that most blades moved between regions as finished items through down-the-line exchange, as they did elsewhere at this time (Hirth and Cyphers 2020; Joyce and Henderson 2010:196).

Ceramics also provide valuable information about interregional interaction. Although most ceramics were made locally, the emulation of decorative styles indicates which areas were interacting and sharing information on a regular basis (Henderson and Beaudry-Corbett 1993a, 1993b; Robinson 1989). The most precise way of examining ceramic exchange, however, is through petrographic and geochemical analyses that measure how far vessels moved from their original points of manufacture (Hodge et al. 1993; Neff et al. 2006; Rattray 1991). The most important Late Formative trade ware was Usulután

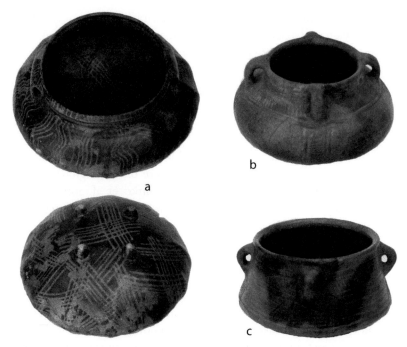

FIGURE 2.3. *Late Yunque ceramics from the Burial 1-17 at Salitrón Viejo: (a) top and bottom views of an Usulután vessel, (b–c) incised ware.* Courtesy, *IHAH; edited by Kenneth Hirth.*

ceramics (figure 2.3a), a decorated resist ware that was widely traded across the broad expanse of southeastern Mesoamerica (Andrews 1976; Demarest and Sharer 1982, 1986).

A chemical characterization study of Usulután ceramics from eleven regions of Honduras and El Salvador using instrumental neutron activation analysis (INAA) provides valuable insights into how this ceramic moved through interregional trade (Goralski 2008). Although it was originally thought that Usulután ceramics were manufactured in El Salvador (Andrews 1976; Demarest and Sharer 1982), INAA analysis established that they were produced in multiple locales across Honduras. Second, the analysis revealed that resist decorated ceramics from other areas consistently entered regions where they were manufactured locally. Third, while Usulután ceramics come in a variety of vessel types, one primary form that circulated between regions consisted of shallow plates and bowls with out-flaring walls that could be stacked and transported in an economical way. Fourth and finally, INAA analysis revealed that Usulután ceramics moved between regions over distances of 150 km or more (Goralski 2008:272–278).

Decorated ceramics were used regularly in inter-household celebrations and public feasts across Honduras. This tradition began during the Early Formative and continued into the Classic period with the appearance of well-made polychrome wares (Joyce 2017; Joyce and Henderson 2007). It should come as no surprise, therefore, to find Usulután ceramics occurring primarily as service ware. INAA analysis revealed that Usulután ceramic vessels made in the El Cajón region were traded into both the Comayagua and Ulúa valleys. Similarly, Usulután ceramics produced in the Comayagua valley were also widely traded, reaching areas of Santa Bárbara, Copán, Lake Yojoa, Naco, and El Cajón (Goralski 2008:table 6).

So, how were trade items used in these chiefdom societies? The importance of feasting can account for the interregional movement of ceramic service wares (Goralski 2008:283) and their inclusion in mortuary contexts where feasting accompanied burial of the dead. Obsidian was a utilitarian item (Dixon et al. 1994:74; Joyce and Henderson 2002:12) as opposed to an exotic good that elite aggrandizers would seek if they were building status through individualized social networks. But here some caution needs to be exercised. If trade goods were used to develop aggrandizers networks along the lines suggested by Jonathan Friedman (1982; Friedman and Rowlands 1978), then exotic wealth goods (e.g., jade and shell earflares, pendants, belts, and beads) should be prominent elements of mortuary offerings as elites elevated and separated themselves from the rest of the population. In reality, this did not occur. Exotic trade goods were included in a few early burials at Los Naranjos and Playa de los Muertos, but this practice decreased in importance during the Late Formative.

A more enduring use of imported wealth goods was as offerings associated with the construction of monuments. The earliest dedicatory offerings identified thus far are from Puerto Escondido, where two caches of imported goods were placed under a platform built between 1400 and 1100 BC. One offering consisted of twenty-one obsidian flakes and nodules, while the other was a belt made of sixteen shell ornaments (Joyce and Henderson 2002:12). Jade was used in architectural dedications at Puerto Escondido during the Middle Formative (Joyce and Henderson 2001:10) and as an offering under the column sculpture at the site of La Guacamaya (Gordon 1898b; Robinson 1989:189). Another notable architecture offering was the placement of two human crania, a greenstone celt, and red pigment at the base of Structure IV at Los Naranjos (Joyce 1999:38).

The Formative was a period of significant cultural development in north-western and west-central Honduras. Social differentiation is evident, marking the appearance of elite leadership with influence that extended to the regional level. Most impressive was the mobilization of labor to construct large-scale civic-ceremonial architecture in several key sites. The chiefdom societies that developed during the Formative period spread across Honduras during the subsequent Classic period.

THE CLASSIC PERIOD (AD 250–1000)

The Classic period covers approximately 750 years, which can be subdivided into subphases depending on the variability found in local material assemblages. While significant chronological work has been conducted on Honduran ceramics, phase divisions within the Classic are difficult to align between regions because of the variability they display (e.g., Henderson and Beaudry-Corbett 1993b). No attempt is made here to generalize about cultural processes across regions beyond a bipartite division of the Classic period into Early (AD 250–600) and Late (AD 600–900) subphases. The Terminal Classic (AD 900–1000) is referred to in general terms but is not examined in detail because it is not a well-represented occupation in the El Cajón region. Even with a two-period comparison of the Early and Late Classic, direct comparison between regions is challenging.

The Classic period is noted for its ceramic richness. This is the era when polychrome ceramics became popular in a wide variety of decorative styles. Various types of polychromes appeared at Copán (Viel 1978, 1983), while west-central Honduras saw the development of the elaborate and diverse groups of Ulúa and Sulaco polychromes.[14] These ceramics had a high aesthetic appeal and were widely traded between regions. Despite continuing efforts to improve the chronological precision of regional ceramic typologies (table 2.1), the diversity of types and the absence of large numbers of radiocarbon dates remain significant obstacles for direct interregional comparisons.

A hallmark of the Classic period was demographic growth across Honduras. Population densities increased in *every* region, and settlement pattern evidence suggests that the highest population levels in Honduran prehistory were reached during the Late Classic period. Populations were organized as chiefdom societies of different sizes, with the rate of population growth varying from region to region. Some regions (Naco, El Cajón, Santa Bárbara) witnessed continuous growth (Benyo and Melchionne 1987:55; Hasemann 1998:figures 8.3–8.5; Urban 1986; Wells and Davis-Salazar 2008:201), while others (Ulúa valley, Comayagua valley) appear to have lost population during the Early Classic, only to see it surge during the Late Classic (Dixon 1989b; Robinson 1989:195). It is difficult to judge whether this reflects different regional demographic trajectories or the need to refine ceramic chronologies.

Settlement pattern information suggests that Late Classic populations were organized into networks of differential social control. Most regions display a three-tier settlement hierarchy based on site size, with some monumental architecture present at the upper and intermediary tiers (Dixon 1989b:figure 5; Schortman and Urban 1987b:13).[15] Sites in the upper levels of site hierarchies have civic-ceremonial architecture and elite who supervised community events (Joyce 2014:25). Investigators working in the Naco and the Ulúa valleys have identified four- and five-tier settlement hierarchies (Joyce and Sheptak 1983; Pope and Robinson 1987:table 3; Robinson 1989; Wells and Davis-Salazar 2008:201), with most of the variation in site composition at the small end of the demographic spectrum. Although complex site hierarchies may suggest greater levels of social control, the most difficult task is determining the boundaries of regional chiefdoms with any degree of precision.[16] We believe that some small chiefdoms in west-central Honduras may have contained only a few hundred to a thousand people, while the largest chiefdoms like Yarumela during the Late Formative may have approached 5,000–10,000 members. But these are rough estimates based more on inference than on hard data. Certainly, the size of chiefdoms fluctuated with the nature of the integrative mechanisms employed and the charismatic ability of their leaders. Competition between regional centers would have increased as populations grew, so it is no surprise to see some Terminal Classic centers in the Ulúa and Comayagua valleys relocate to defensible locations.[17]

One measure of social complexity that can be discussed with some precision is the size and organization of the largest communities in regional settlement systems. Domestic residences during the Classic period were located on low house mounds that make it possible to estimate population within sites.[18] Table 2.5 estimates population size from mound counts at large sites from several regions during the Classic period. There are two caveats to these figures. First, there is always the possibility that the numbers of domestic structures at Classic period sites are underrepresented if some were constructed directly on ground surface without a basal platform. Research in the El Cajón region, however, suggests that virtually all domestic residences were constructed on low house mounds. Second, there is the difficulty of estimating population from individual structure counts. Here, population is calculated from mound counts using a conservative range estimate of three–five persons per structure.[19] These

TABLE 2.5. Mound counts at large Classic period regional centers in west-central Honduras

Site Name	Region	Number of Mounds	Estimated Population	Reference
LATE CLASSIC				
Gualjoquito	Santa Bárbara	47[a]	141–235	Schortman et al. 1986:265
Currusté	Ulúa valley	200–250	600–1,250	Hendon, Joyce, and Lopiparo 2013:8, 81; Joyce 2014:39
La Guacamaya	Ulúa valley	250	750–1,250	Robinson, personal communication, 2020
La Sierra	Naco valley	468	1,404–2,340	Wells and Davis-Salazar 2008:202
	Cuyumapa, Yoro	250	750–1,250	Joyce, personal communication, 2020
Carpules de Valladolid	Comayagua	102[a]	306–510	Dixon 1989a:105
Guarabuquí	El Cajón, Sulaco River	159[a]	477–795	Hirth et al. 1981:cuadro 1
Intendencia	El Cajón, Humuya River	152[a]	456–760	Hirth et al. 1981:cuadro 1
Salitrón Viejo	El Cajón, Sulaco River	360[a]	1,080–1,800	Hirth et al. 1981:cuadro 1
Travesia	Ulúa valley	250–500	750–2,500	Hendon et al. 2013:8
TERMINAL CLASSIC				
Tenampua	Comayagua	400–500	1,200–2,500	Dixon 1987:142; Popenoe 1935
Cerro Palenque	Sula valley	500 approx.	1,500–2,500	Joyce 2014:41

a. Represents counts of mapped Late Classic platform structures able to support a domestic residence.

estimates include large-range structures that are believed to have supported the residences of elite families (Canuto and Bell 2008; Edward Schortman, personal communication, 2021).

Despite the limitations of these estimates, table 2.5 provides an interesting perspective on how some of the largest Classic period sites in northwest and west-central Honduras ranged in size. First, population varied greatly from region to region, reflecting differences in agricultural productivity and the size of chiefdoms that developed in the regions. The site of Gualjoquito was the largest Late Classic site in the Santa Bárbara region but only had 47 domestic structures compared to 468 at the site of La Sierra in Naco. This variation is also evident in the Comayagua valley where Carpules de Valladolid, the largest site in the region, was only one-third to one-quarter the size of primary centers in the Ulúa valley, the Naco region, and El Cajón.[20] Three sites are listed for the El Cajón region to illustrate how site size varied within a region between primary (Salitrón Viejo) and secondary centers (Guarabuquí and Intendencia).

Table 2.5 also demonstrates that even the largest sites generally do not exceed 500 households in size. Travesía was the largest and most important site in the Ulúa valley during the Late Classic, with an estimated population of between 250–500 structures (Joyce 1983). This is less than the early estimate of Doris Stone (1941) but is more realistic in terms of a systematic evaluation of archaeological remains.[21] When structure counts are converted to population estimates using 3–5 persons per residence, even the largest centers did not exceed on-site populations of 2,000–2,500 persons. This is true even for the Terminal Classic period, when social pressures led to population nucleation at Cerro Palenque in the Ulúa valley and at Tenampua in Comayagua.[22] But not all primary sites were large. Even the largest Late Classic sites in the Santa Bárbara and Comayagua regions had populations in the range of only 200–500 residents, noticeably less than were found in other regions (table 2.5).

Population grew throughout the Classic, and so too did the number of centers with civic-ceremonial architecture. Architectural plans varied from site to site, but several changes occurred in site planning after the Late Formative period. First, the overall scale of civic-ceremonial construction was smaller. Rectangular range mounds supporting elite residences appear frequently at sites but normally do not exceed 2.5–3.0 m in height. Gone are the large-scale constructions like those documented at Los Naranjos and Yarumela (e.g., table 2.2). Second, there was a decline in the use of stone monuments in civic-ceremonial contexts compared to the Formative period. Fewer stone monuments are found; where they occur, they are more abstract in composition. One monument type recovered from the Ulúa valley at Travesía and Cerro Palenque is a geometrically carved stela depicting a goggle-eyed grotesque (figure 2.4a, c–e) (Hendon et al. 2013:figure 6.9; Hirth 1988:figure 9; Stone 1941:figures 49–50). Uncarved stelae occur at other sites in the Ulúa valley (figure 2.4b), reflecting a shift in the way ideological information was communicated during the Classic period.[23] The Meambar Stela, carved in a hybrid rock art style (figure 2.5), likewise exhibits a google-eyed grotesque and appears to date to the Classic period (Hirth et al. 1990:figure 4).[24]

One architectural innovation during the Classic was the appearance of ballcourts in many areas of Honduras. Ballcourts occur in a range of sites,[25] with

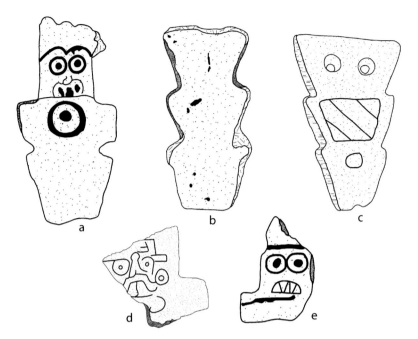

FIGURE 2.4. *Late Classic monuments from the Ulúa valley: (a–b) monuments from Travesía, (c) monument from Cerro Palenque, (d–e) monuments from Travesía. Illustration by Emily Kate and Kenneth Hirth.*

most located in the larger, more influential communities where elites resided.[26] About the only area where ballcourts have not been identified is in the El Cajón region. Table 2.6 summarizes the widespread distribution of ballcourts in twenty-two sites throughout northwestern and west-central Honduras.

The ball game was important throughout Mesoamerica, where it was played both in and outside of formal courts (De Borhegyi 1980; Scarborough and Wilcox 1991).[27] However the ball game was played, it was an important event, with social, ritual, and political importance (Fox 1996; Kowalewski et al. 1991; Santley, Berman, and Alexander 1991).[28] As John Fox (1996:483) has noted, the ballcourt was "a place with powerful supernatural associations . . . [and] served as a stage for rituals in which political conflict was mapped onto and resolved through cosmological drama." Christopher Begley (1999) has argued that the ball game and the ritual complex associated with it provided a context where the elite negotiated social relations within their communities and associated themselves with the elite in other areas. Susan Gillespie (1991:317) has noted that the ball game and the courts where it was played represented

FIGURE 2.5.
The Meambar Stela

places where social boundaries were defined. The variation found in ballcourt orientations in west-central Honduras has been interpreted as reflecting the different seasons when games were held (Hendon, Joyce, and Sheptak 2009; Joyce n.d.). Whenever these events were scheduled, the ball game provided the basis for community, inter-community, and perhaps even interregional interaction between attending groups.

One continuity in ritual activity between the Formative and Classic periods was the incorporation of feasting into socio-religious celebrations and its use in the initiation of public construction projects (Begley 1999; Joyce 1999:18, 2014:123; Wonderley 1985). Middens in public areas are the most common evidence for feasting events in large and small sites. One such deposit was identified underneath the ballcourt at San Juan Camalote (Joyce, Hendon, and Sheptak 2008:294). Although this deposit was probably associated with the ballcourt's construction, it is likely that feasting was carried out alongside the game itself. One pattern associated with feasting appears to be the destruction of cooking and serving vessels used during the celebration at the end of the event (Hendon,

TABLE 2.6. Location of ballcourts in west-central Honduras

Area	Site	Age	Number of Ballcourts	Reference
Comayagua	Quelepa	Late Classic	1	Stone 1957:figure 28
Comayagua	Tenampua	Terminal Classic	1	Popenoe 1935:566
Naco region	La Sierra	Late Classic	1	Wells and Davis-Salazar 2008:202
Naco region	La Palmarejo	Late Classic	1	Wells and Davis-Salazar 2008:203
Lake Yojoa	Los Naranjos	Late Classic	2	Baudez and Becquelin 1973:figures 54–61
Santa Bárbara	Gualjoquito	Late Classic	1	Schortman et al. 1986:270
Ulúa valley	Campo Dos (CR-132)	Late Classic	1	Hendon, Joyce, and Lopiparo 2013:62
Ulúa valley	Curusté	Late Classic	1	Hendon, Joyce, and Lopiparo 2013:8
Ulúa valley	La Guacamaya	Late Classic	1	Robinson 1989:189
Ulúa valley	Quebrada Camalote	Late Classic	1	Hendon, Joyce, and Lopiparo 2013:80
Ulúa valley	Travesía	Late Classic	1	Robinson 1989:189
Ulúa valley	Cerro Palenque	Terminal Classic	1	Joyce 2014
Ulúa valley	Rio Blanco	Late Classic	1	Hendon, Joyce, and Lopiparo 2013:80
Cataguana valley	PACO-2	Late Classic	1	Joyce et al. 1989:table 2
Cataguana valley	PACO-5	Late Classic	1	Joyce et al. 1989:table 2
Cataguana valley	PACO-9	Late Classic	1	Joyce et al. 1989:table 2
Cataguana valley	PACO-11	Late Classic	1	Joyce et al. 1989:table 2
Cataguana valley	PACO-14	Late Classic	1	Joyce et al. 1989:table 2

continued on next page

TABLE 2.6.—*continued*

Area	Site	Age	Number of Ballcourts	Reference
Cataguana valley	San Juan Camalote (PACO-15)	Late Formative	1	Joyce et al. 1989:table 2
Cataguana valley	PACO-17	Late Classic	1	Joyce et al. 1989:table 2
La Venta valley	Róncador	Late Classic?	1	Robinson 1989:189
Cacaulapa valley	El Coyote	Late Classic	1	Wells 2007:39
Total ballcourts			23	

Joyce, and Sheptak 2009:7). Soil chemistry provides additional indications of feasting. Phosphate mapping[29] has identified high concentrations of decomposed organic debris in the central plaza at El Coyote in the Cacaulapa valley, which is interpreted as a product of public feasting (Canuto and Bell 2013:13).

Interregional trade continued as an important activity during the Classic period, with widespread production and distribution of polychrome ceramics. High-value items moved between regions in small quantities that included jade and greenstone items, marine shell from the Pacific and Atlantic Coasts, and marble vessels. Ulúa marble vessels are believed to have been produced at or near the site of Travesía (figure 2.1) and then traded as elite items over a wide area, from Belize and the lowlands of Guatemala to the Nicoya Peninsula in Costa Rica (Luke and Tykot 2007; Luke et al. 2003). The identification of a copper workshop at the site of El Coyote is an example of the production of high-value goods for exchange during the Terminal Classic period (Urban et al. 2013).

High-value goods continued to be included as offerings in the construction of buildings as part of dedication rituals (e.g., Benyo and Melchionne 1987:57; Schortman and Urban 1987b:18). A huge deposit of over 4,500 censer fragments together with a cache of Spondylus shells, sculpture fragments, and small clay cups were recovered from a ritual deposit at La Sierra in the Naco valley (Schortman and Urban 1994:410). This contrasts sharply with the offerings from mortuary contexts, where most burials lack rich offerings. The absence of elaborate burial offerings suggests that wealth inequality was not great and that individual procurement and control of prestige goods was not an important route to power and prestige during the Classic period (Joyce n.d.).

There is evidence for small-scale craft production of utilitarian goods in individual households. Specialized craft production[30] refers to the manufacture of goods intended for consumption outside the unit of production (Hirth 2006:7–8). Excavations at La Sierra identified evidence for several workshops making obsidian blades, ceramic censers, pottery, figurines, textiles, and ground stone implements (Wells and Davis-Salazar 2008:203). The same pattern has been identified in the Ulúa valley, where small-scale craft production was identified in several settlements that included the manufacture of stone tools from local chert and imported obsidian (Joyce n.d.).

Obsidian had circulated through interregional trade across Honduras since the Early Formative, and the range of sources exploited documents the scope of the networks through which it moved (Hirth 1985: Joyce et al. 2004; Wonderley 1985:15). The analysis of 123 obsidian artifacts from the three Classic period sites in the El Cajón region[31] revealed that obsidian reached this area from the Honduran sources of La Esperanza and Guinope and the Guatemalan sources of Ixtepeque and El Chayal (Hirth 1987b:cuadro 3). As in the preceding Formative period, obsidian moved as both nodules and pressure blades. The manufacture of blades from La Esperanza obsidian implies the presence of craft specialists somewhere in Honduras. At present, there is no convincing evidence for a resident obsidian blade specialist producing pressure blades at a major site in west-central Honduras. Instead, many prismatic blades appear to have been traded as finished items or to have been produced by itinerant blade producers known to have existed in other areas of Mesoamerica (Hirth 2006: 134–135, 2008). What is significant is that analysis of obsidian from the three sites in the El Cajón region indicates the operation of independent procurement networks at the household level.[32]

Some of the best indirect evidence for craft specialization is found in the high-quality polychrome ceramics that were produced and circulated between regions during the Classic period. Polychrome ceramics were made locally in every region but continued to be widely exchanged in the same way earlier Usulután ceramics had. Evidence for ceramic production has been identified at the site of Campo Dos along the lower Chamelecón River and at Salitrón Viejo, where Sulaco polychromes were produced (Beaudry et al. 1989; Hendon, Joyce, and Lopiparo 2013:67). Ulúa polychromes were particularly important and were distributed widely across eastern Mesoamerica, from Belize and eastern Guatemala to El Salvador and Nicaragua (Joyce n.d.:22). The reason for their popularity was their striking decorative designs (figure 2.6) and their use in both public and mortuary feasting activities.[33]

FIGURE 2.6. *Ulúa polychrome vessels from the Comayagua Museum.* Courtesy, *IHAH; edited by Kenneth Hirth.*

Ceramics were exchanged and gifted through household-to-household networks along natural communication corridors. Cópador and Gualpopa ceramics from Copán moved down the Chamelecón drainage into sites in west-central Honduras (Dixon 1989b:264; Schortman et al. 1986:262; Urban 1993a, 1993b; Viel 1983). The Sulaco (Bold Geometric) polychromes produced in the El Cajón region (figure 2.7) were distributed south into the Comayagua valley and north along the Ulúa River all the way to the Atlantic Coast (Baudez 1966:312; Robinson 1989:181; Schortman and Urban 1987b:19). Despite the intricate painting, incising, and plastic decoration incorporated into different types, polychrome ceramics were not a restricted luxury item. Both commoner and elite households had access to polychrome ceramics (Beaudry-Corbett

FIGURE 2.7. *Sulaco polychrome vessels, also known as Bold Geometric. Top: a complete Sulaco polychrome jar.* Courtesy, *Middle American Research Institute, Tulane University; edited in Photoshop by Kenneth Hirth. Bottom: (a) Sulaco polychrome jar rims, (b) Sulaco polychrome bowl rims. Photos by Kenneth Hirth.*

1987). Furthermore, the widespread distribution of polychrome styles across Honduras confirms the high level of communication that existed between regions during the Classic period (Begley 1999:153; Henderson and Beaudry-Corbett 1993b). Tracing the networks and the distances over which ceramics moved will have to await the implementation of more precise geochemical source analyses of Ulúa polychromes and other ceramic types.[34]

SUMMARY

Three characteristics were identified at the beginning of this chapter as important elements to consider when discussing the organization of chiefdom societies: the size and scale of integration, the level of stratification and inequality, and the centrality and nature of chiefly decision making. All three of these features are interrelated, but they can be manifested in different ways in the archaeological record. While the information from northwestern and west-central Honduras is far from complete, several interesting patterns have begun to emerge.

Scale of integration is an important dimension of socio-political systems that can be examined if system boundaries can be established from the distribution of archaeological sites, artifactual remains, or textual references in the case of the Maya. Unfortunately, this type of information is difficult to obtain. Boundaries defining the extent of chiefdoms are hard to identify given the extensive interregional exchange of ceramics, which makes social and economic boundaries blend into one another. One precise measure of social integration that archaeologists work with is community size. The available information suggests that even the largest and most influential centers rarely exceeded 2,000–2,500 people during the Classic period (table 2.5). The data are less clear for earlier periods, but it is possible that even large Formative period sites were below these levels. Only at Yarumela has Formative period domestic debris been mapped over an area 30 ha in size. Even modest densities of 10–25 persons per ha produce a population of only 300–750 residents. Clearly, more work is necessary to establish the size of Formative communities across Honduras.

Stratification and inequality can develop along different pathways (Flannery and Marcus 2012; McGuire 1983), and three patterns are beginning to emerge in the archaeological data. The wealth inequality found in a few elite burials during the Formative period appears to have decreased over time. Burials with jade and shell jewelry and elaborate ceramic vessels and figurines like those found at Playa de los Muertos, Cuyamel caves, Copán, and Los Naranjos largely disappeared after 300–400 BC. Most Classic period burials lack mortuary offerings, and even those found in elite residential structures often have only a single greenstone bead or ceramic vessel. Wealth inequality does not provide sharp divisions between elite and non-elite as we move from the Late Formative into the Classic period.

A high level of *wealth equality* rather than inequality is reflected in the distribution of artifact assemblages between the largest and smallest sites in different regions. Valued resources were available to all levels of the population. Cacao could be grown locally, and non-local obsidian moved through trade networks as a preferred material for cutting tools beginning in the Early Formative period. Well-made ceramic vessels that included Usulután resist wares and elaborate polychromes are found in the humblest households, indicating that decorated ceramics used in feasting and other domestic and public rituals were not restricted to the elite. The continuity of access to imported goods, especially decorated ceramics, suggests that control of personal wealth was not the basis for establishing hierarchies of authority for the emergence and spread of chiefdom societies across Honduras.

Finally, there appears to have been a shift in the way leadership narratives were communicated to the broader population between the Formative and Classic periods. During the Early and Middle Formative periods, some of the largest sites incorporated stone sculpture into their ritual centers. These sculptures often depicted anthropomorphic images that linked emerging leaders with spiritual forces that reinforced their ascendant position of authority in society (Joyce and Henderson 2002:15). The incorporation of Olmec imagery in both sculptural treatments and ceramic assemblages during the Early Formative was one way to reinforce elevated status (Joyce and Henderson 2010:195). This changed during the Classic period. Not only did the number of sites with carved monuments decrease, but the representations became more abstract or were replaced with blank stelae, possibly with painted designs (figure 2.4b). This coupled with a decrease in elaborate burial offerings suggests that pathways to individual power were de-emphasized during the Classic, leading to more collective forms of leadership and authority.

Centrality of decision making focuses on leadership and the structure of authority in society. Insight into the nature of decision making in Honduran societies can be gleaned from three types of information: the hierarchical structure of regional settlement patterns, the mobilization of labor for community purposes, and the integrative focus of community activities. Population growth from the Formative to the Classic period resulted in the emergence of two- and three-tier settlement systems in most regions. What the strength of the linkage between communities was remains unclear, but the focus of inter-action appears to have been collective ritual. The construction of large-scale civic-ceremonial platforms at Yarumela and Los Naranjos suggests that lead-ers drew on labor from their surrounding regions. Nevertheless, the decline in the scale of public constructions from the Formative period to the Classic period makes one wonder whether leaders' ability to mobilize regional labor may have decreased over time. One constant, however, was the continued importance of communal feasting. Evidence of feasting has been recovered repeatedly in the plaza areas where ritual celebrations took place as well as on the preconstruction surfaces where large platform mounds were constructed. One can suppose that feasting lubricated all social interaction and ritual events at both community and regional levels.

So, how centralized was decision making in pre-Columbian Honduran societies? While ritual and feasting were important components of these soci-eties, the expression of elite leadership appears to have been relatively weak. Archaeologists who want to find strongly centralized social hierarchies in Honduran societies can point to the large, monumental constructions at Los Naranjos and Yarumela. However, the presence of monumental constructions that include ballcourts at some small village sites suggests a more socially het-erarchical structure during the Classic period. In contrast to strongly hier-archical societies, heterarchies have multiple and often overlapping sources of authority and influence (Crumley 1995; Ehrenreich, Crumley, and Levy 1995). These overlapping pathways of authority can include various forms of social influence, from the role of shamans in directing religious rituals to eco-nomic specialists producing goods for distribution or use in ritual practices. Rosemary Joyce (n.d.) argues that heterarchy is the best model for modeling inequality in Honduran societies.

The question that remains to be answered is, how similar or different were the processes of cultural development in the El Cajón region compared to neighboring areas of Honduras. Chapter 3 describes the physical setting of the El Cajón region and discusses the scale, organization, development, and level of integration of the prehispanic society within it.

3

The El Cajón region is located along the Central Honduran corridor, a natural communication route that connects the Atlantic Coast to the Gulf of Fonseca on the Pacific Ocean by way of the Ulúa, Humuya, and Goascorán Rivers (see figure 2.1). This corridor was an important avenue for interregional interaction between the two coasts throughout the pre-Columbian past (Squier 1855; Yde 1938:11). The El Cajón region covers 1,200 km² of mountainous territory that includes portions of the Sulaco and Humuya Rivers and the upland area between them. The region was named for the El Cajón high dam and hydroelectric power facility that was constructed below the intersection of the Sulaco and Humuya Rivers, creating a 94 km² reservoir area behind the flood wall (figure 3.1). The El Cajón region represents the environmental and cultural impact zone of this modern development project, the limits of which are displayed in figure 3.2. The imminent destruction of archaeological sites within the reservoir zone prompted the Instituto Hondureño de Antropología e Historia (IHAH) to initiate the Proyecto Arqueológico El Cajón (PAEC)[1] to rescue archaeological remains from this previously unstudied portion of the country (Hirth, Lara-Pinto, and Hasemann 1989, 1990).

Most of the archaeological sites in the region are located in the sharply incised valleys of the Sulaco and Humuya Rivers. Local relief ranges from 200–300 m mean sea level (MSL) on the valley floors to 1,500–1,700 m MSL in upland areas.[2] These elevation differences

Pre-Columbian Society and Ecology in the El Cajón Region

https://doi.org/10.5876/9781646424757.c003

Montañuelas

FIGURE 3.1. *The El Cajón high dam and reservoir area. Top: view of the El Cajón high dam under construction as the reservoir was filling. Bottom: satellite image of the partially filled reservoir behind the dam. Google Earth, Image CNES / Airbus, Image © 2021 Maxar Technologies. Photograph by Kenneth Hirth.*

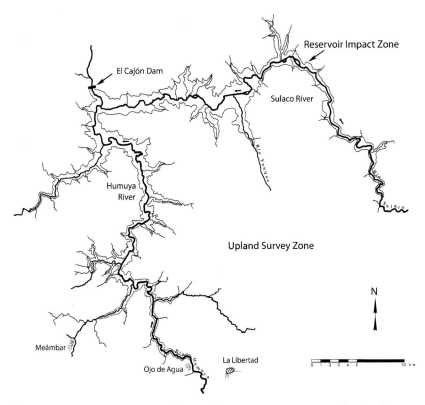

FIGURE 3.2. *El Cajón study area showing the reservoir impact zone and upland survey area between the Sulaco and Humuya Rivers*

created a mosaic of plant and animal resource zones that ranged from a tropical deciduous forest on the valley floor to pine-oak-sweetgum forest in upland areas. To develop a comprehensive understanding of pre-Columbian adaptation in the region, research was expanded beyond the reservoir impact zone (RIZ)[3] to include the upland areas, where a different array of resources could be exploited for subsistence and interregional exchange (figure 3.2).

The research adopted an ecological perspective that sought to understand how pre-Columbian groups interacted with their natural, social, and built environments. To that end, the following discussion begins by examining the natural environment, the resources available within that environment, and how groups could have exploited them. This is followed by an overview of the region's occupational history and how it is chronicled from the archaeological remains. The discussion then shifts to chronicling prehispanic development along the Sulaco River. It examines the organization of the largest and most important community at Salitrón Viejo and places its growth in the context of community development in the region.

UNDERSTANDING THE LANDSCAPE

The El Cajón area can be classified as an early mature landscape. The Sulaco and Humuya Rivers and their tributaries are enclosed in narrow to V-shaped valleys with small alluvial floodplains (figures 3.3 and 3.4). Local relief can exceed 600 m, with steep slope gradients of 12–40 degrees rising from the valley floor. Climate is tropical, with annual rainfall between 1,250 and 1,650 mm depending on local rain shadow effects (Loker 1989a:43). Most precipitation occurs between May and October and is only interrupted by the midsummer drought known as the *canícula*, which lasts between three and six weeks in July or August. Erosion is severe across steep slopes in the uplands, leading to thinner soils that are high in clay content. Upland areas are drained by numerous ravines but contain springs that provide sources of permanent drinking water (Hirth and Cosgren 1989:23). The result is a dissected environment, with variable rainfall that affected both natural vegetation and cultivation practices.

Contemporary plant communities are strongly affected by topography, rainfall, and soil conditions. Intensive plant surveys conducted by David Lentz (1984, 1989b) identified five plant communities that are the basis for reconstructing what the botanical environment resembled during prehispanic times.[4] Two of these, the circum-riverine and tropical deciduous forest zones, occupy the valley bottoms of the major permanent rivers (figure 3.4). The circum-riverine community occupies the banks of river courses and supports a range of majestic tree species—including the guanacaste (*Enterolobium cyclocarpum*), granadillo (*Dalbergia tucurensis* Donn), and negrito (*Simarouba glauca*), which produce edible fruit—as well as a range of useful shrubs and herbaceous plants.

The tropical deciduous forest community occupies the deep alluvial soils of the valley vegas that flank the circum-riverine zone. This community represents the climax vegetation of the valley bottoms and contained the commercially important trees mahogany (*Swietenia macrophylla*), cedar (*Cedrela* sp.), Honduran chestnut (*Sterculia apetala*), and San Juan (*Roseodendron donnellsmithii*). This community also included seven or eight important fruit-bearing trees that were important for the diet. The most prominent of these are the zapote (*Pouteria mammosa*), anona (*A. squamosa* L.), and ramon (*Brosimum alicastrum* Sw.) (Lentz 1989b:table 4.7). Unfortunately, most of the original

FIGURE 3.3. *The narrow Humuya River channel*

forest habitat had been destroyed by farming and lumbering activities at the time the research was initiated and had to be reconstructed from remnant forest stands (Lentz 1989b). Nevertheless, in prehispanic times, this community would have extended from the valley bottoms to elevations as high as 600–900 m MSL following stream courses where well-watered alluvial soils were present (Loker 1989b:143). Archie Carr (1950) notes that this type of situation

FIGURE 3.4. *The Sulaco River channel, its wider vegas, and circum-riverine botanical community*

promotes animal habitat diversity and provides a corridor connecting plant communities found at higher elevations.

Two pine-oak communities are in the upland areas of the El Cajón region. The pine-oak forest occupies the thinner soils on slopes up to approximately 1,000 m MSL. This is the most extensive plant community in the uplands today and contains the fruit-bearing tree known as nance (*Byrsonima crassifolia*), which was important in the diet of prehispanic groups. The forest canopy is relatively open and supports a range of grasses, shrubs, and herbaceous plants that have been reduced in diversity because of modern livestock grazing. Above 1,000 m MSL, cooler temperatures support a pine-oak-sweetgum forest. The pine and oak species in this zone are different from those found below 1,000 m MSL (Lentz 1989b).

The region's fifth plant community is one of secondary growth that covers previously cultivated land gone to fallow. Vegetation in these areas consists of a mixture of scrubs, grasses, and a range of plants adapted to disturbed habitats and periodic upheavals along watercourses. While representing a habitat awaiting its return to cultivation, this community includes some very useful fruit-bearing species, including coyol (*Acrocomia mexicana* Karw.), pepenance

(*Diospyros cuneata* Standley), and ciruela (*Spondias mombin* L., *Spondias. purpurea* L.) (Lentz 1982, 1989b:table 4.7).

Agriculture was the primary subsistence adaptation of groups in the El Cajón region, and its importance is reflected in the location of prehispanic settlement on good agricultural land. The best agricultural land occurs in small alluvial pockets along the Sulaco, Humuya, and Yure Rivers. These alluvial pockets, referred to as vegas, normally range from 1 ha to 20 ha in size, depending on their location and the dynamic forces at work in the rivers where they are located (Norville and Collins 1989).[5] William Loker's (1986:table 4.8) study of contemporary agricultural productivity revealed that alluvial vega lands had the highest maize productivity in the region, as well as the capacity to be cultivated continuously for ten–twenty years without fertilization (250).[6] Agriculture is also possible on the thinner soils of upland slopes and in alluvial pockets along the stream courses that descend from higher elevations. But the difference in maize productivity is notable. The mean maize productivity of vega lands is 1,831 kg/ha compared to 1,165–1,333 kg/ha in upland areas (Loker 1989b:table 6.10). But in addition to higher yields, vega lands were preferred because they could sustain longer continuous cultivation and had much shorter fallow cycles to regain their productivity compared to upland areas.[7]

Contemporary agriculture employed traditional slash-and-burn techniques without chemical fertilizers, and most contemporary farmers only cultivated a single crop each year, although some double cropping was possible. The second maize crop, when attempted, is called the *postrera*; its success was dependent on the amount of precipitation that occurred in October and November and the strategies farmers used during planting.[8] Farmers in the El Cajón region report that yields from the *postrera* were low and risky, with the crop often failing. While planting the *postrera* had decreased in the region over time, it would have been a viable means of increasing agricultural yields in pre-Columbian times. A bean crop was often planted during the *postrera* period between early September and mid-October—in a separate field, intercropped with the *postrera* maize planting, or intercropped with the maturing or harvested fields of the spring maize crop.

Cultivators understood how to maximize the productivity of their vega fields. Several types of squash—including ayote (*Cucurbita pepo*), calabaza (pumpkin), and the tecomate gourd used for storage (*Lagenaria* sp.)—were inter-planted along the edges of maize fields during the spring maize crop (*milpa de primavera*). Under good conditions, farmers could cultivate up to 2.5 ha of land in the valley bottoms using hand tools. The principal constraint to land cultivation in this environment was weeding time. The result was that the cultivation of 2.0–2.5 ha using hand tools could produce a good return to a household for the 630–788 labor hours (or 89–112 days) needed for cultivation, depending on where fields were located and the fertility of the soil (Loker 1989b:153–155). Evidence for the three primary domesticates maize, beans, and squash was recovered from archaeological contexts in the El Cajón region (Lentz 1989a).

Agriculture was important, but it was not the only subsistence activity of prehispanic groups. Archaeological investigations revealed that prehispanic populations practiced a mixed economy that included hunting, foraging, fishing, and arboriculture. The turkey and the dog were two important domesticates that provided important protein sources across Mesoamerica, including the Maya to the west (Turner and Harrison 1978:351–352). But both were absent from paleofaunal collections in the El Cajón region, where protein was supplied by a combination of hunting and fishing (Fernandez 1987).

Faunal remains indicate that hunting in upland areas and along the margins of agricultural fields was very important. Deer (*Odocoileus* spp) was the most important meat source recovered at archaeological sites in the region, followed by peccary (*Tayassu* spp.). Deer are notorious consumers of maize and would have been actively hunted near agricultural fields, while peccary populate the pine-oak upland and secondary growth areas. Fifteen other vertebrate species were consumed and recovered from archaeological contexts. They included the opossum (*Didelphis marsupialis*), turtles (*Testudinata indet*), crocodiles (*Caiman cocodrilum*), agouti (*Dasyprocta punctata*), tepezcuintle (*Cuniculus paca*), armadillo (*Dasypus novencinctus*), and rabbit (*Silvilagus* spp.). Small species such as iguana (*Iguanidae indet.*) and a range of bird species were also consumed in high numbers (Fernandez 1987; Lentz and Alexander 1986). Finally, the El Cajón region abounds in tropical birds—including parrots, toucans, and macaws—which would have been an important source for feathers used in ritual and trade. The quetzal was prized in prehispanic times for its long green feathers; while they were not identified in the region at the time of study, the El Cajón uplands are included in its natural distribution (Hanson 1982; Monroe 1965).

Riverine resources were also important in the diet. Fish bone (*Osteichthyes indet.*) recovered from excavation and flotation samples was the most frequent protein source recovered from domestic contexts after deer. Indigenous fish species are the same as those found along the Usumacinta River in Guatemala (Goldman 1973:19). Large numbers of freshwater bivalves (*Nephronaris* sp.) and a gastropod known as jute (*Pachychilus* sp.) were consumed during the dry season when they could be readily collected along the banks of permanently flowing streams and rivers.[9] A range of other water mollusks and crustaceans were also identified, indicating that all large and small protein sources were included in the diet. In addition to direct consumption, jutes can be used in the preparation of a fermented beverage.

Wild resources were another facet of subsistence practices in the El Cajón region, and a range of wild but edible plants such as frijolillo (*Cassia* spp.) and blackberry (*Rubus* spp.) were identified in the excavations. The quantity of fruit recovered indicates that arboriculture also was important. Given the utilization of fruit species, it was somewhat surprising that no remains of either avocado or cacao were recovered in the paleobotanical collections. Instead, there was a strong reliance on wild tree fruits, which were very likely encouraged or left to grow in abandoned fields (Lentz 1989a:189). Foremost among these was coyol palm (*Acrocomia mexicana*), which along with pine charcoal constituted the most common plant remains recovered from archaeological contexts. Coyol fruits can be eaten fresh or cooked, the nuts can be processed into oil, and the fresh endocarp can be used to make a fermented drink (Conzemius 1932; Roys 1931; Williams 1981:249–250).[10] Coyol wine is obtained from the trunk of the mature palm tree. To produce this wine, the palm is cut and part of the trunk is hollowed out so the sap can accumulate and be extracted. Coyol wine is still consumed in Olancho as part of traditional gatherings and feasts.[11] Coyol palms are intentionally planted around the houses of the Jicaque because of their varied uses (Lentz 1987). Other edible fruits recovered include the zapote (*Pouteria mammosa*), nance (*Byrsonima crassifolia*), capulin (*Muntigia calabura*), negrito (*Simarouba glauca*), and ciruela (*Spondias* sp.) (Lentz 1989a:193–195).

The overall picture is one of broad-based subsistence practices that combined the cultivation of domestic plants with hunting, foraging, and the selective retention or planting of usable wild fruit-bearing trees. On the whole, groups in the El Cajón region resided in a productive environment. They were slash-and-burn agriculturalists who cultivated maize, beans, and squash, which they combined with a strong tradition of hunting both large and small animals. The primary subsistence focus was on resources grown, collected, or hunted on the valley bottoms. But plant products were extracted and animals hunted in upland areas to provide a wholesome and predictable diet to sustain them throughout the year.

Residents used a range of other resources that occurred in good supply to shape their built environment. Cobbles, which were readily available in ravines that descend from the uplands, were used in wall and platform construction. Timber was abundant; most buildings were wattle-and-daub constructions, with pine supplying most of the firewood. Several species of palm occur in El Cajón, including *suyuate* (*Brahea dulcis*), and their thatch was probably employed as roofing material (von Hagen 1943:43). Cut stone masonry was not used in construction, but lime plaster was identified at Salitrón Viejo in the Iglesia Precinct, where it was employed for some flooring material and to seal or decorate adobe walls (see chapter 4).

Cryptocrystalline rocks such as chert outcrop in a number of areas along the Sulaco and Humuya Rivers, where nodules could have been recovered by any household that needed them.[12] A dark red (7.5R 3/8), dusky red (10R 3/3–4), and reddish-gray (10R 3/1) chert was used to manufacture expedient flaked stone tools and some bifaces. Obsidian was widely used for both blades and flakes, all of which was imported from source areas in Honduras and Guatemala (Hirth 1985, 1987b, 1988). Microcrystalline rock used to manufacture ground stone tools was available in ravine cuts and upland areas. These tools include footed and unfooted grinding slabs (metates), grinding stones (manos), pestles, and stone bowls. Most ground stone items were manufactured from basalt, tuff, or rhyolite; a small number of items were made from granite, trachyte, sandstone, and dense limestone. Unifacial knives made from andesite were common, as were bark beaters made from a range of different stone types. Highly polished celts and wedges were manufactured from very hard microcrystalline aphinitic and phaneritic rocks. Some of these materials appear as rare occurrences in river gravels of the Sulaco and Humuya Rivers, although most were likely imported into the region as finished products (Hirth and Cosgren 1989:31–35).

A range of exotic and semi-precious materials that entered the region by trade were identified in excavations. Some marine shell and one shark's tooth were recovered (Fernandez 1987:2), which probably reached the El Cajón region through exchange with groups to the north along the Ulúa River. A large quantity of carved and polished lapidary goods—including beads, pendants, earflares, plaques, and other items—was recovered from Salitrón Viejo. These items were manufactured from a variety of jade, greenstone, talc, serpentine, albite, and granular marble, which are described and discussed in chapter 5. The materials came from a range of geologic source locales, including the Motagua River located 185 km west of the El Cajón region (Bishop, Sayre, and van Zelst 1986). The variety of materials indicates that residents at Salitrón Viejo were active participants in long-distance interregional exchange. A fragment of one marble vessel was among these materials; it was most likely manufactured at the site of Travesía in the Ulúa valley.

THE OCCUPATIONAL HISTORY OF THE EL CAJÓN REGION

The occupational history of the region was reconstructed using settlement survey and stratigraphic excavation, combined with the analysis of material remains and radiocarbon dating from select archaeological contexts (appendix A). A regional chronology was constructed to provide a time line for development and to examine socioeconomic interaction within and between contemporaneous communities (see table 2.1). Ceramics were the focus for constructing a chronology because of their sensitivity to change and the ability to use style to correlate chronological periods with ceramic phases in adjacent regions. Classification followed a modified type-variety approach (Gifford 1960; Smith et al. 1960), with equal priority given to paste and decoration (Hirth, Kennedy, and Cliff 1989 1993; Kennedy 1987).[13]

The prehispanic occupation was divided into two major divisions: the Yunque period (or phase) (400 BC–AD 400) and the Sulaco period (or phase) (AD 400–1000). The Yunque period was divided into Early and Late subphases on the basis of ceramic characteristics that included the production of ceramics with bichrome, resist, incised, and appliqué decoration on coarse cream and fine tan pastes. The Sulaco period was subdivided into Early, Middle, and Late subphases, reflecting the development of painted polychrome ceramics within the region and throughout Honduras. The well-known Ulúa polychrome types (e.g., Joyce 2017) appear as trade wares in the region alongside the locally made and more abundant Sulaco polychrome types, also known as Bold Geometric ceramic wares (Baudez 1966; Beaudry et al. 1989; Stone 1957:32–33). These regional occupation phases are summarized in table 2.1.

Regional settlement history was reconstructed by phasing the ceramic remains recovered from test excavations across the region. Two surveys were implemented to identify prehispanic settlement patterns: a 100 percent survey of the 94 km² reservoir impact zone (Hasemann, Dixon, and Yonk 1982; Hirth et al. 1981) and a highland survey (Hasemann 1983) that sampled 4 percent of the 1,200 km² of the mountainous uplands between the Sulaco and Humuya Rivers (figure 3.2). Large-scale excavations were carried out at the four largest sites in the region: Salitrón Viejo (Hirth 1981), Intendencia (Lara-Pinto and Sheptak 1985), Guarabuquí (Messenger 1982, 1984), and La Ceiba (Benyo 1986). Additional excavations were carried out at twenty-four sites along the Sulaco and Humuya Rivers as part of a regional testing program (Hasemann 1998; Hasemann, Dixon, and Yonk 1982).[14]

Notable differences were observed in the distribution of prehispanic sites throughout the region. Although groups practiced a mixed subsistence strategy, agriculture was the most important activity affecting site location. While upland zones were important for hunting and foraging, only 10 of the 143 prehispanic sites recorded in the region were located in the highlands outside the valley bottoms. Since the best agricultural land was on the vega terraces in the valley bottoms, this is where most prehispanic sites were located. Similarly, the presence of larger vegas along the Sulaco River led to differences in the size, number, and patterning of communities compared to the Humuya drainage.

More sites were located along the Humuya (n = 71) than the Sulaco River (n = 62), but they are noticeably smaller and more widely dispersed. The Humuya River valley is narrow (e.g., figure 3.3) and the river is dynamic, resulting in only small pockets of cultivable land along its margins. As a result, archaeological sites tended to be located on lower hillslopes so all available vega lands could be cultivated. The site of Intendencia (PC109) had 220 structures, making it the largest site on the Humuya River and the second largest community in El Cajón (Lara-Pinto and Sheptak 1985). However, it was the *only* large community identified along the 66 km of the Humuya River and its two major tributaries. The next largest site along the Humuya River had fewer than 50 structures (Lara-Pinto and Hasemann 1982). The occupation of Intendencia and many other sites along the Humuya dates primarily to the Middle and Late Sulaco phases and reflects a relatively late utilization of the area, a result no doubt of its limited agricultural potential vis-à-vis other areas.

The Sulaco River valley, by contrast, is wider and has larger pockets of cultivable vega land (figure 3.4). This resulted in the development of larger sites situated directly on vega terraces. Sites also appear organized into a well-developed hierarchy of large, intermediate, and small sites around the principal community of Salitrón Viejo. The site of Salitrón Viejo grew to become the largest and most important community in the El Cajón region, with over 400 visible architectural features. The site is located on a 1.5 km² parcel of vega land on a river terrace where the Rio Yunque joins the Sulaco River. This is the largest expanse of high-quality agricultural land in the El Cajón region and is the reason why Salitrón Viejo developed there.

THE SITE OF SALITRÓN VIEJO

Archaeological investigations indicate that Salitrón Viejo (figure 3.5) was the central community in a regional chiefdom of several thousand people in the El Cajón region. It was both the longest occupied and largest community in a hierarchy of sites that differed from one another in size and architectural complexity. The scale and layout of domestic and civic-ceremonial architecture provide important clues about how Salitrón Viejo was internally organized

FIGURE 3.5. *Map of Salitrón Viejo (PC1) and major areas within the site*

and linked to surrounding communities along the Sulaco River. Five other large sites, each with over 100 mapped structures, were located on the Sulaco River within a 13 km radius of Salitrón. Three of these sites had monumental structures over 2 m in height that were laid out around formal plazas where ritual and social activities were carried out. These sites grew in complexity over time, reaching their maximum size during the Middle Sulaco phase, after which population and regional integration declined.

Salitrón Viejo was mapped, and systematic excavations were carried out over four years to clarify important aspects about the function of different areas within the site. Mapping and excavation identified 410 architectural features that are summarized in table 3.1.[15] Three hundred and ninety of these 410 architectural features were earth and cobble platform structures that supported perishable structures on their summits or were used to delimit important areas of the site. Three hundred and thirty of these platform structures were small

TABLE 3.1. Architectural features at Salitrón Viejo

Architectural Feature	Iglesia Precinct	North Precinct	West Group	South Group	Total
Civic-ceremonial	22	8	—	—	30
Domestic residence	—	—	156	174	330
Range structures	1	—	4	6	11
Special non-residential	5	13	1	—	19
Walls	5	—	5	2	12
Ramps	4	1	—	3	8
Total structures	37	22	166	185	410

FIGURE 3.6. *Typical house mound platforms in the El Cajón region*

domestic house mounds. An additional 11 large Range structures were identified, which are believed to have supported residential buildings occupied by
elite members of the community. The architectural layout of Salitrón Viejo is
presented in figure 3.5. It depicts four distinct areas that served different functions over the length of the site's 1,400-year occupation.

Interpreting what figure 3.5 indicates about the organization of Salitrón
Viejo requires understanding how its built environment was shaped over time.
A pervasive practice across the region was the construction of domestic resi-
dences on low earthen house mounds 40–60 cm or more in height (figure 3.6).

Houses were thatch or wattle-and-daub constructions. Residential mounds were raised in elevation over time as floors were resurfaced and domestic residences were rebuilt. Residences were also abandoned as families underwent generational changes or relocated to new locations. A regular feature of new family formation was the construction of a new house mound. When this occurred, previously abandoned mound structures were partially or completely dismantled, recycling their fill into the construction of a new residential platform. One residential structure was identified at Salitrón Viejo that was in the process of being dismantled and used for fill in other structures at the site.[16]

The continual recycling of house mound construction was observed at all sites and has several implications for interpretations of material culture in the El Cajón region. One result was that the fill of any given platform mound contained artifacts from one or more earlier constructions and did not reflect the behavior carried out by its occupants. Another was the destruction of interments buried under the floors of domestic structures. The combined result of these two processes was the recovery of many unarticulated human bone fragments, referred to as mortuary occurrences from mound fill, which were portions of human burials that were broken up when they were removed with the fill from recycled structures (Benyo, Storey, and Hirth n.d.). A third implication was that all the site maps produced in this study reflect community organization during their last, maximum episode of growth, which usually conformed to the Middle or Late Sulaco occupations. Finally, the practice of architectural recycling meant that most early structures had less chance of surviving than later ones. The exception to this practice was where early civic-ceremonial structures continued in use or were buried by later construction. Most small domestic structures were not preserved, which created difficulties in estimating the size of a site's early occupation. To resolve this problem, the project relied on material recovered from preconstruction levels under later mound constructions that contained cultural refuse from earlier occupations.

These considerations are important when viewing the organization of Salitrón Viejo depicted in figure 3.5. The site layout is a palimpsest of *all* phases of occupation and subsequent modifications over 1,400 years of occupation. Salitrón Viejo had four distinct architectural components: the Iglesia and North Precincts and the South and West Residential Groups. These four areas had different functions and are used as descriptive locations in the discussion below. The Iglesia and North Precincts were important ritual areas, while the West and South Groups contained the site's residential population (Hasemann 1987; Hirth 1981, 1989a). Stratigraphic excavations clarified that the structures in these four areas were not exactly contemporaneous in their construction and use.

TABLE 3.2. Civic-ceremonial structures in the Iglesia and North Precincts

Site Area	No. of Structures[a]	No. of Monumental Structures (> 2 m)	Total Construction Volume[b]
Iglesia Precinct	37	9	19,544
North Precinct	22	1	1,575
West Group	4	4	6,791
South Group	6	6	4,984
Total	69	20	32,894

a. Includes platform and ramp structures.
b. Includes the Acropolis platform.

The Iglesia Precinct was the site's central civic-ceremonial zone that hosted important ritual activities for all occupants. It began as a large open plaza that was 95 m long (E–W) and 45 m wide (N–S), delimited by platform structures on its four sides. It is here that the earliest evidence for feasting and other ritual activities was recovered. The importance of the Iglesia Precinct as the site's main ritual center was demonstrated in three ways. The first was the scale of civic-ceremonial architecture in the Iglesia Precinct, which contained thirty-seven structures representing 19,544 m³ of construction fill (table 3.2). The second was the construction of the Acropolis platform over the original plaza surface to mark its importance as a special place within the site. The third was the deposit of many jade and marble artifacts as cache offerings to dedicate and sanctify the Acropolis platform and other structures within the precinct (Hirth 1988; Hirth and Hirth 1993). The sequence of construction activities in the Iglesia Precinct is discussed in detail in chapter 4. The wealth items and how they were used in these offerings are discussed in chapters 5 and 6.

The North Precinct was a second civic-ceremonial zone located on the northern periphery of Salitrón Viejo that appears to have been used for receiving groups from outlying communities. It is a large open plaza, defined on its northern and eastern sides by the river terraces and on its south and west sides by a series of low linear platforms, terrace walls, and rock alignments. Twenty-two structures were constructed to define this precinct (table 3.2). The plaza of the North Precinct is 160 m long (E–W) and 75 m wide (N–S). It is the largest plaza in the El Cajón region and contains eight small civic-ceremonial platform mounds, only one of which reached 2 m in height. Excavations in the North Precinct recovered jade and marble artifacts deposited in the plaza floor as well as in dedicatory caches associated with Structures 38 and 40 (figure 3.7). No domestic debris was associated with structures in the North Precinct plaza, which underscores its role as a special ritual and assembly area.

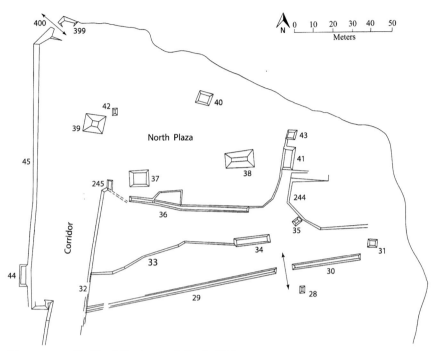

FIGURE 3.7. *The North Precinct at Salitrón Viejo*

The South and West Groups are residential clusters where the bulk of the site's population resided. The central focus of each residential group was a large open plaza defined by several rectangular Range structures that were 20–40 m on a side and 2–4 m in height. These were earthen platforms with exterior cobble walls and outset stairways that ascended from the plaza (figure 3.8). Perishable wattle-and-daub buildings that were occupied were constructed on their summits that were occupied by the group's elite. Plaza areas were used for dances, celebrations, and other social activities carried out by their residents. Excavations in the center of the West Group plaza uncovered several midden deposits that included food preparation equipment, broken service vessels, and burnt food remains that appear to be the result of group feasting. It is assumed that residents of the South Group engaged in similar practices, although no excavations were carried out within its plaza.

Most residential structures in these groups were low, square or rectangular house mounds under 1 m in height (figure 3.6). House mounds vary in orientation rather than aligning with Range structures in the groups' central plazas. Residential structures are tightly nucleated and are separated from one

FIGURE 3.8. *A sub-monumental Range structure (< 2 m in height) with outset stairway at Intendencia (Structure 6)*

another by distances of 5 to 8 m. The reason for this close spacing is unclear, but when population estimates are calculated, they are compatible with or exceed population densities found in many Mesoamerican urban centers (Hirth n.d.).

House mounds in these groups represent individual residences and do not articulate into paired structures or patio groups, as was noted at several other large sites in the survey zone.[17] It is likely that the South and West Groups represent small clans of related kinsmen, the interpretation for which is based on their clear separation as distinct residential groups, each with its own central plaza. The corporate nature of the South Group is also implied by the presence of three paved ramps that ascend the eastern river terrace leading into the group from the Rio Yunque. Two of these ramps provided access into the central plaza of the South Group.[18]

Both residential groups were established early in Salitrón's occupational history. The precise date is difficult to reconstruct because of the constant recycling of small domestic structures into later constructions. Nevertheless, excavations across the West Group plaza did not uncover concentrations of domestic material that would be expected if early house mounds were leveled to create a plaza in a previously occupied area. The construction of Structure 66, a small Range platform at the southwest corner of the West Group alongside an open area, may reflect the beginning of a third residential group (figure 3.5).

COMMUNITY DEVELOPMENT AT THE REGIONAL LEVEL

The entire reservoir impact zone and portions of the adjacent uplands were surveyed to reconstruct settlement history in the El Cajón region (Lara-Pinto and Hasemann 1982). All visible features were mapped, and sites were classified based on the size and scale of their architectural constructions. In most cases there was a direct correlation between a large number of house mounds and the presence of formal plazas, monumental constructions, or both. George Hasemann (1998:151) identified three platform types in the El Cajón region: non-monumental platforms that are less than 1 m in height, sub-monumental platforms that are intermediate-scale structures 1 to 2 m tall, and monumental structures over 2 m high. Monumental structures were special purpose constructions with civic-ceremonial or elite functions. Monumental structures were further subdivided into rectangular Range platforms that supported elite residences and square pyramidal structures that were ceremonial in nature.

The earliest settlement in the El Cajón region occurred along the Sulaco River. This area was occupied continuously between 400 BC and AD 1000 and displays considerable variation in site size and architectural diversity. Occupation along the Humuya River does not appear until the Late Yunque phase (AD 0–400) and was populated more slowly because of limited agricultural land. As noted above, the only large community along the Humuya River was the site of Intendencia (PC109), which reached its maximum size during the Late Sulaco phase (figure 3.9) (Haseman, Dixon, and Yonk 1982; Lara Pinto and Sheptak 1985). While sites across the El Cajón region share a common ceramic assemblage, it is unclear how closely sites along the Humuya River interacted with Salitrón Viejo or were incorporated into its sphere of regional interaction compared to those along the Sulaco River.

The prominence of Salitrón Viejo is evident in the scale of its built environment. Most monumental civic-ceremonial structures in the El Cajón region were 2 to 3 m in height and employed 250–800 m³ of fill in their construction. The largest structures in secondary centers could use up to 1,500–1,700 m³ of fill, but that was rare. Table 3.3 and figure 3.10 summarize the number of civic-ceremonial structures and their construction volume at sites in the El Cajón region. The difference between Salitrón Viejo and other sites in the region is striking. Twelve sites along the Sulaco River had at least one civic-ceremonial structure that was 2 m in height, with Cueva Grande (PC59) having as many as five.[19] By comparison, Salitrón Viejo had sixty-nine civic-ceremonial and related special purpose structures, twenty of which were 2 m or more in height: nine in the Iglesia Precinct, one in the North Precinct, four in the West Group, and six in the South Group (table 3.2). Salitrón Viejo contained three-quarters

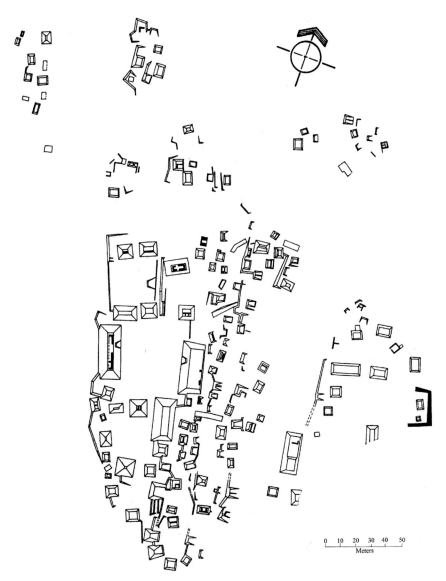

FIGURE 3.9. *The site of Intendencia (PC109) on the Humuya River*

of all civic-ceremonial constructions along the Sulaco River (table 3.3), and 45 percent of them were over 2 m in height. An even sharper contrast is evident for the Humuya River, where only eight monumental structures were identified in five sites.

TABLE 3.3. Sites with monumental civic-ceremonial architecture in the El Cajón region

Site	No. of Civic-Ceremonial Structures	Construction Volume	
		Cubic Meters	Percent
SULACO RIVER			
PC1	69	32,894	62.1
PC3	1	721	1.4
PC4	2	493	0.9
PC7	1	503	1.0
PC12	1	1,523	2.9
PC13	3	1,700	3.2
PC15	3	1,666	3.1
PC37/38	2	1,078	2.0
PC59	5	3,730	7.0
PC71	2	967	1.8
PC72	1	354	0.7
PC75	1	587	1.1
PC85	2	1,564	3.0
HUMUYA RIVER			
PC105	1	423	0.8
PC109	3	2,744	5.2
PC131	1	354	0.7
PC138	2	1,319	2.5
PC139	1	339	0.6
Sulaco River sites	93	47,780	90.2
Humuya River sites	8	5,179	9.8
Total sites	101	52,959	100.0

The role and importance of civic-ceremonial architecture is reflected by the amount of energy used to construct it (Abrams 1994). Table 3.3 summarizes this effort in cubic meters of mound fill used in monumental structures across the region. Civic-ceremonial construction at Salitrón Viejo employed an estimated volume of 32,894 m^3 of fill in civic-ceremonial structures across the site (Hirth 1987a). This is twelve times greater than the 2,744 m^3 found at Intendencia (PC109), the largest site on the Humuya River, and almost nine

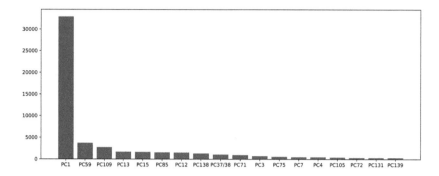

Figure 3.10. *Comparison of the scale of civic-ceremonial construction at Salitrón Viejo and other sites along the Sulaco River. Illustration by Kacey Hirth.*

times more than the 3,730 m³ at Cueva Grande (PC59), which has the second-most monumental constructions on the Sulaco River (Hasemann 1998; Hirth 1996a). The total investment in civic-ceremonial constructions at *most* sites along the Sulaco River ranges between 500 and 1,500 m³ of construction fill, which is 20–60 times less than what was found at Salitrón Viejo (figure 3.10). Figure 3.11 provides a comparison of the scale of civic-ceremonial construction between Salitrón Viejo and all sites along the Sulaco and Humuya Rivers. When viewed comparatively, Salitrón Viejo had 1.6 times the volume of monumental construction of all the sites along the Sulaco and Humuya Rivers combined (table 3.3). This difference is even greater when civic-ceremonial construction is compared by phase (see chapter 7).

Regional survey located sites, but the thick tropical vegetation required test excavations to date them. To this end, a regional excavation program was directed by George Hasemann (1985, 1998; Haseman, Dixon, and Yonk 1982) to test both architectural and non-architectural areas of sites and to reconstruct regional demographic growth over time. Because funding was limited, the project focused on the Sulaco River settlements, with only selective testing of sites along the Humuya River.[20] For this reason, the discussion of settlement complexity focuses primarily on communities along the lower Sulaco River, with limited reference to the Humuya River and its tributaries.

Table 3.4 summarizes the five-tier settlement typology used to classify sites in the El Cajón region, and figure 3.12 illustrates the distribution of major sites along the lower Sulaco and Humuya Rivers. The practice of dismantling earlier platform mounds meant that the settlements depicted in figure 3.12 most often represent their last occupation during the Middle and Late

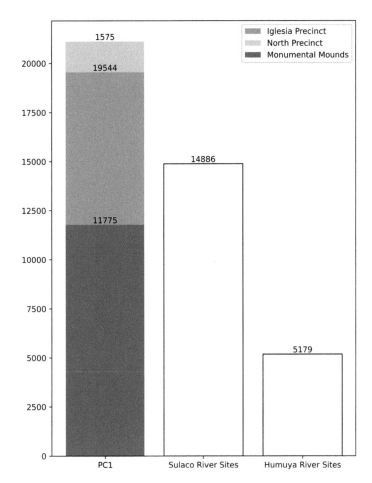

FIGURE 3.11. *Comparison of the scale of civic-ceremonial construction at Salitrón Viejo to all sites along the Sulaco and Humuya Rivers. Illustration by Kacey Hirth.*

Sulaco phases. Information on sites during Early Yunque through Early Sulaco phases had to be reconstructed from non-architectural deposits and preconstruction surfaces. Finally, many of the small hamlet communities in the region were not excavated and could not be dated. The result is that the following discussion underrepresents the number of sites and the size of the population that would have been present during any given time. Nevertheless, the available settlement information captures the broad pattern of community development in the El Cajón region over time.

TABLE 3.4. The El Cajón settlement hierarchy

Site Type	Total No. of Structures	Non-monumental Structures	Sub-monumental Structures	Monumental Structures
Hamlet	1–49	1–49	None	None
Simple village	15–91	The majority	None	1 Range structure, no defined plaza
Complex village	47–75	The majority	None	2 Range structures around an incipient plaza
Secondary regional center	36–209	The majority	Present	Range structures, pyramid structure, defined plaza
Primary regional center	> 300	The majority	Present	Exceeds all sites in the scale and complexity of architecture

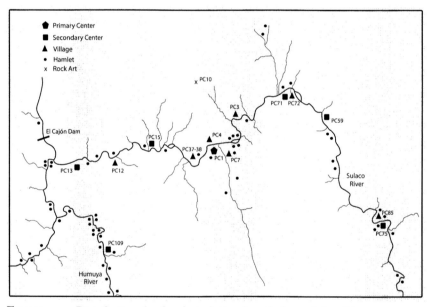

FIGURE 3.12. *Distribution of archaeological sites along the lower Sulaco River. Illustration by Kenneth Hirth and Ryan Middlemore.*

THE EARLY YUNQUE PHASE (400–0 BC)

Salitrón Viejo was the first community occupied in the El Cajón region. Its location is no surprise as it was situated on the largest segment of productive agricultural land in the region, at the intersection of the Sulaco and Yunque

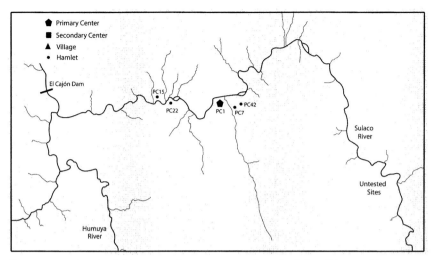

FIGURE 3.13. *The Early Yunque settlement pattern along the Sulaco River and lower Humuya River. Illustration by Kenneth Hirth and Ryan Middlemore.*

Rivers (figure 3.13). Not only was the Salitrón vega an attraction for pioneer agriculturalists, but it provided support for its resident population throughout the length of its occupation. Ceramics during the Early Yunque phase include bichrome, incised, and resist decorated wares and share strong stylistic similarities with types reported for the Eden 1 phase at the neighboring site of Los Naranjos (see table 2.1) (Baudez and Becquelin 1973; Beaudry-Corbett 1993). Usulután-style resist decoration is prominent on several ceramic paste types, of which Muérdalo Orange is the most frequent (see figure 2.3a). Coarse cream wares are prevalent, with impressed appliqué, incised, and punctate decoration. Also appearing by the end of the phase is a double slip orange-on-white ceramic type known as Bolo Orange, which imitated resist decoration using a different set of techniques. Some of the earliest stylistic ceramic markers resemble those found in Toyos-phase deposits at Playa de los Muertos that include white, red-on-white, red-on-tan, and red-on-black ceramic types (Hirth, Kennedy, and Cliff 1989; Kennedy 1981, 1987; Kennedy, Messenger, and Yonk 1982).

Salitrón Viejo covered 2 ha and was the largest site in the region. The recycling of abandoned house mounds into later constructions has erased most traces of domestic occupation during this phase. Only two house mounds on the far western periphery of the site survived that could be dated to the Early and Late Yunque occupation.[21] Site area during this phase was reconstructed from material excavated from preconstruction surfaces and indicates

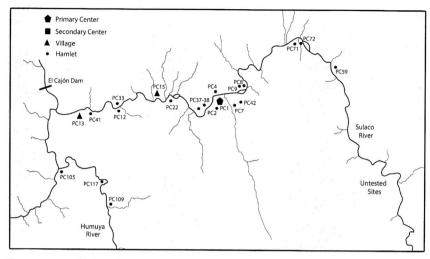

FIGURE 3.14. *The Late Yunque settlement pattern along the Sulaco River and lower Humuya River. Illustration by Kenneth Hirth and Ryan Middlemore.*

an occupation dispersed over the area from the Iglesia Precinct to the western edge of the West Group. Two small house clusters were also located in the South Group, one on its eastern edge overlooking the Yunque River and the other along its western margin.

The Iglesia Precinct was established at this time. Several structures defined its central plaza, and evidence for feasting was identified, indicating early ritual activity (see chapter 4). The size of the site together with evidence for ritual activity indicates that Salitrón Viejo was the most important center in the El Cajón region. Four other communities (PC7, PC15, PC22, PC42) were also occupied along the Sulaco River during the Early Yunque phase (figure 3.13). Three of these sites were small hamlets, two of which (PC7, PC42) were situated in the large vega immediately east of and adjacent to Salitrón Viejo, while the third (PC22) was a two-hour walk downriver. A small occupation was also identified at the site of Guarabuquí (PC15), although it is difficult to estimate its size because of the scale of later construction (Cliff 1990a).

The Late Yunque Phase (AD 0–400)

The Late Yunque phase was a period of major cultural development, with Salitrón Viejo emerging as the center of a regional chiefdom in the El Cajón region. Regional population increased dramatically, with thirteen new sites settled along the Sulaco River (figure 3.14). The role of Salitrón Viejo as the region's primary socio-political center is evident in the amount of labor invested in the construction of its civic-ceremonial architecture. Five small sites appear for the first time along the Humuya River and, despite shared ceramic similarities,[22] it is unclear if they were incorporated into the Salitrón chiefdom developing along the Sulaco River.

Late Yunque ceramics continued the tradition of bichrome, incised, and resist decoration—sharing strong stylistic similarities with Eden II assemblages at Los Naranjos (see table 2.1) (Baudez and Becquelin 1973; Beaudry-Corbett 1993). Usulután-style resist decoration in the Muérdalo and Bolo Orange types continued but disappeared by the end of the phase. Chilanga-style ceramics that combined red painting with resist decoration occur, but in very low numbers. An important type known as Tamaro Incised (see figure 2.3b–c) appears, which combined incised decoration with well-burnished cream to brown surfaces.[23] Several orange slipped types appear for the first time, spanning the Late Yunque and Early Sulaco phases. One of these is Ladrillo Orange, a well-fired monochrome ceramic with a red-orange slip that occurs in flat-bottom out-flaring wall bowls with solid nubbin or hollow mammiform supports. Sulaco Orange ware appears for the first time at the end of the phase, which ushered in the Bold Geometric or Sulaco ceramic family. Sulaco Orange is a monochrome ceramic with two decorative variants: resist decoration like that found on Muérdalo types and an orange-on-orange panel decoration of contrasting hues (Hirth, Kennedy, and Cliff 1989, 1993; Kennedy 1987).

All four areas of Salitrón Viejo show evidence of occupation during the Late Yunque phase. Major construction occurred in both the Iglesia and North Precincts, which served as civic-ceremonial areas at both the site and regional levels. The Iglesia Precinct was at the center of social and ritual activity in Salitrón Viejo and underwent a series of extensive architectural modifications. The sequence of construction is discussed in detail in chapter 4, but three aspects of these activities are particularly noteworthy. First, a cluster of platform mounds was constructed on the eastern end of the Iglesia Precinct that includes a Range structure believed to have supported the residence of the ruling elite family at Salitrón Viejo. Second, it was during this period that the Acropolis platform was built, converting the original ground-level plaza into an elevated Acropolis that emphasized its socio-religious importance. Third, the construction of civic-ceremonial architecture involved the procurement of thousands of jade and marble artifacts to dedicate the buildings.

The North Precinct was a second civic-ceremonial area that played an important role in Salitrón's regional chiefdom. Its importance is underscored by its size. At 160 m long (E–W) and 75 m wide (N–S), it has the largest formal plaza in the El Cajón region. The edge of the river terrace on which Salitrón Viejo is located provided natural boundaries for this plaza on its north and east sides, while a series of low lineal platforms define its southern and western borders. Archaeological excavations established that all of the structures in the North Precinct were constructed and utilized during the Late Yunque phase.[24] They include the eight platforms within the North Plaza, the three lines of parallel platforms along its southern flank, and the two parallel platform lines that define a north–south corridor that connected the North Precinct to the rest of the site (figure 3.7). The civic-ceremonial role of this area was underscored by (1) the recovery of dedicatory caches containing 349 jade and marble artifacts around structures in the plaza, (2) the distribution of multiple large brazier fragments on every excavated structure and across the plaza floor, and (3) the absence of domestic occupation in this area.

An important feature of the North Precinct was that it was removed from, yet formally connected to, the main residence areas of Salitrón Viejo. Two low platforms (Structures 36 and 244) defined the southern edge of the plaza, while two additional lines of platforms (Structures 29–30 and 33–35)[25] provided additional physical and conceptual separation of the North Precinct from the Iglesia Precinct and the rest of the community (figure 3.7). These constructions create the impression that this separation was intentional. Several postholes identified on Structures 29 and 30 suggest that they supported a small palisade, a practice also noted in the East Courtyard of the Iglesia Precinct.

While situated on its northern periphery, the North Precinct was connected to the rest of the site in two ways. First, two low parallel platforms (Structures 32 and 44–45) form the sides of a corridor or processional way that connected the southwest corner of its plaza to the area between the Iglesia Precinct and the West Residential Group (figures 3.5, 3.7). In terms of architectural design, the presence of streets and corridors is as much about controlling or channeling the movement of people as it is for providing access between architectural areas (Rapoport 1969). Second, two narrow openings were identified between Structures 34–35 and 29–30 that align with one another and appear to be accessways that also channeled population movement.[26] Both openings align with the northern ramp of the Iglesia Precinct (see 394c in figure 4.1) and imply that access between the two areas was controlled.

We believe the North Precinct was a special area set apart from the rest of Salitrón Viejo that was used to host assemblies of individuals from neighboring communities. Excavations recovered concentrations of organic refuse along six of the low platforms on the periphery of the North Precinct that may be the remains of feasting activity or relocated fill but not permanent residence.[27] The role of the North Precinct as an area of ritual engagement for groups along the Sulaco River is supported by its location within the site and the construction of a paved ramp (Structure 400) and a flanking platform (Structure 399) at the northwest corner of the plaza. This ramp, although badly eroded, was originally about 3 m wide and at least 10 m long. It ascended the northern slope of the river terrace, providing an entrance into the precinct for groups arriving at Salitrón Viejo along the Sulaco River (figure 3.7).

Throughout the El Cajón region, ramps provided more than just access. They also emphasized the importance of the group they were associated with, in much the same way causeways functioned among the Maya. This is why there are four ramps associated with the Iglesia Precinct, three ramps providing access to different areas of the South Residential Group, and ramps associated with the largest residential clusters at both La Ceiba (PC13) and Guarabuquí (PC15). Structure 400 would have been unnecessary if the North Group was a ritual precinct used exclusively by residents of Salitrón Viejo. The fact that it leads down to the Sulaco River suggests that the North Group was a ritual area used to reinforce social relationships with other communities along the Sulaco and Humuya Rivers that were incorporated into Salitrón Viejo's regional chiefdom.

Domestic debris was recovered from preconstruction surfaces over the greater extent of the South and West Groups (figure 3.5). Both plaza areas were laid out and used by their residents during the Late Yunque period. Concentrations of domestic refuse were recovered from preconstruction surfaces around the periphery of the plazas but not within them. Eight of the nine large Range structures that border the two large plazas were excavated.[28] Several of these structures have Late Yunque materials in their preconstruction surfaces, but none of the range mounds were constructed at this time. If range mounds supported elite domiciles, then the only elite residence at Salitrón Viejo during the Late Yunque phase was Structure 6, located in the eastern end of the Iglesia Precinct (figure 3.5). What this pattern indicates is that important community spaces were defined socially before they were formalized with special monumental architecture. It also suggests that residents of the West and South Groups were more closely integrated at the site level through activities carried out in the Iglesia Precinct than they were later on, when Range structures were constructed and occupied around the peripheries of their central plazas.

Significant regional population growth occurred during the Late Yunque phase as existing sites grew in size and new sites were established. Eighteen sites were occupied along the Sulaco River, seventeen of which were within a 12 km radius of Salitrón Viejo (figure 3.14). While this represents a significant increase over the previous phase, the number of sites was certainly greater, since these identifications only reflect excavated material from the regional testing program. Excavations were not extensive except at La Ceiba (PC13) and Guarabuquí (PC15), which were classified as village communities based on their size (figure 3.14). At La Ceiba (PC13), domestic refuse from preconstruction surfaces was distributed over half a hectare. The residential occupation at Guarabuquí (PC15) was less than 2 ha in size. The Salitrón chiefdom was formed at this time and is reflected in the scale and distribution of regional civic-ceremonial architecture. No monumental architecture was constructed at any other site in the region, although Late Yunque ceramics were recovered from preconstruction levels within the areas that later became large civic-ceremonial plazas at La Ceiba or Guarabuquí. The centrality of Salitrón Viejo is evident in the construction of the Iglesia and North Precincts and the absence of civic-ceremonial architecture at other sites during this phase (figure 3.14).

The Early Sulaco Phase (AD 400–600)

Population continued to expand both at Salitrón Viejo and across the region at this time. This phase is marked by the development of Sulaco ceramic wares previously referred to as the Bold Geometeric ceramic tradition (Baudez 1966; Beaudry et al. 1989; Stone 1957:32). Sulaco Orange was produced in both sub-hemispherical ring-base bowls and flat-bottom vases with hollow and rectangular slab tripod supports. The similarity of these two forms to Thin Orange– and Teotihuacan-style vase forms is striking. Sulaco Red-on-Orange Bichrome and Sulaco Trichrome occur in both bowl and jar forms, while Chinda and Marimba Red-on-Natural types appear primarily as jars. Cancique Bichrome and Trichrome types mimic the decorative style of the Sulaco ceramic group, although they were fashioned with a different paste and may be trade wares. Sulaco polychromes using black painting mark the transition into the Middle Sulaco phase (Hirth, Kennedy, and Cliff 1989, 1993).

Salitrón Viejo was fully occupied at this time, with the Iglesia and North Precincts continuing in use as important civic-ceremonial areas. Several platform mounds were constructed on the east end of the Iglesia Precinct that subdivided the Acropolis platform into two areas and may reflect a shift in how the precinct was used. The west end of the Acropolis remained an open plaza that would have been used in community celebrations. This contrasts with the east end of the Acropolis, where several structures enclosed what became

Plaza Two, which appears to have been a restricted elite area (see chapter 4). Structure 6 was located in this plaza (figure 3.5), which was the largest Range structure and the residence of Salitrón's highest-ranking elite family.[29] The North Precinct continued as an assembly area for visiting groups, although there was little new construction in this area. Structure 36 was rebuilt along the southern margin of the North Plaza, and the upper surface of Structure 38 was resurfaced with a new floor (see figure 3.7).

Domestic occupation extended across both the West and South Residential Groups. Most of the house mounds from this phase were recycled by later occupants as platform fill into the domestic structures. Nevertheless, several domestic structures were preserved when they were expanded during the subsequent Middle Sulaco phase. Civic-ceremonial activity continued in and around both the West and South Plazas. A small but concentrated midden dating to the Early Sulaco phase was identified on the north end of the West Plaza that contained a large number of broken service vessels that appear to be the result of feasting activity. Perhaps the most significant development at this time was the initial construction of a Range structure around the plaza margins in both the West and South Groups. These two structures were Structure 120 in the West Plaza and Structure 212 in the South Plaza (figure 3.5).

Regional population grew slightly during this phase with the appearance of two additional village sites along the lower Sulaco River (figure 3.15). Two new sites were established (PC5, PC6) while two others (PC22, PC42) were abandoned, keeping the total number of settlements in the lower Sulaco valley at eighteen. The only noticeable change was that the two new sites were located within 1 km of Salitrón Viejo while one of the abandoned sites (PC22) was 5.5 km downriver, suggesting a slight clustering of population around the region's main community. Several new sites appeared along the Humuya River. Occupation expanded at the site of Intendencia (PC109) while two previous Late Yunque sites (PC105, PC117) were abandoned, suggesting that the population was relocated to Intendencia (figures 3.14, 3.15). All of the sites that developed into large centers along the Sulaco River were occupied at this time, although limited archaeological testing made it difficult to estimate their size during each of the Sulaco subphases. Nevertheless, extensive excavations at La Ceiba (PC13) and Guarabuquí (PC15) indicate increased activity and the beginning of monumental construction in their public plazas (figures 3.16, 3.17). Regional civic-ceremonial activity continued to be focused on Salitrón Viejo, with the North Precinct still playing an important integrative role for communities along the Sulaco River.

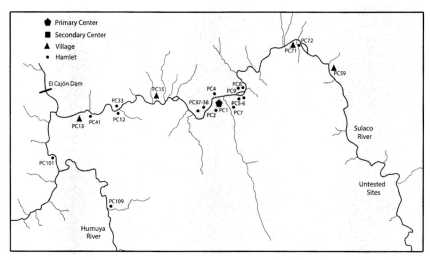

Figure 3.15. *The Early Sulaco settlement pattern along the Sulaco River and lower Humuya River. Illustration by Kenneth Hirth and Ryan Middlemore.*

The Middle Sulaco Phase (AD 600–800)

The Middle Sulaco phase represents the culmination of regional development at two different levels. First, regional population grew and then plateaued, continuing processes that began during the Early Yunque phase. This is reflected in both the size of sites along the Sulaco River and the increased nucleation of domestic structures within them (figure 3.18). Second, this phase is marked by the construction of a significant amount of civic-ceremonial architecture at other sites throughout El Cajón. Salitrón Viejo was still the largest community, but its level of influence appears to have diminished in the wake of increased competition and elite-directed ritual activity at large villages and other secondary regional centers.

The Middle Sulaco ceramic assemblage witnessed the continued development of the Sulaco ceramic group. Sulaco Trichromes characteristic of the preceding phase disappeared and were replaced by the Sulaco polychrome complex, which added black to the red and orange designs painted on a light orange background. Sulaco polychrome jars are decorated with motifs that include knots, lizard and serpent motifs, pyramids, and step-frets. Incision consisting of diagonal or cross-hatched lines appears on tall-neck polychrome jars; these incised areas are often covered with a red slip applied after incision. Chinda Red-on-Natural and Masica Incised types occur as both neckless and long-necked jars. Ulúa polychromes are a rare but important trade ware that

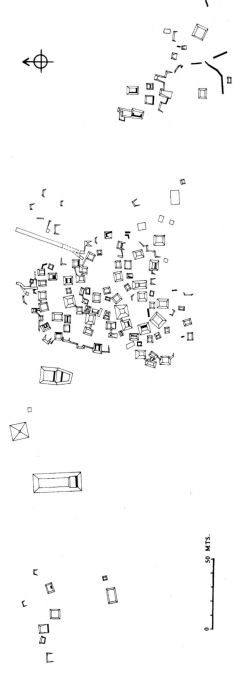

50 MTS.

0

FIGURE 3.16. *The site of La Ceiba (PC13) along the lower Sulaco River*

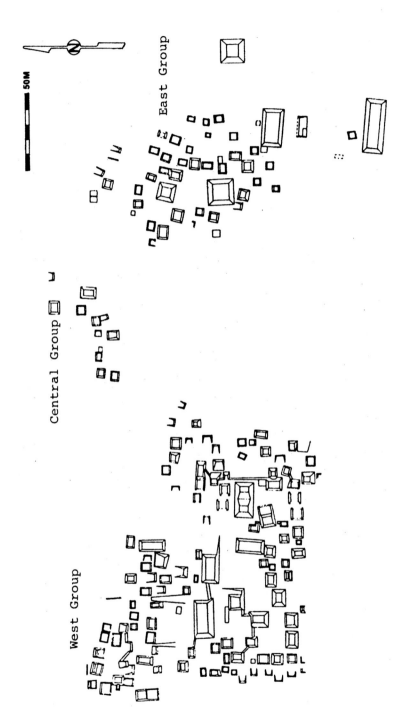

FIGURE 3.17. *The site of Guarabuquí (PC15) along the lower Sulaco River*

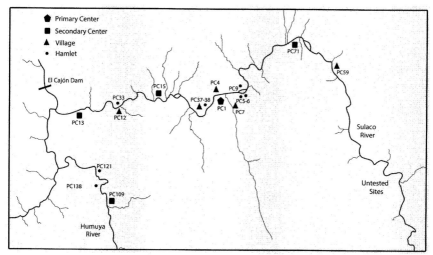

FIGURE 3.18. *The Middle Sulaco settlement pattern along the Sulaco River and lower Humuya River. Illustration by Kenneth Hirth and Ryan Middlemore.*

includes Santa Rita, Yojoa, and Travesía decorative types (Hirth, Kennedy, and Cliff 1989, 1993).

Notable changes are evident in Salitrón Viejo. The Iglesia Precinct was still important, but there is little evidence for activity outside of Plaza Two on the Acropolis's eastern end (figure 3.5). The North Precinct fell out of use except for a small amount of ritual activity around Structure 38 and the presence of refuse along the base of Structures 29 and 30 (figure 3.7).

The focus of elite-directed ritual activity shifted to the plaza areas of the South and West Residential Groups. The construction of Range structures in these areas increased in intensity. Range Structure 212, initiated during the Early Sulaco phase, was expanded and four new range mounds (Structures 209–211, 213) were constructed in the South Plaza (figure 3.5). Structures 209 and 213 were new constructions that were brought to their final dimensions of 2.0 m and 3.4 m, respectively, in height during this phase, while the other three Range structures were expanded during the subsequent Late Sulaco.

The same process was observed in the West Group Plaza. Range Structure 120, initiated during the previous phase, underwent three episodes of expansion and remodeling during the Middle Sulaco. Two additional range mounds (Structures 118 and 119) and one sub-monumental house mound (Structure 121) were constructed on the south side of the West Plaza, all of which underwent at least one remodeling and expansion episode. Each of these additions was done incrementally, often in accordance with rebuilding the structure on its summit or resurfacing its hard-packed clay floor. But the side-by-side construction and remodeling of multiple Range structures throughout this phase speaks to the emergence of new elites in these residential groups that actively engaged in social and ritual activities.

Two important changes are apparent across the region during the Middle Sulaco phase. The first was a stabilization of population levels in sites along the Sulaco River (figure 3.18). No new sites were established. Instead, four previously occupied sites (PC2, PC8, PC41, PC72) were abandoned at the same time larger sites expanded to their fullest extent. This process very likely reflects the resettlement of groups from smaller outlying sites into larger communities, beginning the process of population nucleation observed in other areas of Honduras during the Terminal Classic period (Joyce 2014). The reason for population nucleation appears related to the second change observed at this time: the noticeable increase in the construction of range mounds and other monumental structures in public plazas at sites outside Salitrón Viejo. These two processes are linked, and they parallel the trend observed at Salitrón Viejo of increased elite-directed ritual activity and range mound construction in the West and South Groups. Excavations at La Ceiba (PC13) confirm that Structure 13, a two-tier civic-ceremonial structure, was constructed at this time (figure 3.16). The important sites of Cueva Grande (PC59) and El Mango (PC71) grew in size, and it appears that the monumental structures located on their civic-ceremonial plazas were also initiated at this time. On the Humuya River, the site of Intendencia (PC109) grew to become an important secondary center, with smaller occupations identified at PC121 and PC138 (figures 3.9, 3.18).

The Late Sulaco Phase (AD 800–1000)

The Late Sulaco phase was a period of population decline in the El Cajón region. Population was concentrated in the largest sites, which appear to have grown by relocating smaller settlements into their communities (figure 3.19). Community integration continued to be strong, and the sites of Guarabuquí (PC15) and Intendencia (PC109) (figures 3.9, 3.17) flourished at this time. Nevertheless, after AD 1000 there is no discernible population in the El Cajón region. The region was abandoned, and complex social entities like the Salitrón chiefdom never reappeared in El Cajón. Population shifted instead to the more productive agricultural Comayagua and Ulúa valleys.

Late Sulaco ceramics are characterized by changes in the style and decoration of Sulaco and Ulúa polychromes. Chinda Red-on-Natural and Masica

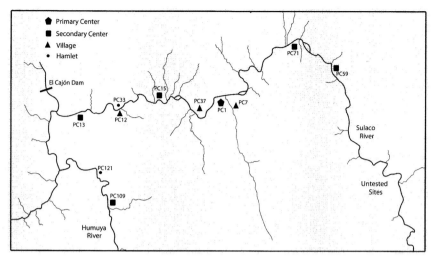

FIGURE 3.19. *The Late Sulaco settlement pattern along the Sulaco River and lower Humuya River. Illustration by Kenneth Hirth and Ryan Middlemore.*

Incised ceramic types were the main utilitarian wares, with the later decreasing toward the end of the phase. Sulaco polychrome is represented by several decorative varieties that include broad-line diagonal painting and black painting along the rims of bowls and jars. Ulúa polychrome continued as an important trade ceramic that includes Nebla and Santa Ana decorative wares. Tenampua-class polychromes are also present and mark the end of the Late Sulaco phase (Cliff 1990b; Hirth, Kennedy, and Cliff 1989, 1993).

Salitrón Viejo was the largest community in the region, but its population declined throughout the period. The Iglesia Precinct remained a prominent area, but there is no evidence of any new construction or rebuilding episodes; further, no ceramics from this phase were recovered from its pavement surfaces or terminal debris that would suggest continual use in public ceremonies. The same was true for the North Precinct, which was completely abandoned and probably was cultivated, as only one Late Sulaco pottery sherd was recovered from the area.

The central plazas of the South and West Residential Groups were the focus of most civic-ceremonial activity. Elite-directed activities continued to mobilize labor for public celebrations and to expand the Range structures flanking their plazas. All five excavated range mounds in the South Plaza continued in use, and Structures 210, 211, and 212 were expanded to their final elevations of 2–3.8 m. The same was true in the West Group plaza, where all three

Range structures were enlarged, bringing them to a height of 3.2 m above the plaza floor. Archaeological excavations identified four discrete phases of construction at Structures 118 and 119 during the Late Sulaco phase. Two phases of construction were also identified at Structure 120 and sub-monumental Structure 121. Civic-ceremonial activity during this period was clearly focused on the residential compounds *within* Salitrón Viejo instead of on activities that unified the site and its relationship with the region.

Regional population shrank, and only eight sites were occupied outside of Salitrón Viejo (figure 3.19). Only the largest Middle Sulaco sites continued to have on-site residence and the construction of monumental architecture. But it was not a period of complete stagnation. Instead, the site of Guarabuquí (PC15) (figure 3.17) reached its maximum size and constructed most of its monumental and sub-monumental architecture (Cliff 1990a; Messenger 1984). The site of La Ceiba (PC13) continued to be important, although its on-site population appears reduced compared to the preceding period. Both Cueva Grande (PC59) and El Mango (PC71) had major occupations during the Late Sulaco phase, when they also reached their maximum population size. The same trend was identified on the Humuya River, where two sites (PC109, PC121) with Late Sulaco occupation were identified. The site of Intendencia (figure 3.9) continued as a large and important secondary center until it was abandoned by the end of the phase (Cliff 1990b).

SUMMARY

The El Cajón region straddles the Central Honduran corridor, which was a major north–south communication route across Honduras in pre-Columbian times. It is not surprising, therefore, that it shared ceramic and cultural similarities with the Ulúa valley to the north, the Comayagua valley to the south, and the Lake Yojoa region to the west. An additional important feature for groups in El Cajón was that the Sulaco River provided a ready communication route into eastern Honduras (Lara-Pinto 2015, 2019) (see figure 2.1). The primary deficiency of the El Cajón region was the limited amount of good agricultural land, which was probably why it was not occupied by farming groups until 400 BC. Nevertheless, the earliest and largest sites in the region are located on the largest and most productive vega lands along the Sulaco River. Developments in El Cajón underscore the fact that societies like the Salitrón chiefdom can develop in areas with a limited agriculture resource base.

Salitrón Viejo was the earliest and largest community to develop in the El Cajón region. It occupied the largest section of rich agricultural land, which attracted and supported a resident population of somewhere between 1,000 and 1,600 people over the greater length of its occupation. The residents of Salitrón invested in the construction of two civic-ceremonial precincts during the Late Yunque phase. The Iglesia Precinct was the site's central civic-ceremonial precinct, which fulfilled the community's most important ritual and ceremonial needs. The North Precinct was a separate special purpose area intended to integrate regional groups into the Salitrón socio-political community. What is important is that a chiefdom emerged within the context of regional interaction. Major construction in both the Iglesia and North Precincts was completed during the Late Yunque period, centuries before regional communities reached their maximum population size and internal differentiation.

A rise in civic-ceremonial construction at sites during the Middle and Late Sulaco phases is correlated with what appears to be a decrease in ritual activity in both the Iglesia and North Precincts at Salitrón Viejo. The centralizing forces found during the Late Yunque phase appear to have weakened over time. Salitrón Viejo remained the largest and most influential community in the region, but a good deal of civic-ceremonial activity and large-scale construction shifted to local communities and residential units like the West and South Groups. The emergence of influential elite in secondary regional centers such as Guarabuquí (PC15), Intendencia (PC109), La Ceiba (PC13), and Cueva Grande (PC59) was a source of competition for the elite of Salitrón Viejo. The result was that the Salitrón chiefdom weakened over time, as the focus of ritual activity shifted inward within regional communities. By the end of the Sulaco period, there was a greater degree of socio-political parity between large communities in the region.

Feasting was the common denominator of civic-ceremonial activity, with midden deposits linked to feasts and feast preparation during all phases of occupation at Salitrón Viejo. We envision that over time, civic-ceremonial activity shifted from centralized celebrations at Salitrón Viejo to a cycle of inter-community feasting at five or more large centers in El Cajón during the Middle and Late Sulaco phases. Public plazas were the focus of these celebrations, where dances and ritual enactments of different types were carried out. The importance of these plazas is underscored by the construction and periodic expansion of the Range structures located around their peripheries. While large by local standards, these platforms were not single-phase constructions. Instead, excavation revealed that they were accretionary constructions, built serially over time by relatively small-scale investments of labor mobilized as communal work groups.

By AD 1000, the El Cajón region was abandoned. While the factors behind this abandonment remain unclear, it parallels cultural events identified elsewhere throughout western Honduras and the adjacent Maya region (Kennett and Beach 2013; Lucero 2002; Smith and Demarest 2001; Webster 2002). One such event was the increased nucleation of population into fewer large regional centers at the end of the Classic period. This process was initially identified by Rosemary Joyce (1985, 2014) in the Ulúa valley at Cerro Palenque. The same population trend is evident in the nucleation of population in the lower Sulaco valley between the Early and Late Sulaco periods. This increased nucleation may have produced increased competition between sites, but it did not result in the relocation of population into more defensible locales, as documented for the Comayagua and Ulúa valleys. Whatever the causes, population eventually moved out of the El Cajón region, presumably into areas that still had larger communities with active ritual lives.

The three chapters that follow refocus discussion on the key features and material evidence of the Salitrón chiefdom that can be measured archaeologically during the Late Yunque phase. Chapter 4 reconstructs the sequence of construction in the Iglesia Precinct, which was the most important civic-ceremonial area in the El Cajón region. Chapter 5 examines the carved jade and marble artifacts used in large-scale offerings in the Iglesia and North Precincts. Finally, chapter 6 looks at the location, composition, and handling of these offerings in different contexts and what they tell us about ritual practice at Salitrón Viejo.

4

The Iglesia Precinct is the most imposing architectural group at Salitrón Viejo. Its central location together with the scale and type of its architecture indicate that it was the most important ritual complex in the El Cajón region. The complex measures 154 m long (E–W) by 80 m wide (N–S) and covers an area of 1.2 ha (figure 4.1). The dominant architectural element in the complex is the Acropolis platform, which is 88 m long (E–W), 78 m wide (N–S), and 2.0–2.10 m in height over its greatest extent. The Acropolis covered the precinct's original plaza, raising its floor 2 m above the living surface of the community, which emphasized its importance in Salitrón Viejo.

This chapter reconstructs and dates the construction of the Iglesia Precinct and provides observations about probable usage areas within it. The Iglesia Precinct was the setting for a good deal of the society's ritual economy, which included large-scale offerings. From a macro-perspective, the Iglesia Precinct provides important information about four different aspects of civic-ceremonial life at Salitrón Viejo and the regional chiefdom over which it held sway.

First and foremost, the Iglesia Precinct was a formidable architectural complex that required considerable effort to construct. While the Acropolis platform and its associated structures did not reach the grandeur of Late Formative constructions at Los Naranjos or Yarumela, the Iglesia Precinct required over 19,000 m^3 of architectural fill to construct (see table 3.2). This

https://doi.org/10.5876/9781646424757.c004

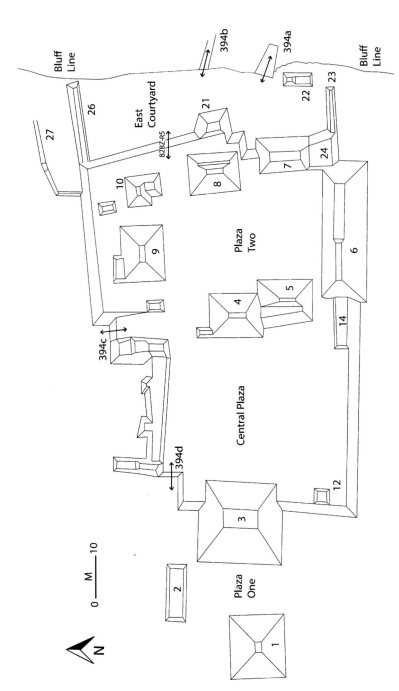

FIGURE 4.1. *Map of the Iglesia Precinct with numbered structures discussed in text. Illustration by Kenneth Hirth.*

required mobilizing labor from Salitrón Viejo and possibly its neighboring communities (see chapter 7). In comparative terms, the volume of construction in the Iglesia Precinct was about two-thirds of what was used in Structure IV, the large Acropolis platform at Los Naranjos.[1] Archaeological evidence indicates that most of the architecture in the Iglesia Precinct was constructed over a 400-year period during the Late Yunque phase.

Second, the Iglesia Precinct was established as the primary ritual center at Salitrón Viejo when the site was first occupied. This area also contained the primary residence of the site's elite between the Late Yunque and Middle Sulaco phases. It would be an oversight, however, to focus on the Iglesia Precinct to the exclusion of the North Precinct, which had the largest plaza suitable for receiving groups from surrounding communities. Sumptuous offerings of jade and marble artifacts were recovered in both of these precincts. The wealth of these offerings together with their architectural layouts reflect the symbiotic use of these areas in the organization of Salitrón Viejo's regional chiefdom.

Third, the Acropolis platform follows an architectural tradition found at other sites in Honduras. Acropolis platforms supported structures and functioned as elevated assembly areas during the Late Formative and Classic periods. Other Acropolis platforms occur at Los Naranjos, Gualjoquito, Jamáltepec, Travesía, Copán, and Yarumela (Ashmore 1987:figure 2; Baudez and Becquelin 1973:figure 10; Dixon et al. 1994:figure 1; Sanders 1986:figure 1; Stone 1941:figure 48). The Acropolis platform is the third largest such platform in west-central Honduras, behind Structure IV at Los Naranjos and Structure 101 at Yarumela.

Fourth and finally, the site of Salitrón Viejo developed into an important regional center between AD 0 and 400. This period is less well-known in west-central Honduras than either the preceding Late Formative or subsequent Late Classic periods.[2] The construction of the Iglesia and North Precincts provides valuable information on three topics: (1) the formation of a complex chiefdom society during this period, (2) the role of ritual as a regionally important integrative mechanism, and (3) how socio-political organization and the focus of civic-ceremonial activity changed over time. As such, it provides valuable information on regional development during an era that is less well documented than other periods of Honduran prehistory.

THE IGLESIA PRECINCT

The Iglesia Precinct consists of the Acropolis platform and the mounds on or alongside this central architectural feature. The complex in its final form was divided into four distinct zones, which are used here for describing the architecture within it. The precinct was organized around its large central plaza; while its boundaries were established at its inception, the four zones within it became differentiated only as construction proceeded over time. These four zones are (1) Plaza One, defined by three structures located at the west end of the Iglesia Precinct; (2) the Central Plaza, which occupies the western half of the Acropolis platform; (3) Plaza Two, which occupies the eastern half of the Acropolis platform; and (4) the East Courtyard, located below the east edge of the Acropolis platform (figure 4.1).

Plaza One is defined by three mounds (Structures 1–3) situated around a patio adjacent to the west side of the Acropolis platform. While Plaza One is small, it contains the earliest and tallest structures in the Iglesia Precinct.[3] The Central Plaza in its final form was 53 m (E–W) by 64 m (N–S) in size and was used for an array of ritual and public gatherings. Excavations uncovered several buried structures within the matrix of the Acropolis[4] that defined the limits of the Central Plaza during the Early and Late Yunque phases before the platform was constructed. Plaza Two is a group of seven mounds on the east end of the Acropolis platform (Structures 4–10) that enclosed an area 18 m (E–W) by 45 m (N–S) in size. This area contains Structure 6, which is the Range structure believed to be the location of the site's earliest elite residence. The East Courtyard is located between the east side of the Acropolis and the edge of the river terrace overlooking the Rio Yunque. Four mound structures (21–24) were constructed in this courtyard.

The Iglesia Precinct is the central architectural group at Salitrón Viejo (see figure 3.5). Structures 1 and 3 in Plaza One are the tallest structures at Salitrón Viejo (figure 4.2) and were the first civic-ceremonial mounds individuals would encounter as they entered the site along the corridor leading from the North Precinct (see figure 3.5). Access onto the Acropolis was restricted to a few entrance points. Primary access was provided by two paved ramps on the west and north sides of the Acropolis (figure 4.1). The west ramp (394d) provided access from the West and South Residential Groups, while the north ramp (394c) is located opposite a set of paired openings that connect with the North Precinct. Two additional paved ramps (Structures 394a, 394b) ascend the river terrace overlooking the Rio Yunque and enter the East Courtyard. From there, a stairway on the east side of the Acropolis (Feature 82BZ-R5) provided access onto its upper surface.

The non-symmetrical configuration of the Acropolis platform was the result of it being built in multiple episodes rather than a single construction event. The irregular configuration is particularly evident along its northwest side, where the platform's expansion engulfed and covered an earlier structure.[5]

FIGURE 4.2. *Structures 1 and 3 in Plaza One of the Iglesia Precinct looking north*

Excavations were designed to identify the broad construction sequence of the Iglesia Precinct with less attention paid to individual small structures within it. A large sample of architecture was exposed that included eighteen structures and large portions of the Acropolis platform.[6] In the process, excavations revealed the use of two different construction techniques: the early use of adobe walls and a later reliance on cobble wall construction combined with earthen and cobble fill. Two types of floor surfaces were identified on the platform: cobble pavements and a conglomerate of crushed rock in a wet lime and clay mixture. The floor surfaces of both Plaza One and the East Courtyard were hard-packed earth floors (Hirth, Lara-Pinto, and Hasemann 1984:17). River cobbles were used both in wall construction and as fill in the Iglesia Precinct. Unfortunately, the tropical growth that covered the complex after abandonment broke up floor surfaces and dislodged cobble wall alignments, which made architectural reconstruction a challenging endeavor even with large-scale clearing and stratigraphic cuts.

The growth of the Iglesia Precinct can be separated into six construction stages based on the superposition of architectural features, floors, and wall alignments. These construction episodes were dated and aligned with the El Cajón chronology (see table 2.1) using radiocarbon dates from stratigraphic units together with the analysis of 23,926 ceramic sherds retrieved from 81 features and stratigraphic contexts. Structures were built and expanded in different construction stages. To register sequential construction, structures spanning multiple building episodes were labeled by number and alphanumeric designation beginning with the earliest substructure encountered. For example, the initial construction of Structure 3 was labeled 3-subA, with subsequent expansions and rebuilding episodes labeled 3-subB, 3-subC, and so on, until it reached its final form. The final construction episode was simply labeled with the number assigned during site mapping (e.g., Structure 3). Structures over 1 m in height were often constructed as multi-tier buildings with a stairway on one side. Features were labeled by year, excavation area, and feature number. Feature 4, excavated in 1981, in Operation F would be labeled Feature 81F-R4. Nevertheless, cobble wall construction did not preserve well, so structures are represented by their basal dimensions in the figures that illustrate the six growth phases. Likewise, only structures that were tested archaeologically are incorporated into the architectural reconstruction. As a result, some small structures originally mapped in the Iglesia Precinct and shown in figure 4.1 are not included in the phase reconstruction presented here.

IGLESIA PRECINCT CONSTRUCTION STAGE 1 (EARLY YUNQUE PHASE)

The first evidence for ritual activity in the Iglesia Precinct dates to the site's initial occupation between 300 and 100 BC (figure 4.3). All activity deposits and construction during Stage 1 were on the original ground surface; they were either covered by the Acropolis platform or destroyed during subsequent remodeling episodes, making it difficult to determine their contemporaneity with precision. What is particularly interesting is that traces of early ritual activity including feasting were recovered across the entire extent of the Iglesia Precinct. No domestic structures were in this area[7] except for the Range structure, which appeared during Stage 2. From its inception, the Iglesia Precinct was a special civic-ceremonial space. Three structures were identified during this stage: Structures 2-subA and 3-subA located in Plaza One and Structure 21-subA on the precinct's far eastern end (figure 4.3).

Structure 3-subA is located on the east side of Plaza One and was the first construction in the Iglesia Precinct. It was a low cobble and earthen platform 7.0 m long (N–S), 6.75 m wide (E–W), and 90 cm tall. Two jade beads were recovered from the structure's interior construction matrix. The heaviest concentrations of features from Stage 1 were in preconstruction strata that extend across Plaza One and underneath Structures 1 and 3 (figure 4.1). These materials lay directly on the sterile subsoil and include several midden concentrations, a refuse pit dug into sterile soil, a hard-packed earthen floor, and a portion of the wall and floor of a perishable building.[8]

Structure 2-subA was a low oblong earthen mound located on the north side of Plaza One (figure 4.3). It was built without retention walls and supported several perishable wattle-and-daub buildings that were rebuilt during the structure's use-life to at least the end of the Early Sulaco phase (Stage 5).

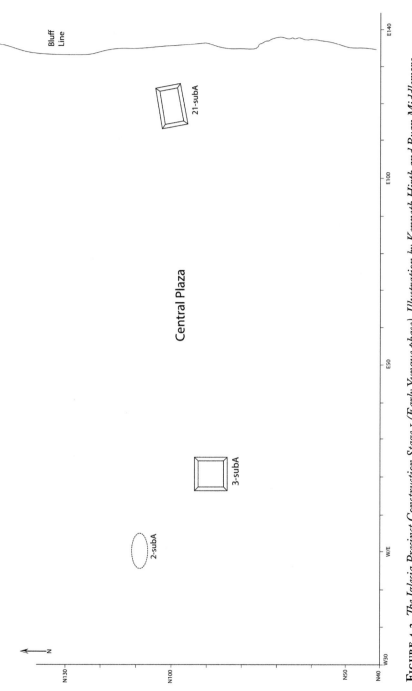

Figure 4.3. *The Iglesia Precinct Construction Stage 1 (Early Yunque phase). Illustration by Kenneth Hirth and Ryan Middlemore.*

The structure was 9.0 m long (E–W), 4.5 m wide (N–S), and 25.0 cm high. It grew through the gradual accumulation of refuse on the floor of the structure on its summit. Stage 1 construction was initiated by laying down a 10–12 cm layer of sterile clay over which a crushed stone floor and cobble pavement raised the mound to a height of 25 cm. The placement of several large cobbles along the south side of this floor appears to have anchored wooden poles used in the structure's perishable building.

The main function of this structure was food preparation. Seven metates and three mano fragments were recovered on its floor, along with abundant quantities of broken ceramics, lithics, burnt bone, carbonized botanical remains, coyol nuts, jute shells, ash, and wood charcoal. Despite clear evidence for food preparation, it was not a domestic structure since house mounds were always built using stone retention walls to stabilize the area on which the residential building was constructed (e.g., figure 3.6).[9] It appears instead to have been a food preparation area used for periodic feasting in the Iglesia Precinct. The earliest radiocarbon date recovered from midden deposits in the pre-architectural strata of Plaza One dates to 2δcal 418–96 BC (94%) (table 4.1:SMU1934).

Structure 21-subA was the third early structure in the Iglesia Precinct that was located in what became the East Courtyard. It was 9 m long (E-S), approximately 5 m wide (N-S), and 40 cm tall. The south side of the structure was damaged when a portion of it was mined away and used as fill in later construction in the Iglesia Precinct. The upper surface of the platform had an earthen floor that was covered with a 1–2 cm layer of a hard stucco-like material that provided a durable surface. An adult male burial approximate twenty-two years of age (Burial 1-33) was recovered from preconstruction deposits along the south side and beneath Structure 21 (Benyo, Storey, and Hirth n.d.). Buried midden deposits from the East Courtyard produced a radiocarbon date of 2δcal 389–55 BC (95%) that was associated with the use of this structure (table 4.1:SMU2296).

IGLESIA PRECINCT CONSTRUCTION STAGE 2 (EARLY TO LATE YUNQUE TRANSITION)

This stage represents a significant increase in construction activities across the Iglesia Precinct between 100 BC and AD 100. Structures 3-subA and 21-subA were expanded, Structure 12-subA was built at the southeast corner of Plaza One, and five new structures were initiated at the east end of the Iglesia Precinct in the area that became Plaza Two. All new structures were built

TABLE 4.1. Radiocarbon dates from the Iglesia Precinct

Sample	Analysis Type	Provenience	Iglesia Area	Iglesia Construction Stage	¹⁴C yr (BP) ± 1σ	cal BC–AD (2σ) Oxcal 4.4 (IntCal20)
PSU7061	AMS	PCI, AL-1-E	Plaza 2, Str. 9-subA	6b	1265±20	AD 672–777
PSU7690	AMS	PCI, AL-1-D	Plaza 2, Str. 9-subA	6b	1610±15	AD 417–538
SMU1933	C14	PCI, AL-1-D	Plaza 2, Str. 9-subA	6b	1445±60	AD 436–679
PSU6408	AMS	PCI, AL-2-O	Plaza Two, Str. 9	Fill	1990±20	42 BC–AD 80
PSU6411	AMS	PCI, M-41-B	Plaza Two	6a	1585±20	AD 425–545
SMU2295	C14	PCI, M-41-B	Plaza Two	6a	1590±50	AD 384–593
PSU6406	AMS	PCI, G-137-c	Str. 12, south pedestrian surface	5	1760±20	AD 238–352
PSU7058	AMS	PCI, G-100-c	Str. 12, north pedestrian surface	4	1760±20	AD 238–352
SMU2035	C14	PCI, G-100-c; G-101-d,e	Str. 12, north pedestrian surface	1–4	2118±219	766 BC–AD 327
PSU6407	AMS	PCI, G-198-D	Str. 395, west pedestrian surface	3–4	1880±20	AD 119–223
PSU6405	AMS	PCI, 1984-R30	Plaza Two, preconstruction surface	3	1960±20	AD 8–123
PSU7060	AMS	PCI, M-37-J	Plaza Two, preconstruction surface	2–3	2015±20	50 BC–AD 61

continued on next page

Table 4.1.—*continued*

Sample	Analysis Type	Provenience	Iglesia Area	Iglesia Construction Stage	^{14}C yr (BP) ± 1σ	cal BC–AD (2σ) Oxcal 4.4 (IntCal20)
SMU2294	C14	PC1, M-37-J	Plaza Two, preconstruction surface	2	2070±50	200 BC–AD 62
PSU7059	AMS	Burial 1-17	Str. 3	2	2060±20	164–1 BC
SMU1932	C14	Burial 1-17	Str. 3	2	2085±40	199 BC–AD 12
PSU7057	AMS	PC1, F-5-AV	Plaza One, preconstruction surface	2	1995±20	44 BC–AD 77
PSU6409	AMS	PC1, 1984-R96	Plaza One, preconstruction surface	2	2050±20	110 BC–AD 21
PSU7056	AMS	PC1, 1984-R15	Plaza One, preconstruction surface	disturbed	130±15	AD 1682–1937
PSU7691	AMS	PC1, 1984-R15	Plaza One, preconstruction surface	2	1960±15	AD 17–121
PSU7698	AMS	PC1, 1984-R15	Plaza One, preconstruction surface	3	1740±15	AD 248–378
SMU1934	C14	PC1, 1984-R15	Plaza One, preconstruction surface	1–2	2250±70	418–96 BC
SMU2296	C14	PC1, AD-1-F	East Courtyard	1	2180±70	388–52 BC

along the margins of the Central Plaza, which was 85 m long (E–W) by 43 m wide (N–S) during this phase (figure 4.4).

Structures 3-subB and 3-subC. Structure 3-subA was enlarged twice during this phase using adobe blocks and earthen fill to expand it laterally and vertically. Structure 3-subB was the first construction episode that produced

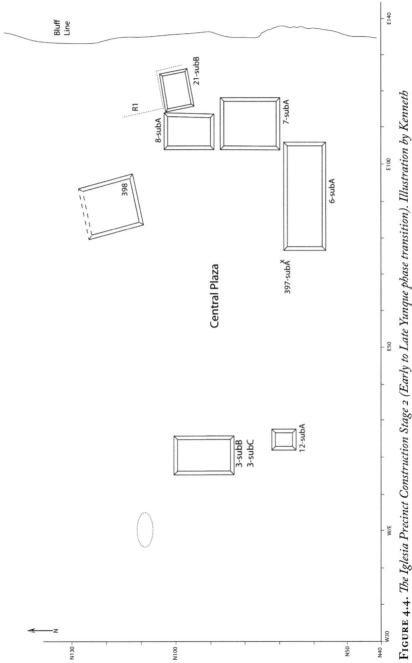

Figure 4.4. *The Iglesia Precinct Construction Stage 2 (Early to Late Yunque phase transition). Illustration by Kenneth Hirth and Ryan Middlemore.*

FIGURE 4.5. *Adobe wall construction on the west side of Structure 3*

a platform mound 15.0 m long (N–S), 8.25 m wide (E–W), and 2.1 m high. Adobe blocks that were 45–55 cm long, 18–20 cm high, and 18–20 cm thick were used to fashion its exterior walls. The exterior surface of the adobe walls was sealed with multiple layers of lime over a clay mixture to create a smooth white surface (Hirth, Lara-Pinto, and Hasemann 1984:16) (figure 4.5).[10] Adobe was also used in the adjacent later construction of Structure 1-subA.

Structure 3-subB was associated with an adult burial (1-17) of indeterminate gender (figure 4.6) (Benyo, Storey, and Hirth n.d.). A large bonfire was prepared on the surface of Structure 3-subA, creating a thick layer of ash on which Burial 1-17 was interred (Benyo, Storey, and Hirth n.d.). Associated mortuary offerings included three ceramic vessels (see figure 2.3), a jade bead, and a stucco-covered wooden vessel. Two radiocarbon dates were run on material from this burial that provide dates of 2δcal 164–1 BC (95%) and 2δcal 199 BC–AD 12 (94%) (table 4.1:PSU7059, SMU1932). This burial was then covered with fill and structure 3-subB was raised to its height of 2.1 m.

The process was then repeated in the second building episode that produced *Structure 3-subC*. A secondary burial of an adult female approximately

Figure 4.6. *Excavation of Burial 1-17 and offerings. Burial is in pedestaled area.*

thirty-seven years of age and a three-year-old child (Burial 1-16 A&B) was laid on the surface of Structure 3-subB (figure 4.7) (Benyo, Storey, and Hirth n.d.). This burial was then covered with 50 cm of earth, over which a partially fired red clay floor (Floor 3-subC1) was prepared that brought Structure 3-subC to a height of 2.6 m, making it the tallest structure in the Iglesia Precinct during Stage 2.[11] Burial 1-16 A-B was interred with an offering containing eight ceramic vessels, which also included one stucco-covered ceramic vessel (figure 4.8), two stucco-covered wooden vessels, one jade bead, and one fragmented carved marble artifact (Carías de López 1996). This was the largest mortuary offering found at Salitrón Viejo and throughout the El Cajón region during all phases.[12]

Structure 2-subA continued to be involved in preparing food for feasts. Six pit hearths were identified in the floor of Plaza One that were covered

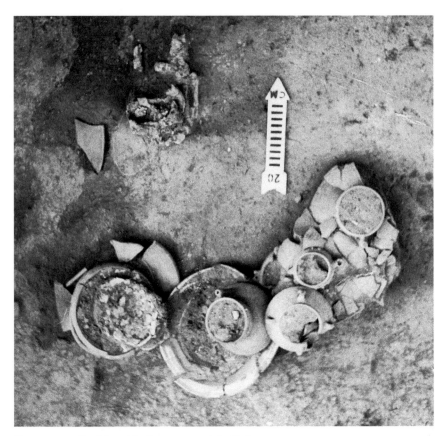

FIGURE 4.7. *Burial 1-16 in Structure 3 with offerings*

later by the construction of Structure 1. Each of these hearths had three shallow depressions dug into the plaza floor where fires were built and pots were placed for cooking.[13] Quantities of coyol remains were associated with these hearths that may have been used to boil fruit for direct consumption or been part of the process for making a fermented beverage (Ramírez Hernández et al. 2013).[14] An AMS radiocarbon date from one of these hearths dated to 2δcal 110 BC–AD 21 (94%) (table 4.1:PSU6409).

The Central Plaza was the focus of civic-ceremonial activities at this time, and six new structures were constructed on its periphery (figure 4.4). New constructions included Structures 6, 7, 8, 12, 397, and 398—the latter two of which were later covered by the Acropolis platform. Structures 397 and 398 were identified by stratigraphic explorations, although excavations did not define their complete dimensions.[15]

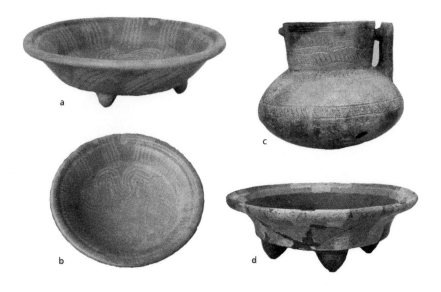

Figure 4.8. *Four Late Yunque ceramics from Burial 1–16 in Structure 3 at Salitrón Viejo.* Courtesy, *IHAH; edited by Kenneth Hirth.*

Structure 12-subA was a small platform located at the southwest corner of the Central Plaza. When the Iglesia Precinct was mapped, this structure appeared to be a low altar on the surface of the Acropolis (figure 4.1), but excavation revealed that it was an intact mound buried within the platform's matrix. Structure 12-subA was a small cobble wall platform 4.8 m long (N–S), 3.8 m wide (E–W), and 65 cm high. It was constructed on a 15 cm layer of reddish-brown clay laid down over an earlier Stage 1 midden. The upper floor of 12-subA was a pavement of closely fitted river cobbles where a large amount of carbon, burnt bone, ceramics, and one jade bead was recovered.

A considerable amount of construction activity occurred at the east end of the Iglesia Precinct in the area that became Plaza Two. Three structures were constructed on the east side of the precinct (7-subA, 8-subA, 21-subB), one along its southeast edge (6-subA), and one along its northeast side (398) (figure 4.4).

Structure 21-subB was expanded to 9.0 m long (E–W), approximately 7.0 m wide (N–S), and 1.8 m tall. An important aspect of this building episode was the use of adobe blocks along its south side (figure 4.9), like those used in the construction of Structures 3-subB and 3-subC. A low footing wall 30 m in length (82BY-R1/R2/ R4) was identified around the structure's northern

FIGURE 4.9. *Structure 21-subB: (a) adobe wall showing recycling of structure fill, (b) adobe blocks within the wall*

and eastern perimeter that was the abutment of a wooden palisade or screening wall (figure 4.4). One jade bead and fragments of a conical jade flare and zoomorphic pendant were found inside and at the base of this footing wall.

Structure 6-subA was a rectangular cobble wall Range structure constructed at the southeastern margin of the Central Plaza (figure 4.4). It was 27 m long (E–W), 10 m wide (N–S), and 1.8 m high. A cobble pavement was constructed on its summit where a 20 cm layer of occupational midden was identified. Range structures are believed to have supported elite residences. This together with the occupational midden recovered from its floor suggests that Structure 6-subA was the residence of the community's highest-ranking elite family, perhaps even the residence of the individuals in Burials 1-16A and B and 1-17 located in Structures 3-subB and 3-subC.

Structures 7-subA and *8-subA* were located on the east end of the Central Plaza. *Structure 8-subA* was located adjacent to Structure 21-subB. It was 7.25 m wide (E–W), 12–13 m long (N–S), and 2.0 m high. The structure was built using a combination of cobble and adobe wall construction, the former on its east side with adobe walls on the west. Heavy carbon and ash deposits were identified on the west side of 8-subA that lie beneath a compact earthen floor (Feature 84-R34) that defined a 3 m wide pedestrian surface around its base. Portions of a gravel subfloor were identified on the summit of 8-subA1 (Feature 84-R37).

Structure 7-subA was a cobble wall platform 15.0 m long (N–S), 12.0 m wide (E–W), and 2.0 m tall constructed in the southeast corner of the Iglesia Precinct. A fire hearth 100 cm long and 80 cm wide was identified on the pedestrian surface at the base of its west wall (81M-R2) that contained a heavy concentration of carbon, burnt clay, bone, and jute shells. Two radiocarbon samples were analyzed from this hearth that date to 2δcal 50 BC–AD 61 (95%) and 2δcal 200 BC–AD 62 (93%) (table 4.1:PSU7060, SMU 2294). These two samples provide *terminus ante quem* dates for the construction of the Eastern Acropolis platform, which covered the hearth during Stage 3.

Structure 397-subA was constructed near the northwest corner of Structure 6-subA (figure 4.4). Excavations identified it as a low platform 30 cm high with a burnt clay floor across its upper surface (Feature 81G-R19). Like Structure 12-subA, the upper surface of this structure was covered with a 30 cm layer of mixed cultural debris containing ceramics, carbon, and burnt daub.

Structure 398 was located at the northeast corner of the Central Plaza (figure 4.4). It was a large cobble walled platform 14.0 m long (N–S), at least 12.0 m wide (E–W), and 1.75 m high. Two floors were associated with this structure. The initial structure was 1.55 m tall and had a compact earthen floor on its summit and a smooth layer of mud plaster covering the face of its south wall.

The platform was then resurfaced with 20 cm of fill, topped by a burnt clay floor that brought the structure to a height of 1.75 m. A bench 75–80 cm in height was attached to its southern exterior wall (Feature 81M-R15).

IGLESIA PRECINCT CONSTRUCTION
STAGE 3 (LATE YUNQUE PHASE)

The construction of the Acropolis platform was initiated in Stage 3, but the platform was not built as a single architectural feature. Instead, it was constructed sequentially in three episodes (Stages 3–5) that gradually expanded its size until it covered all of the original (Stage 2) area of the Central Plaza. How quickly each construction stage was carried out is unclear because there may have been incremental construction episodes within each stage.[16] Nevertheless, sequential construction is indicated by (1) the presence of finished walls within the fill of the Acropolis platform that had pedestrian surfaces or prepared cobble pavements at their bases, (2) the accumulation of refuse on these surfaces, and (3) variability in the ceramics recovered in the construction fill, suggesting that some time elapsed between finishing one segment of the Acropolis platform and resuming construction on another. The use of sequential construction is consistent with what is expected for a small-scale society like the Salitrón chiefdom. While groups from outlying communities may have participated in the construction of the Iglesia Precinct, the scope of the work required did not surpass the labor available within the Salitrón community if it was broken down into a series of punctuated activities spaced over several years or decades. The amount of work involved in the Acropolis construction is discussed in chapter 7.

Construction of the Acropolis began in the eastern half of the Iglesia Precinct, where six structures were already present during the preceding stage (figure 4.10). The Eastern Acropolis platform adjoined and covered most of these structures. The platform was 78 m long (N–S), 34 m wide (E–W), and ranged from 2.0 m to 2.25 m in height depending on the underlying topography. The platform was constructed of earth and cobble fill, with a pavement of flat river cobbles on its upper surface (Feature 81M-R4). The west side of the Eastern Acropolis was an adobe wall (Feature 84G-R12) constructed using a double course of adobe blocks set on a cobble base. An interior retention wall (Feature 84-R50) in the Acropolis fill suggests that the platform was constructed in two closely spaced sequential building episodes, as no floor or pedestrian surface was identified at its base.[17] Late Yunque ceramics and organic debris were spread across the

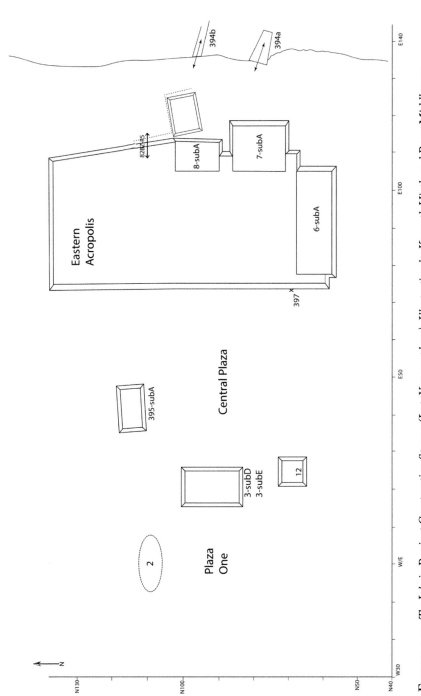

Figure 4.10. *The Iglesia Precinct Construction Stage 3 (Late Yunque phase). Illustration by Kenneth Hirth and Ryan Middlemore.*

preconstruction surface beneath the Stage 3 Acropolis platform. An AMS radiocarbon sample drawn from this pre-architectural surface produced a *terminus ante quem* date of AD 8–123 2δcal (95%) (table 4.1:PSU6405).

The construction of the Eastern Acropolis divided the Central Plaza into two parts: an elevated section to the east and the original ground surface plaza to the west. It also reduced the size of the original Central Plaza by 40 percent, to 54 m (E–W) × 43 m (N–S). The only identifiable access onto the Eastern Acropolis platform at this time was a 1.5 m wide cobble stairway (Feature 82BZ-R5) that ascended its east side (figure 4.10). Two access ramps (Structures 394a, 394b) ascended the sloping bluff from the Yunque River and provided access to the east side (figure 4.10). Their date of construction is unclear, although they are no later than Stage 3, as the Yunque River was the closest source of river cobbles used to construct the Acropolis platform.

The Eastern Acropolis platform engulfed Structure 398 but did not completely cover Structures 6-subA, 7-subA, 8-subA, and 397-subA. Instead, the Eastern Acropolis was constructed to the height of Structures 7-subA and 8-subA, which left the buildings on these two structures level with the new Acropolis surface. In fact, the height of these two platform structures may have determined the elevation of the Acropolis platform. This is evident by the way the south side of the Acropolis platform was modified to conform to the elevation of Structure 6-subA, which was only 1.8 m tall. Instead of being constructed to a constant height of 2.0 m and covering 6-subA, the surface of the Acropolis descended 20 cm from north to south so that it articulated with the cobble pavement on its summit. The matching of the elevation of the Eastern Acropolis platform with the height of these three structures indicates that the perishable buildings on their summits continued in use without immediate rebuilding during Stage 3.

Structure 397 was located in the southeast corner of the Central Plaza alongside the Acropolis platform. A final building episode was initiated by excavating a fire pit (Feature 81G-R18) 46 cm long, 32 cm wide, and 11 cm deep into the cultural debris that had accumulated on its surface. This fire pit was then covered by fill and a cobble pavement (Feature 81G-R17) that brought Structure 397 to its final height of 70 cm. Excavations did not attempt to determine the structure's lateral dimensions.

Building activity continued on the west side of the Iglesia Precinct, where three preexisting structures (2-subA, 3-subC, 12-subA) were expanded and one new structure (395-subA) was constructed.

Structures 3-subD and 3-subE. Structure 3-subC was expanded in height by adding an additional tier in two building episodes without expanding its lateral size. The initial building episode (3-subD) added 45 cm of fill onto the Stage 2 surface, which was finished with a burnt red clay floor (Feature 82G-R18). This brought the height of Structure 3-subD to 3.05 m. The only artifact associated with this structure was a small pyrite sequin or mirror fragment (Melgar, Gallaga, and Solís 2014) recovered from its floor (F 5.48b). The second stage of construction added 60 cm of fill to the height of the platform and was sealed with a hard-packed earthen floor, which brought Structure 3-subE to its final height of 3.65 m above Plaza One. A secondary burial of a twenty-six-year-old adult female (Burial 1-15) was included in the fill of this second construction episode. No mortuary offerings were included with this interment (Benyo, Storey, and Hirth n.d.).

The upper tiers of both 3-subD and 3-subE were again built using adobe blocks and were sealed with a layer of white lime, as in Stage 2 construction.[18] Enough of the finished adobe wall was preserved to identify several episodes of refinishing that extended 3.06 m up the structure's western facade (figure 4.5). Careful cleaning revealed that the white lime surfacing extended onto the floor of Plaza One while the structure walls were resurfaced twice as its upper tier was increased in height.

Structure 2 reached its final dimensions of 14 m long (E–W), 7 m wide (N–S), and 50 cm high at this time. Nevertheless, ceramics recovered from the summit of Structure 2 indicate that it was used periodically during the Early and possibly the Middle Sulaco phases.[19] Three AMS radiocarbon dates recovered from Plaza One date the most intensive use of this structure to the period from 2δcal 44 BC to AD 378 (95%) (table 4.1:PSU7057, PSU7691, PSU7698). The association of this structure with ritual activity is indicated by the recovery of six fragmented jade artifacts as isolated finds within the structure's upper floor.

Structure 12 was brought to its final form and is the best-preserved structure at Salitrón Viejo. Its importance in the Iglesia Precinct is underscored by its unusual form. It has a sloping *talud* wall surmounted by a small outset vertical *tablero* constructed using flat *lajas* and small cobbles set in a wet clay mortar mixed with small pebbles (figures 4.11, 4.12, 4.13). The *talud-tablero* architectural design has not been reported at other non-Maya sites in Honduras and was unique even at Salitrón Viejo. The structure was oriented to true north and was 6.15 m long (N–S), 5.25 m wide (E–W), and 2.15 m tall. One jade bead was recovered from the cobble floor of Structure 12-subA, and an additional six jade artifacts, two granular marble artifacts, and one non-jade lapidary artifact were incorporated into its construction fill. Of particular interest was the recovery of three broken earflare fragments and one jade bead from each

FIGURE 4.11. *Structure 12, northeast corner. Note south wall of the Stage 4 West Acropolis intersecting the east side of Structure 12.*

of the four corners of the structure's *talud* wall, where they were embedded in the mortar between cobbles just below the upper t*ablero.*

The *talud* walls of Structure 12 were 1.45 m tall, with an upper *tablero* 65–70 cm in height. This produced a *talud* to *tablero* ratio of 2.2:1. The *talud*'s inward-sloping walls reduced the structure's upper surface to an area 5.25 m by 4.45 m in size. The *talud* walls were constructed on a foundation of large wide cobbles, which adjoined a pavement on its east side. The *tablero* was constructed using three courses of white limestone *lajas* 20–40 cm in length, 2–5 cm thick, and spaced 15 cm apart that projected 10 cm beyond the upper edge of the *talud* wall (figure 4.12). The two lower rows of *lajas* extended 20–25 cm into the fill

FIGURE 4.12. *West side and southwest corner of Structure 12 with pedestrian surface. Note* talud-tablero.

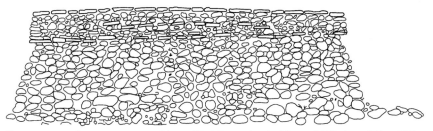

FIGURE 4.13. *Structure 12, east side profile. Illustration by Kenneth Hirth and Shae Rider.*

of the *tablero* and were anchored by the third row of *lajas* and a pavement of cobbles that acted as a counterweight to hold them in place. The area between the *laja* layers was filled with small pieces of white limestone set in a red clay mortar to create an attractive contrasting design. Although Structure 12 is small, its architectural design is vaguely reminiscent of Teotihuacan influence, although the *talud-tablero* proportions are different.

Structure 395-subA was a rectangular cobble wall platform constructed along the northwest periphery of the Central Plaza (figure 4.10). No traces of this platform were noted during original mapping because it was completely covered by the Acropolis platform during Stage 5. The dimensions of this structure are estimated at 10.5 m long (E–W), 6.0 m wide (N–S), and 1.6 m high. The west wall of Structure 395-subA was well preserved and built in *talud* like Structure 12 but without a superimposed *tablero*. An AMS radiocarbon sample from the pedestrian surface on the west side of the structure provided a date of 2δcal AD 119–223 (94%) (table 4.1:PSU6407).

IGLESIA PRECINCT CONSTRUCTION
STAGE 4 (LATE YUNQUE PHASE)

This stage involved a considerable amount of building in the Iglesia Precinct that included the continued expansion of the Acropolis platform (figure 4.14). The Eastern Acropolis platform was expanded 15.0 m to the west, and the Western Acropolis platform was constructed so that it was attached to Structure 3-subE. Several structures were expanded across the Iglesia Precinct, which included enclosing the area of the East Courtyard. Construction activities in the Iglesia Precinct did not go on simultaneously but were carried out in between work on the Acropolis platform.

The Eastern Acropolis platform was extended 15.0 m to the west in two closely spaced construction episodes (figure 4.14). The first episode added a 5.5 m by 78 m extension to its west side. The retention wall for this extension (84-R20) may have been left exposed for a short period of time, but it was not a finished external wall. The second construction episode added another 9.5 m to the west side of the Eastern Acropolis, which ended in a finished cobble wall (Feature 81G-R17) that had a hard-packed pedestrian surface at its base. After this second extension was completed, a continuous stucco floor surface was prepared across the 84-R20 retainment wall, indicating that both building episodes were closely spaced in time. A 4 m wide ramp (Structure 394c) was constructed at the northwest corner of the platform that provided access to the summit of the Eastern Acropolis. This ramp aligns with the two accessways leading to the North Precinct (see figure 3.5), indicating a relationship between these two areas.

Two low platform mounds were constructed at the northeast and southeast corners of the Acropolis platform that enclosed the East Courtyard. Both structures supported either a privacy palisade or perishable wattle-and-daub (*bajareque*) buildings on their summits. Structure 26 on the north side of the courtyard was 21.0 m long (E–W), 4.0 m wide (N–S), and 50 cm high. Structure 23 on the south side was 25.0 m long (E–W), 4.0 m wide (N–S), and 50 cm high and was attached to the south side of Structure 7 using a small platform (Structure 24) (figures 4.1, 4.14).

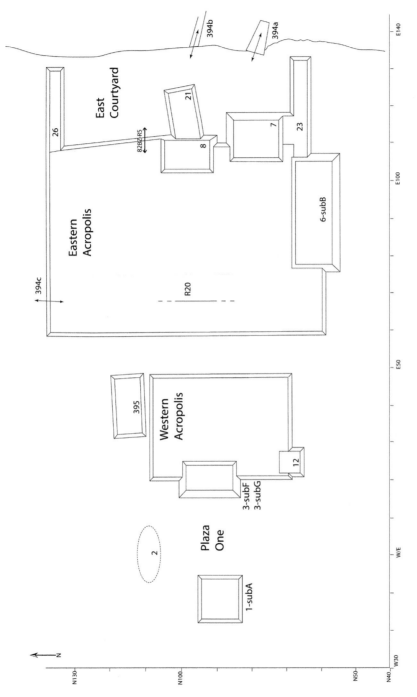

Figure 4.14. *The Iglesia Precinct Construction Stage 4 (Late Yunque phase). Illustration by Kenneth Hirth and Ryan Middlemore.*

The Western Acropolis platform was constructed alongside and attached to Structure 3-subE. It was 38 m long (N–S), 25 m wide (E–W), and 2.0 m high, matching the Eastern Acropolis platform to which it would be attached during Stage 5. This platform covered a large portion of the Central Plaza, articulating with the north side of Structure 12, but it stopped before engulfing the south side of Structure 395. A total of 127 jade artifacts were deposited in the platform's construction fill, including 13 artifacts that were placed behind its east wall along the plaza's east–west centerline. The position of this offering was important, as it was the location for additional offerings when the Acropolis platform was completed during Stage 5.

The Western Acropolis platform covered the north side of Structure 12 and part of its east side (figure 4.11). Two carbon dates were recovered from the north pedestrian surface of Structure 12 underneath the platform. A high-precision AMS sample provided a *terminus ante quem* date for the Western Acropolis platform of 2δcal AD 238–352 (95%) (table 4.1:PSU7058). A low-precision radiometric date from deeper midden deposits along the north side of Structure 12 provided a occupation range of 2δcal 766 BC–AD 327 (94%) (table 4.1:SMU2035). The importance of Structure 12 was highlighted by the offerings associated with it. For its size, this structure had more carved jade and marble artifacts associated with it than any other structure in the Iglesia Precinct except the Acropolis platform. More than 200 pieces were recovered on its buried pedestrian surfaces, in the adjacent fill under the Western Acropolis platform, and on the summit of the structure in what appears to be a termination ritual (see chapter 6 for discussion).

Structures 3-subF and 3-subG. These two construction episodes added a third tier to the structure along with a stairway of flat white *lajas*. Both construction episodes continued to employ adobe construction, and they added 1.7 m of height without changing the structure's basal dimensions. The first episode (3-subF) raised the height of the structure by 55 cm and had a hard-packed earthen floor (Feature 82G-R4) on its summit. The second episode (3-subG) added an additional 1.15 cm to the structure. The stairway (Feature 82G-R2) was added to the south side of Structure 3-subG and provided access to its summit from the Western Acropolis platform. As in previous construction episodes, a thin white lime wash was used to seal the adobe walls of the structure. A secondary burial of a young adult female approximately twenty-six years of age (Burial 1-14) was incorporated into the construction fill of structure 3-subG; it lacked associated offerings (Benyo, Storey, and Hirth n.d.). A quantity of jade and marble artifacts was recovered from the 3-subG construction episode, but none of the artifacts were associated with Burial 1-14 (see chapter 6).

FIGURE 4.15. *Profile of Structure 1 showing cobble and adobe construction of Structure 1-subA*

Structure 395 was expanded on its west and south sides, bringing its overall dimensions to approximately 14.5 m long (E–W), 7.0 m wide (N–S), and 1.6 m high. The north edge of the Western Acropolis platform did not extend all the way to Structure 395. Instead, it left a corridor 15.0 m long (E–W) and 1.5–2.0 m wide between Structure 395 and the north side of the platform that provided access to the area between the Eastern and Western Acropolis platforms. Why this area was left open is unclear, but a cobble pavement was laid down in this corridor that represented the pedestrian surface over which individuals passed. The north side of Structure 395 may have been modified and possibly cut back during the completion of the Acropolis platform in Stage 5.[20]

Structure 1-subA was constructed on the west side of Plaza One. Structure 1-subA was a low adobe wall platform with cobble fill[21] that was 10.5 m long (N–S), 10.5 m wide (E–W), and 1.4 m tall (figures 4.14, 4.15). Two floors were identified on the upper surface of Structure 1-subA. The initial floor was a dense red clay and gravel layer 16–20 cm thick, associated with a wattle-and-daub structure. This floor was subsequently resurfaced with a single layer of cobbles capped by a second red clay floor, bringing Structure 1-subA to a height of 1.4 m. An array of occupational debris, including a large metate, was recovered from this floor. An AMS radiocarbon date from the preconstruction surface under Structure 1-subA provided a date of 2δcal AD 248–378 (95%) (table 4.1:PSU7056).

Three structures were expanded and rebuilt in Plaza Two at this time. During the preceding stage, the Eastern Acropolis platform was constructed to the height of Structures 6-subA, 7-subA, and 8-subA without disrupting the structures on their summits. All three structures were rebuilt during Stage 4.

Structure 6-subB was expanded to 29.0 m long (E–W), 12.5 m wide (N–S), and 2.2 m in height above the floor of Plaza Two. To increase the size of its upper summit, the south side of this Range structure was extended beyond the edge of the Eastern Acropolis platform (figure 4.14). Access to the summit of 6-subB was provided by a stairway that ascended its north side from Plaza Two.

Structure 7 reached its final form in a single construction episode at this time. It was a cobble wall platform that was 15.0 m long (N–S) and 12.0 m wide (E–W) and that rose 2.2 m above the floor of Plaza Two. It was positioned directly over substructure of 7-subA and had an upper surface area that was 9.5 m (N–S) by 6.0 m (E–W). Because Structure 7-subA was built on the pre-architectural ground surface, its east side rose to 3.6 m above the floor of the East Courtyard.

Structure 8 was built to final form as a two-tier platform in a single construction episode. The platform was 15.00 m long (N–S), 9.00 m wide (E–W), and 2.75 m in height above the floor of Plaza Two. The area between Structures 8 and 21 was filled in and leveled, which connected Structure 21 to the east side of Structure 8.[22]

IGLESIA PRECINCT CONSTRUCTION
STAGE 5 (LATE YUNQUE PHASE)

The Acropolis platform was completed during this stage by filling in the area between the Eastern and Western Acropolis (figure 4.16). The south edge of the Western Acropolis was extended 10 m to form a continuous line with the south edge of the Eastern Acropolis platform. This expansion covered the south side of Structure 12 with fill, preserving its *talud-tablero* architecture. An AMS radiocarbon date from its southern pedestrian surface provided a *terminus ante quem* date of 2δcal AD 238–352 (95%) (table 4.1:PSU6404). This assay is identical in calibrated radiocarbon years to the date taken from the pedestrian surface on the north side of the structure covered by the Western Acropolis during Stage 4 (table 4.1:PSU7058). The contemporaneity of these

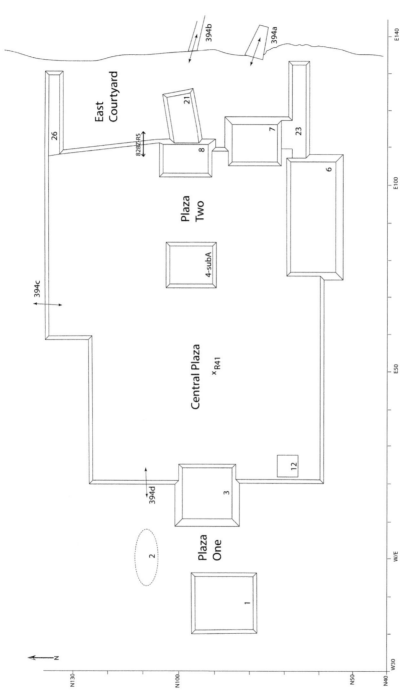

Figure 4.16. *The Iglesia Precinct Construction Stage 5 (Late Yunque phase). Illustration by Kenneth Hirth and Ryan Middlemore.*

two dates indicates that little time transpired between construction events on the Acropolis platform in Stages 4 and 5.

The north edge of the Acropolis was extended 17.0 m, engulfing and burying *Structure 395*. The paved corridor between Structure 395 and the Western Acropolis platform was filled in and replaced with a paved ramp (394d) that provided access onto the summit of the Acropolis platform and into what was now the new Central Plaza from the west (figure 4.16). The completion of the Acropolis platform was a very important event and involved large-scale offerings as part of its dedication ritual. Foremost among these was a large deposit of 1,303 artifacts (Feature 81G-R41) along the east–west centerline of the Central Plaza (figure 4.16). Offerings also accompanied the construction of other structures in the Iglesia Precinct during this stage.

An important undertaking coincident with the completion of the Acropolis platform was the rapid expansion of *Structure 1*, which transformed it into the second tallest platform mound in the Iglesia Precinct. All the evidence suggests that this growth took place in two building episodes using cobble wall construction during Stage 5.[23] The first building episode produced Structure 1-subB, which was constructed as a two-tier platform mound 17.0 m long (N–S), 14.0 m wide (E–W), and 3.3 m tall. A 2.0 m wide stairway was constructed on its south side that was fashioned using white limestone *lajas* for risers.

The second construction episode brought Structure 1 to its final form by adding a third tier to the structure, followed by three floor resurfacing events on its summit. Forty cm of fill were deposited behind a low cobble wall to form the third tier, which was finished with a hard-packed earthen floor. More than 200 jade and marble artifacts were associated with this construction episode, the majority of which (n = 183) occurred in 15 small caches[24] placed around the periphery and under this floor (see chapter 6). Two additional hard-packed and burnt earthen floors mark subsequent floor resurfacing, which culminated in the preparation of a closely articulated pavement of small cobbles (81F-R34) on the top of the structure. While the basal dimension of the structure remained at 17.0 by 14.0 m in size, these activities brought Structure 1 to a final height of 4.4 m above the surface of Plaza One. A layer of occupation debris consisting of charcoal, burnt bone, ceramic, lithic debris, and *bajareque* covered the structure's upper cobble floor.

Structure 3 was also expanded and brought to its final dimensions of 16.00 m long (N–S), 15.00 m wide (E–W), and 5.35 m high. The structure may have been a little higher, but the floor on its upper summit had eroded away. This stage of construction departed from the previous use of adobe block and employed cobble wall construction to broaden the basal dimensions of the structure along its west side (figure 4.16).

Construction also continued in Plaza Two. *Structure 6* was expanded to its final dimensions of 32.0 m long (E–W), 15.0 m wide (N–S), and 2.2 m above the floor of Plaza Two. The structure was extended 2.5 m along its south side, where it had the form of a three-tier cobble wall platform that rose 4.0 m above ground surface. A cobble pavement covered its upper summit, and a second set of stairs may have been added to its south side to provide access to the building's summit from outside the Iglesia Precinct.

Structure 4-subA was a new construction located on the west side of Plaza Two. Its construction initiated the process of enclosing and separating Plaza Two from the rest of the Acropolis platform. This initial construction was a cobble wall platform mound 12 m long (N–S), 10 m wide (E–W), and 90 cm tall. A hard-packed clay floor was identified on its summit.

IGLESIA PRECINCT CONSTRUCTION STAGE 6 (EARLY TO MIDDLE SULACO PHASES)

Stage 6 was the final episode of construction and use in the Iglesia Precinct (figure 4.17). By the Middle Sulaco phase, most discernible ritual activity shifted to the West and South Residential Groups (see figure 3.5). Construction brought civic-ceremonial structures in Plaza Two to their final form and increased the separation of this area within the Iglesia Precinct. Activities in Plaza Two seem less open to the community as a whole. Two altars were constructed in Plaza Two and the floor of the plaza was modified, creating two small sunken patios referred to as M1 and M2 in front of Structures 6 and 7. These two patios emphasized the importance of these two structures while at the same time highlighting different display and worship activities within Plaza Two.

Structure 4 was completed by adding a second level to the previous structure. The basal dimensions of the structure remained 12.0 m long (N–S) and 10.0 m wide (E–W), with the second-level addition bringing the structure to its final elevation of 2.8 m. Although the upper portions of this structure were badly eroded, topographic contours suggest that the second level was 8.0 m wide (E–W), with a 2 m wide frontal platform facing onto Plaza Two.

Structure 5 was a new construction located at the southwest corner of Plaza Two immediately alongside Structure 4 (figure 4.17). It was built as a two-level platform using cobble wall construction that was 14.50 m long (E–W), 12.00 m wide (N–S), and 3.15 m tall. Unlike other structures in Plaza Two, its lower

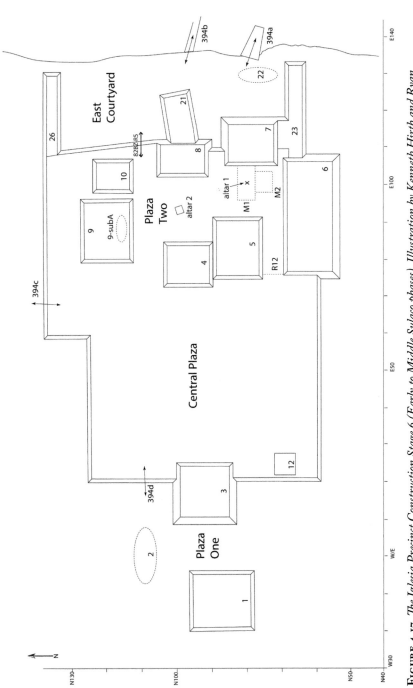

Figure 4.17. *The Iglesia Precinct Construction Stage 6 (Early to Middle Sulaco phases). Illustration by Kenneth Hirth and Ryan Middlemore.*

level faced onto the Central Plaza, with a stairway on its west side constructed using white limestone *lajas*. A low cobble wall 7 m long, 90 cm wide, and 28–40 cm high was built between the southwest corner of Structure 5 and the northwest corner of Structure 6. Registered as Structure 408 (figure 4.17), this wall appears to have been the basal abutment for a wooden palisade or screening wall that closed off access to Plaza Two from the Central Plaza. This made the area between Structures 4 and 9 the only means of entering Plaza Two from the Central Plaza.

Structure 9 was a new construction located on the north side of Plaza Two. Although superimposed over Structure 398, there was no direct architectural link between them.[25] This structure was constructed in several building episodes during this stage. *Structure 9-subA* was an unconsolidated layer of earth 60 cm in thickness that was deposited directly on the cobble pavement of Plaza Two. The form of Structure 9-subA strongly resembles the low earthen mounds of Structure 2 in Plaza One and Structure 20 in the East Courtyard (see below). Like both of these structures, it appears to have had food preparation functions. A circular hearth and a large quantity of food remains were recovered from this deposit.[26] Three AMS radiocarbon dates from this hearth date its use to the Early and Middle Sulaco phases, from 2δcal AD 417–538 (95%) to 2δcal AD 672–772 (90%) (table 4.1:PSU7690, PSU7061, SMU1933), indicating that Structure 9-subA was used repeatedly throughout Stage 6. The latest of these assays provides a *terminus ante quem* date for the construction of Structure 9-subA (table 4.1:PSU7061).

Structure 9-subB was built directly over the unconsolidated deposit of 9-subA as a two-tier platform 15.0 m long (E–W), 13.0 m wide (N–S), and 1.9 m tall. A second building episode (9-subC) raised this structure by 50 cm, bringing it to a height of 2.4 m above Plaza Two. A burnt clay floor was located on the structure's summit where a fragmented jade pendant was recovered. An infant burial (Burial 1-32) was recovered underneath and sealed by this clay floor (Benyo, Storey, and Hirth n.d.). An early AMS carbon sample from platform fill under this floor dates to 2δcal 42 BC–AD 80 (93%) (table 4.1:PSU6408). It appears that some of the fill used in constructing this structure was recycled from the fill of Structure 21 in the East Courtyard, which accounts for the early AMS date (figure 4.9a).

Final construction added a third level to the platform, bringing Structure 9 to its final dimensions of 15.00 m long (E–W), 13.00 m wide (N–S), and 3.45 m tall. Its summit was 5.00 m wide (N–S) and was surfaced with a well-preserved burnt clay floor. A stairway of white limestone *lajas* rose from Plaza

Two to its summit. Carved jade and marble artifacts were recovered from the fill of this final construction phase (see chapter 6).

Structure 10 was constructed as a small, single-phase platform mound at the northeast corner of Plaza Two immediately east of Structure 9. It was 9.5 m long (N–S), 7.0 m wide (E–W), and 1.75 m tall.[27]

Structure 22 is in the East Courtyard and was dated to this stage from associated polychrome ceramics recovered in its fill. It was a low, unconsolidated earthen mound 11 m long (N–S), 4 m wide (E–W), and 80 cm high that was built without retention walls. In both form and function, it strongly resembles Structure 2 on the north side of Plaza One and Structure 9-subA in Plaza Two. It supported a wattle-and-daub (*bajareque*) building on its summit. Whether it was used for periodic food preparation for feasts or was a permanent cooking facility for residents in Plaza Two is unclear.

Plaza Two was used for ritual activity during this stage. Two recessed floor areas labeled as Patios M1 and M2 were located on the south side of Plaza Two, one of which (M1) contained a shaped monument identified as Altar 1. A second low platform identified as Altar 2 was located at the north end of Plaza Two in front of Structure 8 (figure 4.17).

Patios M1 and M2 are located adjacent to one another. Patio M1 is located in front of the stairs of Structure 7. It is 9.0 m long (E-W) and 5.6 m wide (N-S) and is recessed 20.0 cm below Plaza Two's cobble pavement. Patio M2 is also located in front of Structure 7 and alongside Structure 6. It is 5.5 m long (E-W) and 4.6 m wide (N-S) and is recessed 55.0 cm below the cobble pavement of Plaza Two. While adjacent to one another, their different elevations highlight different use areas. Patio M1 contained a composite monument identified as Altar 1 (Feature 81M-R3), while Patio M2 had a circular cobble hearth (Feature 81M-R1) that was 64 cm in diameter and constructed on the patio floor. Two radiocarbon samples were analyzed from this hearth that provide dates of 2δcal AD 425–545 (95%) and 2δcal AD 384–593 (95%) (table 4.1:PSU6411, SMU2295).

Altar 1 is a boulder monument composed of three large rocks grouped together on the floor of Patio M1. It appears to have been a large boulder with a cylindrical depression pecked into its surface; the larger of these depressions was a conical orifice 16 cm in diameter and 55 cm in length that passed through the boulder's short axis. At some point the boulder was broken into sections through the conical perforations. Three sections were then trimmed and reunited to create a trefoil arrangement that was 110 cm long (E–W), 72 cm wide (N–S), and 55 cm high (figure 4.18). The presence of carved horizontal lines on two of the stones suggests that the boulder sculpture had a

FIGURE 4.18. *Excavation of Altar 1 on the cobble pavement of Plaza Two*

simple design carved around its exterior prior to breakage. Altar 1 was associated with Structure 7, and it is possible that the original boulder monument was as well. The recovery of a few flakes around the base of Altar 1 indicates that some shaping was done on the floor of Patio M1 as part of the monument's dedication.

Breaking the boulder through its conical-shaped orifices left remnant flute scars on each of the three stone sections. When the three stones were reassembled, the widest portion of each cup-shaped orifice was oriented downward, possibly signifying emptying or overturning of the boulder's original function. Offerings were placed under these flutes on and beneath the patio's cobble surface. Four ceramic vessels and a cache of jade artifacts were interred in a subfloor offering under the largest exposed flute on its west side. The rim of the uppermost vessel was situated even with the patio surface and then covered with a ceramic lid so it could receive periodic offerings (figure 4.19). A necklace of 109 beads with a central pendant was recovered from the uppermost vessel in this cache (see figure 5.50a). Thirty carved jade and marble artifacts were recovered from this altar and 21 pieces in another vessel in the subfloor offering. A large broken metate was also recovered immediately alongside this altar (figure 4.18).

FIGURE 4.19.
*Altar 1: (a)
offering under the
cone-shaped volute
of Altar 1, (b)
closeup of subfloor
offering*

FIGURE 4.20. *Plaza Two looking south from Structure 9 toward Structure 6. Altar 2 is in the foreground and at the center of the plaza.*

Altar 2 was in the center of Plaza Two between Structure 4 and Structure 8 (figures 4.17, 4.20). It was a low platform 2.2 m long (N–S), 1.9 m wide (E–W), and 25.0 cm high. The unique feature of this platform was that all four sides and its upper surface were fashioned from white limestone *lajas* 40 cm × 30 cm in size (figure 4.20). Broken polychrome ceramics were recovered from the platform's fill that confirm its construction in the Middle to Late Sulaco phases. The platform is oriented N12W, which conforms to the original orientation of Structure 398 and not to the N–S alignments of the other structures in Plaza Two. No offerings were associated with this structure. Its primary purpose appears to have been the preparation and display of food, probably related to the feasting that was common among traditional Lenca groups (Chapman 1985:87, 109–122; Herrera y Tordesillas 1944–1947:6:23). Two manos and four metate fragments were recovered around the base of Altar 2, with a fifth metate fragment located on its upper surface. The proximity of Structure 9-subA and the hearth used in preparing food is another link to food preparation and feasting.

SUMMARY

The Iglesia Precinct was the most important civic-ceremonial zone in the El Cajón region. This is evident from both the scale of construction and the way the precinct was integrated into the community of Salitrón Viejo. Archaeological testing established that both the Iglesia and North Precincts were important civic-ceremonial areas that were constructed and used simultaneously during the Late Yunque phase. Both have large central plazas, but their placement within the site and their architectural layouts are distinctly different. While the Iglesia Precinct was located adjacent to the residential population of Salitrón Viejo, the North Precinct was located at the site's periphery close to the Sulaco River. The North Precinct plaza is the largest assembly area at Salitrón Viejo and together with its associated boundary platforms (Structures 29–30, 36, 45) is more than twice the size of the Iglesia Precinct (see figure 3.7). We believe it was used for receiving groups from the surrounding region that were integrated into the Salitrón chiefdom through ritual ceremonies and other social interactions. For Salitrón to maintain its position as a regional center, outlying groups had to be incorporated into meaningful social and ritual gatherings. The North Precinct was a place where some of these interactions took place.

The Iglesia Precinct was a planned architectural zone. Although it expanded gradually over time, it did not grow in a haphazard fashion. The Iglesia Precinct was laid out around an open plaza that took its final form through six sequential construction stages. The east-to-west orientation of the Iglesia Precinct was established during the Early Yunque phase (Stage 1) with the construction of Structures 3 and 21 on the western and eastern margins of its large central plaza.[28] Subsequent structures were built around the periphery of the Central Plaza during Stage 2 and were later covered by the Acropolis platform.

Regional survey identified a distinctive pattern of civic-ceremonial architecture in the El Cajón region (Hasemann 1998; Hasemann, Dixon, and Yonk 1982). The largest communities throughout the region have a public plaza that often combines two types of architectural constructions: square ceremonial mounds with limited upper surface areas and rectangular Range mounds that supported structures associated with the local elite. Both structure types were constructed in the Iglesia Precinct early in its architectural history. Structures 3 and 21 were conical mounds while Structure 6 was an early Range structure (figure 4.4). The presence of these structures in the Iglesia Precinct indicates that it was the center of both ritual activity and early elite residence at Salitrón Viejo from the end of the Early Yunque phase.

The presence of conical mounds in civic-ceremonial areas extends back to the Middle Formative period across Honduras, and they are always associated with incipient plaza organization in the El Cajón region. All of the secondary centers along the Sulaco River (PC13, PC15, PC59, PC71, PC75) have at least one conical mound in an incipient plaza group (see figure 3.12) (Hasemann 1987:90–91, 1998). Range structures are more numerous than conical mounds at Salitrón Viejo, and they increased in number over time as they were constructed in the West and South Residential Groups during the Middle through Late Sulaco phases.

A notable feature of the Iglesia Precinct was the short time span over which it was constructed. Of course, short is a relative term. The preceding discussion grouped construction activities into six architectural stages based on the stratigraphic superposition of architectural features and building alignments. Chronological evaluation combined twenty-one radiocarbon dates with ceramic analysis from more than eighty-one stratigraphic contexts. Together, these analyses revealed that the majority of the construction took place during the Late Yunque phase (AD 0–400). The earliest civic-ceremonial activity dates to the latter half of the Early Yunque phase, but it was not until the beginning of the Late Yunque phase that large-scale construction activity took place coincident with the formation of the Salitrón chiefdom. The Acropolis platform was the focus of construction activity during Stages 3–5. When viewed sequentially, all of the building during Stages 2–5 took place within the 400-year span of the Late Yunque period. Stage 6 represents construction activities carried out during the subsequent 400 years of the Early and Middle Sulaco phases.

While building activities were grouped by stages in this discussion, construction activities were probably carried out as a series of small projects spaced out over time within these stages. The only possible exception was the construction of the Acropolis platform, which involved more concentrated effort than the work required for expanding a small mound. Even the Acropolis, however, was constructed in serial fashion. This should not be a surprise, since the amount of labor that could be mobilized was limited. While construction in the Iglesia Precinct decreased during Stage 6, it remained a prominent area for collective activities in Salitrón Viejo.

Platform mounds in the Iglesia Precinct were constructed in two different ways that have chronological significance. Adobe walls occur early in the Iglesia sequence and were gradually replaced by more cobble wall construction over time. Structure 3 was largely constructed with adobe walls whose outer surface was sealed with a layer of lime to create a smooth white surface (figure 4.5). While not a true stucco, the wet lime mixture was also used to create a smooth and durable floor on the upper surface of the Acropolis platform (Hirth, Lara-Pinto, and Hasemann 1984:17). It is important to note that adobe was not used outside the Iglesia Precinct.

While not as versatile as adobe, river cobbles were readily available and could be pulled directly from the Sulaco and Yunque Rivers. Unfortunately, cobble walls were only as strong as the clay mortar that held them in place.

These walls did not preserve well and were easily dislocated by the root systems of post-abandonment tropical vegetation. It was good fortune that the *talud-tablero* construction of Structure 12 was preserved within the Acropolis platform (figures 4.11–4.13). *Talud-tablero* construction was not identified in any other structures in the Iglesia Precinct, which probably reflects its function as a special purpose shrine. But Structure 12 shows that sophisticated construction was possible even using cobbles as the primary construction material. *Talud-tablero* design has not been reported elsewhere in west-central Honduras and suggests interaction with areas of Mesoamerica further to the west. Whatever the origin of this design, Structure 12 is unique within the Iglesia Precinct for both its form and the quantity of jade and marble artifacts associated with it. While small, it has more jade and marble artifacts associated with it than does any other platform structure at Salitrón Viejo (see chapter 6).

Architecture defined the civic-ceremonial space of the Iglesia Precinct, but four lines of evidence document its ritual use. The first is the evidence for food preparation for public consumption in feasts associated with ritual celebrations and communal work projects. Five structures were identified that were involved in food preparation at some level (Structures 2, 9-subA, 22, 397) and food display (Altar 2). These structures had large quantities of associated organic refuse, food processing artifacts, or both. Furthermore, oven features and hearth areas were identified in both Plazas One and Two. The importance of feasts in social and ritual interaction is discussed more fully in chapter 7.

Censors were used across Mesoamerica to burn incense and make offerings, and they are important indicators of the places where ritual behavior occurred. Censorware occurs in two ceramic types at Salitrón Viejo: as large stationary vessels (figure 4.21) and smaller handled vessels (Carías de López 1996). Both can have appliqué spikes and striated lines adorning their exteriors.[29] Sixty-nine spiked censors were identified in the collection, and their distribution is summarized in table 4.2. The data reveal that most of both censor types are associated with structures and in areas where we would expect rituals to be conducted: the Iglesia and North Precincts and around Range structures in the West and South Residential Groups. Similarly, the only area where large stationary censorware vessels outnumbered handled censors was in the Iglesia Precinct. While rituals were also carried out in domestic structures, areas of public ritual were evident by concentrations of these unique vessels.

Carved stone monuments have been reported in a few large sites in west-central Honduras but are relatively rare after the Formative period. Nevertheless, they were important ritual furniture that marks the location of ceremonial activities. Altar 1 was the only carved stone monument identified

FIGURE 4.21. *Large stationary spiked censor with lid from Salitrón Viejo being restored*

TABLE 4.2. Location of spiked censorware at Salitrón Viejo

Area	Handled Censors		Stationary Censors			
	Number	Percent	Number	Percent	Total	Percent
Iglesia Precinct	7	16.6	13	48.1	20	29.0
North Precinct	5	11.9	2	7.4	7	10.1
West Group plaza	25	59.5	12	44.5	37	53.6
West Group domestic	2	4.8	0	0	2	2.9
South Group plaza	1	2.4	0	0	1	1.5
South Group domestic	2	4.8	0	0	2	2.9
Total	42	100	27	100	69	100

in the El Cajón region except for a petroglyph site in the uplands (figure 4.22). The fact that Altar 1 was intentionally broken and rededicated within the elite residential area suggests two possible interpretations. First, the breakage and

Figure 4.22. *Petroglyph rock engraving at site PC10*

rededication may reflect a cyclical notion of time such as that practiced in areas of Mesoamerica to the west (Hirth 1988). Second, the placement of the monument in Plaza Two may suggest that it was associated with elite rituals that did not involve the entire community.

Finally, the ritual importance of the Iglesia Precinct is documented by the large quantity of jade and marble artifacts used as ritual offerings in the dedication of the Acropolis platform and other associated structures. A total of 2,371 whole and fragmented lapidary regalia and precious wealth goods were included in these offerings. The stylistic features of these goods and how they were distributed in caches throughout the Iglesia Precinct and across Salitrón Viejo are presented in chapters 5 and 6.

5

This chapter examines the artifacts recovered in ritual deposits at Salitrón Viejo that were manufactured in various styles and from an array of different materials. Most of these objects were jade beads, pendants, earflares, and a miscellanea of other high-value items of personal adornment used throughout Mesoamerica. In the El Cajón region, these materials do not occur with individuals in burials, and they were not associated with wealth accumulation strategies of aspiring elites. Instead, high-value goods were used as offerings in monuments that defined civic-ceremonial space. While they were status and wealth items in other areas of Mesoamerica, here they were used for offerings to the spiritual forces that framed their reality. Although most of these items were well finished, that was not a requirement for use in ritual contexts. Unfinished beads and pendants along with natural rocks were also included in offering clusters at Salitrón Viejo. The quality and rarity of the items, together with the effort needed to obtain them, enhanced their value as offerings to the gods.

It is important to state at the outset that none of the high-value items discussed below were manufactured at Salitrón Viejo. No evidence for lapidary work was found in either domestic or non-domestic contexts at Salitrón Viejo or elsewhere in the region. Crafting areas were not identified and partially worked raw material was not recovered, except from a few pieces of raw material that were included in offerings with other finished goods. Finally, no lapidary tools were

The Jade, Marble, and Ritual Offerings

recovered such as drills, grinding slabs, grinding compounds, and the other implements needed for flaking, cutting, and polishing finished items (e.g., Andrieu, Rodas, and Luin 2014; Digby 1972:figure 4; Gazzola 2007:59–62; Hirth 2009b). Instead, all of the artifacts recovered were manufactured elsewhere and arrived at the site in finished form through some form of trade. What local residents would have used as exchange items to procure these goods is unclear, but they probably consisted of perishable products for which there is no clear archaeological evidence (see chapter 7).

Procurement through trade is reflected in the diversity of raw material represented in the collection. While most lapidary goods were manufactured of jade, other materials were also used, including micaceous jade, granular marble, and a miscellanea of other stone types such as serpentine, talc, limestone, pyrite, slate, volcanic tuff, soapstone, fine-grained marble, and quartzite. Table 5.1 summarizes the raw material categories expressed in terms of minimum artifact counts (MAC) recovered in the assemblage (see below). No attempt was made to identify source locations for these materials, beyond using instrumental neutron activation analysis (INAA) to confirm that the jade originated from the Rio Motagua source area (Bishop, Sayre, and Mishara 1993:57; Bishop, Sayre, and van Zelst 1986; Foshag 1957). The geology of Honduras remains understudied and source locales remain unknown for most of the semi-precious rock types recovered at Salitrón Viejo. Regardless of their mineralogical composition, the beads, pendants, and other ornamental items fashioned from marble and other non-jadeite greenstone (e.g., quartz, serpentine, talc) had value as social jade in pre-Columbian society (Bishop, Sayre, and Mishara 1993:32; Lange 1993:1; Tremain 2014).

Considerable diversity is evident in the artistic styles and manufacturing techniques represented in the lapidary regalia. Goods that were produced in a single community of practice often display consistency in artisan *techné* with regard to thematic and technological style (Abell 2020; Costin 2016; Kovacevich 2015; Lara-Pinto 2019; Wendrich 2012; Wenger 1998). This consistency was not reflected in the Salitrón assemblage. Considerable variation is evident in the Maya, non-Maya, Olmec, highland Guatemalan, and even Costa Rican influences found in the collection, which reflects multiple manufacturing areas and the distances over which these goods were exchanged. Differences can be seen in the design of imagery, how pieces were executed, and the variation in anthropomorphic, zoomorphic, and geometric themes represented. Diversity is also evident in the manufacturing technologies employed to produce finished goods. This variation includes alternative combinations of cutting, flaking, pecking, drilling, and polishing techniques like

Table 5.1. Artifacts by raw material category recovered in ritual offerings in the El Cajón region

Material	Salitrón Viejo	Regional Sites	Total Artifacts	Salitrón Viejo: Artifacts after Refitting	Cajón Region: Artifacts after Refitting
Jade	2,313	6	2,319	2,065	2,071
Micaceous jade	209	—	209	203	203
Granular marble	302	—	302	290	290
Fine marble	1	—	1	1	1
Other metamorphic	12	—	12	12	12
Obsidian eccentrics	3	—	3	3	3
Chert/calcedony	10	—	10	10	10
Pyrite	1	—	1	1	1
Quartzite	3	1	4	3	4
Slate	37	—	37	4	4
Non-jadeite	290	15	305	290	305
Shell	—	1	1	—	1
Total	3,181	23	3,204	2,881	2,904

the variation found in the two technological traditions used to manufacture conical and tubular earflares.

The following discussion has two objectives. First, it identifies the artifact categories and describes their size and manufacturing attributes. Second, it illustrates their stylistic features, which are important because carved images had significance to the people who used them. The El Cajón assemblage is important because it is a large in situ collection that dates to a short period of time during the Early Classic period. As such, it helps date similar pieces from less secure archaeological contexts, including those in museum collections. (As a supplement to the technical drawings of artifacts presented here, photographs and additional discussion can be found in Hirth and colleagues 2023.) As an assemblage, these pieces reflect the enormity of effort a small chiefdom society invested in the activities associated with its ritual economy. The chapter concludes with a discussion of similarities between the El Cajón collections and materials found elsewhere in eastern Mesoamerica.

JADE, COLOR, AND THE PRE-COLUMBIAN WORLD

Jade refers to a range of microcrystalline metamorphic gemstones formed under high pressure and relatively low temperature. The term *jade* is used to refer to both jadeite, a mineral of the pyroxene group that is a sodium aluminum silicate, and nephrite, a silicate of calcium and magnesium.[1] The mineralogical composition, however, was not important in the pre-Columbian world. Pre-Columbian groups valued a variety of precious and semi-precious stones (e.g., turquoise, amber, serpentine, jadeite) that ranged from emerald green and dark green to greenish-blue, yellow, red, and white to black (Sahagún 1963:221–228). A range of stone types were used to manufacture jewelry that served as symbols of rank and authority as well as items of ritual importance. What pre-Columbian people admired most were green and blue-green stones that were translucent and had the ability to be polished to a high luster.

While the Spanish were interested primarily in gold, they recognized the value native societies gave to the stones they referred to as *piedra de yjada/ijade* (RAE 2021), which were believed to have curative properties (Foshag 1957:9; Taube and Ishihara-Brito 2012:136).[2] The term *jade* is used by archaeologists to refer to a wide range of metamorphic greenstone with a MOHS hardness of 6.0–7.0. It is in this general sense that the term *jade* is used here. Greenstone of different mineral compositions was valued by Mesoamerican people because it symbolized life and growth in the natural world. But jade with the same mineralogical source occurs in a variety of hues that range from white and pink to green, blue-green, gray, and black, depending on its composition.

Color was important in the pre-Columbian world, not for the aesthetic properties of different hues but for the symbolic meaning it added to the individuals, monuments, and architecture it adorned. Color in Mesoamerica was used to denote directionality, lineage associations, day/night differentiation, preciousness, and sacredness (Boone 1985:174). Green symbolized life, and greenstone had properties of being alive. Jade was believed to attract and absorb moisture and to give off a "fresh breath" that made plants around it grow better (Sahagún 1963:222). All greenstone was valued, and it was from its associated life-giving properties that jade objects were used as ritual offerings across the pre-Columbian world.

Although green was the preferred color, it is relatively rare in jade deposits at Salitrón Viejo. For this reason, the color of artifacts was documented to evaluate whether there was a selective preference for green hues in ritual offerings. While important, initial examination of the collection revealed considerable variation in hue, strength and modeling of color, and the light or dark tones of artifacts. Fifteen color categories were used to capture this

TABLE 5.2. Color ramps and categories used to describe the jade assemblage

Ramp	Light		Medium		Dark
1	Cloudy white	Light gray	Medium gray	Dark gray	Gray/black
2	Pale yellow-green	Greenish-gray	Gray-green	Olive green	Green brown-black
3	Mottled green	Apple green	Emerald green	Blue-green	Dark forest green

variation and to characterize artifact hues along three color ramps. No model was available for characterizing color variation at the time the study was conducted, although that has changed with the widespread use of Munsell color codes (Andrieu, Rodas, and Luin 2014; Kovacevich and Callaghan 2019). The use of these color ramps made it possible to generalize about the collection as a whole, resist the temptation to illustrate only the greenest pieces (e.g., Proskouriakoff 1974:plates I–IV), and avoid implying that all the jades in the Salitrón assemblage were green when they were not.

Tables 5.2 and 5.3 summarize the color categories used, while figure 5.1 illustrates the color range. The three ramps in table 5.2 are organized along a gradient from light to dark, with the light colors located on the left and darker hues to the right. Ramp 1 contains *gray* tones that vary from cream and cloudy white to gray/black. Ramp 2 contains *gray-green* colors ranging from pale yellow-green to green brown-black. Ramp 3 is the group with *strong green* hues that, based on the discussion provided by Fray Bernardino de Sahagún (1963:221–228), should represent the most sought-after materials across the pre-Columbian world. These colors range from mottled green and white jade at the light end of the spectrum through apple and emerald green to blue-green and dark forest green. The weakness of this classification is that it only registers the dominant hues and ignores many of the subtle veins of color found in specimens. The values in table 5.3 employ Munsell color codes so these ranges can be compared to other collections (see also figure 5.1).

Color was coded for 90.6 percent of the artifacts in the collection. All of the 290 granular marble materials were cloudy white to light gray except where there were small veins of green in the material (see below). The remaining jade and non-jade artifacts were sorted into the three color ramps. The gray tones of Ramp 1 (n = 1,038) constitute 44.3 percent of these materials, compared to 19.2 percent (n = 450) for the weak gray-green of Ramp 2 and 36.5 percent (n = 854) for the strong green tones of Ramp 3. Together, the green tones of

TABLE 5.3. Munsell color ranges for color categories

RAMP 1: GRAY TONES		
1a	Cloudy white	This is the lightest color range in the assemblage. Colors range from a clear white (N9/) to very light gray (N8/). Color patterning is uneven, with gentle mottling.
1b	Light gray	Color varies from very light gray (N7/- 10YR 8/2) to light gray (5Y 7/1) and light greenish-gray (5GY 7–8/1). Color patterning is even, with little evidence of mottling or veining.
1c	Medium gray	This category varies from medium-light gray (N6/) to light gray (5Y 6/1) and greenish-gray (5GY 6/1). Color patterns are often uneven and contain both diffuse and sharply contrasting hues. Pieces may be heavily veined with darker hues of brownish gray (5YR 5/1–2) and medium gray (N5/).
1d	Dark gray	The background color is consistently dark gray (N4–5/) to bluish-gray (5B 4–5/1). The initial impression is that this is a solid tone, although close inspection reveals slight mottling, with small amounts of medium-light gray (N6/).
1e	Grey/black	Color is a very dark gray to grayish-black (N2–3/). Little mottling with lighter hues of either gray or dark green is evident in this material.
RAMP 2: WEAK GREEN		
2a	Pale yellow-green	Color in this category ranges from a pale yellowish-green (10GY 7/2; 5Y 7/1) to pale and light green (5G 7/2–4). Occasional inclusions of dark yellowish-green (10GY 4/4) also occur.
2b	Greenish-gray	This category is a yellow-green (5GY 6/2) to greenish-gray (5GY 6–7/1), light blue-gray (5Y 6/1), and light olive gray (5Y 6/2). The paleness of this color combined with an iridescent finish can give artifacts a silvery cast.
2c	Gray-green	Background color ranges from greenish-gray (5G 6/1) and bluish-gray (5B 6/1) to medium-dark gray (N4–6/) and greenish-black (5G2/1). Little to no veining is evident and color is even, except where large crystals produce highlights of color ranging from green (10G 4–5/2) to dark yellowish-green (10GY 4/4).
2d	Olive green	The background color varies from olive gray (10Y 4/2, 5Y 4/1) to dark greenish-gray (5GY 2–4/1) with lighter greenish highlights (5GY 5–6/1). Color patterns range from even in the darker hues to slightly mottled or cloudy without clear borders between color changes.
2e	Green brown-black	This dark color category ranges from greenish-black (5G 2/1) and dark brown (5YR 2–3/2–3) to grayish-black (N2/).
RAMP 3: STRONG GREEN		
3a	Mottled green	This category has sharp mottling between a very light gray (N7–8/) and white background (N 9/), with accent colors that range from moderate (5G 5–6/6) and light to pale green (5G 7/4; 5G 6–7/2). Included here are mottled blue-gray varieties that use bluish-gray (5B 8/1; 5B 5–6/1) and medium gray (N 5/).

continued on next page

TABLE 5.3.—*continued*

RAMP 3: STRONG GREEN		
3b	Apple green	This material is noted for its even green color that ranges from light pale green (5G 7/2; 10G 8/2) to green (5G 6/4; 10G 6/2) or greenish-gray (5G 6/1). This is the most translucent material in the collection and will transmit light through up to 5 mm. Some surfaces tone or weather to a light gray or white (N 8–9/).
3c	Emerald green	This material is notable for its bright solid green color without large veins or darker intrusions. Color ranges from grayish-green (5G 5–6/2; 5G 5/4) to moderate and emerald green (5G 4–6/6). This material is somewhat translucent and can be polished to a high luster.
3d	Blue green	The background color of this category is often a greenish-gray (5GY 6/1), with highlights ranging from light bluish-gray (5B 6/1) to pale blue-green (5BG 5–7/2), pale blue (5B 6/2), and moderate blue-green (5BG 5–6/6). The blue-green tones often appear as a distinct vein from the background color.
3e	Dark forest green	This is the darkest category in the strong green range. Background color is a dark grayish-green (10G 4/2) to dusky green (5G 3/2), with occasional streaks or mottling of dark yellowish-green (10GY 4/4). Green hues can be mixed with light brownish-gray (5YR 6/1) or dusky yellow-green (5GY 5/2).

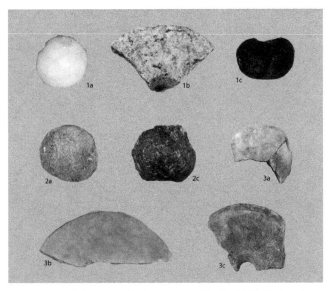

FIGURE 5.1. *Raw material types and color types within the El Cajón lapidary assemblage: (1a) cloudy white quartzite, (1b) light gray jadeite, (1c) gray-black non-jadeite, (2a) pale yellow-green micaceous jade, (2c) gray-green jadeite, (3a) mottled green jadeite, (3b) apple green jadeite, (3c) emerald green jadeite. Photograph by Kenneth Hirth.*

Ramps 2 and 3 represent 55.7 percent of all the artifacts in the collections. Apple green (n = 602) was the modal color used to manufacture lapidary artifacts, followed by medium gray (n = 529). This illustrates a preference for green hues when available irrespective of the rock's mineralogical characteristics.

THE ARTIFACT CATEGORIES

Table 5.4 summarizes the number of high-value artifacts recovered in the collection, their conversions to MAC, and their corresponding breakage patterns. A total of 3,204 high-value artifacts were recovered in excavations in the El Cajón region. In the aggregate, the collection constitutes slightly more than 150 kilos (330 lbs) of jade, marble, and other semi-precious materials. All but 23 of these artifacts were recovered from the site of Salitrón Viejo. Because many artifacts were broken when they were placed in offerings, a program of refitting was undertaken to produce a count that more closely reflected the MAC in the collection. Three hundred of the artifacts could be refit to other pieces, which reduced the MAC in the sample to 2,904 items for the whole El Cajón region. Table 5.4 shows that a large percentage of the artifacts were intentionally fragmented upon deposition and, while an effort was made to refit broken artifacts, many conjoining pieces were unaccounted for. Only minimum artifact counts are used in the artifact descriptions except where specified to minimize the effect breakage could have on over-representing the size of the assemblage.

Artifact descriptions are organized into four classes based on material type: jade, micaceous jade, granular marble, and other non-jadeite materials (figure 5.1). Artifacts in these classes are described in terms of form and stylistic characteristics. Separating artifact groups by material type created some redundancy in the classification, as similar artifacts were created in different raw materials. Nevertheless, lapidary craft production begins with raw material whose physical properties may require different technologies to create finished goods. Likewise, artisans often prefer to use local raw materials over distant ones to minimize the cost of procurement. Beginning an analysis from the perspective of the raw material has the potential of capturing different local carving traditions and themes expressed within them. This approach helped identify several differences in the artifacts manufactured from micaceous jade and granular marble.

Jade artifacts encompass a range of jadeite and albitic gemstone with a MOHS hardness of 6.0–7.0. They are the most numerous items in the collection (table 5.1) and occur in the greatest array of forms, some of which were

TABLE 5.4. Artifact counts and fragmentation rates in the El Cajón assemblage

Material	No. of Pieces	Total AAR[a]	Fragmented AAR[a]		Complete Artifacts	
			Number	Percent	Number	Percent
All jade	2,528	2,274	1,131	49.7	1,143	50.3
All marble	303	291	249	85.6	42	14.4
Other	373	339	67	19.8	272	80.2
Total	3,204	2,904	1,447	49.8	1,457	50.2

a. AAR represents artifacts after refitting.

replicated in marble and the other non-jade materials. Micaceous jade is a secondary jade category that is described separately because of its distinctive color and appearance from other stone in the collection. Many of the artifacts fashioned from this material are unique in both form and style and may represent a distinct community of practice in eastern Mesoamerica. Marble is a third class of material that occurs in both fine and granular crystalline forms. All the marble artifacts except for one Ulúa marble vase fragment occur in the granular material. This material does not preserve well in tropical conditions due to acidic soil conditions, and many of these artifacts were badly eroded, making stylistic characteristics difficult to identify. They are important, however, because they reflect a separate community of practice and regional carving tradition in Honduras distinct from that found in the Ulúa valley (Gordon 1921; Luke and Tykot 2007; Luke et al. 2003). The fourth material class is a heterogenous group of other non-jadeite materials that combines a range of low-frequency materials that include slate, steatite, serpentine, volcanic tuff, siltstone, chert, obsidian, and sandstone. Individually, these materials do not represent significant accumulations, but together they reflect the diversity of stone types included in ritual deposits.

Artifacts were classified into form categories common throughout Mesoamerica. These include plain and carved beads, large and small pendants, bead pendants, earflares, disks, eccentrics, and small sculptures. The characteristics of these artifact classes are identified below, along with whether they were prepared with singular or paired suspension holes (figure 5.2). Carved pieces were further classified into stylistic classes based of whether they had geometric designs or images that could be classified as zoomorphic or anthropomorphic forms. Aspects of style are discussed, but in some cases, images were so abstract that even the identification of zoomorphic and anthropomorphic features was challenging. Table 5.5 summarizes the MAC counts of artifacts in the collection by material type.

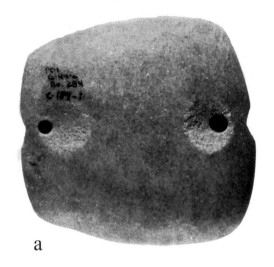

a

b

FIGURE 5.2. *Two forms of drilling suspension holes on pendants: (a) paired suspension holes using bidirectional drilling with a solid drill, (b) a single suspension hole created with bidirectional drilling using a tubular drill.* Courtesy, *IHAH; edited by Kenneth Hirth.*

JADE ARTIFACTS (N = 2,071)

A total of 2,319 artifacts manufactured of jade were recovered in the El Cajón region before refitting (table 5.1). Artifact classes are described below, with plain types presented first followed by carved examples. Unless specified, dimensions are calculated only for unbroken, complete artifacts.

Undecorated Plain Beads

Beads are the most common items in the collection (table 5.5) and were one of the earliest decorative artifacts produced and used across Mesoamerica (Garber et al. 1993; Hammond et al. 1979; Lange 1993:3; MacNeish, Nelken-Terner, and de Johnson 1967:133). Form categories were defined using metric criteria and the orientation of the bore hole drilled for suspension. Beads in which the suspension hole was drilled through their narrowest axis were classified as spheroid and discoidal forms. Most suspension holes were drilled biconically, and the metric proportions presented for beads were calculated

TABLE 5.5. The El Cajón ritual assemblage

Artifact Class	Jade	Micaceous Jade	Marble[a]	Non-Jadeite	Totals
PLAIN BEADS					
Spheroid	568	119	7	141	835
Discoidal	32	17	1	117	167
Oblong	137	12	—	6	155
Tubular	1	2	—	—	3
CARVED BEADS					
Collared	7	—	—	—	7
Squash form	3	—	—	—	3
Carved oblong	10	—	1	—	11
Carved tubular	4	2	—	—	6
BEAD PENDANTS					
Plain	5	—	4	1	10
Geometric	7	1	1	6	15
Curvilinear anthropomorphic	14	1	1	2	18
Triangular anthropomorphic	16	—	—	—	16
Stylized anthropomorphic	3	—	—	—	3
Hunchback	—	—	3	—	3
Zoomorphic	19	36	—	—	55
Stylized zoomorphic	10	—	—	—	10
Human hands	5	1	—	—	6
FLARES					
Conical	278	—	4	—	282
Tubular stemmed	188	1	2	—	191
Tapered	10	—	—	—	10
Earflare fragments	138	—	2	—	140
PENDANTS					
Plain	280	4	116	12	412
Ring pendants	42	—	—	—	42
Geometric	19	—	57	—	76
Zoomorphic	27	7	15	1	50
Hunchback	37	—	1	—	38

continued on next page

TABLE 5.5.—*continued*

Artifact Class	Jade	Micaceous Jade	Marble[a]	Non-Jadeite	Totals
PENDANTS—*continued*					
Anthropomorphic	26	—	8	—	34
Crescent pectorals	24	—	—	—	24
Flat plaques and disks	7	—	—	—	7
Concave plaques	4	—	—	—	4
Unfinished pendants	10	—	1	—	11
OTHER ITEMS					
Human effigy figures	1	—	4	4	9
Mozaic tesserae	2	—	—	—	2
Celts	1	—	—	2	3
Unidentified pieces	127	—	54	12	193
Nodules and flakes	9	—	8	17	34
SPECIAL MATERIALS					
Ulúa marble vase	—	—	1	—	1
Slate disks	—	—	—	4	4
Pyrite sequin	—	—	—	1	1
Bifacial eccentrics[b]	—	—	—	3	3
Obsidian/chalcedony nodules and flakes	—	—	—	10	10
Total	2,071	203	291	339	2,904

a. All artifacts are granular marble except for the carved Ulúa marble vase, which is fine marble.
b. Two obsidian and one chalcedony eccentric.

against the length of their suspension drill holes. *Spheroid* beads are those in which the bead's height-to-width ratio ranges from 1:1 for round beads to 2:1 for oval or disk-shaped examples. *Discoidal* beads are narrower and have a height-to-width ratio of 2.1:1 to 4:1. *Oblong* beads have suspension holes drilled through their long axis where the proportion of length to vertical height ranges from 1.01:1 to 3:1. *Tubular* beads are those in which the ratio of length to height is greater than 3:1.

Spheroid Beads (498 complete, 69 fragmented, 1 unfinished)

These beads are similar to the spheroid beads described by Tatiana Proskouriakoff (1974:18–22). There are few perfectly round beads in the collection; most are slightly disk shaped and flattened at the drilling poles. They range greatly in size, from 6 mm to 71 mm in diameter (Mo = 20 mm, Md = 26 mm, Ave = 27.7 mm). The distribution of bead size is bimodal, with peak ranges occurring between 16–24 mm (n = 214) and 29–37 mm (n =148), which represent three-quarters (73.1%) of all spheroid beads. Most beads (65.1%) have oval to rectangular frontal profiles, followed by trapezoidal (12.9%) and triangular (6.8%) shapes. There are 60 large spheroid beads in the collection, with diameters between 40 mm and 71 mm. Large spheroid beads were often prominent elements in offering deposits.

Spheroid beads are generally well finished, with high to medium polish. The majority are bilaterally drilled (83%) using a solid drill. Nearly 60 percent (58.4%) of complete and fragmentary spheroid beads were manufactured from gray jade, with dark gray (n = 121) and medium gray (n = 106) the two most common hues. Strong green jade was used to manufacture 26.5 percent of these beads, over half of which were mottled green jade. This is interesting because spheroid beads account for nearly 60 percent (58.3%) of all the mottled green jade artifacts in the collection. Clearly, the contrasting green and blue hues against a white background were highly desirable for bead manufacture. One unfinished spheroid bead was recovered whose drill hole was not completed.

Discoidal Beads (21 complete, 11 fragmented)

These beads are narrower and more disk-like than spheroid forms, with a frontal height that is two to four times greater than their width. Complete discoidal beads range from 17 mm to 41 mm in diameter (Mo = 21 mm, Md = 23 mm, Ave = 22.7 mm). Frontal profiles are oval to ellipsoidal in shape (55.6%), and a few beads are narrower at the top than they are on the bottom, creating a triangular or teardrop (11.1%) profile. Discoidal beads are not as well finished as spheroid beads, with only about half having any polish on their frontal surfaces. Most beads were bilaterally drilled using a solid drill bit. The majority of discoidal beads (81.3%) were manufactured from gray jade, with dark gray as the modal color.

Oblong and Tubular Beads (oblong: 116 complete, 21 fragmented; tubular: 1 complete)

These bead categories are longer than they are high and were drilled longitudinally in line with their greatest dimension. Complete examples range from 15 mm to 68 mm in length (Mo = 30 mm, Md = 32 mm, Ave = 33.3 mm). The height of oblong beads ranges from 6 mm to 53 mm, with bimodal frequencies of 22 mm and 25 mm, a median of 23 mm, and an average diameter of 23.8 mm. Most oblong beads are round to ovate in cross-section (67.7%), followed by trapezoidal and triangular forms (12.9%). None of the oblong beads have a length-to-height ratio that exceeds 2.6:1. The single tubular bead in the collection has a length-to-height ratio of 3.1:1. All examples are well finished, with medium to high polish on their fronts and backs. Most beads were bilaterally drilled using a solid drill bit. Oblong beads occur in all three color tones: gray tones are the most common (48.1%), followed by weak green (30.1%) and strong green (21.8%). Gray-green is the modal color, and the tubular bead is medium gray.

Collared Beads (3 complete, 4 fragmented)

These beads are distinctive by having one or two incised or carved bands that extend around their circumference at one end of the bead. They are oblong to square in shape and range from 15 mm to 39 mm in width (figure 5.3d–e). Five of these beads (71.4%) are strong green in color.

Squash Beads (3 complete)

Three spheroid beads were carved in the form of four-lobed squash. They ranged from 21 mm to 35 mm in width and 21 mm to 37 mm in height (figure 5.3a–c). Two were polished to a medium luster, while the third was unpolished. Two of the squash beads were dark gray in color, while the third was gray-green.

Carved Oblong Beads (9 complete, 1 fragmented)

Like plain oblong beads, these artifacts are longer than they are tall. Nine were biconically drilled, while one was perforated unilaterally using a tubular drill. Complete examples range from 15 mm to 51 mm in length (Ave = 31.4 mm). Beads vary in shape depending on the imagery depicted. Zoomorphic images are the most common and include fish, a serpent, and a rabbit displayed in profile (figure 5.4a–b, d–l). The only non-zoomorphic image was that of an elaborate geometric bar. All surfaces were finished to a medium or high luster. Beads are evenly distributed across gray (44.5%), weak green (33.3%), and strong green (22.2%) hues.

Carved Tubular Beads (1 complete, 3 fragmented)

Carved tubular beads are rare, with only one complete and four partial examples in the collection. The longest complete example was 75 mm in length and was carved as a contorted acrobat with his feet placed on the top of the head (figure 5.5a), a position Karl Taube (1983:172, 2005:figure 2) attributes to the maize god. The remaining three fragmented beads were small but elaborately carved, one of which had X-images on either end (figure 5.5b). The acrobat and

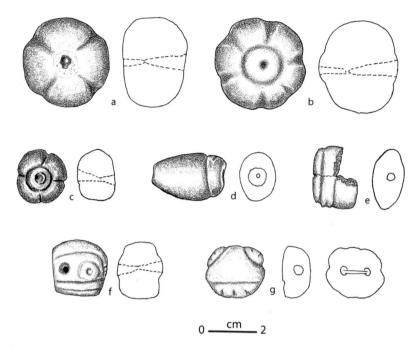

FIGURE 5.3. *Carved jade and non-jadeite beads and bead pendants: collared, geometrically incised, and squash beads (a–c), squash beads (d–e), collared beads, (f–g) geometric bead pendants. Illustration by Cynthia Ott and Kenneth Hirth.*

the geometric bead were gray, and the two other tubular beads were strong green. All carved tubular beads were polished to a medium or high luster.

BEAD PENDANTS

Bead pendants are characterized by off-center drilling that together with stylistic information was used to define several shaped categories (cf. Smith and Kidder 1951:figure 57). Complete examples range from 14 mm to 41 mm in height (Md = 24 mm, Ave = 29 mm) and 11 mm to 52 mm in width (Md = 24.0 mm, Ave = 24.8 mm). Bead pendants include a range of plain and carved forms with geometric, anthropomorphic, and zoomorphic images. The carving on some bead pendants is highly stylized, making it difficult to separate human from animal imagery. Despite this limitation, bead pendants are fairly evenly divided between anthropomorphic and zoomorphic images. The jade used in

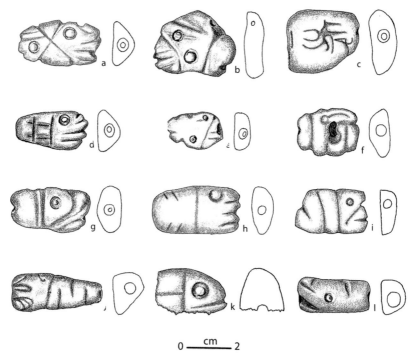

FIGURE 5.4. *Carved jade oblong beads and bead pendants. Illustration by Cynthia Ott and Kenneth Hirth.*

bead pendants ranges from weak green (44.1%) to gray (32.3%) and strong green (23.7%). Human head portraits were divided into curvilinear, triangular, and stylized groups. Zoomorphic bead pendants fall into two groups: naturalistic and stylized images. Finally, there is a small group of bead pendants that depict human hands.

Plain Bead Pendants (3 complete, 1 fragmented, 1 unfinished)
These are single pieces of shaped and polished jade that were drilled off-center to hang below the line on which they were strung. All items are either teardrop or ovate in shape. Plain bead pendants range from 23 mm to 37 mm in height and 20 mm to 52 mm in width, depending on the orientation of the drilling. One piece was incompletely drilled and unfinished. These items occur in equal proportions across all three major color groups (table 5.2).

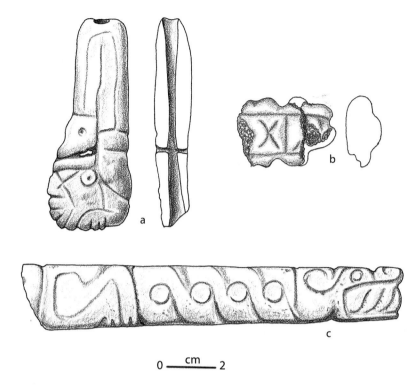

FIGURE 5.5. *Carved tubular beads: (a–b) jade beads, (c) micaceous jade serpent bead. Illustration by Anne Dowd, Cynthia Ott, and Kenneth Hirth.*

Geometric Bead Pendants (6 complete, 1 fragmented)

Geometric bead pendants have a variety of embellishments, ranging from raised panels and carved surfaces to incised lines and markings made with solid and tubular drilling (figure 5.3f–g). They range from 20 mm to 37 mm in height and 11 mm to 44 mm in width, depending on the orientation of drilling. Five of the seven items were fashioned from gray jade, while the other two are strong green.

Curvilinear Anthropomorphic Bead Pendants (11 complete, 3 fragmented)

These bead pendants are well-executed carvings that depict human heads and faces in both frontal and profile views. They have lozenge-shaped eyes and rounded noses (figures 5.6, 5.7). Mouths were defined either as slightly curved lines within oval lips or as horizontal slits with drill holes at the corners. Most display some form of headdress or hair design. Several depict earflares. They

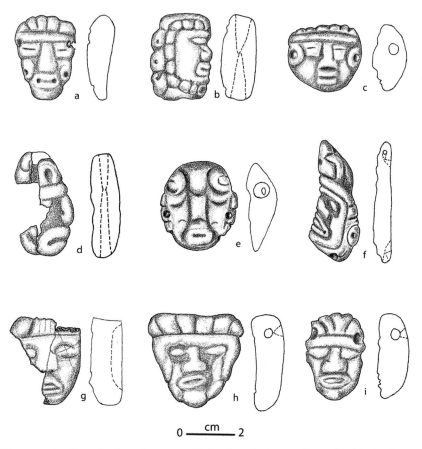

FIGURE 5.6. *Carved jade anthropomorphic bead pendants: curvilinear head portraits. Illustration by Cynthia Ott and Kenneth Hirth.*

range from 21 mm to 41 mm in height and 18 mm to 39 mm in width. Heads carved in profile were often drilled so the face would be oriented downward when strung (figures 5.6b, d, f; 5.7a–c). Frontal views include figures 5.6a, c, e, and g–i and 5.7d–f. The colors represented in these bead pendants are strong green (50%), weak green (28%), and gray (22%).

Triangular Anthropomorphic Bead Pendants (14 complete, 2 fragmented)

Bead pendants in this category used a lineal carving style to depict human faces (figures 5.8, 5.9). The artisans creating these pendants relied on straight cut incisions and tubular drilling to depict images on these bead pendants. They were executed in both frontal and profile views. Two diverging lines on

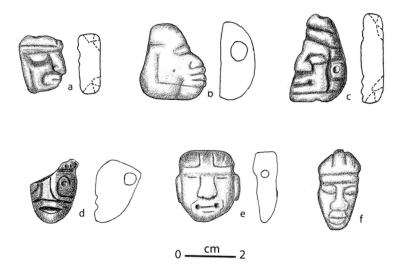

FIGURE 5.7. *Carved jade anthropomorphic bead pendants: curvilinear head portraits.*
Illustration by Cynthia Ott and Kenneth Hirth.

frontal portraits formed the central portion of the face, defining the nose and sides of the mouth. One diagonal line defined this same area on profile heads. The mouth was defined by two or three horizontal lines, and eyes were formed using tubular drills. Triangular heads were depicted without headdress elements, although hair was suggested by a central crest on top of the head created by incisions. Pendants are from 24 mm to 41 mm in height and 17 mm to 30 mm wide. Most examples were fashioned from weak green jade (71.6%), followed by gray (14.2%) and strong green (14.2%).

Stylized Anthropomorphic Bead Pendants (3 complete)

These bead pendants are executed in a minimalist style and are classified here as anthropomorphic because they suggest human faces (figure 5.10). They are executed simply,[3] with eyes formed by drilling and a horizontal slit for the mouth. The three examples in this style range between 30 mm and 35 mm in height and 13 mm to 24 mm in width. One of the items is gray in color, while the other two are weak green jade.

Zoomorphic Bead Pendants (18 complete, 1 fragmented)

Zoomorphic bead pendants have carved imagery that represents different species of real or imaginary animals. Carvings employ a curvilinear style that shaped the form of the animal depicted. Common images include birds,

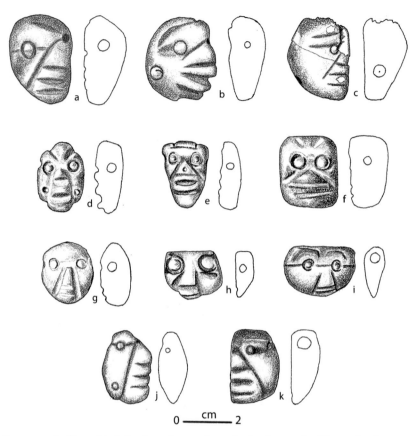

Figure 5.8. *Carved jade bead pendants: triangular head portraits. Illustration by Cynthia Ott and Kenneth Hirth.*

canids, monkeys, serpents, reptiles, fish (figure 5.11), and a unicorn-like creature that may represent a manatee (figure 5.11g, i–j). Birds can be identified by bulging eyes placed on the side of elongated faces that represent beaks. Eyes were usually created using solid drill holes except for two canid bead pendants whose eyes were created using tubular drilling (figure 5.11a–c, h). One zoomorphic bead pendant (figure 5.11d) was carved with a throat bib reminiscent of the bib-and-helmet style associated with Terminal Formative and Early Classic carvings elsewhere in Mesoamerica (Garber 1983:figure 2a, 2c). While this artifact lacks the helmet element associated with human portraits, a similar simian bib-and-helmet pendant was recovered from Chichen Itzá

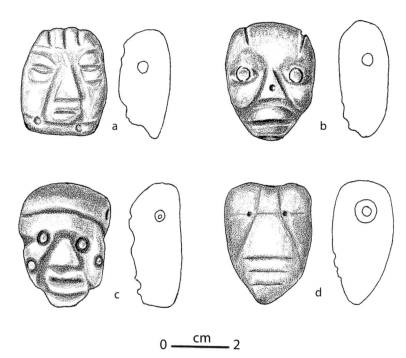

FIGURE 5.9. *Carved jade bead pendants: triangular head portraits. Illustration by Cynthia Ott and Kenneth Hirth.*

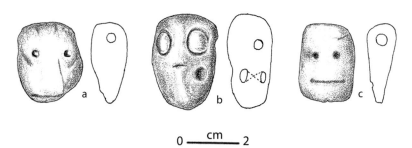

FIGURE 5.10. *Carved jade bead pendants: stylized head portraits. Illustration by Cynthia Ott and Kenneth Hirth.*

(Proskouriakoff 1974:plate 53a7). These pendants range between 14 mm and 39 mm in height and 11 mm and 43 mm in width, depending on the animal depicted. The majority are weak green in color (60%), with the remainder manufactured from gray (20%) and strong green (20%) shades of jade.

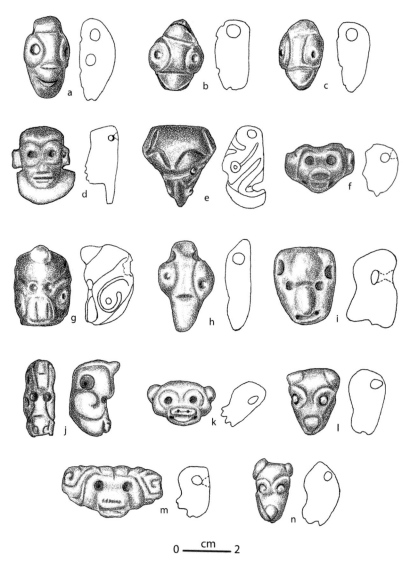

FIGURE 5.11. *Naturalistic zoomorphic bead pendants. Illustration by Cynthia Ott and Kenneth Hirth.*

Stylized Zoomorphic Bead Pendants (9 complete, 1 near complete)

These bead pendants are carved in a minimalist style, like stylized anthropomorphic portraits. As a result, it is difficult to identify the specific type of animal beyond eliminating human forms from consideration (figure 5.12). The carving

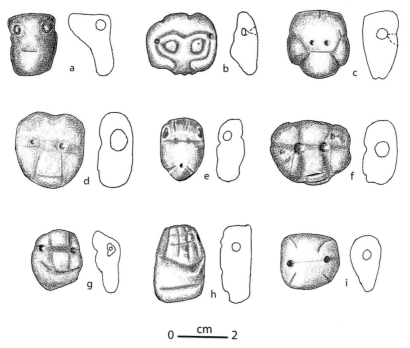

FIGURE 5.12. *Stylized zoomorphic bead pendants. Illustration by Cynthia Ott and Kenneth Hirth.*

style is quite varied. Eyes are most often portrayed by solid drilling, although some tubular drilling was noted. A horizontal line was used on some examples to define eye placement (figure 5.12d–g, i). In some cases, the facial features created with horizontal and vertical lines are so abstract as to border on geometric decoration (figure 5.12h). One bead pendant (figure 5.12a) has a pronounced facial protrusion and is reminiscent of stylized bird pendants found in Costa Rica. Artifacts range from 21 mm to 29 mm in height and 17 mm to 32 mm in width. Examples are distributed fairly evenly across all three color ramps (table 5.2).

Human Hand Bead Pendants (5 complete)

This group of bead pendants occurs in two forms. One category is represented by a carved image of a hand suspended from a hole near the wrist (figure 5.13a, d). The other four are images of hands incised on the surface of a square- to rectangular-shaped bead (figure 5.13b–e). Items in this category range between 22 mm and 28 mm in height and 18 mm and 30 mm in width. These bead pendants occur in all three color categories, from gray to strong green (table 5.2).

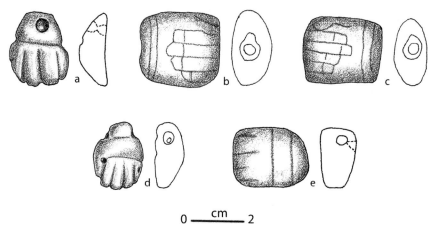

Figure 5.13. *Human hand beads and bead pendants. Illustration by Cynthia Ott and Kenneth Hirth.*

Earflares

Earflares are the second most common artifact in the collection after beads (table 5.5). They are well documented across Mesoamerica as a primary adornment worn by high-ranking members of society. What is interesting is that most earflares were intentionally broken when deposited as offerings. This combined with the practice of interring fragments of the same earflare in different deposits was a complicating factor in estimating MAC in the collection.[4] For that reason, the MAC estimates provided here are based only on counts of the robust earflare stem used in chapter 7 for estimating the amount of labor invested in their production.[5] Three flare groups were identified, with several profile classes within each group (figure 5.14). These three groups were conical flares, stemmed tubular flares, and tapered flares. To avoid misassignment, disk fragments were often tabulated separately as earflare fragments (table 5.5). Nevertheless, most of these fragments were broken from the thin discs of stemmed tubular flares. The three classes of flares were manufactured using combinations of distinct shaping and finishing techniques that reflect separate communities of practice with different technological traditions.

Conical Flares (21 complete, 257 fragmented, 225 estimated MAC)

Conical flares are the most numerous types in the collection. They are included in this category because of their general resemblance to stemmed earflares, although their size and weight make it unlikely that they were worn

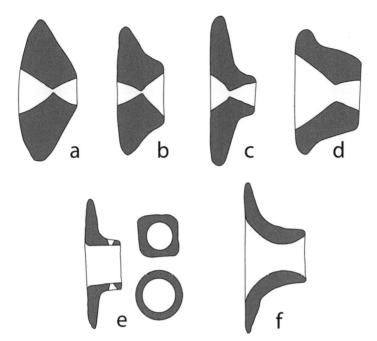

FIGURE 5.14. *Conical, tubular, and tapered flare profiles: (a–d) conical flare types 1–4, (e) tubular earflares, round and square tubes, (f) tapered earflare. Illustration by Cynthia Ott and Kenneth Hirth.*

in an ear lobe. This group of flares was first identified and described as earplug flares at Kaminaljuyú (Kidder, Jennings, and Shook 1946:125–126). Four subtypes were identified in the El Cajón collection based on the shapes illustrated in figure 5.14a–d. All conical flares are robust and heavy. The twenty-one complete conical flares range from 132 g to 548 g in weight,[6] and it is possible that they were worn as ornamental items on a belt or headdress instead of in the ear (Digby 1972:17). An important feature of conical flares is that they were manufactured using a different technological sequence than the stemmed tubular flares and tapered flares described below.

The technology used to shape these flares is related to that used to produce jade celts and axes. Flare preforms were created by percussion flaking and were brought into final form using pecking and grinding. Cutting was used to flatten the front face of these flares, although it is also possible that conical flares were shaped around a large initial flake or flat pebble. Traces of flaking were identified on thirty-one conical flares, with pecking evident on eighty-three others. Twenty-four of the flares with flaking also display remnant pecking that was not completely removed by further finishing. Frontal surfaces were generally polished to a medium to high luster. The use of flaking and pecking to shape these artifacts was harsh, and nearly one-quarter of all the conical flares have fractures from pecking on their surfaces.

The distinctive feature of conical flares was their central throat, which was prepared by biconical drilling. Drilling was conducted by rotating the flare on a preformed jig with a conically shaped projection. Repeating this operation on both sides of the flare created a biconical perforation along its center axis. One of these drilling jigs was recovered at Kaminaljuyú (Kidder, Jennings, and Shook 1946:figure 153a), where it was apparently used to manufacture conical flares. While the faces, sides, and backs of conical flares were polished, biconical drill holes forming the throat were unfinished and show clear traces of grinding.

Four types of conical flares are illustrated in figure 5.14a–d. Flare Types 1–3 (blocky, stubby, shaped disk) lie along a continuum from Type 1 flares, where there was no attempt to create a tubular stem on its posterior side (figures 5.14a, 5.15a), to Type 3, which achieves a T-shaped profile with thinned frontal disks and a well-formed stem (figure 5.14c, 5.16). Type 2 flares (figure 5.15b) are an intermediate category, with some shaping of the frontal disk but not enough thinning on the posterior of the flare to create a distinctive stem. Open mouth flares are the fourth type (figures 5.14d, 5.15c); they have a large frontal throat and the very narrow disk. Open mouth flares (Type 4) most closely resemble tapered flares in overall form (figure 5.14f) but were manufactured like other conical flares using pecking and grinding techniques.

Conical flares vary in frontal form. Most have round silhouettes (38.5%), although ovate (12.3%) and square, pentagonal, and rectangular shapes (10.7%) are also found. Type 3 flares (n = 140) are the most common and represent 62.2 percent of all conical flares recovered. This is followed by Type 2 (n = 55, 24.4%) and Type 1 (n = 26, 11.6%) flares. Type 4 flares are rare (n = 4) and represent only 1.8 percent of the collection. The frontal hole or throat of conical flares typically ranges from 18 mm to 36 mm in diameter for Types 1–3. Open mouth (Type 4) flares are an exception and have frontal throats between 51 mm and 58 mm in width. The distribution of colors is clearly bimodal across these four flare types. Strong green tones are found in 50.6 percent of conical flares, followed by gray (46.5%) and weak green (2.9%).

Stemmed Tubular Earflares (5 complete, 183 fragmented, 58 estimated MAC)

These earflares are well represented and are called flat face earflares by Proskouriakoff (1974:29) and Type B flares at Kaminaljuyú (Kidder, Jennings,

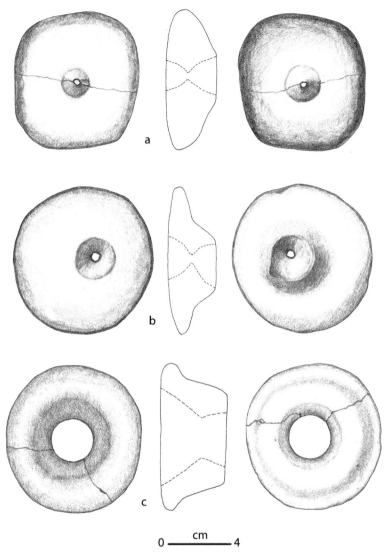

cm
0 ——— 4

FIGURE 5.15. *Conical flares, front and back views: (a) Type 1, (b) Type 2, (c) open mouth. Illustration by Cynthia Ott and Kenneth Hirth.*

and Shook 1946:figures 143–145). The main features of these flares are a flat frontal face, a pronounced stem at the back of the flare to extend through the ear lobe, and a cylindrical hole produced using a tubular drill that extends through the stem (figures 5.14e, 5.17a). Adrian Digby (1972:fig. 4) proposed

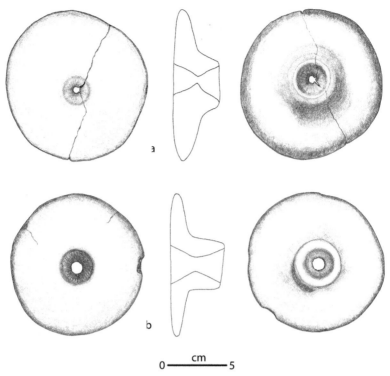

FIGURE 5.16. *Conical flares Type 3, front and back views. Illustration by Cynthia Ott and Kenneth Hirth.*

that tubular drilling on a preform was the first step in manufacturing these flares, followed by cutting the preform in half and shaping the stem using straight cuts followed by smoothing edges and grinding off ridges. The result was the creation of earflares with a strong T-shaped profile. The frontal shape of these flares varies and is evenly divided between symmetrical (round, square, rectangular) and non-symmetrical (ovate, irregular curvilinear) shapes.

Stemmed tubular earflares were divided into two subtypes based on whether the stem was square or round (figure 5.14e). Square stem flares are almost twice as numerous (n = 57) as round stem flares (n = 30). Contrary to Digby's manufacturing reconstruction, roughly one-quarter of flares have a small ledge on the interior of the stem created when tubular drilling initiated from the face side ceased and was resumed from the back side of the stem. Most instances of bidirectional drilling were found on square stemmed flares. Both round

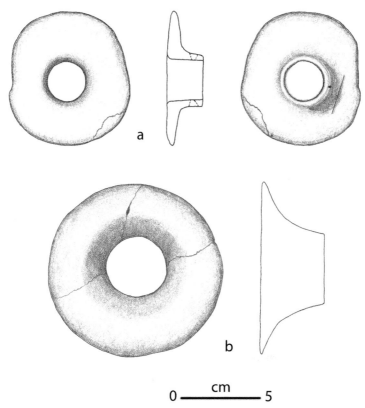

FIGURE 5.17. *Tubular and tapered flares: (a) round stemmed tubular earflare, (b) tapered earflare. Illustration by Cynthia Ott and Kenneth Hirth.*

and square stemmed flares may have two small opposing perforations drilled through the sides of the stem that were used to affix the flare when worn.

Dimensions are similar for square and round stemmed flares. The front face of flares, from the edge of the disk to the tubular drilling hole, ranges from 20 mm to 32 mm in width. Tubular holes range from 20 mm to 32 mm in width, which creates flares that are 62 mm to 134 mm across their face.[7] Earflare stems range from 9 mm to 33 mm in length and 31 mm to 51 mm in width for both round and square varieties. Tubular flares are more gracile than conical flares, with the complete examples in the collection weighing between 20.8 g and 89.9 g. The majority of stemmed earflares were manufactured of jade in strong green hues (89.8%), compared to those in gray (8.5%) and weak green (1.7%).

Moreover, there was a clear preference for apple green jade, which constitutes nearly three-quarters (79.0%) of all tubular flares.

Tapered Earflares (2 complete, 8 fragmented)

These are the least frequent type of earflares in the collection. They are notable for having wide mouths where the curvature of the throat expands gradually toward the lip of the flare (figures 5.14f, 5.17b). They were labeled Type A earflares at Kaminaljuyú (Kidder, Jennings, and Shook 1946:figures 143, 146) and resemble the wide-throated flares recovered from Chichen Itzá (Proskouriakoff 1974:29–30). They occur in both large and small forms. Large flares range from 65 mm to 111 mm in diameter at the mouth and 28 mm to 44 mm from front to back. One small example had a mouth diameter of 35 mm and a depth of only 14 mm. These flares employed a more complex shaping process than either conical or stemmed tubular flares because they required creating a gentle curvature from the back to the front of the flare. Color information was recorded for eight flares in this category: six were manufactured from emerald green (n = 3) or apple green (n = 3) jade and the other two from medium gray jade. All were polished to a high luster.

Pendants

Pendants occur in both plain and carved forms (table 5.5). They were shaped to emphasize the greatest exposure of material, which resulted in their often being two to three times broader than they were thick. A large quantity of pendants was recovered, either alone or in groups but usually not as central elements in a string of beads. They were separated into categories to identify differences in shape and decorative style. The shaped categories include geometric, zoomorphic, anthropomorphic, and hunched or hunchback pendants; ring pendants; crescent pectorals;[8] and flat and concave plaques. What made analysis challenging is that many pendants, like earflares, were intentionally fragmented when deposited in offerings. Despite attempts at refitting, a large number of carved pendant fragments were not recovered in project excavations across Salitrón Viejo.

Plain Pendants (114 complete, 166 fragmented)

Plain pendants are the most common type in the collection (table 5.5). They are blocky in form and include a range of symmetrical and asymmetrical shapes. The most common are rectangular/square (27.8%) (figure 5.18c, d), ovate (18.0%) (figure 5.18b), biconvex (8.3%), and teardrop/triangular (5.3%). Common asymmetrical forms include trapezoidal (13.5%) and irregular

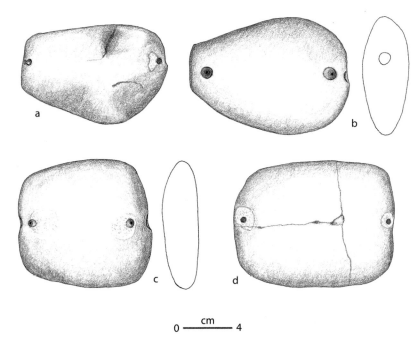

FIGURE 5.18. *Plain pendants reverse sides: (a) trapezoidal pendant with natural configurations evident, (b) oval pendant, (c–d) rectangular pendants. Illustration by Cynthia Ott and Kenneth Hirth.*

outlines (figure 5.18a) that follow the natural contours of the stone (18.0%). Pendants range from 16 mm to 160 mm in width (Ave = 67.7 mm) and 20 mm to 100 mm in height (Ave = 53.2 mm).

Pendants were suspended using both singular and pairs of biconically drilled suspension holes in equal numbers. The use of two biconically drilled suspension holes (figures 5.2a, 5.18a–d) was efficient and minimized the amount of drilling time. Why paired suspension holes were not used more often than traverse drilling along the entire width of the pendant is curious from a technological perspective and most likely relates to the technological procedures preferred by different communities of practice. Nevertheless, pendants using single-suspension holes were notably narrower than those that used paired-suspension holes. The majority of plain pendants were fashioned from jade with gray tones (55.6%), followed by strong green (36.6%) and weak green (7.8%). Apple green is the dominant color represented in the strong green category (74.5%).

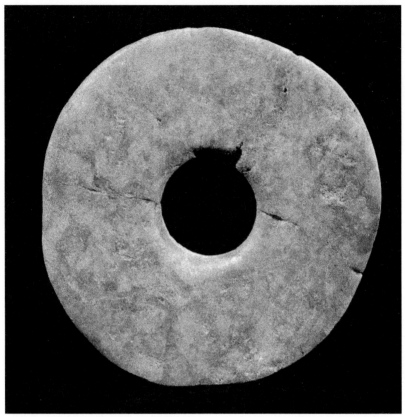

FIGURE 5.19. *Circular jade ring pendant*

Ring Pendants (5 complete, 37 fragmented, 23 estimated MAC)

Ring pendants are a unique category of carefully shaped pendants (figure 5.19). They were fashioned from flat sawn slabs of jade that are 3 mm to 17 mm thick. Ring pendants range from round to slightly ovate in shape, with an average thickness of 7.7 mm. Complete and near complete examples range from 68 mm to 127 mm in diameter, with a central hole 27 mm to 58 mm wide. Most ring pendants were intentionally fragmented; because of their thinness, they break into multiple small pieces. Two small suspension holes were drilled from front to back at their centerline that provided a means of suspension. The fronts and backs of ring pendants were polished to a high or medium luster, and there was a clear preference for strong green (73.3%) in ring pendants, followed by gray (16.7%) and weak green (10.0%).

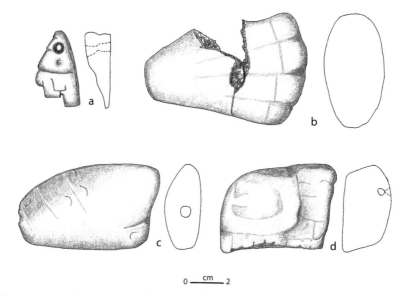

FIGURE 5.20. *Geometric Jade Pendants. Illustration by Cynthia Ott and Kenneth Hirth.*

Circular motifs were important symbolic elements across Mesoamerica, and they occur in a variety of materials and contexts ranging from ceramics and mural paintings to architectural embellishments. Nevertheless, circular jade pendants are rare and have been reported at relatively few archaeological sites. Places where they occur include a pair of carved ring disks from Teotihuacan (Evans 2010:15), six complete pendants at Cerro de las Mesas (Drucker 1955:54), and eight flat rings and miscellaneous fragments from the Cenote at Chichen Itzá (Proskouriakoff 1974:plate 36e). An interesting feature of ring pendants at Salitrón Viejo is that one-third of them occur as paired items in the same or adjacent offering deposits.[9] Paired rings are often interpreted as an expression of the storm god at Teotihuacan, whether they are located in headdresses or as part of other costume elements (Evans 2010:18; Langley and Berlo 1992:248–252; Miller 1973).

Geometric Pendants (4 complete, 1 complete unfinished, 14 fragmented)
These pendants have incised or carved geometric designs in both curvilinear and rectilinear style (figure 5.20). Decoration consists of lateral cuts, straight and curvilinear lines, scrolls, and circular motifs created using a tubular drill.[10] Both horizontal and vertically oriented pendants were identified, with dimensions ranging from 41 mm to 96 mm in height and 59 mm to

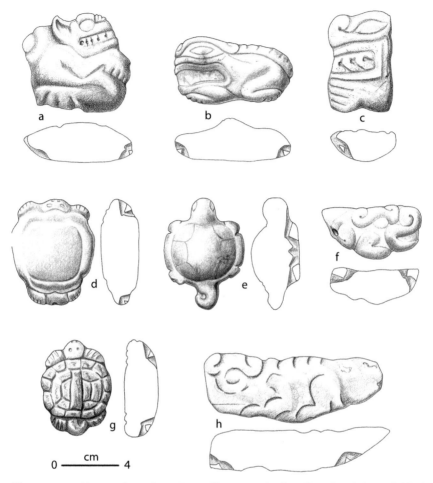

FIGURE 5.21. *Zoomorphic jade pendants. Illustration by Anne Dowd and Kenneth Hirth.*

120 mm in width. One geometric pendant (figure 5.20a) may be an abstract Costa Rican–style bird pendant (Aguilar 2003:34; Baudez 1977:137–138). All three colors occur, with strong green (57.9%) predominating followed by gray (36.8%) and weak green (5.3%).

Zoomorphic Pendants (22 complete, 5 fragmented)

These pendants depict stylistic attributes that are zoomorphic in nature (figures 5.21, 5.22, 5.23, 5.24). The animals identified include alligators or reptiles (figure 5.21b, f, h, 5.23f), bats (figure 5.21a), birds (figures 5.22e, h; 5.23b), turtles

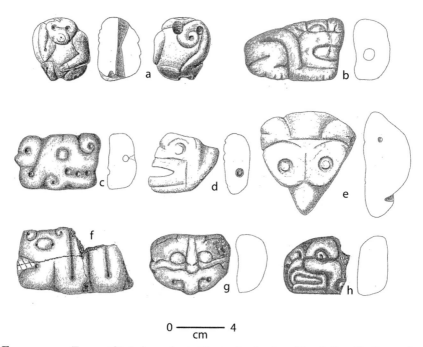

FIGURE 5.22. *Zoomorphic jade pendants. Illustration by Anne Dowd, Cynthia Ott, and Kenneth Hirth.*

(figure 5.21d–e, g; 5.23c–d), monkeys (figure 5.22a), serpents (figure 5.22f), jaguars (figure 5.22g), fish (figure 5.22d), an insect, possibly a grasshopper (figure 5.24e), and a marine mollusk (figures 5.23e). Most images are carved using low incising or shallow sculpting on one side. Examples carved on all sides include an image of a monkey (figure 5.22a), the head of a bird (figure 5.22e), and several turtles that incorporated the curvature of the shell into the carving (figures 5.21d–e; 5.23d). Three highly stylized pendants (figures 5.23a, 5.24a–b, d) were placed in this category because they display curved eyebrows, fangs, or other elements used in realistically carved animal images.

Pendants vary in size depending on whether they depict the entire animal, its head, or just a few salient characteristics. Horizontal orientations were used to display the entire animal, while pendants taller than they were wide show either the face or other aspects of the animal. Complete pendants range from 27 mm to 84 mm in height and 22 mm to 124 mm in width. Pendants were suspended using both single and paired biconical suspension holes. As a rule, single biconical suspension holes were used on pendants where the hole did not exceed 50 mm in length and was positioned along the top of the pendant.

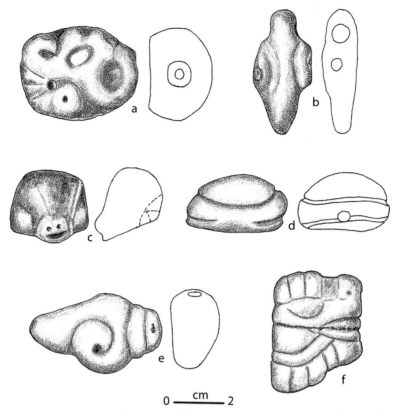

Figure 5.23. *Zoomorphic jade pendants. Illustration by Cynthia Ott and Kenneth Hirth.*

Paired suspension holes were always used on horizontally oriented pendants that were 67–124 mm in width. All pendants were polished to a medium to high luster. The unfinished pendant depicts the face of a feline (figure 5.22g) and lacks suspension holes.

The carving style is curvilinear and varied in the way elements were portrayed. Nevertheless, several stylistic features are distinctive. Reptiles were represented with a double scroll over the eye (figures 5.21b, f, h; 5.22c, f; 5.23a), and alligators were portrayed with plate scales along the spine of their backs (figures 5.21b, h; 5.24c). Eyes were carved as lozenges or represented by solid or tubular drilling. The corners of mouths on some figures were marked by holes made with a solid drill that also marked the division between teeth (figures 5.21a, c; 5.22c, g; 5.23a, f). The colors represented in carved zoomorphic pendants were distributed across all three color groups. Strong green jade hues were the most prevalent (44%), followed by gray (36%) and weak green (20%).

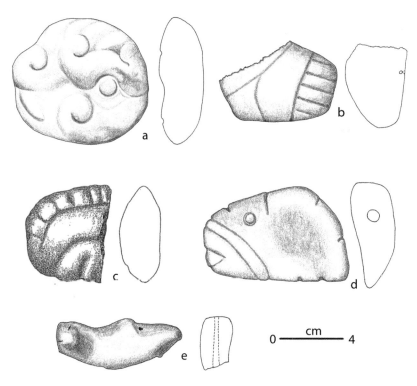

Figure 5.24. *Stylized and partial zoomorphic jade pendants. Illustration by Anne Dowd, Cynthia Ott, and Kenneth Hirth.*

Hunchback Pendants (21 complete, 16 fragmented)

Anthropomorphic pendants in the form of hunchbacks or dwarfs are one of the most important pendant classes in the collection. We refer to these images interchangeably in this work as hunched or hunchback figures, for several reasons. First, the term *hunchback* has been used by numerous scholars to identify these images in Mesoamerica, and we retain its use here (e.g., Ashmore 1980:40; Digby 1972:26; Easby 1992:136–138; Inomata and Houston 2001; Miller 1985; Proskouriakoff 1974:94; Thompson 1970). Second and more specific, it is the direct translation of the Spanish word *jorobado* used for the images in Honduras. Nevertheless, we recognize the disparaging connotations the terms *hunchback* and *dwarf* may have in modern parlance. What is important to note is that individuals with shortened or unusual stature had an elevated and exalted status in the pre-Columbian world, and that is what distinguished them as special (see discussion in chapter 8). The unique style

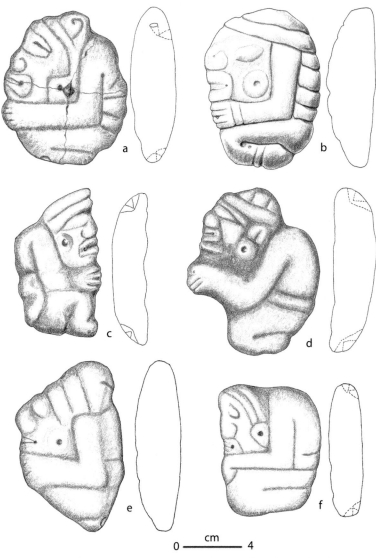

FIGURE 5.25. *Hunchback pendants. Illustration by Anne Dowd, Cynthia Ott, and Kenneth Hirth.*

and posture displayed in these pendants make them distinctive and readily identifiable. Similar examples have been recovered at Copán (Digby 1972), Quirigua (Ashmore 1980:40), Kaminaljuyú (Kidder, Jennings, and Shook 1946), Chichen Itzá (Proskouriakoff 1974:figure 51a-4), Altun Ha (Pendergast

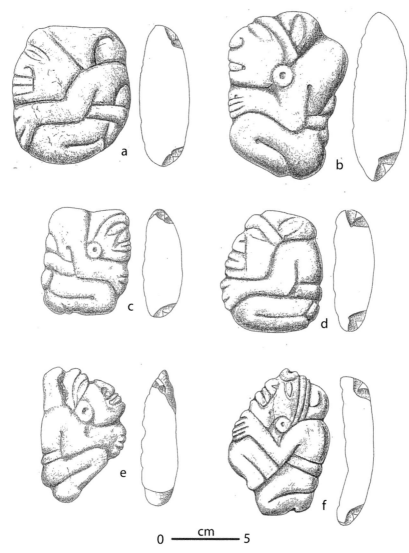

FIGURE 5.26. *Hunchback pendants. Illustration by Anne Dowd and Kenneth Hirth.*

1979:2:89), and Asunción Mita (Ashmore 1980:39), as well as in Costa Rica (Balser 1961:213; Stone 1977b:figure 78a). The hunched or hunchback pendants from Salitrón Viejo were manufactured in a variety of raw materials, and their large number underscores their importance in the population's religious life. Figures 5.25, 5.26, 5.27, and 5.28 reveal the variation in the form and style of these jade pendants.

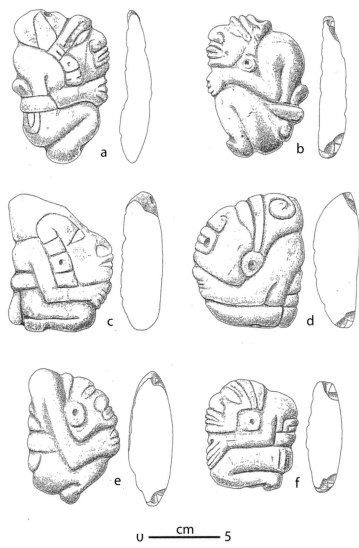

cm
0 — 5

FIGURE 5.27. *Hunchback pendants. Illustration by Anne Dowd and Kenneth Hirth.*

Images are identified as hunched or hunchback figures based on the crouching or stooped-over posture that all the figures portray. Several scholars have suggested that these figures represent dancers or dwarfs (Miller 1985:141–142; Thompson 1970). This identification is based on their consistent stooped and inclined carriage and the occasional depiction of a hump or spinal deformity protruding above or behind the head (figures 5.26b–c; 5.27b, e). Pendants range

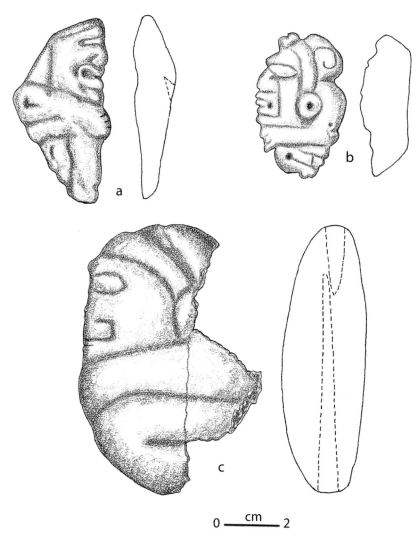

FIGURE 5.28. *Two miniature hunchback pendants (a–b) and one fractured hunchback pendant (c). Illustration by Cynthia Ott and Kenneth Hirth.*

from 46 mm to 118 mm in height and 29 mm to 103 mm in width when they are oriented in an upright position. All pendants, however, had their suspension holes located at the tops and bottoms of the figures so that suspended figures would have been oriented horizontally in a facedown position.

Figures in profile are portrayed in a kneeling position, leaning forward with their hands placed under the chin, thumbs upward, in an expression of praise or supplication. Figures are usually portrayed wearing a belt and loin cloth, a portion of which is visible along the back of the figure. They are often shown wearing earflares to denote their importance and some sort of cap or head covering depicted either as a scroll (figures 5.25a; 5.26a–b, d, f; 5.28b) or a head band, sometimes with a feather decoration (figure 5.26b, d). The face is carved in a curvilinear style, with the eye rendered using incision or as a raised lozenge. Figures have a pronounced aquiline nose, and the mouth is depicted as closed or slightly open, displaying the tongue or teeth. Solid drilling was used to define the center of earflares and occasionally the corners of mouths. The face on two pendants (figures 5.25d; 5.26d) is defined with a diagonal line reminiscent of triangle face figures (see below), but this is relatively rare. Most hunched figure pendants are carved from gray jade (77.1%), followed by apple green jade (14.3%) and weak green (8.6%).

Anthropomorphic Pendants (16 complete, 10 fragmented)

This category covers a range of pendants carved in curvilinear and abstract styles. Pendants range from 44 mm to 98 mm in height and 21 mm to 123 mm in width. Because many pendants depict human faces, nearly three-quarters of complete pendants were taller than they were wide. Two-thirds of the pendants had paired suspension holes located at either end of their centerline axis. Pendants with single biconical or tubular drilling had suspension holes situated off-center along their upper register so the carved image would orient properly when suspended.

Twenty-three pendants are carved in a curvilinear style, illustrated in figures 5.29, 5.30, 5.31, and 5.32. Three pendants display the bodies of acrobats or divers (figure 5.32b–d), while a fourth depicts a human hand (figure 5.30e). Faces are shown in both frontal and profile views, with one image depicting tattoos on the side of the face (figure 5.31d). Three pendants are carved in a clearly Maya style (figure 5.32a, c–d). Three others employ a more angular, triangular format (figure 5.33) where the face was shaped with straight cuts like triangular face bead pendants (see figures 5.8, 5.9). Half of anthropomorphic pendants are carved from gray jade (50.0%), followed by strong green (36.4%) and weak green (13.6%).

Crescent Pectorals (13 complete, 11 fragmented, 17 estimated MAC)

This class of pendants has not been reported elsewhere in Honduras outside of Salitrón Viejo (figures 5.34, 5.35, 5.36, and 5.37). They are typically hemispherical in shape, with a carefully cut scallop or rounded notch located at the center of the pendant's upper margin. They range between 110 mm and 161

Figure 5.29. *Anthropomorphic pendants. Illustration by Anne Dowd, Cynthia Ott, and Kenneth Hirth.*

mm wide, 51 mm and 96 mm high, and 9 mm and 25 mm thick. The central notch is 9–39 mm wide and 9–32 mm deep, depending on whether it was fashioned with a large circular drill or lateral cuts that were rounded during the finishing process. Two-thirds of crescent pendants have two V-shaped notches cut into their sides that divide the pendant visually into an upper and lower register that could be decorated in different ways. An important technological feature is that they were fashioned from sawn slabs of jade that were shaped, decorated, and polished to a medium to high luster.

In form, these pendants represent the flat stylized nose ornaments referred as *narigueras de mariposa* in western Mesoamerica. The Nariguera de Mariposa is a Middle Classic symbol associated with the rain god Tlaloc and Teotihuacan

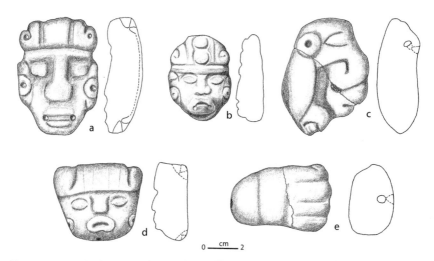

FIGURE 5.30. *Anthropomorphic pendants. Illustration by Anne Dowd, Cynthia Ott, and Kenneth Hirth.*

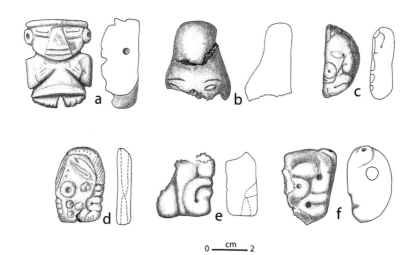

FIGURE 5.31. *Anthropomorphic pendants. Illustration by Anne Dowd, Cynthia Ott, and Kenneth Hirth.*

influence (Hernández Reyes 1974; Kidder, Jennings, and Shook 1946; Parsons 1967–1969; Sejourne 1962). Crescent elements also occur as painted motifs on polychrome ceramics throughout Honduras (Joyce 2017; Viel 1978:119). All pendants in the Salitrón collection have two small suspension holes located

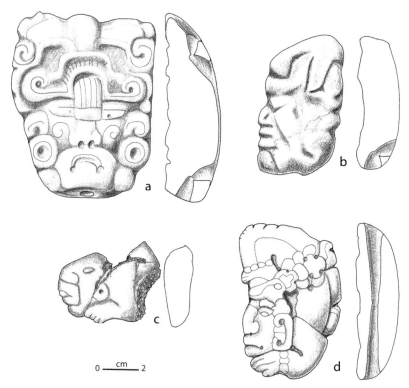

Figure 5.32. *Anthropomorphic pendants in Maya style. Illustration by Anne Dowd, Cynthia Ott, and Kenneth Hirth.*

at or near their upper edge and positioned on either side of the central scallop. These suspension holes were drilled biconically from the top edge to the back of the pendant, so they were hidden from view. Fully three-quarters of all crescent pectorals were manufactured of gray jade (75.0%), followed by weak green (20.8%) and strong green (4.2%) hues.

Pectorals were separated into four classes on the basis of design. Seven plain pectorals were identified, two of which have paired V-shaped lateral side notches that are 7–10 mm in depth (figure 5.34). Crescent pendants with geometric decoration (n = 13) are the most numerous but vary in form, size, and decoration (figures 5.35, 5.36a–b). They occur both with and without lateral side notches and with large and small central scallops. Pendants are commonly decorated with three or more singular or concentric circles created by a tubular drill (figure 5.35). The largest complete pendant (154 mm × 96 mm) has a composite silhouette form that combines a rectangular upper register with a lower

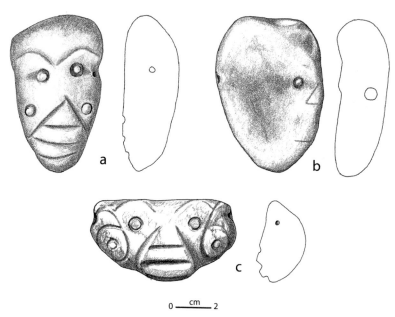

FIGURE 5.33. *Triangle head pendants. Illustration by Anne Dowd, Cynthia Ott, and Kenneth Hirth.*

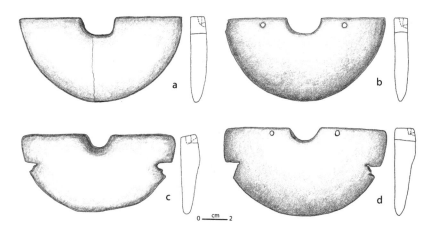

FIGURE 5.34. *Plain crescent pectorals. Illustration by Cynthia Ott and Kenneth Hirth.*

hemispherical shape; this composite silhouette is replicated in the pendant's central scallop (figure 5.35g). Two artifacts employed incised lines to decorate their surface (figure 5.36a–b). In one case, a horizontal line was incised along

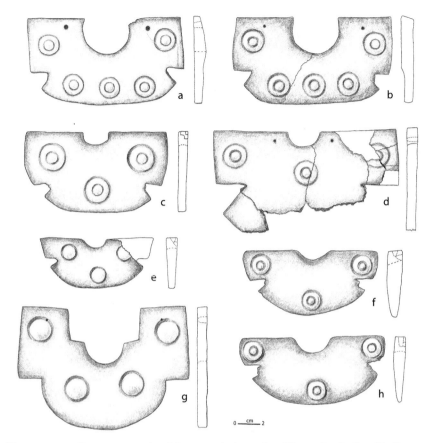

Figure 5.35. *Crescent pectorals with geometric decoration. Illustration by Cynthia Ott and Kenneth Hirth.*

the centerline of the pendant to divide it into two registers that were decorated with different motifs (figure 5.36b).

Two crescent pendants with human faces were created using straight and angled tubular drilling (figure 5.36c–d). Both faces have circles incised below the eyes that represent earflares. While both pectorals lack V-shaped side notches, the upper register of one pendant (figure 5.36d) has sculpted indentations that frame the upper register of the face as a horizontal bar. In the other, the pendant's lower register was rounded to represent the chin or jawline (figure 5.36c). The use of tubular drilling to create geometric designs and human faces can be found on several flat pectorals recovered from the Cenote at Chichen Itzá (Proskouriakoff 1974:plate 51b).

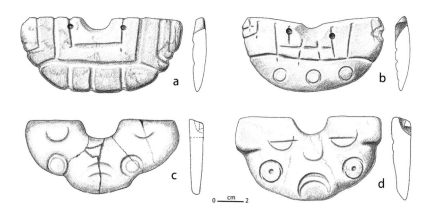

FIGURE 5.36. *Crescent pectorals with geometric decoration and human faces. Illustration by Anne Dowd, Cynthia Ott, and Kenneth Hirth.*

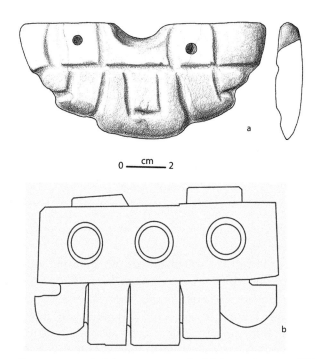

FIGURE 5.37. *Crescent pectorals: (a) crescent pectoral with jaguar imagery, (b) Banda de Tlaloc nose ornament from Teotihuacan. Illustration by Anne Dowd, Ryan Middlemore, and Kenneth Hirth.*

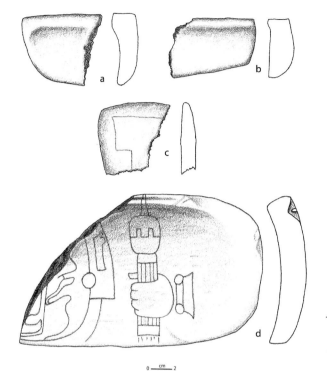

FIGURE 5.38. *Flat and concave plaques: (a–b) concave plaques, (c) flat plaque with T-shape incision, (d) concave plaque with incised Olmec image. Illustration by Anne Dowd, Cynthia Ott, and Kenneth Hirth.*

One crescent pectoral was identified with stylized jaguar imagery (figure 5.37a). An incised horizontal line separates the pectoral into upper and lower registers. Carving in the lower register was used to shape two L-shaped fangs located on either side of a U-shaped mouth element. Two rectangular lozenges carved in the upper register resemble eyes, which together with the fang elements create the impression of a face. The composition of this pendant closely resembles the Banda de Tlaloc nose elements (figure 5.37b) associated with Teotihuacan culture across Mesoamerica (Angulo 1969). L-shaped fang-like elements are also present on one of the incised geometric pendants (figure 5.36a) and may represent the same jaguar theme.

Flat Plaques and Disks (4 fragmented plaques, 3 complete disks)

Flat plaques and disks are grouped together because they were both manufactured from sawn slabs of jade. All flat plaques were fragmented, so dimensions are not available. Two are plain, while the other two have geometric decorations. One of the plaques was incised with a T-shaped design (figure 5.38c), which is similar to some flat plaques at Chichen Itzá (Proskouriakoff 1974:plates 50a,

65b). The other plaque was decorated with circular designs created using a tubular drill like those found on crescent pectorals as well as some flat plaques at Chichen Itzá (plates 36a, 51b). The three small disk pendants were shaped from thinly sawn pieces of jade and are 15–33 mm in diameter and 2–4 mm thick. Three plaques were fashioned from strong green jade, while the fourth was gray. Two of the disks are medium gray in color, while the third is emerald green.

Concave Plaques (4 fragmented)

Four concave plaques were manufactured for use as pendants. Three of these plaques were plain (figure 5.38a–b), while the fourth was incised with an Olmec-style figure (figure 5.38d). These plaques have distinct concave surfaces that are often referred to as clam shell pendants in the Olmec area (Andrews 1987; Drucker, Heizer, and Squier 1959:plate 27; Healy and Awe 2001; Proskouriakoff 1974:36, plate 38a). While exact dimensions could not be determined, plain plaques ranged from 27 mm to 35 mm in width, while the incised example was 71 mm wide. The incised Olmec image depicts a face in profile located inside a cartouche representing a cave motif, with a torch or blood letter held in the hand in front of the face. The concave surfaces of all four plaques were finished to a high luster. The incised plaque was fashioned from emerald green jade. Two of the plain plaques were fashioned from apple green jade, while the third was manufactured from gray jade.

Unfinished Plain Pendants (8 complete, 2 fragmented)

All ten of these pendants were deposited in ritual deposits in unfinished form. They were classified as unfinished because drill holes were incompletely executed or never attempted, or the pendant was abandoned before completion. The fact that artifacts were unfinished did not result in their being handled differently from finished artifacts in ritual deposits.

Human Effigy Figure (1 fragmented)

One fragment of a human effigy figure was identified. Although incomplete, it appears to be a seated figure. It was very likely similar in form to those produced in non-jadeite materials (see figure 5.48b).

Mozaic Tesserae (2 pieces)

Two small tesserae were identified that were probably part of a larger mosaic artifact. These tesserae were 4–5 mm in size and 1 mm thick. Both were emerald green in color. Although no other tesserae were recovered, both of these items were located in the same deposit as three slate disks (see figure 5.44b) that may have been the backing on which these items were glued.

Jade Celt (1 complete)

One small celt was identified that was 38 mm long, 14 mm wide, and 8 mm thick. It was rectangular in shape and manufactured from apple green jade.

Unidentifiable Pieces (127 fragmented)

These fragments could not be conjoined with other jade artifacts across the site. Most appear to be pieces of pendants and possibly a few earspools. All of these pieces were between 6 mm and 37 mm in length and 4 mm and 25 mm in width. Strong green is the predominant color represented by these fragments (50.8%), followed by gray (44.1%) and weak green (5.1%). Apple green represents fully 86.7 percent of the strong green hues.

Jade Nodules and Flakes (3 complete nodules, 6 fragmented flakes)

Eight small jade nodules and one jade flake were recovered with other materials in ritual offerings. The nodules range from 14 mm to 43 mm in diameter and 8 mm to 19 mm thick. There is no evidence that jade nodules were used to fashion any of the finished artifacts in the collection. Instead, six of the nodules were fragmented using bipolar percussion alongside other finished artifacts within deposits. Of the nine items, six were strong green and three were gray jade.

MICACEOUS JADE ARTIFACTS (N = 203)

This category of jade is described separately because of its unique visual characteristics that make it stand out as a distinctive raw material used in lapidary production. The items produced from this material are unique in both type and style from other artifacts in the collection, which suggests that they represent a separate community of lapidary practice using stone their artisans preferred and had access to. The distinguishing feature of this material is the presence of mineral crystals or platelets 1–2 mm in size that look like small pieces of mica embedded in the stone (figures 5.1, 2a). Shaping and polishing the stone exposed these platelets, creating a noticeable sparkling effect that is recognizable to the naked eye. Polishing does not achieve a high surface luster on this material. Instead, the appearance of luster is provided by the platelets exposed across the artifact surface.[11] The most common items were beads, bead pendants, and a few pendants (table 5.5). Earflares are rare. Artifacts in this material occur overwhelmingly in weak green hues (95%), followed by strong green (4%) and gray (1%).

Spheroid, Discoidal, and Oblong Beads (139 complete, 9 fragmented)

Plain beads occur in spheroid, oblong, and discoidal forms. Spheroid beads are the most numerous (n = 119), followed by a few discoidal (n = 17) and oblong (n = 12) types (table 5.5). Spheroid beads range from 8 mm to 35 mm in width, although most are small, with an average width of 14.8 mm. Discoidal beads range from 5 mm to 33 mm in height and 2 mm to 14 mm in width. Oblong beads are 7–52 mm wide.

Plain and Carved Tubular Beads (4 fragmented)

Two plain and two carved tubular bead fragments were recovered (table 5.5). The two carved examples were undulating serpents that followed the same format, which combined curved lines with tubular drill marks to depict undulating coils. The longest fragmented serpent bead was 141 mm long (figure 5.5c).

Carved Bead Pendants (39 complete)

All bead pendants manufactured from this material depict carved images. Like other bead pendants they were drilled off-center, allowing the carved image to hang in a consistent orientation when suspended. Bead pendants of this material are small, ranging between 14 mm and 29 mm high and 8 mm and 22 mm wide. All but three were carved as small animal heads (table 5.5). The three exceptions consisted of one geometric bead pendant decorated with horizontal and vertical incised lines, an image of a human hand (figure 5.13a), and a possible anthropomorphic image that was like figure 5.6i.

The overwhelming majority of these bead pendants (n = 36, 92.3%) depict zoomorphic images displayed in frontal view (figures 5.39, 5.40, 5.41, and 5.42). Their identification as zoomorphic images is based on four features: elongated facial profiles, the placement of ears on the top or upper corners of the face, a slightly prognathic facial snout, and the location of the mouth under the snout at the bottom of the bead pendant. Pendants were often shaped as elongated rectangular or triangular forms. Facial features were represented by lateral incisions and circular drill marks. Eyes were depicted by small holes drilled within or above horizontal or diagonally incised lateral cuts that defined the nasal break of the face. Suspension holes were often placed within the lateral cuts to define ears at the upper corners of heads.

The consistency of the imagery suggests that bead pendants were intended to depict specific categories of animals. Figure 5.39 illustrates bear-like animals that may represent kinkajous. Eyes are represented by drill holes located in a horizontal incised line on the lower register of the face, with the mouth placed out of view under the bottom of the snout. Figure 5.40 depicts faces that resemble monkeys. Ears are located at the upper corners and above a

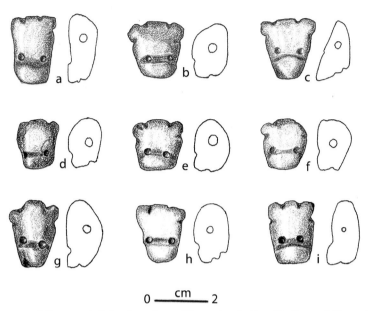

FIGURE 5.39. *Micaceous jade bead pendants. Illustration by Cynthia Ott and Kenneth Hirth.*

V-shaped cut at the midline of the face. Figure 5.41 depicts variations on these bear and monkey images and one possible humanoid face (figure 5.41e), where the eye is represented by a small horizontal cut instead of a solid drill indentation. A final group of zoomorphic carvings is depicted in figure 5.42. While too abstract to associate with any specific type of animal, they all have elongated faces, with two incised lines that define the lower facial register.

Stemmed Tubular Earflares (1 fragmented)

While earflares are common in other forms of jade, they are rare in this material. Only one fragmented earflare was recovered, which had a square posterior stem.

Pendants (5 complete, 6 fragmented)

One complete and three fragmented plain pendants were recovered. Seven zoomorphic pendants were also identified, six of which are depicted in figure 5.43. The zoomorphic images depict a jaguar (figure 5.43a), a serpent (figure 5.43b), a bird (figure 5.43e), a turtle (figure 5.43d), and a bear-like animal (figure 5.43f). A more abstract carving was also identified that may be the stylized head of a bird (figure 5.43c).

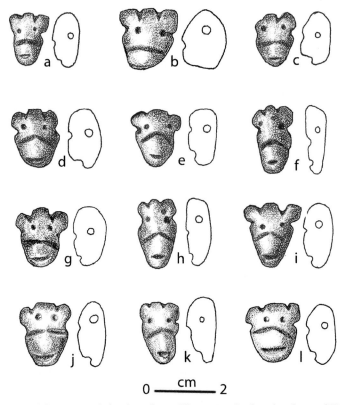

FIGURE 5.40. *Micaceous jade bead pendants. Illustration by Cynthia Ott and Kenneth Hirth.*

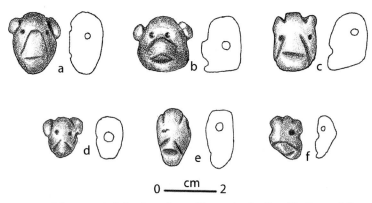

FIGURE 5.41. *Micaceous jade bead pendants. Illustration by Cynthia Ott and Kenneth Hirth.*

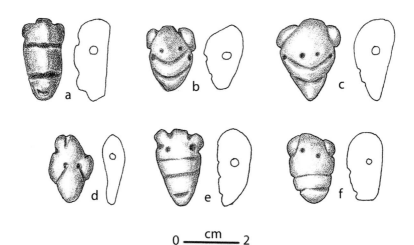

FIGURE 5.42. *Micaceous jade bead pendants. Illustration by Cynthia Ott and Kenneth Hirth.*

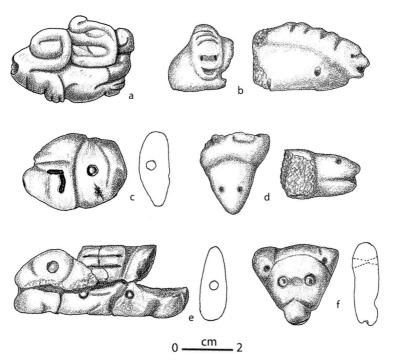

FIGURE 5.43. *Micaceous jade zoomorphic pendants. Illustration by Anne Dowd, Cynthia Ott, and Kenneth Hirth.*

Marble Artifacts (n = 291)

Marble deposits occur in many areas across north and west-central Honduras (Williams and McBirney 1969), and marble was an important resource for pre-Columbian people. Marble sources in the Ulúa valley were used to fashion the well-known Ulúa marble vases (Luke, Tykot, and Scott 2006; see also Gordon 1921; Luke and Tykot 2007; Stone 1938).[12] The marble used in Ulúa vases is a fine-textured white stone and is referred to here as fine marble. The majority of the marble occurring in the El Cajón collections is a much coarser granular marble (figure 5.44a, c–d). Its granular texture is the product of small cleavage plains that are visible under low (8–10×) magnification. Thin bands of quartz with malachite inclusions run through some of this material, which artisans took advantage of, shaping the artifact so the natural green veins in the rock were exposed on its surface (figure 5.44a). Granular marble ranges from white (N9/, 8/1 5YR) to light gray buff (10YR 8/2) in color, with a MOHS hardness of 3.5–4.0. The attractiveness of this material for lapidary artifacts may have been its softness and workability, along with its white color that was associated with death and sacrifice (Dupey García 2015). While the source location for this material has not been identified, Robert Fakundiny (1970) reports several siliceous marble outcrops in the Montaña de Comayagua south of the El Cajón region between La Libertad and the Comayagua valley. These outcrops run from fine- to coarse-grained marble, with a snowflake texture and with malachite and azurite crystals occurring in cracks of at least one deposit (Fakundiny 1970:166, 190). While it is uncertain whether this was the source of the granular marble recovered in the El Cajón collections, it is a potential area of future study.[13] George Byron Gordon (1898b:13) reported three beads and one zoomorphic pendant made from a flaky limestone with streaks of green crystals from the site of Guacamaya that may be this same material.

A total of 291 marble artifacts were recovered in the El Cajón region (table 5.5). One fragment of an Ulúa marble vase was recovered that was manufactured of fine marble. The remainder—most of which were pendants—were manufactured of granular marble. Beads, bead pendants, earflares, and effigy images were also recovered in small numbers. Granular marble artifacts, unfortunately, do not preserve well in tropical conditions and tend to disintegrate, breaking along internal cleavage planes.[14] The most severely eroded pieces can lose their shape entirely.

Plain and Carved Beads (2 complete, 7 fragmented)

Very few beads were identified in granular marble. Seven spheroid beads were recovered, only one of which was complete. They ranged from 9 mm to 45 mm

Figure 5.44. *Granular marble and slate artifacts: (a) granular marble using natural green silica layer as the surface of an earflare, (b) slate plaque with cinnabar coating, (c–d) granular marble pendants. Illustration by Kenneth Hirth.*

in diameter, with suspension holes created using a tubular drill. One complete discoidal bead was recovered that was 17 mm high and 8 mm wide. One carved oblong bead had an incised line and a small tubular drill mark on its surface.

Plain Bead Pendants (3 complete, 1 fragmented)

All four plain bead pendants had a single suspension hole drilled through their short axis. Bead pendants were both rectangular and trapezoidal in form. They ranged from 35 mm to 45 mm in height and 25 mm to 36 mm in width.

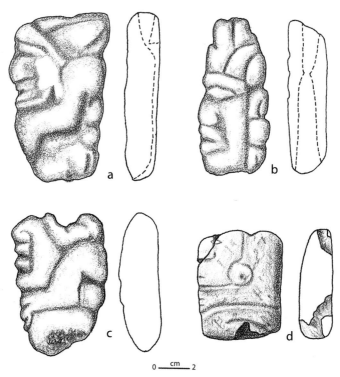

Figure 5.45. *Granular marble bead pendants. Illustration by Anne Dowd, Cynthia Ott, and Kenneth Hirth.*

Decorated Bead Pendants (4 complete, 1 fragmented)

These bead pendants are decorated in geometric and anthropomorphic images (table 5.5). One bead pendant was decorated with simple incised geometric lines. The other four have anthropomorphic images that are depicted in figure 5.45. Three are hunchbacks (figure 5.45a, c-d), while the fourth is a human head carved in a more Mayoid style (figure 5.45b). These hunched or hunchback images conform to the same conventions found in their jade counterparts. All three are shown in left profile, with a stooped posture and hands tucked underneath their chins. One image depicts a hump or spinal deformity behind the figure's head (figure 5.45d). While all bead pendants are depicted vertically in figure 5.45, their suspension holes were oriented so they hung facedown when suspended like jade hunchback pendants.

Earflares (8 fragmented)

A few earflares of granular marble were recovered. Both conical (n = 4) and tubular flares (n = 2) were identified, all of which have short anterior stems (table 5.5). Earflares manufactured of granular marble have not been reported from other sites in Honduras. The only dimension of these flares that could be measured consistently was the width of the disk, which ranged from 22.0 to 27.5 mm. An example of a conical flare manufactured of granular marble is illustrated in figure 5.44a. What is particularly creative about this artifact is that it was shaped behind the malachite rich green layer that served as the frontal surface of the flare.

Plain Pendants (16 complete, 100 fragmented)

Plain pendants are the most common artifact recovered in granular marble (table 5.5). Shapes include rectangular/square (45.9%), oval or ellipsoidal (29.2%), trapezoidal (8.3%), triangular (8.3%), and natural shapes (8.3%). Like other pendants, they were generally drilled to hang in a horizontal orientation. Their dimensions are 50–87 mm wide, 35–61 mm high, and 11–42 mm thick. Large pendants were suspended using pairs of conical drill holes on their sides (cf. figures 5.18, 5.44d), although examples of single holes drilled from the front to the back were also identified.

Geometric Pendants (3 complete, 54 fragmented)

Pendants with geometric decoration are common, although they are almost always fragmented. Common designs include incised lines arranged in steps and grecas (figure 5.46a) and combinations of scrolls and lozenges (figure 5.46b). Scroll patterns are twice as frequent (64.3%) as linear decorations (35.7%) in these pendants. Most geometric pendants are oriented horizontally and have biconical drill holes on either end of their long axis. Pendants were 65–100 mm long, 40–70 mm high, and 15–47 mm thick.

Carved Zoomorphic Pendants (3 complete, 12 fragmented)

These pendants have images or attributes associated with animals carved on their surfaces. All zoomorphic images were carved in a curvilineal style using shallow incising. The animals include birds (figure 5.46c), alligators, rabbits (figure 5.46d), and felines (figures 5.22b, 5.46f). Complete pendants are 54–70 mm high, 65–80 mm wide, and 22–29 mm thick. Paired suspension holes were located above the midline on the edges of pendants. Erosion has weathered the surface features and reduced clarity of detail, but on the whole they were carved following the same general conventions used for other zoomorphic

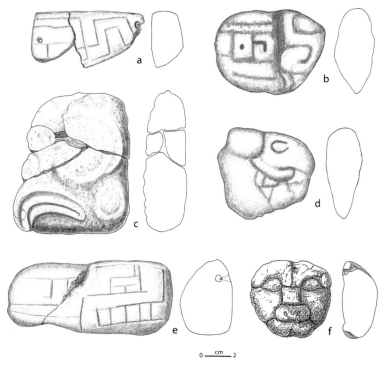

FIGURE 5.46. *Granular marble and non-jadeite geometric and zoomorphic pendants. Illustration by Anne Dowd, Cynthia Ott, and Kenneth Hirth.*

pendants in the collection. Gordon (1898b:figure 16) illustrates a broken zoo-morphic pendant in the form of a feline from the site of La Guacamaya that is very likely granular marble.

Anthropomorphic and Hunchback Pendants (2 complete, 7 fragmented)

Nine anthropomorphic pendants in a curvilinear style were recovered, seven of which are shown in figure 5.47. Most depict facial views (figure 5.47b–g), although full figures are also represented (figure 5.47a). Individuals are often shown wearing headdresses and earflares. One image depicts a face emerging from the jaws of an animal, possibly a serpent headdress (figure 5.47f). The full-figure image (figure 5.47a) resembles the *camahuile* figures from highland Guatemala (Ichon and Arnauld 1985:figure 21). Pendants were suspended using biconically drilled holes. Complete pendants range from 66 mm to 120 mm high, 53 mm to 94 mm wide, and 22 mm to 34 mm thick. One fragmented pendant depicts a hunched or hunchback figure.

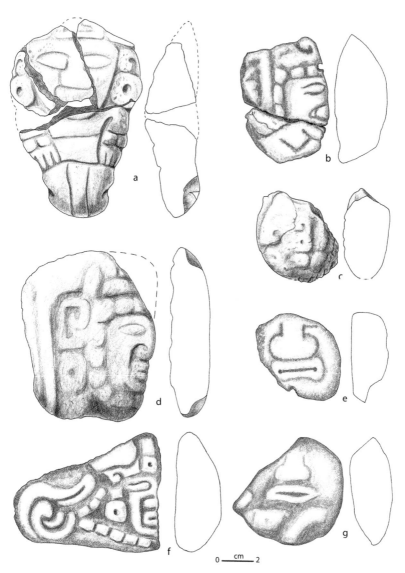

Figure 5.47. *Granular marble anthropomorphic pendants. Illustration by Anne Dowd, Cynthia Ott, and Kenneth Hirth.*

Unfinished Pendant (1 complete)

One unfinished geometric pendant was identified that was carved with scroll designs. While complete, it did not have drill holes needed for suspension. It is 89 mm long, 46 mm wide, and 35 mm thick.

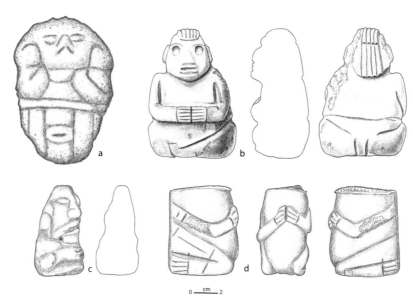

FIGURE 5.48. *Granular marble and non-jadeite human effigy figures. Illustration by Anne Dowd, Cynthia Ott, and Kenneth Hirth.*

Human Effigy Figures (2 complete, 2 fragmented)

Four human effigy figures were identified that were carved both in full-figure (figure 5.48a) and profile views (figure 5.48c). These images mimic the posture of hunched figures with their hands positioned under the chin or on their chests. They are granular marble versions of better-preserved effigy images carved from non-jadeite materials (figure 5.48b, d). Figure 5.48a was not drilled and resembles *camahuile* figures of highland Guatemala portrayed with their hands across their chests and with a pointed base (Ciudad Ruiz 1986:figure 3; Ichon and Arnauld 1985:figure 21). Complete effigies ranged from 66 mm to 117 mm high, 40 mm to 79 mm wide, and 34 mm to 38 mm thick.

Unidentifiable Pieces (54 fragmented)

While these pieces could not be associated with other granular marble artifacts in the collection, they appear to be fragments of other pendants. As a group they are 14–29 mm long and 11–28 mm wide. The disintegration of these pieces due to weathering made matching them with other pendant pieces very difficult.

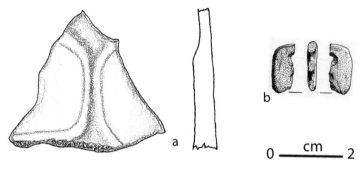

FIGURE 5.49. *Ulúa marble vase and pyrite artifact: (a) carved Ulúa marble vase, (b) pyrite artifact. Illustration by Cynthia Ott and Kenneth Hirth.*

Nodules and Flakes (6 complete, 2 fragmented)

Eight pieces of unworked granular marble were recovered alongside other materials in ritual offerings. Two of the rocks were intentionally fragmented. The other six were unmodified stones that ranged from 32 mm to 55 mm long, 30 mm to 52 mm in wide, and 18 mm to 34 mm thick.

Ulúa Marble Vase (1 fragment)

A single Ulúa marble vase fragment was recovered from Structure 121 in the West Residential Group at Salitrón Viejo (figure 5.49a). It is the only artifact in the collection that was manufactured of fine-textured white marble. The artifact displays carved circular lozenges like those found on other Ulúa marble vases. The fragment is 42 mm high, 47 mm wide, and 8 mm thick. The vase fragment was recovered from a deposit containing polychrome vessels that can be assigned to the Middle Sulaco period (AD 600–800) (Luke 2003; Luke and Tykot 2007).

OTHER ARTIFACTS (N = 339)

The variety of materials used to manufacture luxury goods was so extensive that it was unproductive to try to separate them into individual geologic categories. Instead, the rest of the different stone types were grouped into a single category of non-jadeite and non-marble artifacts. Most of these artifacts are beads, many of which were likely created in different areas of eastern Mesoamerica by artisans using varied raw materials. Although grouping these artifacts together is descriptively expedient, it has the effect of shrouding the diversity and richness of crafting traditions throughout Honduras and the variety of raw materials used in production. This is unfortunate, but there is no alternative until the geology of the region is better known and archaeological research can identify the communities where they were made. Some of the material in this composite category includes quartzite, serpentine, talc, limestone, volcanic tuff, soapstone, siltstone, sandstone, schist, diopsite, obsidian, chert, slate, pyrite, and marine shell.[15]

Plain Spheroid Beads (126 complete, 15 fragmented)

These beads range from 4 mm to 28 mm in width, with an average diameter of 13.1 mm. None of the beads were manufactured from materials with strong green colors. The majority were medium gray (86.5%), with the remainder in various tones of weak green (13.5%).

Plain Discoidal and Oblong Beads (120 complete, 3 fragmented)

One hundred fifteen complete and two fragmented discoidal beads were recovered that range from 5 mm to 13 mm in height. Five complete and one fragmented oblong bead were also recovered that were 12–30 mm in length (Ave = 20.3 mm), with an average diameter of 8.3 mm. Most of the discoidal beads (n = 109) were part of one necklace with a central plain bead pendant that was included in the Middle Sulaco cache associated with Altar 1 in the Iglesia Precinct. The beads in this necklace ranged from 5 mm to 8 mm in height and were 1 m to 4 mm thick (figure 5.50a). Beads with larger diameters (8 mm) were interspersed between small-diameter beads (5 mm) when strung together.[16] Beads this small are rare in the El Cajón collection.

Bead Pendants (7 complete, 2 fragmented)

One plain and eight carved bead pendants were identified (table 5.5). The plain bead pendant was key-shaped in form and was the central element of the necklace recovered from Altar 1. Its shape is reminiscent of stylized bead pendants from Costa Rica (see figure 5.20a), although it may also represent an animal tooth. Other bead pendants were decorated with geometric and anthropomorphic designs. Geometric bead pendants (n = 6) occur in triangular, rectangular, and hemispherical forms that are 11–23 mm high, 11–25 mm wide, and 6–17 mm thick. Decoration consists of solid drill hole indentations, circles made with tubular drills, and incised lines (figure 5.3f). Two fragmented anthropomorphic bead pendants were also recovered. Carved bead pendants are represented in equal proportions in gray and weak green colors.

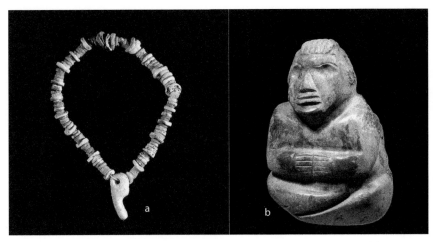

FIGURE 5.50. *Non-jadeite artifacts: (a) necklace with pendant from Altar 1, (b) human effigy figure. Photographs by Kenneth Hirth.*

Plain Pendants (3 complete, 9 fragmented)

Unadorned pendants occur in oval and round forms as well as the natural shape of the stone. Pendants are oriented in a horizontal position and are 30–86 mm wide, 30–55 mm tall, and 12–15 mm thick. All are gray or weak green in color.

Carved Zoomorphic Pendant (1 complete)

The single zoomorphic pendant is rectangular in shape, with the image carved using a combination of straight cuts. The image is highly stylized (figure 5.46e) and appears to represent an alligator or a large fish. The pendant is 129 mm long, 55 mm wide, and 40 mm thick. The pendant illustrated in figure 5.46e shows how it was broken when interred as an offering.

Human Effigy Figures (1 complete, 3 fragmented)

These figures have flat bases, which allowed them to sit upright without additional support (figure 5.48b, d). All effigies are seated with their hands positioned on their chests or stomachs. One figure is sitting in a cross-legged position (figures 5.48b, 5.50b), while another has its legs folded under the body like hunchback figures (figure 5.48d). The face of the complete effigy (figure 5.48b) was composed using straight cuts and conforms to the style of triangle face pendants. Solid drilling shaped the eyes, and straight cuts were used to leave a crest of hair on the top and back of the head. These figures appear to be three-dimensional depictions of the same images represented in hunched and hunchback pendants. Nevertheless, none of the effigies depict any form of spinal deformity. The effigy in figures 5.48b and 5.50b was shaped from a hard metamorphic stone; while it was complete, numerous small flakes were removed by impact fractures on the head and across the figure's left shoulder that may have been produced to break it when the image was interred. This effigy is 107 mm high, 75 mm wide, and 43 mm thick.

Celts (2 fragmented)

Two celts manufactured from metamorphic stone were recovered from Structures 121 and 122 in the West Group. Both were in non-ritual contexts and were olive green in color.

Unidentifiable Pieces (12 fragmented)

These fragments could not be associated with other incomplete lapidary artifacts at Salitrón Viejo. Most were pieces of plain pendants. They range from 5 mm to 38 mm long, 5 mm to 29 mm wide, and 2 mm to 15 mm thick. They are all gray (67%) and weak green (33%) in color.

Nodules and Bipolar Flakes (11 complete, 6 fragmented)

Seventeen metamorphic and other non-jadeite rocks were recovered in ritual offerings. Six of these were fractured using bipolar percussion, but there is no evidence that they were employed in lapidary production. Unbroken nodules are 18–91 mm long, 13–55 mm wide, and 10–22 mm thick. The predominant colors of these rocks were medium gray (76.9%) and olive green (23.1%).

Slate Disks (35 fragmented, 4 MAC)

Thirty-five slate fragments that came from four heavily fragmented slate disks were identified in ritual deposits. These disks were 140–160 mm in diameter and 2–6 mm thick. None of the disks were complete, and it is believed that additional fragments were deposited in contexts at the site that were not excavated. Holes were drilled around the perimeter of several of the disk fragments, which suggests that feathers or other forms of adornment were affixed to them. Red hematite and a yellow substance (pyrite?) coated the surfaces of several disks (figure 5.44b). The two jade tesserae were found in association with fragments of these disks on the west side of Structure 12, which suggests that at least one of them may have been the backing for a mosaic.

Pyrite Sequin/Mirror (1 fragmented)

A small pyrite artifact was recovered from the occupation floor of Structure 3-subD in the Iglesia Precinct. The artifact was 18 mm long, 7 mm wide, and

a   b

FIGURE 5.51. *Lithic bifacial eccentrics: (a) sinuous biface of green obsidian, (b) hooked chert biface. Photograph by Kenneth Hirth.*

4 mm thick (figure 5.49b). Two holes were drilled in the center of the artifact, which suggests that it was a sequin or small mirror that was sewn on clothing before it broke.

Obsidian and Chalcedony Bifacial Eccentrics (3 fragmented)

Two obsidian eccentrics were recovered in the Acropolis platform. While the two pieces did not refit, they are segments of large sinuous bifaces. Most significant, both bifaces were manufactured of green obsidian from the Sierra de las Navajas source in Central Mexico. The largest sinuous blade was 164 mm long and 10 mm thick (figure 5.51a). The other segment was 38 mm long and 19 mm thick. The form of the eccentrics, the source from which they came, and the presence of transverse-parallel pressure flaking indicate that they are trade pieces from Central Mexico (Spence 1996). Transverse-parallel pressure flaking is a highland technology and is not found on eccentric bifaces in the Maya area. They are identical in form to sinuous bifaces representing lightning or serpent figures recovered at Teotihuacan (Pastrana and Hruby n.d.; Serra Puche and Solís Olguín 1994:108–109, 117). The chalcedony biface (figure 5.51b) was in the form of a hook that is 40 mm long, 23 mm wide, and 8 mm thick.

Obsidian and Chalcedony Nodules and Flakes (6 nodules, 4 flakes)

Obsidian occurs in many domestic contexts, and one obsidian flake was included in one cluster cache in the Acropolis platform. Likewise, nine chalcedony artifacts were also recovered from the Acropolis platform[17] that included three complete flakes and six fragmented nodules broken into pieces by direct percussion. The six calcedony nodules were recovered from a cache at Structure 40 in the North Precinct. All of the calcedony items were manufactured from olive green and pale yellow-green stone.

SUMMARY

The El Cajón lapidary assemblage provides a unique opportunity to examine the diversity of artisanal and technological style as well as the themes reproduced in high-value goods circulating throughout eastern Mesoamerica over a short period of time. The vast majority of the assemblage dates to the end of the Late Yunque period, when large numbers of jade, marble, and other precious items were deposited in dedication rituals associated with the completion of the Acropolis platform. Radiocarbon dating has assigned the greatest amount of these materials to between cal AD 238 and 352 (see table 4.1) during Stages 4 and 5 of the Iglesia Precinct construction sequence (see chapters 4 and 6). This places the collection at the interface between the Proto-Classic and Early Classic periods in the Maya chronology, coincident with the Bijac phase occupation at Copán (Fash 2001:64). As such, it provides valuable information on the high-value goods circulating between areas of eastern Mesoamerica at this time. It also provides an opportunity to critique what has been said about jade carving style in eastern Mesoamerica.

A number of scholars have discussed aspects of the eastern Mesoamerican jade carving style during the Late Preclassic and Early Classic periods (Digby 1972; Easby 1961:77, 1992; Proskouriakoff 1974:12; Rands 1965:575; Taube and Ishihara-Brito 2012). While valuable, most of this discussion has focused on artifacts excavated at sites in the Maya region or curated in museum collections. This presents something of a conundrum for this study, for two reasons. First, while the El Cajón collection is contemporaneous with materials used in other studies of Mesoamerican jade carving, it is clearly outside the Maya region. The societies in west-central Honduras were organized very differently than the more hierarchical Maya, and one has to question whether the same thematic issues concerning rank and ruler aggrandizement would be reflected in their use of jade regalia. While a few jade carvings were produced in Maya style (figures 5.32a, c–d), they are rarer than might be expected given the importance of Mayan groups at Copán, the distances over which jade was traded, and the proximity of the Motagua valley jade deposits for many of the artifacts manufactured.

Second, the size of the collection far exceeds that reported from most other sites in eastern Mesoamerica[18]; when examined from a holistic perspective, this suggests the existence of several contemporaneous and independent jade carving traditions at this time. Some of the items in the El Cajón collections have not been reported in large quantities from Maya sites. Others reflect different ideological themes and a range of techniques used to produce them (Hirth and Hirth 1993). Whether this will be confirmed through future archaeological excavations in Honduras remains to be seen, but it appears that the production of jade artifacts associated with the Maya style was a very localized activity. Research in the Motagua valley (Rochette 2009a, 2009b) as well as at Cancuen (Andrieu, Rodas, and Luin 2014; Kovacevich and Callaghan 2019) and Copán (Widmer 2009) reveals that the manufacture of jade artifacts was a segmented production process. Beads and earflares were roughed out by commoner artisans in workshop locales and then exchanged or gifted to other centers where carvings were finished, with artisans adding site-specific iconography that met the ideology of local elites. Under these conditions, a considerable degree of variation can be expected in the stylistic execution of Maya pieces.

The El Cajón materials are interpreted here following a communities of practice approach (Abell 2020; Wenger 1998, 2011). A community of practice is "a collection of people who engage on an ongoing basis in some common endeavor" (Eckert 2006:683). A community of lapidary practice would represent a community of artisans who learn how to manufacture items through the process of generational learning and interaction with older skilled artisans. The knowledge, skill, and ability of artisans are referred to as *techné* (Costin 2016) and in pre-Columbian settings were learned at the elbow of kinsmen and other individuals who practiced their craft. In Mesoamerica, crafting was most often carried out within the household, with skills and abilities passed down from parents to children (Hirth 2009a, 2016). This was especially the case for the production of luxury goods like lapidary items, where production took a long time (cf. Luke, Tykot, and Scott 2006; Reents-Budet 1998) and where jade objects might very well have been finished by the elite who used them (Berdan and Anawalt 1997:230; Brumfiel 2008).

Under these conditions, a community of lapidary practice should reflect several characteristics. First, artisans would use raw materials that were locally and readily available; when they were not, they would reduce the number of stone sources used to minimize the effort expended in procurement (Clark and Parry 1990; Hirth 2008). This is reflected at Cancuen by the narrow range of color in raw material entering its jade workshop (Andrieu, Rodas, and Luin 2014:table 4). Second, because artisans made their own tools, they would have employed technologies appropriate for working the raw material used, and best practices would have been learned and shared across the community. Third, style and themes of expression were also learned, with the maintenance of tradition more important than innovation, especially regarding themes dealing with the sacred.

Diversity in raw material usage, the technology employed, and artistic themes expressed is *not* what would be expected within a single community of artisans producing lapidary goods with a high symbolic loading. Maintenance of stylistic tradition is often a priority in crafting communities, and individuals who deviate from established norms often suffer social discrimination (Reina 1963; Reina and Hill 1978). High levels of diversity would not be expected in a consumer site like Salitrón Viejo if the community got all of its finished lapidary goods from a single region or community that followed a unified tradition of production. Instead, vectors of diversity are evident in the El Cajón collection, which are discussed below. Identifying patterns of diversity is the first step in determining whether artisans with different carving traditions supplied the high-value goods obtained by the residents of Salitrón Viejo.

Raw material diversity is perhaps the easiest dimension of variation to identify. Motagua valley jade, micaceous jade, and granular marble were the three primary materials used, along with a miscellanea of non-jadeite lithics that included talc, serpentine, quartz, and other materials. The Motagua valley jade source lies approximately 180 km west of the El Cajón region and represents just over 70 percent of the lapidary items recovered (tables 5.1, 5.5). The exact source of micaceous jade remains unknown, and while mica inclusions have been reported in materials in the Motagua valley (Taube and Ishihara-Brito 2012), the unique bead pendants carved from this material have not—reinforcing our belief that the artisans using it may represent a distinct and localized carving community (see technology discussion below).

Marble is naturally available throughout Honduras, and fine marble deposits in the Ulúa valley were used to produce the widely traded Ulúa marble vases (Luke et al. 2003; Stone 1938). But that is not the granular marble represented in the El Cajón collection, which can deteriorate from weathering to the point of making artifact identification difficult. We suspect that the source for this material was the Montaña de Comayagua located 60 km south of Salitrón Viejo, where marble deposits laced with veins of malachite and azurite crystals occur (Fakundiny 1970:166, 190) (e.g., figure 5.43a). The location of other utilized stone resources remains unclear, although the presence of a few beads manufactured from talc is interesting because a source of green talc was identified along the Tulito River in northeastern Honduras (Begley 1999:175). Even if this source was not used for the talc beads in the El Cajón collection, it reflects the existence and operation of a separate lapidary tradition, since talc artifacts are reported throughout eastern Honduras and the Bay Islands (Strong 1935:62, 148).

Technology is a second dimension of *techné* shared in a community of artisanal practice. The technology employed in crafting is always matched to the raw material artisans used. A range of different drilling techniques was noted in the collection that included using tubular and solid drills and the differential use of single or paired perforations to suspend lapidary ornaments. Two completely different manufacturing technologies were used in shaping conical and tubular flares, which reflect very distinct communities of lapidary practice. Conical flares (figures 5.14a–d, 5.15, 5.16) were shaped using percussion flaking followed by heavy pecking to shape the flare. Flares were then biconically drilled from either side to produce the hole passing through the stem before grinding and final polishing. These flares were left robust, since excessive thinning would lead to breakage as percussion flake scars were removed by pecking.

A very different production sequence was used in the manufacture of the more gracile tubular stemmed and tapered earflares (figures 5.14e–f, 5.17). For these flares, a preform was prepared that combined sawing with tubular drilling. The back of the flare was shaped by lateral cuts to form a round or square stem. Illustrations of this manufacturing process are available in several publications that model creating a gracile earflare with a notable T-shaped profile (Andrieu, Rodas, and Luin 2014:figure 7; Digby 1972:figure 4).

While variation in production steps is possible, the processes of manufacturing tubular and conical flares were strikingly different. From a technological perspective, they employ very different production strategies, with conical flares more closely aligned with the manufacture of ground stone celts than with the sawn and polished tubular earflares. The few earflares manufactured from granular marble in the collection also used conical drilling to create the passage hole through the flare. The size and weight of conical flares made from jade make it unlikely that they were worn as ear ornaments. Nonetheless, in 1502, during Columbus's fourth exploration trip, the north coast of Honduras beyond Trujillo was called the "Costa de las Orejas" because the people encountered there had such heavily pierced ears that an object the size of a chicken egg could be placed in the ear lobe (Lara-Pinto 1980:45). The twenty-one complete conical flares in the collection range from 135 g to 549 g in weight,[19] compared to T-shaped tubular earflares, the largest of which did not exceed 90 g.[20] It was the weight of conical flares that led Alfred Kidder and colleagues (1946:125) to suggest that they were used to adorn idols, while Adrian Digby (1972:17) believes they were belt ornaments. While conical and tubular flares resemble one another somewhat in form, their manufacture represents two different and independent lapidary production traditions with different end usages.

Diversity in style is a third attribute that can be reflected in different communities of artisanal practice. The Early Classic jade carving style has been characterized by pieces that (1) were shaped to the outline of the original stone, (2) were low relief carvings that cut away the edges of the stone, (3) had uneven surfaces that followed the green color of the stone, (4) were thick with smooth, rounded backs, and (5) depicted human portraits organized using a T-shaped structure to the central face and nose (Digby 1972; Proskouriakoff 1974:12; Rands 1965:575–576). These characterizations are insightful, but they assume the existence of a single unified style, even in the face of considerable variability in themes and forms of expression. Robert Rands (1965:577) observed that regional schools of jade working would be difficult to define because of jade's importance and the role long-distance trade played in its procurement and movement. Nevertheless, several dimensions of stylistic variability can be observed that suggest the coexistence of multiple communities of lapidary practice in eastern Mesoamerica during the Proto-Classic and Early Classic periods.

The human countenance was an important feature of early Maya jade carvings. Head pendants were important costume elements of high-ranking individuals depicted on Maya monumental art, and human representations make up the majority of the identifiable images in the Maya jades recovered from Chichen Itzá (Proskouriakoff 1974). While a great deal can be said about the subtleties of the way eyes and mouths were formed in individual carvings, two main differences can be identified in how human portraits were rendered in the El Cajón collection. Two separate carving styles were represented in the curvilinear and triangle face compositional styles described above.

The curvilinear style is represented in both bead pendants and normal pendants. As the name suggests, curvilinear incised lines were used to create realistic images. Human faces were rendered with lozenge-shaped eyes, rounded noses, and coffee bean–shaped mouths fashioned with horizontal slits and occasional drill holes at their corners. Headdress and hair elements can be present and a number of examples depict earflares, which reinforces the impression that they portray high-ranking individuals (figures 5.29b–e, 5.30a–d, 5.47a, c–d, f). A curvilinear carving style is used to depict the greater array of hunched and hunchback images (figures 5.25–5.28) as well as zoomorphic pendants and bead pendants (figures 5.22, 5.23).

The triangular style is different in that it relied on linear cuts to shape the central elements of the face. Two diverging diagonal lines were used on frontal portraits to define the nose and the sides of the mouth (figures 5.8d–i, 5.33a–b). Profile heads used a single diagonal line to define this same area (figure 5.8a–c, k). Eyes were rendered using small tubular drills, and mouths were formed by one or more horizontal lines. What is lacking on these carvings are depictions of headdresses. Most of the figures are bare-headed, earflares are rare, and when hair is implied, it is usually illustrated by straight incisions that form a central crest along the top of the head (figures 5.8d–f, 5.9a–b, 5.48b). Like the curvilinear style, the triangle face format can also occasionally be found on zoomorphic carvings.

It could be argued that the difference between the curvilinear and triangle styles was a matter of artistic ability rather than different carving traditions. This argument is not convincing, since several of the best curvilinear hunchback carvings in the collection also incorporate the triangle format to define the side of the face (figures 5.25d, 5.26d). The triangular style occurs early and has been recovered in Late Preclassic contexts at Cerros, Belize (Garber 1983:figure 2) and is strongly represented in the *camahuile* effigy figures found across highland Guatemala (Ichon 1989; Orellana 1981:158–159; Wauchope 1948:127). Artisans usually worked in small groups, and there were often strong forces mediating against change in styles (e.g., Reina 1963). The diversity in styles suggests that many crafting communities were involved in the creation of lapidary goods at Salitrón Viejo. The argument that different lapidary traditions were the source of the variability observed in carving styles is supported by the absence of the triangular facial portrait in granular marble carvings (figures 5.45, 5.47, 5.48a, c).

Stylistic diversity is also evident in several artifact categories that have not been reported previously in other areas of Mesoamerica. One such group is the zoomorphic bead pendants manufactured from micaceous jade (figures 5.39–5.42). No artifacts in this style have been reported from the Maya area to the west or from sites in lower Central America. Yet at Salitrón Viejo, these artifacts are both numerous and stylistically consistent. What is particularly notable from a community of practice perspective is that these carvings do not occur in Motagua valley jade, in granular marble, or in other non-jadeite materials. They only occur in micaceous jade, where they were probably manufactured by the small group of artisans that only used this material.

Crescent pectorals are another unique and stylistically rare class of lapidary artifacts. These pendants resemble the iconic nose ornaments referred to as *narigueras de mariposa* associated with Teotihuacan culture (figures 5.34–5.37). In addition to their form, this class is technologically distinct from most of other artifacts in the collection as the pendants were shaped from sawn slabs, a practice that was more common during the Late Classic period. Another feature unique to crescent pectorals was the use of tubular drilling to create circular decorative elements (figure 5.35) and facial features (figure 5.36). Most crescent pectorals were manufactured from gray Motagua valley jade and were not imitated in any other material. These artifacts did not circulate widely, and related items have only been identified at two sites: two plain crescent pectorals were found at Kaminaljuyú (Kidder, Jennings, and Shook 1946:figure 146k, l) and another, together with sawn plaques with tubular drill decoration, were recovered from the Cenote at Chichen Itzá (Proskouriakoff 1974:plates 50a4, 51b2). A third possible fragment is illustrated without provenance from Los Naranjos, Honduras (Baudez and Becquelin 1973:figure 146e).

Several distinctive and recognizable styles were identified in the collection. Four Olmec-style clam shell plaques (figure 5.38) were recovered that are probably legacy pieces, carved during the Middle Formative period and procured through trade. The few carvings that are stylistically Maya were obtained from workshops schooled in that style or produced for that population (figures 5.32, 5.45b, 5.47c). No pieces of clear Costa Rican derivation were identified, although one geometric pendant (figure 5.20a) bears some resemblance in form to avian pendants from the region (Canouts and Guerrero 1988:plate 32).

Finally, it is interesting that some of the same themes, images, and iconographic content are depicted in similar and different ways in distinct lapidary media. The most prominent and persistent image is that of the hunched or hunchback figure. These images constitute 11.9 percent of all the carved images in the collection (table 5.6). They are portrayed as profile figures in pendants manufactured of Motagua jade (figures 5.25–5.28), as bead pendants and sculptures in granular marble (figures 5.45a, c–d; 5.48c), and as sculpture in other non-jadeite materials (figure 5.48b, d).[21] They occur in a crouched or sitting position, with their hands under their chins or across their bellies. Costume is limited to a breechcloth, ear ornaments, and sometimes a cap on the head.[22] When depicted as an effigy sculpture, they display a crest of hair down the center of their head in what is often called a Mohawk haircut (Miller 1985). Mary Butler (1935:644) observed almost ninety years ago that the hunchback figure with these characteristics was an important element in Native American spiritual beliefs that stretched from Tennessee to Costa Rica. Hunched or hunchback pendants in jade have been recovered from the Yucatan Peninsula to Costa Rica (Stone 1977b:figure 78a), and jade was clearly a potent component of the belief system of Late Formative and Early Classic groups across this region.

Beads, bead pendants, earflares, and pendants were manufactured in most raw materials in the collection.[23] Earflares were primarily manufactured in jade, although they are also found in reduced numbers in both micaceous jade and granular marble. Earflares were closely associated with rank in the Maya area, so it is not surprising that many of the earflares in the collection were fashioned from Motagua valley jade in strong green hues. The fact that there

TABLE 5.6. Thematic representations in the El Cajón lapidary assemblage

Category	MAC[a]	Percent
Geometric	109	30.9
Zoomorphic	119	33.9
Hunchback	42	11.9
Anthropomorphic	82	23.3
Total	352	100.0

a. Minimum artifact counts

are proportionately fewer earflares in granular marble compared to plain and decorated pendants was likely a result of the structural characteristics of the marble used to create them.[24]

Finally, the images depicted provide a glimpse of the emic themes important in the people's spiritual life. An examination of lapidary goods from the Cenote at Chichen Itzá (Proskouriakoff 1974) reveals that anthropomorphic figures were the dominant image represented in lapidary carvings compared to zoomorphic ones. Of the more than 400 zoomorphic and anthropomorphic images illustrated in the Cenote catalog, 85 percent are human images.[25] This makes sense, given the importance placed on rank and status in Maya society. A total of 352 carved images were identified in the El Cajón collection, which are summarized in table 5.6. These images are not heavily anthropocentric but are divided evenly among anthropomorphic, zoomorphic, and geometric motifs. Anthropomorphic carvings together with hunchback imagery represent 35.2 percent of the assemblage (n = 124) compared to zoomorphic carvings (n = 119) at 33.9 percent (table 5.6). When hunched and hunchback figures are separated because of their possible association with spirit beings, the anthropomorphic imagery declines to 23.3 percent. These differences suggest that human portraits displaying rank and status were not as important in west-central Honduras as they were in the Maya region further to the west. The reason for this may have been a greater emphasis on animistic beliefs focused on protective animal spirits, a topic that is discussed in chapter 8.

If diversity is the spice of life, then the El Cajón lapidary assemblage is very spicy. But despite the variation in raw materials, lapidary techniques, and stylistic themes, there is consistency in the ways high-value goods were used in the El Cajón chiefdom. Three salient behavioral patterns are evident. First, most of all the high-value lapidary goods entering the El Cajón region were intended for ritual use. While they were manufactured as objects of personal adornment, they may not have been widely used for that purpose since they are not associated with individuals in mortuary contexts. Second, their use is closely associated with the construction and dedication of ceremonial space. Third and finally, their use as ritual offerings often resulted in the intentional destruction or desecration of the objects themselves. All three of these behaviors, together with where they were located within Salitrón Viejo, are discussed in chapter 6.

6

In the pre-Columbian world, items manufactured of jade and marble had high social, economic, and symbolic significance. Beads, earflares, and pendants were used for personal adornment to distinguish individuals of high rank who are portrayed on stelae, on bas-relief carvings, in murals, and on ceramic vessels. The materials discussed in chapter 5 describe the high-value items used in the social and ritual life of Salitrón Viejo. What is remarkable about these materials is not only the size of the collection but the fact that they were recovered from in situ contexts that provide insight about their usage in Honduran society.

More than 2,559 of the 2,881 items recovered at Salitrón Viejo were finely finished jade and marble artifacts (see table 5.1). Larger collections of jade artifacts have been recovered from the Aztec Templo Mayor in Tenochtitlan (Lopéz Lujan 2005) and the Cenote at Chichen Itzá (Proskouriakoff 1974). But both of these collections are from the capitals of large state-level societies. What is striking about the El Cajón materials is that a large quantity of valued status markers was accumulated by a small community the size of Salitrón Viejo. In this regard, the deposits are more in line with the offering recovered at Blue Creek, Belize, where over a thousand pieces of jade were associated with a mortuary interment dating to AD 500 (Guderjan 1998). Salitrón Viejo at the height of its development had somewhere between 1,000 and 1,600 persons, depending on how house mound counts

The Patterning of Ritual Deposits at Salitrón Viejo

https://doi.org/10.5876/9781646424757.c006

are converted to population estimates (Hirth n.d.). This was an extraordinary accumulation of wealth goods for a site that had only 150–200 households and a population under 1,000 persons when they were assembled during the Late Yunque phase.[1] No evidence was found at Salitrón Viejo for on-site production of these goods. Instead, all of these items were obtained through trade.

This chapter examines the usage patterns of high-value goods at Salitrón Viejo and has two objectives. It begins by identifying the depositional contexts in which wealth goods were recovered in each of the four areas of Salitrón: the Iglesia and North Precincts and the West and South Residential Groups. This is followed by an examination of how these goods were deposited, either as isolated occurrences or as clusters of items within these areas. These depositional patterns provide insight into how goods were used and what they imply about ritual behavior in the settings in which that behavior was practiced. As discussed below, the majority of the high-value materials recovered at Salitrón (86.3%) were from the Iglesia Precinct (n = 2,487). The construction of the Acropolis platform distinguished this area as the region's central civic-ceremonial precinct. To facilitate discussion, the Iglesia Precinct is subdivided into its eastern and western divisions and those materials associated with the construction of the Acropolis platform (table 6.1).

THE WESTERN IGLESIA PRECINCT

This area includes the structures located in Plaza One as well as those on the western margins of the Central Plaza that were subsequently buried by the construction of the Acropolis platform. Five structures were in this area: Structures 1–3, 12, and 395. The materials associated with these structures were recovered as individual pieces and caches of artifacts in contexts that included (1) surfaces underneath structures, (2) pieces within the construction fill, (3) pieces on pedestrian surfaces of plazas and around structures before they were covered by the Acropolis platform, (4) items associated with burials in Structures 3-subB and 3-subC, and (5) as a termination offering on the summit of Structure 12.

STRUCTURE 1

A total of 213 artifacts were recovered from this structure (table 6.1). One bead and a jade fragment were recovered from the Stage 4 construction fill of Structure 1-subA. Most of the materials from this structure (n = 183) were recovered in 15 artifact clusters from its final Stage 5 construction episode.[2]

TABLE 6.1. Summary of ritual artifacts in the Iglesia and North Precincts

Site Area	Jade	Granular Marble	Obsidian and Chert	Other Semi-Precious	Total
WESTERN IGLESIA PRECINCT					
Structure 1	115	85	—	13	213
Structure 2	3	—	—	3	6
Structure 3	129	68	—	15	212
Structure 12	247	25	—	7	279
Structure 395	4	—	—	2	6
ACROPOLIS PLATFORM					
East platform: Stages 3–4	2	—	—	2	4
West platform: Stage 4	125	—	—	2	127
Acropolis platform: Stage 5 Primary Offering	1,167	16	7	114	1,304
Acropolis platform: Stage 5	7	—	—	1	8
Acropolis platform: Stages 3–5	151	11	—	4	166
EASTERN IGLESIA PRECINCT					
Structure 8	2	—	—	—	2
Structure 9	3	10	—	1	14
Structure 21	3	—	—	—	3
Plaza 2	2	—	—	—	2
Plaza 2–Altar 1	21	3	—	116	140
East Courtyard	1	—	—	—	1
Subtotal Iglesia Precinct	1,982	218	7	280	2,487
NORTH PRECINCT					
Structures 29 and 30	3	—	—	—	3
Structure 37	1	—	—	—	1
Structure 38	160	65	—	9	234
Structure 40	52	2	6	7	67
Structures 44 and 45	3	—	—	—	3
Plaza deposit	36	3	—	2	41
Subtotal North Precinct	255	70	6	18	349
Total Artifacts	2,237	288	13	298	2,836

These clusters contained from 6 to 34 artifacts that were deposited beneath the floor on the east side of the structure (figures 6.1, 6.2). Twelve additional artifacts were recovered from fill that had been dislodged from clusters on the northeast side of the structure, while an additional 16 artifacts were recovered from the mixed terminal debris eroding off its summit. While the artifact composition of these clusters varied, it is interesting that 7 of the 15 clusters had one or two unmodified jade or granular marble nodules included in artifact caches. Although the majority of beads and bead pendants were complete (85.2%), most of the other artifacts from this structure were intentionally broken when they were deposited (81.1%).

Two aspects of the artifacts from Mound 1 are noteworthy. First, while beads are the most common artifact recovered in ritual deposits at Salitrón Viejo (see table 5.5, 40.5%), they were not the predominant offerings in this structure. Instead, there was a preference for plain pendants (n = 77) over beads (n = 45). Second, a high percentage of the artifacts recovered (39.3%) were granular marble. This is notable because these materials represent almost one-third (29.3%) of all the granular marble artifacts recovered at the site. Portions of a slate disk[3] were recovered from the Stage 5 construction that conjoined with pieces recovered from the western pedestrian surface of Structure 12.

STRUCTURE 2

Six jade artifacts were recovered from limited excavations at this structure that could be divided into early (n = 2) and late (n = 4) occupation episodes. All of the artifacts were fragments and occurred as individual finds embedded in the structure's earthen floor. Structure 2 is believed to have been used for preparing food for feasts, and it is possible that these artifacts were deposited in the floor of the structure as part of feast preparation or celebration activities.

STRUCTURE 3

The importance of this structure is reflected by the 212 artifacts recovered as offerings from its five construction episodes (table 6.1). Jade constitutes most of the offerings (60.8%) from this structure, followed by granular marble (32.1%) (table 6.1). The largest number of items was incorporated into its Stage 4 expansion when the Western Acropolis platform was constructed and attached to its east side.

The initial (Stage 1) construction of Structure 3-subA during the Early Yunque phase was a low cobble and earthen platform 90 cm high. The only

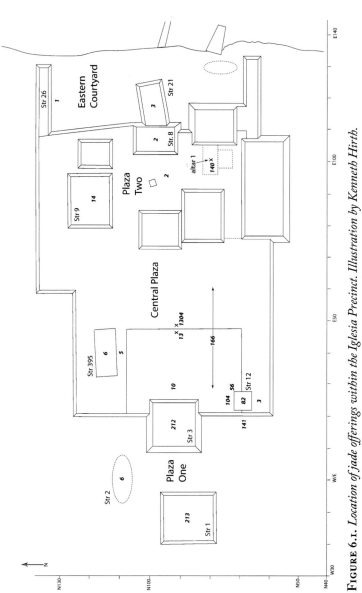

Figure 6.1. *Location of jade offerings within the Iglesia Precinct. Illustration by Kenneth Hirth.*

FIGURE 6.2. *Cache of jade earflares and pendants in the Stage 5 construction on the summit of Structure 1. Photograph by Kenneth Robinson.*

associated offerings with this structure were two jade beads that were incorporated in platform fill. Two burials (1-16, 1-17) were placed in the structure during its Stage 2 expansion, both of which had mortuary offerings of ceramic- and stucco-covered vessels but only one bead in each (see figures 4.6, 4.7). Ten jade artifacts were recovered from the Stage 2 construction fill, six as individual pieces and four others in a single cluster (#2136) containing pieces of two earflares and two pendants. The structure was raised 1.05 m in height in two building episodes (3-subD, 3-subE) during Stage 3, and the only artifact associated with this stage was a pyrite sequin recovered from the floor of 3-subE (figure 5.49b).

A total of 188 artifacts were associated with the expansion of Structures 3-subF and 3-subG during Stage 4; 124 were recovered from the structure's construction matrix and 64 from redeposited fill from this stage. Pendants and earflares were the dominant items, while beads were relatively rare. Eleven small artifact clusters associated with the 3-subG construction episode were located on the east side of the structure where they overlooked the Western Acropolis platform.[4] These eleven clusters represent a unique offering event, with granular marble artifacts constituting 82.9 percent (n = 34) of their 41 artifacts. Eleven jade pendants and earflare artifacts were recovered from redeposited construction fill from Stage 5.

STRUCTURE 12

Structure 12 was a small platform 6.15 m long (N–S), 5.25 m wide (E–W), and 2.15 m tall. For its size, it has the highest quantity of offerings (n = 279) recovered from any structure in the Iglesia Precinct. Offerings were recovered from four contexts: (1) from the structure's interior fill, (2) in deposits from its northern pedestrian surface covered during Stage 4 by the Western Acropolis platform, (3) from a termination ritual on its summit, and (4) in offerings on the west side of the structure deposited when Structure 12 was completely covered during Stage 5.

Structure 12 was constructed in two phases. A single jade bead was deposited under the stone pavement of Structure 12-subA during its Stage 2 construction. An additional thirteen artifacts were incorporated in the fill of the Stage 3 *talud-tablero* structure. Nine pieces were scattered throughout the structure's earthen fill, while three earflares and a jade bead were positioned between the cobbles that formed the exterior corners of the structure. The Western Acropolis platform engulfed the structure during Stage 4 and completely covered it in Stage 5. A ritual deposit of 68 artifacts was identified on the structure's summit; it appears to be a termination ritual dating to Stage 4. Sixty-five of these artifacts were deposited in a cluster at the structure's center, which primarily contained tubular earflares (n = 28) and non-matching

FIGURE 6.3. *Five clusters of artifacts deposited during Stage 5 on the west side of Structure 12. Photograph by Paul Webb.*

earflare fragments (n = 22). All of the artifacts were intentionally broken except for one tubular earflare located at the center of the deposit.

Another set of offerings containing fifty-six artifacts was recovered from the pedestrian surface on the north (n = 40) and northeast (n = 16) sides of Structure 12. All of these artifacts except for two beads and one zoomorphic pendant were intentionally broken. Thirty-one of these artifacts were recovered in three distinct caches along the base of the structure's north wall. Seven other artifacts were recovered from a fourth cache offering on the northeast side of the structure. It is likely that all of these materials were deposited as termination offerings when the Western Acropolis platform covered the north and northeast sides of Structure 12 during Stage 4.

A final set of 141 artifacts was recovered from the pedestrian surface on the west side of Structure 12 (figures 6.1, 6.3). One hundred and thirty-five items (95.7%) were recovered in ten discrete artifact clusters deposited in small pits dug into the western pedestrian surface.[5] These clusters contained from 5 to 29 objects and included a range of artifact types, with plain and ring pendants (33.3%) the most frequent. These deposits are more difficult to date because they were not associated with architectural construction episodes. Nevertheless, the recovery of fragments from three slate disks matches those found on the summit of Structure 1, which dates them to Stage 5 contemporaneous with the completion of the Acropolis platform. Like Structure 1, these deposits contained larger quantities of granular marble artifacts (n = 22, 15.6%) compared to other offerings associated with Structure 12.[6]

STRUCTURE 395

This structure was located at the northwest corner of the Iglesia Precinct bordering the Central Plaza. Five lapidary artifacts (three beads, a plain jade pendant, and a small carved fragment) were recovered from its Stage 3 construction (Structure 395-subA). A single plain jade pendant was recovered from the structure's Stage 4 construction fill.

THE ACROPOLIS PLATFORM

The Acropolis platform was the central architectural feature in the Iglesia Precinct and required a considerable amount of labor and material to build. Offerings were also used to sanctify new constructions and to de-sanctify structures that were buried in its fill. These offerings were not evenly spread throughout the Acropolis construction. Instead, the vast majority were concentrated in the Western Acropolis platform within the Central Plaza, which was the Iglesia's general assembly area.

The Acropolis platform was built in three episodes. The Eastern Acropolis platform was constructed during Stages 3 and 4, the Western Acropolis platform was built during Stage 4, and the two areas were merged into one platform during Stage 5. The recovery of artifacts by sector and stage is summarized in table 6.1. A total of 1,609 high-value items were recovered from deposits in the Acropolis platform. Many of these artifacts were intentionally broken when they were deposited either as isolates or clusters of items included in construction fill.

The Eastern Acropolis platform was initiated in Stage 3 (see figure 4.10), and only one fragmented earflare was associated with its construction. The platform was expanded 15 m to the west during Stage 4, when two beads and one jade pendant fragment were incorporated into its fill.

The vast majority of offerings were recovered from the western half of the Iglesia Precinct.[7] The Western Acropolis platform was constructed during Stage 4, covering the Central Plaza and partially burying Structure 12 and its northern pedestrian surface. Offerings were incorporated into its construction matrix in various places. One hundred and four artifacts were recovered in its fill immediately alongside Structure 12. Twenty-two artifacts were scattered

Figure 6.4. *Bead offering caches in the central Stage 5 offering in the Acropolis platform. Photograph by Kenneth Hirth.*

throughout the platform matrix,[8] while 82 others were grouped in eleven distinct cluster caches placed between cobbles within the fill.[9] Most of these artifacts were conical and tubular flares (n = 46) and unmatched earflare fragments (n = 31). All but 5 of these 104 artifacts were intentionally fragmented when deposited.[10] Ten jade artifacts were distributed as isolated pieces in platform fill around Structure 3. Finally, 13 jade artifacts were placed in the fill along the east-to-west centerline immediately behind the platform's east wall (figure 6.1). The 13 jade artifacts in this offering included 6 fragmented earflares, 4 plain pendants, 2 ring pendants, and 1 bead.

The Acropolis platform was completed during Stage 5 by filling in the area between the Eastern and Western Acropolis platforms and expanding its north and south sides. In the process, both Structures 12 and 395 were covered and not rebuilt. Completion of the Acropolis platform was certainly a great event and would have been commemorated with feasts and celebrations by community members and individuals from throughout the region. The importance of its completion and dedication as a ritual space is reflected in the quantity of offerings recovered from the Stage 5 construction.

The largest single group of offerings in the Iglesia Precinct dates to Stage 5. It was placed along the east–west centerline against the exterior wall of the Western Acropolis platform and immediately opposite the earlier Stage 4

Figure 6.5. *Two crescent pectorals and a jade cache in the central Stage 5 offering in the Acropolis platform. Photograph by Kenneth Hirth.*

offering. This offering was made as the final act of completing the Acropolis platform. A total of 1,304 artifacts were deposited as individual artifacts and cluster offerings placed within the cobble fill of the Acropolis platform.[11] Forty cluster caches containing 1,165 artifacts were included in this offering (figure 6.1).[12] The cobble fill of the Acropolis provided a good matrix for these cache offerings, with groups of artifacts placed in the spaces between cobbles (figures 6.4, 6.5). In this way, offerings were stacked up from the base of the wall to within 15 cm of the platform's upper surface. An additional 139 artifacts were recovered as isolates or dislodged artifacts in the fill around these clusters.

In addition to its large size, this offering contained a higher percentage of jade objects than other areas of the Iglesia Precinct. Fully 89.5 percent of

Figure 6.6. *Earflare offering in the central Stage 5 offering in the Acropolis platform. Photograph by Kenneth Hirth.*

the artifacts were jade and micaceous jade, while only 1 percent were manufactured from granular marble (n = 16, 1.2%). The preference for jade in these offerings reflects the importance of the Central Plaza in the Iglesia Precinct.

The quality and diversity of artifacts in this deposit were also very high. Some of the best carved pendants (e.g., hunchback, zoomorphic) in both Maya and non-Maya style were recovered here (see, e.g., figures 5.5a, 5.25, 5.26, 5.29, 5.32). Most of the crescent and ring pendants (see figures 5.19, 5.34–5.36) were found in this deposit, along with 53 conical flare fragments, 83 tubular earflare fragments, and 41 non-matching earflare fragments (figure 6.6). All three of the eccentric bifaces (one chert, two obsidian) occur in this deposit (see figure 5.51). Some artifact classes were handled differently here than in other places in the Iglesia Precinct. Fully 95.5 percent of the 916 beads and bead pendants were unbroken compared to the other artifact classes. Whether this was due to bead robusticity is unclear, but differential breakage patterns are evident, with 90.4 percent of earflares intentionally fragmented in this deposit.

Smaller amounts of jade were deposited in other areas of the Stage 5 Acropolis construction. Three jade artifacts were included in the fill along the south side of Structure 12. Likewise, five lapidary objects were recovered in the construction fill on the platform's north side, four of which were in the corridor that separated Structure 395 from the Western Acropolis platform. Final salvage operations conducted prior to reservoir flooding recovered an additional 166 lapidary items from the preconstruction surfaces underneath Structure 12 and the Western Acropolis platform.[13] Clearly, a great deal of effort and accumulated wealth went into preparing the offerings associated with the completion of the Acropolis platform.

THE EASTERN IGLESIA PRECINCT

The offerings in this area were associated with structures in Plaza Two and the East Courtyard. High-value goods were not abundant compared to the west end of the Iglesia Precinct and were only recovered from Structures 8, 9, 21, and Altar 1. Items were recovered both as individual and clusters of artifacts, with the largest offering associated with Altar 1 at the south end of Plaza Two.

STRUCTURES 8 AND 9

Structure 8 is located on the east side of Plaza Two, where a jade pendant and earflare were recovered from mound fill when the structure was rebuilt to its final form during Stage 4. Structure 9 is the tallest structure in Plaza Two. Fourteen artifacts were recovered here that were associated with the last two episodes of Stage 6 construction. One fragmented jade pendant was recovered from the floor of Structure 9-subC. The remaining thirteen jade and marble artifacts were incorporated into the fill of the structure's final construction phase. Three of these artifacts were recovered underneath the burnt clay floor on the structure's summit, while the other ten were deposited in two adjacent subfloor pits that were excavated through this floor. The artifacts in these clusters consist of nine pendants, one human effigy figure in granular marble, one non-jadeite pendant, two jade pendants, and one jade bead. Twelve of the fourteen artifacts recovered were intentionally fragmented.

PLAZA TWO AND ALTAR 1

Altar 1 is a boulder monument located at the south end of Plaza 2. It was shaped from a single rock that had a large cylindrical opening carved through its center. The monument was broken into three pieces and then rededicated in Patio M1 in front of Structure 7 (see figures 4.17, 4.18). A necklace composed of 109 discoidal beads with a central pendant (see figure 5.50a) together with 30 other artifacts were recovered along with 4 ceramic vessels in a subfloor offering under the large flute on the altar's west side (see figure 4.19b). The uppermost vessel in this offering contained the necklace[14] and was covered by a ceramic plate, while the vessel below contained 21 jade and marble lapidary artifacts, 1 ceramic candelero, and 4 human teeth.[15] An additional 9 jade artifacts were recovered on the plaza floor at the center of the altar where the 3 rocks articulated with one another. A jade earflare and pendant fragment were also recovered on the cobble floor of Plaza Two.

STRUCTURE 21 AND THE EAST COURTYARD

Three jade artifacts were recovered from Structure 21. One was associated with Structure 21-subB, while the other two could not be assigned to a specific construction stage. Only one jade artifact was recovered from the East Courtyard. It was a geometric pendant recovered in a test pit on the southeast side of Structure 26.

THE NORTH PRECINCT

This civic-ceremonial area contains eight structures in the large plaza on the north end of Salitrón Viejo. Offerings were recovered in three different contexts in this area: cache offerings around Structures 37, 38, and 40; artifacts associated with the low platforms that define the limits of the North Group (Structures 29, 30, 44, 45); and items deposited in the floor of the North Plaza (figure 3.7).

STRUCTURE 37

This structure was constructed using sterile fill, indicating that it was the first structure built in the North Precinct. A single fragmented jade bead was associated with this structure.

STRUCTURE 38

This was the largest structure in the North Precinct (see figure 3.7). It was 1.8 m tall and had the largest concentration of artifacts (n = 234) in the precinct. All items were recovered as subsurface offerings around the base of the structure (figure 6.7). Seventy-six artifacts were recovered in eight clusters that contained two to twenty-six items in each group. Two-thirds (68.4%) of the items were jade artifacts, followed by granular marble (27.8%). Earflares and pendants were the primary artifacts recovered, representing 31.6% and 51.7% of the assemblage, respectively.[16] Considerable variability was evident in the types of artifacts recovered from the cluster caches. Three caches only contained items of granular marble, while three others only contained jade.

FIGURE 6.7. *Cache offering of granular marble artifacts associated with Structure 38 in the North Precinct. The larger cache contains granular marble artifacts and the smaller one contains jade. Photograph by George Hasemann.*

STRUCTURE 40

This structure is 1 m high and is located 30 m north of Structure 38 (see figure 3.7). The materials recovered were from surface collections and light excavations across the summit of the structure. Sixty-seven artifacts were recovered, the majority of which were jade earflares (29.9%) and pendants (34.3%). One of the artifacts was a clam shell pendant with an incised Olmec-style design (see figure 5.38d). Six chalcedony nodules were also included in the offering, most likely because of their olive green color.

STRUCTURES 29 AND 30

These two structures are low east-west–oriented platforms that separated the North Precinct from the Iglesia Precinct. Three fragmented jade artifacts from two pendants and one unidentifiable artifact were recovered alongside these structures.

Structures 44 and 45

These structures form the west side of the corridor leading south from the North Precinct into Salitrón Viejo. Three fragmented jade artifacts were recovered from these structures that include a jade bead, a plain pendant, and a ring pendant.

The North Plaza

Forty-one artifacts were recovered from subsurface deposits across the open plaza. All of these artifacts were placed as individual items 20–30 cm below the plaza floor.[17] The majority of artifacts (n = 34) were jade, with pendants the most frequent artifact type recovered (56.1%). Twenty-one of the twenty-three pendants were undecorated, and six were unfinished. The two remaining were granular marble pendants adorned with geometric designs. Unlike many of the items found at Salitrón Viejo, the majority of the artifacts deposited in the North Plaza (80.5%) were unbroken.

THE WEST RESIDENTIAL GROUP

The structures in this group overlie some of the earliest domestic deposits at Salitrón Viejo. All four of its Range structures and 31 of its 156 house mounds were stratigraphically tested to collect materials to date their use and occupation. Three of the four Range structures and 9 of the 31 house mounds had at least one lapidary artifact in their assemblages. While some of the items recovered were from preconstruction levels, most date to the Early to Middle Sulaco periods. Thirty-six high-value items were recovered from these twelve structures (table 6.2). Variation was noted in the distribution of items, which in some cases did not conform to original expectations.

All four Range structures were extensively tested, and fifteen jade artifacts were recovered in three of them. Curiously, Structure 66, the smallest of these Range structures, had ten lapidary artifacts recovered from mound fill. While the number of pieces was high, the items were relatively modest and consisted of seven fragmented beads and three small unidentifiable pieces. Range Structures 119 and 120 had a smaller collection of fragmented artifacts that included two beads, two pendants, and one conical flare—all manufactured of jade.

One surprise was the large number of lapidary items recovered from house mounds. Twenty-one lapidary artifacts were found in commoner domestic contexts, two-thirds of which were fragmented jade artifacts that included six beads, six pendants, a tubular earflare, a tubular bead, a bead pendant, and a

TABLE 6.2. Summary of ritual artifacts in the West and South Residential Groups

Structure Number	Type of Structure	Jade	Granular Marble	Other Semi-Precious	Total
WEST GROUP STRUCTURES					
66	Range structure	6	1	3	10
119	Range structure	3	—	—	3
120	Range structure	2	—	—	2
57	House mound	1	—	—	1
112	House mound	1	—	—	1
114	House mound	1	—	—	1
115	House mound	1	—	—	1
121	House mound	—	—	2	2
122	House mound	5	—	3	8
138	House mound	1	—	—	1
188	House mound	2	—	2	4
396	House mound	2	—	—	2
Subtotal		25	1	10	36
SOUTH GROUP STRUCTURES					
211	Range structure	—	1	—	1
302	House mound	—	—	1	1
306	House mound	4	—	—	4
361	House mound	1	—	—	1
365	House mound	—	—	1	1
369	House mound	—	—	1	1
Subtotal		5	1	3	9
Total		30	2	13	45

fragmented marble vase (see figure 5.49a). What is interesting is that ten of these items were clustered in Structures 121 and 122, located adjacent to one another at the southeast corner of the West Plaza. These two sub-monumental structures had more lapidary goods than the three large adjacent Range structures that border the West Plaza. Another concentration of six artifacts was identified in five adjacent house mounds located within 30 m of one another (figure 6.8).[18] All structures in this cluster were small house mounds 15–60 cm in height. The concentration of wealth goods in this house mound cluster reflects both a level of household inequality and the operation of variable inter-household procurement networks to obtain small quantities of wealth goods.

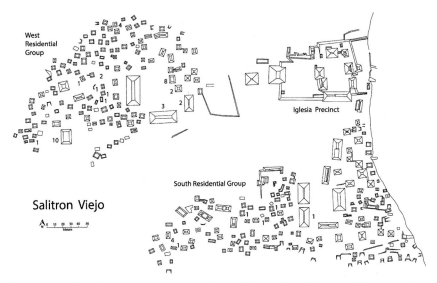

FIGURE 6.8. *Location of jade at structures in the West and South Groups. Illustration by Kenneth Hirth.*

THE SOUTH RESIDENTIAL GROUP

Like the West Group, most of the visible structures in this group date to the Middle and Late Sulaco phases. Five of the 6 Range structures and 34 of its 174 house mounds were stratigraphically tested to date their occupation and to obtain samples of associated material. Of these, only 1 Range structure and 5 house mounds had lapidary goods in their assemblages. The 9 artifacts recovered from these 6 structures are summarized in table 6.2. Only 1 granular marble pendant fragment was recovered from the 5 Range structures in this group. Each of the 5 domestic structures had a single bead in its assemblage along with fragments of a conical flare, a plain pendant, and a ring pendant recovered from the open area between the structures.[19]

PATTERNING AND USE OF WEALTH GOODS

The pattern that emerges from the foregoing discussion is that the overwhelming majority of high-value goods were associated with activities carried out in the two primary civic-ceremonial areas: the Iglesia and North Precincts. Tables 6.1 and 6.2 summarize the distribution of goods across Salitrón Viejo. Fully 98.4 percent of the wealth goods recovered at Salitrón Viejo were from the two civic-ceremonial precincts. The use of these goods in ritual activities is evident from their concentration in non-residential spaces used for community assemblies and public celebrations. While the east end of the Iglesia Precinct was an elite area, the majority of high-value offerings were located in Plaza One and the Central Plaza. The idea that feasting was an important dimension of ritual and civic celebrations is supported by the evidence of large-scale food preparation and display identified at Structures 2, 9, 22, 397, and Altar 2.

Wealth goods were used as dedicatory offerings in the construction and termination of ritual spaces. This is especially clear in the construction of the Acropolis platform and other buildings in the west end of the Iglesia Precinct (figure 6.1). Offerings were also associated with Structures 38 and 40 in the North Precinct. But it is important to identify where wealth goods do *not* occur. The large quantity of wealth goods entering Salitrón Viejo would suggest that the elite were intimately involved in their procurement and use. Although logical, this is not apparent from the contexts where jade occurs. While the artifacts in offerings were objects of personal adornment (e.g., beads, earflares, pendants), they were not regularly included in mortuary contexts with their presumed users. Only one jade bead was included with each of the two burials (1-16, 1-17) in structure 3. Likewise, there is no clear association of jade artifacts with Range structure 6 in the Iglesia Precinct or any of the other Range structures believed to be elite residences in the West and South Residential Groups. Except for Structure 66, there is more jade associated with non-elite house mounds in these groups than with the large structures associated with elite activities. Members of elite families were certainly involved in the procurement of wealth items entering Salitrón Viejo, but they don't seem to have used them in ostentatious personal displays. This has important implications for the organization of the Salitrón chiefdom, discussed in chapter 7.

Finally, there are patterns of intentional breakage associated with the use of wealth goods in the Iglesia and North Precincts. Over half of the artifacts (51.7%) in these two areas were intentionally broken when they were deposited. Fragmentation is evident because from two to six broken pieces of the same item were often recovered from the same context that could be refitted to assemble complete or partially complete artifacts.[20] The rate of fragmentation, however, was not consistent across artifact categories and material types. Granular marble is softer than jadeite; as a result, these artifacts were fragmented at a higher rate than jade artifacts. A comparison between areas of the site reveals a fragmentation rate of 47.8 percent in the Iglesia Precinct compared to 79.0 percent in the North Precinct. But this is due in part to a higher proportion of granular marble artifacts in the North Precinct compared to the Iglesia Precinct.[21]

TABLE 6.3. Fragmentation rates of select artifact categories in the Iglesia and North Precincts

Artifact	Jade Artifacts				Granular Marble Artifacts			
	Complete	Broken	Total	Percent Broken	Complete	Broken	Total	Percent Broken
Beads	781	118	899	13.1	2	6	8	75.0
Bead pendants	108	9	117	7.7	7	2	9	22.2
Conical flares	21	255	276	92.4	0	4	4	100.0
Tubular earflares	5	193	198	97.5	0	2	2	100.0
Pendants: plain	114	162	276	58.7	16	101	117	86.3
Pendants: carved[a]	68	46	114	40.4	8	72	80	90.0
Total	1,097	783	1,880	41.7	33	187	220	86.0

a. Includes anthropomorphic, geometric, and zoomorphic pendants.

Table 6.3 compares fragmentation rates of several jade and granular marble artifact classes in the Iglesia and North Precincts. Most jade beads (86.9%) and bead pendants (92.3%) recovered were unbroken compared to earflares, where 92.0%–97.5% were fragmented when deposited.[22] A different pattern is seen in granular marble, where most of the artifacts were pendants and readily fragmented owing to their softer consistency. Plain and carved artifacts likewise reflect selective breakage patterns. Jade pendants with carved images were fragmented at a lower rate (40.4%) than plain pendants (58.7%) (table 6.3). Most granular marble pendants were broken irrespective of whether they were plain (86.3%) or had carved (90.0%) images (table 6.3).

High-value items were handled in a similar fashion outside the Iglesia and North Precincts. While most of the structures in the West and South Residential Groups date to the Middle and Late Sulaco phases, the pattern of how wealth goods were handled there remained the same. Although the number of artifacts recovered in domestic contexts was small (n = 45), nearly three-quarters (73.3%) were intentionally fragmented, suggesting a continuity of practice in both public and domestic contexts. Similar to artifacts in the Iglesia Precinct, the majority of complete artifacts were beads (n = 12, 92.3%). Where usage patterns differed were in sites outside of Salitrón Viejo. Despite extensive excavation at twenty-eight sites throughout the region, only twenty-three lapidary items were recovered at four sites outside Salitrón Viejo (see table 5.1).[23] The majority of these items (73.9%) were manufactured from non-jade materials that did not include granular marble. Like the West and South Groups, most of these materials date to the Middle and Late Sulaco phases. Where usage differs is that nearly all the artifacts (95.7%) were recovered as complete, unbroken items.

THE SYNCHRONICITY OF RITUAL EVENTS

Fifty percent (50.2%) of the 2,881 high-value goods recovered at Salitrón Viejo were broken pieces. Large numbers of fragmentary pieces provide challenges in any analytical study. To aid interpretation, a program of artifact refitting was undertaken to provide an estimate of the MAC (minimum artifact counts) represented in the collection and to evaluate what artifact fragmentation could inform about ritual behavior.[24] While a slow and time-consuming process, the study of artifact refits has a long and productive history in lithic studies (e.g., Cahen 1987; Inizan et al. 1999:94–96). Analysis of conjoined pieces can provide a wealth of information on the sequence and spatial organization of activities (Franklin and Simek 2008; Iceland 2013; López-Ortega, Rodríguez, and Vaquero 2011; Morrow 1996; Vaquero et al. 2019). The focus of the refit study presented here is on the spatial patterning of conjoined pieces to provide insight into the synchronicity of ritual deposits in Salitrón Viejo. Of course, this assumed that fragments of artifacts were not held over long periods of time for use as memory items in later rituals (e.g., Selsor Walker 1998:95). This assumption seemed reasonable given the frequency of breakage within the collection and was borne out over the course of analysis in all but one instance (see below) as artifact conjoins were identified in simultaneous and adjacent cluster caches.

Three hundred refit matches were identified in the collection. Of these, 224 were *intra-deposit* matches (table 6.4). These conjoins were from artifacts that were broken when they were placed in an offering or scattered across a construction level. These refits are important because they established that items were regularly broken at the moment of deposition. Intra-deposit matches are the largest number of refits because they were the easiest to spot in artifact clusters that were identified in the field and removed to the laboratory as intact units.

A second category of refits was made up of *inter-deposit* conjoins. These consist of artifacts that occur in different in situ deposits that were near one

TABLE 6.4. Conjoining artifacts from ritual deposits at Salitrón Viejo

Location	Stage	Number
INTRA-DEPOSIT CONJOINS		
Various	Various	224
INTER-DEPOSIT CONJOINS		
Str. 12 north side	4	4
Str. 12 summit termination	4	3
Str. 12 west side	5	12
Str. 1 construction	5	4
Centerline: West Acropolis platform	5	39
INTRA-SITE CONJOINS		
Str. 12/West Acropolis platform	4	1
Centerline: West Acropolis platform	4–5	5
Str. 12 west side/Str. 1	5	3
Str. 38/Acropolis platform	4–5	2
Str. 38/North Plaza	4–5	2
Str. 9/Plaza 2	6	1
Total		300

another and reflect simultaneous deposition. There were 62 of these matches (table 6.4): 39 in the primary Stage 5 offering associated with the completion of the Acropolis platform, 16 from the west and north sides of Structure 12, 3 from the termination deposit on the summit of Structure 12, and 4 from cluster caches on the summit of Structure 1. These matches are important because they reinforced the contemporaneity of adjacent cluster deposits. The 12 inter-deposit matches on the west side of Structure 12 established that the 10 artifact clusters recovered there were deposited simultaneously as part of a single ritual event. Likewise, 4 matches were identified between the 15 artifact caches recovered from the summit of Structure 1, which confirmed the contemporaneity of their deposit. Finally, 39 artifact matches were identified between the 40 clusters of jade artifacts that formed the primary offering at the center of the Acropolis platform. These matches reinforced earlier field observations that this large deposit occurred at a single moment in time.

The third class of refits includes *intra-site* artifact matches. These occur in different contexts and over considerable distances from one another within

Salitrón Viejo. Only 14 intra-site artifact matches were identified, but they are important because they establish the contemporaneity or near contemporaneity of rituals carried out in different areas of the site. Nine intra-site matches occur in the Iglesia Precinct, and they date to construction Stages 4 and 5 (table 6.4). They were part of the large-scale simultaneous dedicatory celebrations involved in finishing the Acropolis platform and expanding the structures associated with it. Intra-site artifact matches link 6 ritual deposits in different areas of Salitrón Viejo and provide a glimpse of ritual activities that were carried out as part of large and prolonged ritual events. Figure 6.9 shows how these intra-site artifact matches connect simultaneous ritual deposits in the Iglesia and North Precincts.

Six intra-site artifact matches were associated with the Stage 4 construction of the West Acropolis platform. This platform covered the north side of Structure 12, where fifty-six lapidary items were recovered from the pedestrian surface at the base of the structure under the Acropolis fill. One match was identified between a fragmented bead recovered from the pedestrian surface and its counterpart, which was included in the fill of the West Acropolis platform. Thirteen jade artifacts were also identified in construction fill along the east–west centerline behind the platform's eastern exterior (figure 6.1). Surprisingly, five of these thirteen artifacts were conjoined matches with artifacts in the Stage 5 Acropolis offering on the opposite side of the West Acropolis wall.[25] The five artifacts in the Stage 5 Acropolis offering appear to be legacy or memory artifacts from the completion of the West Acropolis platform. This is important because it indicates that there was very little time between the construction of the West Acropolis platform and the completion of the Acropolis during Stage 5. The five refits were found at different levels in the fill, which eliminated the possibility that they were deposited simultaneously in a side-by-side manner during a single ritual event. This suggests that a few artifacts were retained to commemorate and link the earlier centerline offering with the larger one when the Acropolis construction was completed. The interval between these two events was undoubtedly short, and this is the only instance of legacy offering retention identified at Salitrón Viejo.

Structure 38 is located in the North Precinct. Two pendant fragments recovered from plaza deposits at the base of this structure were refit to pieces recovered from the Acropolis platform in the Iglesia Precinct (figure 6.9). These refits have two important implications. First, they indicate that the ritual offerings associated with Structure 38 were contemporaneous with construction activities in the Iglesia Precinct during the Late Yunque phase. Second,

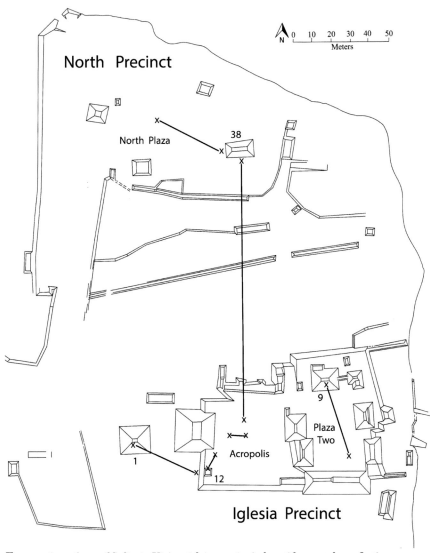

FIGURE 6.9. *Areas of Salitrón Viejo with intra-site jade artifact matches reflecting contemporaneous ritual events. Illustration by Kenneth Hirth.*

they confirm that ritual activities carried out in the North Precinct were part of broader site-wide ritual events. Two additional refits in the North Precinct helped reinforce the identification of coordinated site-wide ritual activity. Pieces of two carved pendants recovered from fill and along the base of Structure 38 matched items deposited individually in the floor of the North Precinct.[26] When all four matches are taken together, they provide a picture of simultaneous ritual activity across the North and Iglesia Precincts.

Three refits were also identified between artifacts recovered from subsurface caches on the western pedestrian surface of Structure 12 and those included in a subfloor cache on the summit of Structure 1 (figure 6.9). Portions of three slate disks were included in two subsurface caches on the west side of Structure 12; they were the only such artifacts recovered at Salitrón Viejo (see figures 6.1, 5.44b). Fragments of these disks matched those recovered on the summit of Structure 1, suggesting that both offerings were deposited as part of simultaneous Stage 5 ritual activities in the Iglesia Precinct.

The final refit occurs in Plaza Two at the east end of the Acropolis platform. A pendant with geometric designs was recovered from an artifact cluster on the summit of Structure 9. Its conjoining piece was recovered from the far southeastern corner of Plaza Two near Altar 1 and reflects ritual activity in the Iglesia Precinct during Stage 6.

THE CHRONOLOGICAL PATTERNING OF RITUAL OFFERINGS

The Iglesia Precinct was constructed and used over a period of 900–1,000 years between the Early Yunque and Middle Sulaco phases (see table 4.1), while the North Precinct was used primarily during the Late Yunque and Early Sulaco phases. Several interesting trends are evident in the timing of ritual deposits at Salitrón Viejo. The greatest demand for high-value goods corresponded to the completion of the Acropolis platform. Fully 91.2 percent (n = 2,627) of the 2,881 items deposited in ritual offerings at Salitrón Viejo date to Stages 4 and 5 of the Iglesia construction sequence (table 6.5). The AMS radiocarbon dates and the five artifact refits between the Stage 4 and 5 centerline deposits of the Acropolis platform indicate that these construction activities were closely spaced in time. The quantity of ritual goods accumulated for this event was immense, and no other celebration in the life of the community required such a large set of offerings.[27]

Jade was the dominant material used for lapidary goods entering the site beginning in the Late Yunque phase (Stage 2). Material from the Motagua valley consistently represents between 70 percent and 80 percent of the

TABLE 6.5. Frequency of ritual offerings at Salitrón Viejo by construction stage

Iglesia Construction Stage	Chronological Phases	Iglesia Precinct	North Precinct	South Group	West Group	Total	Percent
Stage 1	Early Yunque	2	0	0	0	2	0.1
Stage 2	Early–Late Yunque	12	0	0	0	12	0.4
Stage 3	Late Yunque	20	0	0	0	20	0.7
Stage 4	Late Yunque	447	0	1	0	448	15.6
Stages 4–5	Late Yunque	166	345	1	0	512	17.8
Stage 5	Late Yunque	1,667	0	0	0	1,667	57.8
Stage 6	Sulaco	156	0	3	31	190	6.6
Unphased	N/A	17	4	4	5	30	1.0
Total	N/A	2,487	349	9	36	2,881	100.0

TABLE 6.6. Material type of ritual offerings at Salitrón Viejo by construction stage

Iglesia Construction Stage	Chronological Phases	Jade	Granular Marble	Obsidian and Chert	Other Semi-Precious	Total
Stage 1	Early Yunque	—	—	—	2	2
Stage 2	Early–Late Yunque	10	—	—	2	12
Stage 3	Late Yunque	14	2	—	4	20
Stage 4	Late Yunque	363	69	—	16	448
Stages 4–5	Late Yunque	402	81	6	23	512
Stage 5	Late Yunque	1,407	123	7	130	1,667
Stage 6	Sulaco	49	15	—	126	190
Unphased	N/A	23	—	—	7	30
Total	N/A	2,268	290	13	310	2,881

assemblage up through the end of the Late Yunque phase (Stage 5). During the Early to Middle Sulaco phases (Stage 6), the quantity of wealth goods entering the region declined coincident with lessened construction in the Iglesia Precinct. Lapidary goods were not used as dedicatory offerings in the large Range structures in the West and South Residential Groups. Although some jade from the Motagua valley still reached Salitrón Viejo, a greater percentage of lapidary goods consisted of non-jadeite material (table 6.6). While 190 artifacts are reported for Stage 6, the amount entering Salitrón Viejo was much less, since 110 of these items were from one necklace (see figure 5.50a) recovered in the offering at Altar 1.[28]

VARIATION IN OFFERING COMPOSITION

One question of interest is whether there was patterned regularity in the composition of offerings that might indicate a conceptual recipe for the composition of offerings or the presence of a supervisory authority orchestrating their collection. Conversely, variation in offering composition would suggest the participation of multiple independent groups in the assembly of ritual offerings. The participation of multiple independent groups in rituals was suggested by the location of the North Precinct on the periphery of Salitrón Viejo. The low walls screening it from the Iglesia Precinct, the corridor connecting it to the site, and the ramp (Structure 400) leading into the North Plaza from the Sulaco River suggested that it was used to receive groups residing elsewhere in the region (see chapter 3). The degree of independent but coordinated ritual behavior was assessed by examining the variation evident in the composition and treatment of offerings at Salitrón Viejo. It was felt that if ritual activities were coordinated through a centralized authority, there would be more commonality in the composition of offerings than if they were obtained and offered by groups operating independent of one another.

The examination of artifact patterning revealed considerable variability in the content and treatment of artifacts placed in offerings at different locations across the site. Table 6.7 summarizes the fragmentation patterns for the four primary material classes used in ritual offerings in the Iglesia and North Precincts. Notable differences were observed in breakage patterns between these two areas. In the Iglesia Precinct, 45.8 percent of all artifacts in ritual deposits were intentionally fragmented compared to 79.1 percent in the North Precinct. While there are differences in the size of the respective samples, an ANOVA test of variance revealed that the difference in fragmentation practices between the two sectors was highly significant ($F = 14.25$, $p = 0.001$).

There are also notable differences in where different artifact classes occur and how they are handled upon deposition. One hundred twenty-seven lapidary artifacts were incorporated into the fill of the Western Acropolis platform during its Stage 4 construction. Two things stand out about these artifacts. First, all but two of the artifacts were jade, two-thirds of which ($n = 88$, 69.3%) were earflares. Second, fully 94.5 percent ($n = 120$) of these earflares were fragmented when they were deposited in the fill of the platform; this contrasts sharply with the way artifacts were handled in the primary Stage 5 offering

TABLE 6.7. Artifact fragmentation by material type in the Iglesia and North Precincts

Artifact Condition	Jade	Granular Marble	Obsidian and Chert	Other Semi-Precious	Total	Percent
IGLESIA PRECINCT						
Complete	1,081	27	4	237	1,349	54.2
Fragmented	901	191	3	43	1,138	45.8
Subtotal	1,982	218	7	280	2,487	100.0
NORTH PRECINCT						
Complete	49	15	0	9	73	20.9
Fragmented	206	55	6	9	276	79.1
Subtotal	255	70	6	18	349	100.0
COMBINED AREAS						
Complete	1,130	42	4	246	1,422	50.1
Fragmented	1,107	246	9	52	1,414	49.9
Total	2,237	288	13	298	2,836	100.0

deposited alongside the east–west centerline of the Acropolis platform, where only 263 of the 1,304 artifacts (20.2%) were fragmented.

Several other differences were observed in the locations where lapidary goods of different materials were deposited. Two hundred and two micaceous jade artifacts were recovered at Salitrón Viejo. Ninety-five percent of them (n = 192) occur in the Iglesia Precinct, the majority of which (n = 186) were recovered in offerings in the Acropolis platform. Moreover, half of all micaceous jade artifacts (n = 101) occur within four of the forty cluster caches that comprise the primary offering in the center of the Acropolis platform. The high concentration of this material in these caches suggests two things. First, there was a clear preference for their use in the Acropolis offerings; second, there was a high degree of individuality in the composition of cluster offerings in the primary centerline deposit during Stage 5.

Granular marble is the second most frequently occurring material in ritual deposits (n = 290), after Rio Motagua jade (table 5.1). Like micaceous jade, these materials were not evenly distributed in deposits across the site. Unlike micaceous jade, granular marble artifacts were largely absent from offerings in the Acropolis platform. Instead, most granular marble artifacts (89.0%) were associated with platform mounds on the periphery of the Acropolis platform or in the North Precinct. More than 60 percent (61.4%) of these artifacts were associated with Structures 1, 3, and 12 on the west side of the Iglesia Precinct.

An additional one-quarter of these materials (24.1%) are associated with structures in the North Precinct (table 6.6). Eight artifact caches were deposited at the base of Structure 38, three of which only have artifacts manufactured of granular marble; the other five lacked this material. This variation reflects a high level of individuality in the composition of different cluster offerings.

Finally, examination of patterning within ritual deposits would be incomplete without a consideration of color. Color was an intrinsic feature of pre-Columbian ideology associated with life, death, and directionality. Among the Maya, the colors green and blue were associated with maize, fertility, and the center of the world (McAnany 2010:298; Ortíz 1991; Taube 2005). Jade was esteemed because green was associated with life itself. To examine how color was patterned across the lapidary assemblage, artifacts were coded for strength and variation in hues following the Munsell color ranges summarized in tables 5.2 and 5.3. The goal was to characterize color variation within the collection and to evaluate how different artifact classes varied from one another in terms of color associations.

Tables 6.8 and 6.9 summarize color tendencies for the jade and micaceous jade recovered in the collection. No color summary is provided for granular marble, which ranges from white or light gray to light cream/buff in color except where malachite veins provide a greenish hue that was retained when fashioning artifacts. Jade from the Motagua valley is split fairly evenly between gray (46.0%) and strong green (42.8) tones (table 6.8). Nevertheless, the color most frequently represented among jade artifacts is apple green (see table 5.3), indicating a strong preference for this hue when it was available. Micaceous jade is overwhelmingly represented by the middle tones of weak green, with greenish-grey (see table 5.3) the modal color. Artisans using micaceous jade used this color to fashion beads and bead pendants (table 6.9). Non-jade artifacts fall strongly in the gray tones, with medium gray the modal color in these materials.

Some color selectivity was noted for different artifact types. Plain and carved bead categories were distributed across the three color ramps, with gray tones predominating over the other two hues by 2–3:1. The modal color for beads was dark gray (tables 5.3, 6.9). While green hues may have been preferred, the manufacture of gray jade beads could have been the product of production bias where preferred green tones were reserved for specific artifacts such as earflares and pendants. Bead pendants were carved and perforated to hang like a lavalier or the central element in a bead necklace. While the sample size is small, 44.1 percent of bead pendants manufactured from Motagua valley jade were fashioned in weak green hues (table 6.9), even though this color group represents only 10.6 percent of all the material in the collection.[29]

TABLE 6.8. Color variation for jade, micaceous jade, and non-jade materials

Material	Gray Tones No.	%	Weak Green No.	%	Strong Green No.	%	Modal Color Hue	No.	%	Total
Jade	901	46.0	220	11.2	839	42.8	Apple green	599	30.5	1,961
Micaceous jade	2	1.0	190	94.5	9	4.5	Greenish-gray	146	73.0	200
Non-jadeite	135	86.5	21	13.5	0	0.0	Medium gray	135	86.5	156

TABLE 6.9. Color variation for select artifact categories manufactured in jade and micaceous jade

Artifact Type	Gray Tones No.	%	Weak Green No.	%	Strong Green No.	%	Modal Color Hue	No.	%	Total
JADE										
Beads	424	57.2	132	17.8	185	25.0	Dark gray	159	21.4	742
Bead pendants	19	32.2	26	44.1	14	23.7	Gray-green	15	25.4	59
Conical flares	128	46.5	8	2.9	139	50.5	Apple green	135	49.1	275
Tubular earflares	22	11.8	3	1.6	162	86.6	Apple green	142	75.9	187
Plain pendants	149	55.8	21	7.9	97	36.3	Medium gray	72	27.0	267
							Apple green	73	27.3	
Carved pendants	54	54.0	11	11.0	35	35.0	Medium gray	36	36.0	100
MICACEOUS JADE										
Beads	0	0	144	94.7	8	5.3	Greenish-gray	117	77.4	151
Bead pendants	2	5.4	35	94.6	0	0	Greenish-gray	22	59.5	37

A notable color preference was evident in the manufacture of earflares. Two types of flares (conical and tubular) were identified that were manufactured from Motagua valley jade using different technologies. In both cases, strong green jade was the preferred color preference and constituted half of conical flares (50.5%) and 86.6 percent of tubular flares. The model color for both of these flare types was apple green (5G 6–7/1–4, 10G 6–8/2). Conical flares also occur in gray tones (46.5%) almost as frequently as in strong green and may reflect less access by artisans to greener hues. Earflares were important status markers for the elite, which likely accounts for the preference for apple green jade in their manufacture.

Color distributions were also examined for plain and carved pendants. Most plain pendants were shaped from jade in gray tones (table 6.9), although this distribution is bimodal, with the two most frequent colors being apple green (27.3%) and medium gray (27.0%). Carved pendants were classified into design types based on whether they had geometric, zoomorphic, or anthropomorphic representations, the latter of which included the greater array of hunchback imagery. While carved pendants carried symbolically important images, over half were shaped from jade in gray tones, with medium gray the modal hue (table 6.9). While important for their imagery, there was no clear preference for strong green hues in their manufacture.

Unworked nodules and percussion flakes were also included in some offerings alongside finished goods. The reason for their inclusion in ritual deposits was apparently a result of their green color. Two elaborate eccentric biface fragments were recovered, both of which were manufactured of green obsidian from the Sierra de las Navajas source in Central Mexico (see figure 5.51a). Similarly, one chalcedony eccentric biface (see figure 5.51b) and nine flakes and nodules were recovered, all of which were within the weak green color range, with olive green the modal shade (see table 5.3).

Color was an important variable in cognized ritual practice and is reflected in the selection of artifacts used in dedication offerings. Chapter 7 takes a more nuanced look at ritual practice and its role in the development of Salitrón Viejo's regional chiefdom.

Ritual in a general sense refers to a series of behaviors performed in a prescribed order. While most often associated with religious activities, ritual encompasses a broad range of performances that reinforce individual or culturally meaningful ideologies in society (Adams 2005:115; DeMarrais, Castillo, and Earle 1996; Rappaport 1971, 1999:24). As such, these performances are associated with all important life events ranging from birth to death, as well as graduation, marriage, and even shaking hands as a greeting or to formalize a business arrangement (Fischer et al. 2013). When carried out collectively, they communicate information through both verbal and non-verbal means to build or reinforce systems of belief and behavior (Bloch 1978:329; Rappaport 1971:26). Ritual events, whether religious or secular, often use symbolic acts and material objects that help reinforce the message communicated (Douglas and Isherwood 1979:65). While ancient rituals are often difficult to penetrate, it is through these symbolic acts and material objects that archaeologists can reconstruct both their content and importance in past societies.

Ritual economy has been viewed in two ways by archaeologists: as the *ritual of economy* and as the *economy of ritual*. The ritual of economy perspective examines the multifaceted ways ritual practice permeated the production, distribution, and consumption activities of everyday life. It recognizes the all-pervasive nature of ritual in structuring the interaction of individuals with the material and non-material environments in which

The What, How, and Why of Ritual Activity in the Salitrón Chiefdom

https://doi.org/10.5876/9781646424757.c007

they lived (McAnany 2010:13; Watanabe 2007). While important, this dimension of the ritual economy is beyond the scope of what can be examined here. Instead, this study has followed the second perspective and explored the economy of ritual in the Salitrón chiefdom. This approach identifies a dimension of ritual behavior and attempts to calculate its economic cost in terms of the time, labor, and material investment required (Spielmann 2008). While not as encompassing a view of ritual, it is more amenable to archaeological analysis and evaluation (Barber and Joyce 2007; Davis-Salazar 2007; Kovacevich 2007; Kyriakidis 2007; Spielmann 2002; Wells 2007; Wells and Davis-Salazar 2007).

The El Cajón region provides information on different forms of ritual activity: the construction of civic-ceremonial architecture, participation in feasting activities, and the assembly of high-value goods for use in dedicatory offerings. The discussion here situates this information within the broader context of prehispanic society in west-central Honduras and the chiefdom-level groups located there. It explores some of the economic costs behind ritual activities, what they inform about prehispanic religious practices, and what the offerings at Salitrón Viejo imply about the scale and organization of activities where they were practiced. The El Cajón region underwent a gradual abandonment around AD 1000, replicating the contraction of population noted in other areas of Honduras. The changes in ritual practice provide insights into why community integration declined both in the El Cajón region and across Honduras at the end of the Classic period.

CULTURAL COMPLEXITY AND RITUAL DURING THE LATE FORMATIVE AND CLASSIC PERIODS

The Formative period (1600 BC–AD 250) was an era of considerable cultural development across Honduras (see chapter 2). It was the period when some of the largest monumental architecture was constructed and the greatest social disparities in rank were expressed in mortuary interments. Differences in rank are evident in burials at Los Naranjos, where individuals of high rank were distinguished by mortuary offerings that included jade earflares, belts, and necklaces of jade beads. Similarly, it was during the Middle Formative (800–400 BC) that some of the largest platform mounds were constructed at Yarumela, Los Naranjos, and a number of smaller centers in other regions. Ritual centers during the Formative period contained stone sculptures intended to enhance the ritual experience and reinforce mythical beliefs. It also was when ballcourts began to appear across Honduras (Joyce, Hendon, and Sheptak 2008:294).

Population grew during the Late Formative period, with new communities appearing in areas that were previously unoccupied. The El Cajón region was one of those regions. Most of these societies, except perhaps the large centers of Yarumela and Los Naranjos, were organized as small regional chiefdoms. Elaborate burials of high-ranking individuals were largely absent, suggesting that authority based on hereditary descent or control of wealth was not an essential feature of leadership during the Late Formative. An empty Late Formative tomb at Yarumela (Structure 102) was unused or had its occupant intentionally removed to de-emphasize any linkage of the mound with a particular individual (Dixon et al. 1994:83). During the Classic period, chiefdoms in west-central Honduras appear to have been integrated through collective community ritual rather than the aggrandizing actions of powerful Big Men (e.g., Blanton et al. 1996; Hayden 2001b). If powerful leaders were present in these societies, they are largely invisible in the archaeological record.

A primary integrative mechanism of prehispanic Honduran chiefdoms was community feasting. Feasting was a central feature of traditional Lenca society and was described by Antonia de Herrera y Tordesillas (1944–1947:6:23) in the sixteenth century. Feasts were incorporated in the celebrations of religious events and for mobilizing labor within the community. Mobilizing labor in conjunction with the festive consumption of food and fermented beverages is common practice around the world (Erasmus 1956; Hirth 2020) and was a traditional means of conducting communal work across Mesoamerica and Honduras (Rojas Rabiela 1979; Wells 2007; Wells and Davis-Salazar 2008). The role of feasting in reinforcing community solidarity is reflected by archaeological evidence recovered in multiple archaeological sites across Honduras. Sites where feasting has been identified include CR-44, Curusté, and Río Pelo in the Ulúa valley (Joyce 2014:123; Wonderley 1985); El Coyote in the Cacaulapa valley (Wells 2007); San Juan Camalote in the Cataguana valley (Joyce, Hendon, and Sheptak 2008:294); Salitrón Viejo in the El Cajón region (see below); El Cafetal in the El Paraíso valley (Canuto and Bell 2013:13), and Los Achiotes near Copán (Canuto 2004:47), as well as at Copán (Hendon and Ardren 2020).

Feasting also occurred within individual households. It is notable, however, that most of the recognizable evidence of feasting has been recovered from public plazas in association with civic-ceremonial constructions, indicating its importance in community life.[1] Feasting was central in many chiefdom societies because of its multifaceted benefits. It created the need for economic intensification, which ensured that food surpluses and other socially valued goods were produced to meet celebratory needs (Spielmann 2002). Feasting also required and encouraged cooperation in the mobilization of resources from participating households. Sponsorships of feasts by leaders can be political devices—reifying asymmetrical power relations within society, emphasizing the existence of abundance, and bringing people together to create public consensus (Dietler 2001). However they were contextualized and organized, "ritual feasts sanctified the structures of power that are related to the structure of production" (Sabloff 2008:271). They validated the individuals and the relationships, beliefs, meanings, or events in which they were convened.

The social climate across west-central Honduras was one of strong interregional interaction and trade. The Late Formative and Proto-Classic periods are marked by the wide-scale distribution of Usulután ceramics that were manufactured and traded across Honduras and El Salvador and into the Maya region (Andrews 1976, 1977; Demarest and Sharer 1982, 1986; Goralski 2008; Sharer 1978:3:126).[2] During the Classic period, polychrome ceramics such as Cópador and Ulúa polychrome were produced and moved through these same interregional trade routes (Beaudry-Corbett 1987, 1993; Joyce 2017; Robinson 1989:160–180; Viel 1978). Obsidian from sources in Honduras and Guatemala was exchanged as nodules and as cores for making percussion flakes and pressure blades (Aoyama, Tashiro, and Glascock 1999; Sheets et al. 1990; Sorensen and Hirth 1984). Some wealth goods were produced for exchange but on the whole, this type of activity was localized and has only been reported in a few select locales in the Ulúa valley (Joyce and Henderson 2001; Luke and Tykot 2007). Jade and marine shell ornaments moved through interregional networks as gifts and trade items, but they did so in limited quantities, which makes explaining the high concentration of jade and marble artifacts at Salitrón Viejo an interesting challenge.

THE SALITRÓN CHIEFDOM: ORGANIZATION AND INTEGRATION

The El Cajón region is a sharply incised mountainous landscape with good agricultural land located in a few small pockets along the Sulaco and Humuya Rivers. The earliest settlement in the region occurred at Salitrón Viejo at the beginning of the Early Yunque phase, around 400 BC. This is not surprising, since Salitrón is situated on the largest pocket of productive agricultural land along these two rivers. The result was that Salitrón grew quickly into the biggest and most influential community in the region. Other large communities developed in the El Cajón region over time, most of which were located along the Sulaco River where the greatest population, architectural construction, and presence of a hierarchical settlement pattern suggest that groups were part of an integrated social system. At its center was the site of Salitrón Viejo, which was twice the size of, and architecturally more complex than, any other community in the region. All indications suggest that communities along the Sulaco River formed part of a regional chiefdom centered on the community of Salitrón Viejo (Hasemann 1987).

The site of Salitrón Viejo grew to cover about 2 ha during the Early Yunque phase. Its on-site population at this time is unclear because of the practice of recycling earlier house mounds into later construction (see chapter 3). What is clear, however, is that the Iglesia Precinct was already the site's central ritual precinct. The precinct was defined by three platform constructions (Structures 2, 3, and 21), which left an open plaza between them for conducting dances and other community celebrations (see figure 4.3). Structure 3 was the primary civic-ceremonial building in the precinct, while Structure 2 was an unconsolidated earthen platform that supported a building where food was prepared for feasts. This indicates that ritual activity combined with feasting was a central feature of the Salitrón community from its inception. Four other settlements were identified along the Sulaco River that lacked civic-ceremonial architecture (see figure 3.13). It is likely that the Iglesia Precinct was the ritual center for all sites in the region during the Early Yunque phase.

The Late Yunque phase (0–400 AD) witnessed rapid population growth along the Sulaco River. Seventeen communities were occupied along the Sulaco River within a 12 km radius of Salitrón Viejo (see figure 3.14). A few sites were identified along the Humuya River (see figure 3.14), but the Sulaco River communities formed the core of cultural development in the El Cajón region. There is no evidence for the construction of civic-ceremonial architecture at communities outside of Salitrón Viejo, which was clearly the region's main ritual center and the central community of a growing chiefdom.[3] The population of Salitrón Viejo continued to increase, although it is difficult to estimate its size with precision due to mound recycling. It is evident that larger communities found in the region were compact settlements (Hirth n.d.) that, except for Salitrón Viejo, did not exceed 100 persons in size (Table 7.1).[4]

The issue of population size is important because it was during the Late Yunque phase that the largest civic-ceremonial construction projects were initiated at Salitrón Viejo. The Acropolis platform was constructed along with a number of the other structures in the Iglesia Precinct, which was the site's main civic-ceremonial area (see figure 4.4). The North Precinct, located on the northern periphery of Salitrón, was also constructed at this time (see figure 3.5). The location and design of the North Precinct suggest that it was a special purpose civic-ceremonial zone used to receive groups from throughout the region. Together, the North and Iglesia Precincts provided the civic-ceremonial spaces that helped integrate the Salitrón chiefdom into a regional entity. The fact that broken jade artifacts from the North Precinct were refit with artifacts in the Iglesia Precinct indicates that the two areas were used as contemporaneous co-dependent ritual spaces within Salitrón Viejo.

Both the West and South Residential Groups had plaza areas for communal use, although none of their associated Range structures were constructed until the Early Sulaco phase (see chapter 3).[5] In hierarchical terms, Salitrón Viejo was the central administrative center of the chiefdom that was linked to regional communities by ritual events carried out in the Iglesia and North Precincts. Like the populations in the West and South Groups, no outlying communities along the Sulaco River began constructing their own civic-ceremonial architecture until the Early and Middle Sulaco phases.

The limits of the Salitrón chiefdom are difficult to define, both in geographic and demographic terms.[6] Nevertheless, table 7.1 provides conservative population estimates for communities along the Sulaco River during the Late Yunque phase.[7] Late Yunque ceramics were identified in plaza areas at both La Ceiba and Guarabuiquí, which were used for community activities although they lack dedicated civic-ceremonial architecture. The use of available information and an estimate of four persons per household suggests that two-thirds of the regional population resided at Salitrón Viejo at this time (table 7.1). If areas further upriver along the Sulaco River and Humuya River communities were included in the chiefdom, the resident population of Salitrón Viejo may have been closer to half the total regional population.

THE IMPORTANCE OF FEASTING

Feasting was an important feature of traditional Lenca society, and archaeologists have identified feasting deposits in several sites across Honduras. At Salitrón Viejo, evidence of feasting occurs in civic-ceremonial spaces, indicating a linkage between ritual practices and social celebrations. Evidence of feasting, food preparation, and food display was found in two areas: the Iglesia Precinct and the plaza of the West Residential Group. All the evidence occurs within or near plaza areas, as would be expected for communal feasting.

Most evidence of feasting was recovered from the Iglesia Precinct, which contains the most elaborate architectural constructions at Salitrón Viejo. Structure 3 was built of adobe, which was whitewashed to create a distinctive

TABLE 7.1. Regional population estimates for the Late Yunque phase

Site	Number of Households	Population Estimate[a]
PC1 Salitrón Viejo	200–250	800–1,000
PC2	2–3	8–12
PC4	6–8	24–32
PC7	10–12	40–48
PC8	1–2	4–8
PC9	2–3	8–12
PC12 Soledad	10–15	40–60
PC13 La Ceiba	15–20	60–80
PC15 Guarabuquí	15–20	60–80
PC22	10–14	40–48
PC33	5–7	20–28
PC37–38 La Conce	6–8	24–32
PC41	2–3	8–12
PC42	1–2	4–8
PC59 Cueva Grande	10–15	40–60
PC71 El Mango	6–8	24–32
PC72	2–3	8–12
Total	303–393	1,212–1,564

a. Population estimates were based on four persons/household.

public structure. White *lajas* were used to form stairways in Structures 1, 3, 4, and 9; a hard lime plaster was used to consolidate portions of the Acropolis platform floor. Two altars were constructed in Plaza Two, one of which was faced with white *laja* slabs. Structure 12 was constructed using a *talud-tablero* profile, and Structure 395 also had an exterior wall built in *talud*. Despite the care used in these buildings, this district also contains three of the least well-constructed structures at Salitrón Viejo. These are Structures 2, 22, and 9-subA—all of which were associated with food preparation and feasting in the Iglesia Precinct. What makes these three structures distinct from every other structure at Salitrón Viejo is that they are unconsolidated earthen mounds. Even the humblest residential mounds were built using cobble retention walls to stabilize and give them shape. These three structures do not have those walls; instead, their earthen matrix appears to have been built up gradually over time.

Structure 2 is located at the west end of the Iglesia Precinct (see figure 4.1). It was initially constructed during the Early Yunque phase (see figure 4.3) but remained in use as a food preparation area over the life of the site, or at least as long as Plaza One was an important area for celebrations in the Iglesia Precinct. Its association with food preparation is indicated by the ten grinding stones recovered from a single excavation trench placed through the center of the structure.[8] High concentrations of burnt bone, carbonized botanical remains, coyol and jute shells, ash, and wood charcoal were recovered from this structure, along with broken ceramics, lithics, and burnt daub. Furthermore, six pit hearths were identified immediately south of this structure that were dug into the surface of Plaza One. Large quantities of roasted coyol were associated with these hearths, which were aligned in a row—suggesting that they were constructed and used at the same moment of time to roast, cook, or brew food for many people.[9]

Two similar unconsolidated earthen structures that supported perishable buildings on their summits were found at the east end of the Iglesia Precinct. Structure 9-subA was built on the north side of Plaza Two and had a circular stone hearth that was used to prepare food. Ash, charcoal, burnt daub, and carbonized food remains that included burnt bone, jutes, and coyol were distributed across this structure. Three AMS radiocarbon dates from this structure and its associated hearth date its use to the Early and Middle Sulaco phases (see table 4.1:PSU7061, PSU7690, SMU1933). Structure 9-subA was eventually covered during Stage 6 construction events at the same time Structure 22 was built in the East Courtyard and took over food preparation tasks.[10]

Altar 2 in Plaza Two also appears related to feasting activity (see figure 4.20). It was a low platform 4 m² in size whose primary function appears related to food preparation and display. Five metates and two manos were recovered from the surface of the platform despite its small size. The grinding stones together with its proximity to Structure 9-subA suggest that Altar 2 was associated with some type of feasting in the Iglesia Precinct. The last possible food preparation area identified in the Iglesia Precinct was the fire pit and hearth identified on Structure 397.

The other area at Salitrón Viejo where evidence of feasting was found was in the public plaza of the West Residential Group. This plaza is 2,200 m² in size. Approximately 6 percent of the plaza was excavated,[11] which resulted in the identification of a number of features related to feasting. Foremost among these was a large midden deposit 4.5 m in diameter that contained a high concentration of broken and partially complete ceramic vessels dating to the Early Sulaco phase (figure 7.1). The material in this deposit included a high

Figure 7.1. *A large feasting midden (Feature 82CY-R1) deposited on the surface of the plaza of the West Residential Group. Photograph by Kenneth Robinson.*

percentage of service ware, twelve manos, and eleven metates used in food preparation. Three small pit ovens with burnt surfaces and concentrations of associated charcoal were also identified along the west side of the plaza.[12]

The evidence of feasting consists of high concentrations of food residues, food preparation equipment, and cooking facilities located in civic-ceremonial spaces where one does not expect to recover trash from normal domestic activities. The evidence suggests that feasting was an important ingredient of ritual celebrations and festive labor work groups at Salitrón Viejo. Feasting was also carried out in domestic contexts and has been obscured by normal household activity.

TABLE 7.2. Volumetric estimates for the construction of the Acropolis platform

Area	Construction Stage	Construction Volume	Adjusted Volume	Adjusted Labor Estimate in Person-Days
Eastern Platform	3	6,080	5,170	3,977
Eastern Platform	4	2,400	2,400	1,846
Western Platform	4	1,900	1,778	1,368
Final Platform	5	2,736	2,542	1,955
Total	—	13,116	11,890	9,146

CONSTRUCTING A RITUAL PRECINCT

It is logical that feasting would be associated with ritual celebrations. Across Mesoamerica and neighboring regions of Central America, feasting was also important for mobilizing labor for many types of activities (Hurtado de Mendoza and Troy Vargas 2007–2008; Ibarra Rojas 2014). Examples included planting and harvesting community fields, repairing or cleaning irrigation facilities, and, of course, constructing civic-ceremonial architecture (Rojas Rabiela 1979; Zavala 1984–1989; Zorita 1994). It is likely that some food preparation areas in the Iglesia Precinct were where feasts were prepared for mobilizing labor for construction purposes.

The control of labor is central to the study of socio-political organization. In complex societies, the authority of leaders can be judged, in part, by their ability to mobilize people in different ways. Many levels of socio-political control do not leave physical manifestations that can be observed in the archaeological record. One that does is the mobilization of labor for the construction of public buildings, mortuary monuments, palisades, and civic-ceremonial platform mounds. The scale of monumental constructions is an indirect measure of the workforce size mobilized to create them.

The Acropolis platform was the largest monumental construction at Salitrón Viejo, which consists of 13,116 m^3 of earthen and cobble fill (table 7.2). Walls in the Acropolis were constructed primarily using river cobbles set in a clay mortar, although adobe walls were found in several structures as well as in the west wall of the Eastern Acropolis platform.[13] The upper floor of the Acropolis was a heterogeneous mix of different materials that included hard-packed earth, cobble pavements, and a matrix of crushed rock and wet lime plaster (Hirth, Lara-Pinto, and Hasemann 1984:17). Floor types were discontinuous across the Acropolis platform, reflecting the sequential nature of construction that spanned three building episodes.

FIGURE 7.2. *Central Plaza of the Iglesia Precinct looking east from Structure 3. Note the concentration of cobbles used as fill in the Acropolis platform. Photograph by Kenneth Hirth.*

FIGURE 7.3. *Cobble fill of the Acropolis platform. Photograph by George Hasemann.*

The Acropolis platform was constructed primarily using earth and river cobbles that were 25–40 cm in diameter and 10–15 cm thick (figures 7.2, 7.3). These construction materials were close at hand. An abundance of river cobbles together with soil and sand could be collected from the bank of the Yunque River immediately adjacent to the Iglesia Precinct. Experimental studies of the time needed to collect and transport the building materials are used in addition to the architectural reconstruction presented in chapter 4 to model the effort required to construct the Acropolis platform.

THE ACROPOLIS PLATFORM CONSTRUCTION ESTIMATE

Charles Erasmus (1965) has provided one of the most useful studies of labor construction in Mesoamerica (see also Abrams 1994). His goal was to estimate the number of workdays needed to build Maya ceremonial centers. He conducted experiments in Mexico and Guatemala[14] on how long it took local workers to excavate earth using simple digging sticks and to mine stone using hardwood posts that replicated prehispanic technology and working conditions. He conducted the research using two-man teams. The results revealed that one man could excavate 2.6 m^3 of earth in a five-hour day, which another worker could transport over 75 m in the same amount of time. The excavation of rock was equally impressive. Erasmus (1965:286–288) found that one man could mine 1,700 kg of rock in five hours using a wooden lever and transport it using a tumpline or on his head across 125 m during the same day. Similar parameters have been replicated in other experiments in North America (Hammerstedt 2005), Costa Rica (Hurtado de Mendoza and Troy Vargas 2007–2008), and Scandinavia (Andersen 1988).[15]

Archaeological excavation combined with radiocarbon dating established that the Acropolis platform was constructed in three separate stages, beginning in Stage 3 and completed in Stage 5 (see figures 4.10, 4.14, 4.16). Table 7.2 summarizes the construction volume of each stage. The Acropolis, however, was not built *de nuevo* on unobstructed ground. The Central Plaza over which the Acropolis was constructed was defined by platform structures built around its periphery during Stages 1 and 2. Some of those structures were engulfed and covered by the three stages of Acropolis construction.[16] The adjusted calculation in table 7.2 removes the volume of these earlier structures that were partially or completely covered as the Acropolis was constructed. While these adjustments were relatively minor, they provide a nuanced estimate of the work effort needed to build the Acropolis during each stage.[17]

The proximity of the Yunque River provided access to a ready supply of both cobbles and earthen fill that could be mined from the terrace walls of the river channel. Erasmus organized his labor experiment to estimate labor time for both the collection and transportation of building materials. His two-worker teams were able to excavate and transport 2.6 m³ of earth in a five-hour work-day. Increased efficiency could have been achieved if more laborers were used for transportation depending on the distance involved.[18] His energetic calculations of 1.3 m³ of earth/day/person were applied directly to this labor reconstruction because sufficient building material was available within 50–100 m of the building site.[19] These construction parameters are both conservative and realistic, since a five-hour workday fits the tropical climate and could have been carried out during the non-agricultural dry season.

The estimate of 1.3 m³ of earth excavated per person each day was applied to the adjusted volume presented in table 7.2 to obtain an estimate for the number of person-days needed to build each stage of the Acropolis platform. What is immediately apparent is that the three building stages are not identical in the amount of labor necessary to carry them out. The 3,977 person-days invested in Stage 3 construction are approximately the same as the 3,214 person-days estimated for Stage 4. Completion of the Stage 5 platform was a lower number but was still substantial, involving 1,955 person-days. The first two construction stages appear to have been carried out in the same amount of time, while Stage 5 would have taken less time to bring the Acropolis to its final form. It is impossible to estimate how continuous or syncopated the construction was beyond the three-stage architectural reconstruction presented in chapter 4. Interior retention walls were identified in the fill matrix of the Acropolis; while they could have been left exposed for short periods of time, no floors or refuse accumulations were associated with them, suggesting that they were not exposed for any prolonged period as was the case with exterior walls. What can be said based on architectural sequencing and AMS radiocarbon dating is that Stages 4 and 5 were completed relatively close to one another in time.[20] Whether this was a few years or a decade cannot be specified within the archaeological time frames currently available.

The amount of effort needed to build the Acropolis was substantial but well within the capabilities of a small-scale society depending on the pace and timing of construction (Stanish 2017). The larger question is whether the construction of the Acropolis platform was an architectural endeavor that could have been completed by the residents of Salitrón Viejo or whether it required the collective collaboration of other groups in the region. The Late Yunque population of Salitrón Viejo is estimated at between 200 and 250 households. To estimate the workforce available from Salitrón Viejo, it was assumed that each household contributed one male worker to the Acropolis construction project. Table 7.3 provides an estimated time frame for completing this project using the high and low workforce projections of 200 and 250 laborers, respectively.

TABLE 7.3. Estimate of community workdays to build the Acropolis platform

Construction Stage	Labor Estimate in Person-Days	Community Days with 200 Workers	Community Days with 250 Workers
3	3,977	19.9	15.9
4	3,214	16.1	12.9
5	1,955	9.8	7.8
Total	9,146	45.8	36.6

The two projections suggest that all three stages of the Acropolis could have been completed within a period of 37 to 46 days. Stage 3 construction would have taken the longest and would have required a span of 16–20 days to complete, while the final Stage 5 was the shortest, needing only 8–10 days.

In terms of work effort, the residents of Salitrón Viejo could have completed the construction of the Acropolis by themselves if they had chosen to do so. There are several reasons to believe they did not. Incorporating groups from outlying communities in the Acropolis construction on a rotating basis not only would have increased the rapidity of completion but would also have expanded the collective buy-in of outlying communities in the importance of the Iglesia Precinct as the primary ritual area in the El Cajón region (the sunk cost principle). Collective involvement would have promoted a sentiment of corporate ownership that would have helped integrate the chiefdom around ritual activities. Following the tenets of behavioral economics, the work invested helped produce an endowment effect that reinforced a sentiment of corporate ownership of the facilities. While we believe the North Precinct was constructed for receiving outlying groups entering Salitrón Viejo, no evidence of ceremonial feasting was identified there. Instead, all the evidence of feasting during the Late Yunque phase occurs within the Iglesia Precinct. The implication is that groups invited to Salitrón Viejo would have joined in feasting celebrations in the Iglesia Precinct. Integration, therefore, relied on both the ritual celebrations conducted at Salitrón and the historic certainty that groups who participated in the Acropolis construction had collective ownership of the space in which these ritual celebrations were conducted.

ESTIMATING CIVIC-CEREMONIAL MOUND CONSTRUCTION

The Acropolis platform was the largest architectural construction at Salitrón Viejo, but it was not the only one. Many other smaller civic-ceremonial structures were constructed throughout the length of its occupation. Understanding how the scale and location of construction varied over time provides insight

TABLE 7.4. Volumetric estimates for civic-ceremonial construction during the Yunque and Sulaco phases at Salitrón Viejo

Area	Early Yunque Phase No.	Early Yunque Phase Volume[a]	Late Yunque Phase No.	Late Yunque Phase Volume[a]	Early, Middle, and Late Sulaco Phases No.	Early, Middle, and Late Sulaco Phases Volume[a]	Total[b]	Labor Estimate Person-Days[b]
Iglesia Precinct	3	82	12	8,767	4	1,471	10,320	7,938
Iglesia Acropolis	—	—	1	11,890	—	—	11,890	9,146
North Precinct	—	—	19	1,748	—	—	1,748	1,345
West Group	—	—	—	—	4	6,366	6,366	4,897
South Group	—	—	—	—	6	5,373	5,373	4,133
Total	3	82	32	22,405	14	13,210	35,697	27,459

a. Volume expressed in cubic meters of architectural fill.
b. Estimated based on 1.3 m³ of volume per day.

into the changes in socio-political activities throughout the El Cajón region. Table 7.4 summarizes the number and volume of platform structures in the four civic-ceremonial areas of Salitrón Viejo during three phases of occupation. Structures were often built sequentially, and phases of construction were assigned to each of these three phases where they could be identified.[21] While these calculations do not consider the effort expended in constructing the perishable structures on the summits of platforms, this is a quantifiable assessment of the effort expended in constructing civic-ceremonial structures.[22]

The sequence of architectural construction reveals several interesting trends. While the first civic-ceremonial structures at Salitrón Viejo were constructed during the Early Yunque phase, most architectural activity in the Iglesia Precinct occurred during the subsequent Late Yunque phase. Structures in the Iglesia Precinct continued in use during the Early Sulaco phase, but there was a noticeable decline in construction at this time. There is no indication that structures in the North Precinct were expanded or even used during the Middle and Late Sulaco phases. Nevertheless, all the information suggests that the Iglesia Precinct remained the center of civic-ceremonial life up through the start of the Middle Sulaco phase.

A number of platform mounds were constructed in the Iglesia Precinct. Table 7.4 divides the construction effort in the Iglesia Precinct into two parts: the Acropolis platform and the smaller structures built on and around the Central Plaza during different phases. When taken together, these structures are equivalent to 74 percent of the volume of the Acropolis platform (table 7.4). While smaller in stature, these structures had different functions in the social and ritual activities carried out in the Iglesia Precinct. When all phases are combined, these ancillary structures are equivalent to 87 percent of the construction volume of the Acropolis platform.

A shift in the civic-ceremonial focus at Salitrón Viejo began to occur at the end of the Early Sulaco period. Social interaction increasingly shifted to activities in the plazas of each of the two residential groups. Whether this came at the expense of communal celebrations in the Iglesia Precinct is unclear, although some feasting was certainly carried out in Plaza Two. One small Range structure was constructed in each of the West and South Plazas during the Early Sulaco period. These structures were expanded, and other Range structures were built in these plazas during the Middle and Late Sulaco phases. Most important, the effort and volume of construction in each of these residential groups is three to four times greater than what was carried out in the Iglesia Precinct during these same phases. This suggests an increased emphasis on building social solidarity at the level of the residential group or clan during the Middle and Late Sulaco phases.

Despite these changes, Salitrón Viejo remained the largest community in the region. Nevertheless, the reduced level of construction in the Iglesia Precinct suggests a weakening of centralized authority within the site. Coincident with increased civic-ceremonial activity in the West and South Residential Groups was the increase in monumental public constructions in other sites along the Sulaco and Humuya Rivers. While excavations were not as comprehensive at the regional level as they were at Salitrón, they have confirmed that many of the civic-ceremonial structures in the largest sites also date to the Middle to Late Sulaco periods. The sites where this is best documented include Guarabuquí (PC15), La Ceiba (PC13), Cueva Grande (PC59), and Intendencia (PC109) (see table 3.3).

George Hasemann (1987, 1998) documented a complex hierarchy of sites along the Sulaco River during the Middle and Late Sulaco periods. Although the development of a regional site hierarchy is often interpreted as evidence of higher levels of social control (Lightfoot 1987; Spencer 1987:371–372), in the El Cajón region it may reflect an increased focus on civic-ceremonial activity at the level of individual communities instead of their integration into a regional chiefdom centered on Salitrón Viejo. It was during the Late Yunque phase that the Iglesia and North Precincts were the only civic-ceremonial architecture in the region, and monumental structures were not found at any of the other contemporaneous sites identified in the regional testing program (Hasemann 1998) (see figure 3.14).

While reciprocal community feasting probably accompanied the growth of communities during the Sulaco period, it may have resulted in more competition between sites and a general decline in centralized authority at Salitrón Viejo. Populations at Salitrón Viejo remained actively engaged in the construction of civic-ceremonial architecture within their respective residential groups. When taken together, new constructions in the West and South Residential Groups during the Middle and Late Sulaco phases reflect a nearly identical amount of work invested in the construction of Range structures as was involved in building the Acropolis platform (tables 7-2, 7-4). But this work was not concentrated on a central precinct designed to integrate populations at the site and regional levels. During the Middle and Late Sulaco phases, the Range structure in the Iglesia Precinct underwent one remodeling episode. By comparison, the eight excavated Range structures in the South and West Residential Groups underwent a total of twenty-seven construction and remodeling episodes during the same time span. The focus during the Middle and Late Sulaco phases was clearly on enhancing the ritual environment and the prestige of the leaders in their respective co-resident groups.

THE COST OF DEDICATING A SACRED LANDSCAPE

The cost of construction is not just about the rock, soil, adobe block, and labor needed to undertake a building effort. It also includes the costs of mobilizing the workforce and dedicating finished constructions. As discussed above, labor mobilization most likely took place in the context of community feasting, which required the assembly and preparation of a range of consumable resources. The Iglesia Precinct contained buildings of special religious significance that required dedication offerings. Structure 3 was used as a mortuary repository where several important individuals were interred.[23] The first two building stages in the Iglesia Precinct defined a ceremonial field that was eventually elevated in height with the construction of the Acropolis platform. It is no surprise that the Acropolis platform and other structures in the Iglesia Precinct required special offerings to sanctify them as part of a sacred landscape where ritual activities for the gods were carried out.

Ethnographic and archaeological research has documented that prehispanic groups saw the world as a spiritually animated landscape (McAnany 2010; Sandstrom and Sandstrom 2017). Prehispanic people shared a cosmologically informed worldview in which all animate and inanimate objects had a spirit or an inner soul.[24] The same was true of the built environment, which included everything from simple houses to ritual buildings (McGee 1998:41). The construction of buildings using materials removed from their natural environments created an imbalance that was addressed in the spiritual realm with dedication offerings and ceremonies. Whether these dedication offerings were intended to reimburse the earth for resources removed or to enliven new structures with what Evon Vogt (1998:21) called an inner soul, the results were the same. They involved costs in the form of dedication rituals, offerings, and other acts intended to ensoul, engender, or spiritually animate the built environments people inhabited and used (Freidel 1998:189–190).

The life history of buildings replicated the same events observed in the natural world. Birth, death, regeneration, and transformation were events in the life of structures that could be accompanied by offerings and rituals (Monaghan 1998:47). Archaeologists have identified and labeled these offerings dedication and termination rituals. Offerings that resemble regeneration or feeding the spirit of structures have been identified, but they are rare or difficult to recognize since the destruction of one building stage is often the initiation of a subsequent one. Nevertheless, termination rituals were often associated with the defacement, burning, and breaking of artifacts and architectural elements, while dedication events placed items in walls, under floors and stairways, and in corners of structures (Boteler Mock 1998:5–6; Garber 1983; Selsor Walker 1998).

Excavation of the Iglesia precinct uncovered large offerings of wealth goods in different construction stages. A total of 2,487 items were recovered in offerings from civic-ceremonial structures in the Iglesia Precinct (see table 6.1). They were documented in chapters 5 and 6. The nature and context of these offerings suggest that the majority were used in dedications rather than termination offerings.[25] Nevertheless, fully half of the items in them were intentionally broken upon deposition, probably for the purpose of animating the structures where they were deposited. All forms of greenstone were believed to be imbued with life, such that breaking jade artifacts upon deposition may have been intended to release their spirit into the structures where they were placed.

The size of these offerings represents large-scale sacrifices for a community the size of Salitrón Viejo. Like all sacrifices, the acquisition of large quantities of jade and other wealth goods involved a substantial cost in both the time and resources needed to procure them. Understanding the costs of obtaining these goods is important for reconstructing the organization and scale of the ritual economy (Watanabe 2007). Like architectural construction, the scale of offerings provides a measure of the importance of ritual as a unifying activity in prehispanic society.

MODELING RITUAL PROCUREMENT

The lapidary goods recovered at Salitrón Viejo represent the second largest offering of jade and marble artifacts recovered from eastern Mesoamerica. Only the collection from the Cenote at Chichen Itzá is larger (Coggins and Shane 1984; Proskouriakoff 1974). Other sites where large quantities of jade have been recovered include the site of Blue Creek, where a cache of 1,000 jade artifacts was excavated (Guderjan 1998), and the production site of Cancuen (Andrieu, Rodas, and Luin 2014; Kovacevich 2007). Jade was the most highly valued item in eastern Mesoamerica during the Formative and Classic periods (Taube 2005; Taube and Ishihara-Brito 2012), so the accumulation of a large quantity of high-value items in a small community of only 200–250 households during the Late Yunque phase begs the question of how they were obtained and assembled.

Three procurement models are evaluated below for how this collection of wealth goods was assembled at Salitrón Viejo. The first of these is the on-site production model, where finished goods would have been manufactured at Salitrón Viejo. The second is a down-the-line trade model, where individuals obtained finished wealth goods moving through interregional exchange networks. The third model is one of direct trade, where individuals from Salitrón procured finished goods by going directly to communities of artisans or areas where they could be acquired. All three of these models are plausible alternatives and are examined separately as explanations for the wealth goods found at Salitrón Viejo.

On-Site Production

Small scale production of jade ornaments was identified at the site of Puerto Escondido in west-central Honduras as early as the Middle Formative period (1000–900 BC) (Joyce and Henderson 2001:13). This together with a Honduran marble vessel crafting tradition that extends back to the Early and Middle Formative periods (Canby 1949:143; Dixon 1989a:44; Elder 1984:81; Joyce and Henderson 2002:5) made on-site production a possibility to consider.

The possibility of on-site production was suggested by the recovery of a few pieces of unworked greenstone and over a dozen incompletely drilled and unfinished pendants and beads in several offerings. While few in number, the presence of unfinished artifacts together with raw material suggested the possibility of local lapidary work.

The excavation of jade and lapidary production locales in Mesoamerica provides a model for what on-site production looks like (Andrieu, Rodas, and Luin 2014; Hirth 2009b; Kovacevich 2006; Rochette 2009b; Smith and Kidder 1943:165; Widmer 2009). The information from the jade workshops at Cancuen provides the best and most complete model for jade working. The jade workshop at Cancuen had 3,606 pieces of debitage in production contexts but only 184 finished artifacts (Andrieu, Rodas, and Luin 2014:142, 159). The finished artifact to debitage ratio at Cancuen was 1:19.6, or 1.0 finished item for every 19.6 pieces of debitage. This conforms to the expectation that finished goods will always be relatively scarce in workshop contexts, since they were removed when completed for use elsewhere (Clark 1986, 1990). High concentrations of production debris can be expected, even though artisans try to minimize waste. One way to minimize waste was to manufacture bead pendants and other artifacts from pieces of debitage produced from other cutting and sawing activities.

No production debitage or tools used to cut, shape, or polish lapidary goods were recovered from any domestic or elite contexts at Salitrón Viejo. Likewise, no production debris was found at any other site in the El Cajón region, indicating that none of finished jade and marble artifacts were locally made. Eight small jade nodules were identified, five of which were broken in half using bipolar percussion. These nodules and one percussion flake were the only raw material recovered at Salitrón Viejo (see chapter 5). Had jade artifacts been produced on-site, a large amount of production debitage would have been recovered in our excavations and included in offering deposits, as was the case with the small jade nodules recovered. The artifact to raw material/debitage ratio at Salitrón Viejo was 320:1,[26] which is a very sharp contrast to what is found at Cancuen or any other site where lapidary work was carried out (e.g., Hirth 2009b). The implication is that all high-value lapidary goods entered the region through some form of trade.

Procurement through Down-the-Line Exchange

Multiple investigators have documented the operation of strong interregional exchange networks across Honduras beginning during the Early Formative (Baudez and Becqulin 1973; Joyce and Henderson 2001, 2010;

Popenoe 1934) and continuing through the Terminal Classic period (Aoyama, Tashiro, and Glascock 1999; Beaudry-Corbett 1987; Hirth 1988; Joyce 2017; Robinson 1989; Schortman and Urban 1987a; Schortman et al. 1986; Sheets et al. 1990). High-value items including jade, marine shell, marble bowls, and onyx moved through exchange networks that were very likely accompanied by perishable items such as feathers, textiles, and cacao. Utilitarian items including obsidian (Aoyama, Tashiro, and Glascock 1999; Sheets et al. 1990) and ceramics (e.g., Beaudry-Corbett 1987) also moved through these exchange networks. The best evidence of interregional exchange during the Late Yunque phase was the movement of Usulután-style ceramics between regions (see figures 2.3a, 4.8a–b). These ceramics define a horizon style and are a hallmark of ceramic interaction between 400 BC and AD 250. The distribution of Usulután resist ceramics defines what various investigators refer as the Uapala ceramic sphere that extended across El Salvador and Honduras (Andrews 1976:142–144; Demarest 1986; Demarest and Sharer 1986; Goralski 2008; Robinson 1989).

The distribution of Usulután ceramics represents both a network of direct exchange and a system of interregional communication that connected groups across a wide area of prehispanic Honduras. Craig Goralski (2008) has examined this interregional network using instrumental neutron activation analysis (INAA). A sample of 327 Usulután sherds from twelve areas of Honduras and El Salvador was analyzed to determine where these ceramics were manufactured and how far they were traded. The results showed that Usulután ceramics were manufactured at multiple locations in Honduras and were traded over distances of up to 150 km (272). Goralski identified thirteen different Usulután-related paste groups, three of which were associated with ceramic production in the El Cajón region. Particularly important was the identification of the trade of Usulután vessels among the Comayagua, El Cajón, Ulúa valley, and Copán regions. Usulután resist ceramics are found in both elite and non-elite contexts, and Goralski (272) concluded that they were valued because they constituted an important service ware used in feasting celebrations.

The location of the El Cajón region along the Central Honduran corridor (see figure 1.1) gave El Cajón two advantages. It meant that Salitrón Viejo was well connected to interregional exchange networks and also gave it the opportunity to become an important supplier for Usulután ceramics moving between regions during the Late Yunque period. The question is whether these networks would also have provided access to large quantities of wealth goods used in ritual celebrations at Salitrón Viejo. We believe they did not, for two reasons. First, a few jade items have been recovered from Late Formative and Early Classic sites elsewhere in Honduras and Guatemala (Dixon et al. 1994:74; Ichon and Arnould 1985:35; Robinson 1989:189; Smith and Kidder 1951:33; Wonderley 1985:5; Yde 1938:24) but nowhere near the quantity that occurs at Salitrón Viejo. A large volume of jade and marble goods would have had to have moved through trade networks for the community to have accumulated thousands of high-value items for offerings during the Late Yunque phase. The absence of large quantities of these materials in other contemporary sites suggests that jade and marble lapidary goods were rare rather than common items moving through these exchange networks.

Second, jade and marble jewelry were high-value goods, so it is logical that elites would have been involved in their procurement however they were obtained. Although a logical assumption, it is paradoxical that elites in the El Cajón region seem to have been disinclined to incorporate them in their own broader lifestyles. Earflares, beads, and pendants were costume regalia associated with the elite among the Maya. They were visible on carved stelae and included in mortuary contexts, where they were carried into death by the people who wore them. Elite burials are rare in the El Cajón region; where they occur at Salitrón, they do not have offerings of jade beyond a single bead (Kate and Hirth n.d). While jade objects were held in high esteem, they do not appear to have been a primary vehicle that elites used to accumulate individual wealth and social power. It is even possible that many of the wealth items used in offerings were accumulated collectively by households at Salitrón Viejo, with indirect elite involvement.

DIRECT PROCUREMENT THROUGH COLLECTIVE HOUSEHOLD AND COMMUNITY TRADE

The concentration of jade and marble regalia at Salitrón Viejo, together with its relative scarcity at contemporary sites, is not a result of archaeological sampling error. If jade and other wealth goods were readily circulating within interregional exchange networks, then they would appear with greater frequency at other contemporary sites across Honduras. But they do not. Two exceptions to this would be (1) if wealth goods were procured and deposited at important locations in the natural landscape (e.g., springs, caves, mountains) not usually explored by archaeologists or (2) if the wealth goods obtained at Salitrón Viejo represent a unique instance of ritual behavior that was not replicated at other sites in west-central Honduras. Both options are possible.

While the Acropolis platform is a unique architectural feature, the presence of a civic-ceremonial precinct at a major site is not. Other non-Maya civic-ceremonial centers have been tested across Honduras, and those tests have not uncovered large numbers of high-value goods in dedication offerings. Nevertheless, the fact that most of these materials date to the Late Yunque phase (AD 0–400) is a complicating factor, since fewer sites from this period have been excavated than those occupied after AD 500. But there is no doubt that the need for and use of jade at Salitrón Viejo declined and remained relatively low after AD 400 (see table 6.2).

The absence of on-site production makes it clear that jade and other wealth goods entered the region through some form of exchange. But the specific procurement mechanism used to obtain these items remains unclear unless one uses the process of elimination. The Usulután ceramics manufactured in the El Cajón region were distributed through trade connections that extended up to 150 km in all directions. Usulután trade wares are common occurrences in households at all levels of the social hierarchy, which suggests that a relatively large number of vessels moved within and between regions during the Late Yunque phase. The interregional networks through which these ceramics moved were most likely composed of multiple trade partner relationships where individuals engaged in exchange on an intermittent or part-time basis. The individuals who engaged in these interactions were not full-time merchants. Had merchants been involved, they would certainly also have trafficked in high-value trade items like those found at Salitrón Viejo. And if they had, high-value goods would occur in greater frequency at contemporary sites in the El Cajón region and neighboring regions, but they do not.[27]

It is more likely that the offerings recovered in the Iglesia Precinct involved the gradual and planned acquisition of a large quantity of wealth goods over a long period of time as a prelude to the construction of the Acropolis platform. This accumulation would have involved considerable effort on the part of households in the Salitrón chiefdom. The elite of Salitrón Viejo may have taken the lead in organizing trade ventures, but assembling the resources needed for exchange would certainly have involved the collective effort of every household in the community. It is in this sense that many non-elite households may have been involved in procuring a few wealth items to include in the collective offerings recovered at Salitrón Viejo.

A question that needs to be answered is: what aspects of social interaction made it possible for a community of several hundred households to acquire the thousands of high-value wealth items used in Acropolis dedication ceremonies? If not a single community, how many communities in the Salitrón chiefdom contributed offerings to its festive celebrations? No doubt it took hard work and a collective effort. While elites are often associated with the accumulation of wealth used in reinforcing power relationships within chief-doms (Earle 1991, 1997, 2021), there is little evidence that leaders in the El Cajón region used high-value goods in this way. Although elites may have resided on the site's prominent Range structures, there is little evidence of social inequality found in mortuary treatments (Kate and Hirth n.d.) or the differential accumulation of high-value items in elite and non-elite house-holds. But one feature stands out and is often overlooked in the assessment of collective community activities: the higher level of economic integration that can occur in compact village communities of chieftain societies.

Scholars have noted a great deal of variation in the organization and develop-ment of chieftain societies across the Americas and the ancient world (Drennan and Peterson 2006; Drennan and Uribe 1987; Fowler 1989, 1991; Ibarra Rojas 1990, 2014; Lara-Pinto 1980, 1991b, 2021). One trend that is particularly interest-ing is that societies with high-density communities often manifest higher levels of economic integration and specialization than societies with low population densities. The reason is that in aggregated communities, households have the opportunity for more continuous economic interaction than do households in low-density communities. The basis for this is easy to understand: people interact more frequently when they reside in close proximity to one another. The potential for greater economic integration within communities is inversely proportional to the spacing between households. The degree of integration has implications for the development of the political economy and is especially important when large quantities of resources are needed for feasts, celebrations, or obtaining the ritual offerings used in them (Berrey 2015; Berrey, Drennan, and Peterson 2021; Drennan and Peterson 2008).

A notable feature of the four largest settlements in the El Cajón region is that they are all compact, high-density communities. Population densities at the three large communities on the Sulaco River range from 136–227 persons/ ha for the two residential clusters at Salitrón Viejo to 99–175 persons/ha at the sites of La Ceiba and Guarabuquí (Hirth n.d.). While the area of these com-munities was small, the density of their populations was fully compatible with some of the largest urban sites in Mesoamerica, including Teotihuacan. This high level of nucleation may have been the product of maximizing the limited amount of good agricultural land found in the small vegas along the Sulaco and Humuya Rivers. Whatever the reason, these communities were compact, and close household spacing provided the opportunity for high levels of eco-nomic interaction within them.

If jade and marble goods were obtained through trade, the question is: what did these communities produce to use in exchange? It is here that a problem is encountered because whatever high-value goods were involved, they were perishable and left no discernible trace in the archaeological record. As mentioned above, there was no evidence of large-scale craft production; most crafting was confined to the manufacture of items used in the community. One exception was the manufacture of Usulután ceramics, which INAA analysis has shown were widely traded as far south as the Comayagua valley, as far north as the coast of Honduras, and as far west as Copán (Goralski 2008). A cache of thirty-four ceramic molds used in the production of ceramic whistles was recovered at the site of El Mango (PC71) along the Sulaco River, but where these molds were employed in production activities was not determined. The only other clear evidence of crafting was the identification of several small quarry areas along the Sulaco and Humuya Rivers, where local chert was mined and used in the production of stone tools. In no case, however, was the scale of mining or tool production sizable enough to suggest the manufacture of tools for export to other areas or their use in specialized wood working, hide processing, or some other craft that needed large quantities of stone tools (e.g., Anderson and Hirth 2009).

While ceramics were trade items, they were relatively low-value goods that did not have enough intrinsic worth to be exchanged directly for jade and marble goods. Instead, it is more likely that a range of high-value perishable goods also figured into the exchange. A list of some possible trade items is presented in table 7.5. At the top of this list are tropical bird feathers, important in both elite costuming and regal displays. The El Cajón region abounds in brightly colored macaws, parrots, and toucans that nest in the valley slopes or in the adjacent uplands. This list would also have included the prized quetzal (Hanson 1982; Monroe 1965), although that species no longer occupies the El Cajón uplands. Cacao is grown in the uplands around La Libertad and certainly could have been an important trade item. Cotton textiles are another possibility, although no spindle whorls were recovered even though both the Jicaque and Paya of Honduras grew bush cotton and the Paya manufactured woven cotton garments (Conzemius 1932; Lentz 1986, 1993; von Hagen 1943).

The El Cajón uplands are rich in pine, which was the firewood of choice at Salitrón (Lentz 1989a:table 7.1) and could have been used to produce both aromatic resins and charcoal for trade, as occurred further west among the Maya (Lentz et al. 2005; Morehart, Lentz, and Prufer 2005). Medicinal plants and hallucinogens are another possibility, including extracts from the Bufo marinus toad (Furst 1972), which is a native resident of El Cajón. Finally, a range of felines occupied the forests of Honduras, including the jaguar, cougar, ocelot, and margay, whose prized pelts could also have been used for exchange. The

TABLE 7.5. Possible trade items from the El Cajón region

Imperishable items
Usulután ceramics
Figural ceramic whistles

Perishable items
Tropical bird feathers
Cacao
Cotton textiles
Pine charcoal
Aromatic pine resin
Medicinal plants
Hallucinogens
Feline pelts

list is short, but it does identify several valued resources that may have been used to procure high-value trade goods.

ESTIMATING THE ENERGETIC VALUE OF RITUAL OFFERINGS

The evidence from Salitrón Viejo reveals two aspects about ritual behavior. The first is that the final dedication of the Acropolis platform and associated structures in the Iglesia Precinct required a large quantity of wealth goods to complete the construction. The second is that all of these high-value goods were procured through trade from outside the region. While we can only speculate about the perishable goods used in these exchanges (table 7.5), there is no doubt that the residents of Salitrón Viejo and possibly other communities in the region had to assembly a range of goods with an exchange value equivalent to, or at least sufficient to acquire, the jade and marble items recovered.

This poses an interesting question. Is it possible to estimate the value of the offerings obtained by the residents of Salitrón Viejo through an examination of the amount of work needed to produce them? We know that all lapidary items were valued commodities, but we do not have sufficient information from ethnohistoric sources that identifies exchange equivalencies between different categories of high-value goods such as jade, quetzal feathers, shell, cacao, precious metals, embroidered textiles, or plain white clothes (Lara-Pinto 2011, 2019) even if we knew the quantities collected (e.g., Berdan 1992; Freidel,

Masson, and Rich 2017:39–45; Gutiérrez 2013; Tozzer 1941). Although the goods populations in the El Cajón region used in exchange remain unknown, some insight into their relative value can be gained by looking at the energetic value of the goods obtained. One approach is to look at the labor invested in the manufacture of lapidary goods. Unfortunately, the amount of experimental work needed to make a precise energetic estimate of the labor time (or cost) needed to manufacture lapidary goods is very limited. Despite this situation, some preliminary estimates of manufacturing time are presented for several artifact types that can serve as working parameters to frame this question.

Jade, marble, and other categories of greenstone were all precious substances, and some insight into their value can be obtained by considering the amount of labor needed to produce them. Energetic estimates are provided here for three artifact classes manufactured from Motagua valley jade: tubular earflares (see figure 5.17a), ring pendants (see figure 5.19), and crescent pectorals (see figures 5.34, 5.35). These were selected because a good deal of the production work involved in shaping these three artifact classes used sawing technology for which there is some experimental work. A series of experiments on jade sawing was conducted by Pierre Pétrequin and colleagues (2012:275–278) in their research on the production of Neolithic Alpine axes. They determined that it could take as long as 40 hours to saw a 20.5 cm by 9.5 cm by 9.0 cm block of Alpine jade using prehistoric technology.[28] Using this work as a starting point and assuming similar technological efficiency, estimates were developed for these three artifact classes based on their average dimensions. Estimates are conservative, and the details for their calculation are found in the accompanying endnotes. It is estimated that it would have taken 130–140 hours to shape and finish a single large tubular earflare.[29] 90–95 hours to produce a ring pendant,[30] and 80–90 hours to manufacture a crescent pectoral.[31]

Table 7.6 summarizes the MAC for these three artifact classes along with the estimated amount of time needed to produce them. What is immediately apparent is that each of these artifacts takes many hours to manufacture and represents multiple days of work. Using a five-hour workday as the crafting model, a single large tubular earflare could take 26–28 days for an artisan to complete. The large tubular earflares found in the El Cajón collection were labor-intensive items because of the work required to shape the posterior stem and drill the hole through their centers. Ring pendants and crescent pectorals took less time but still range from 18 to 19 days each to manufacture. Together, the effort to manufacture these 98 artifacts would have required 10,970–11,835 artisan hours, or 2,194–2,367 workdays, of labor. These estimates, of course, are based on conservative MAC of only three artifact classes, are only a fraction

TABLE 7.6. Labor estimates for manufacturing jade artifacts

Artifact	No. of Items	Hours of Manufacturing Time per Artifact	Total Hours	Workdays[a]
Tubular earflares	58	130–140	7,540–8,120	1,508–1,624
Ring pendants	23	90–95	2,070–2,185	414–437
Crescent pectorals	17	80–90	1,360–1,530	272–306
Total	98	—	10,970–11,835	2,194–2,367

a. Assumes a five-hour workday.

of all of the lapidary artifacts entering the region, and may significantly under-estimate the labor invested because they do not account for the many fragmented artifacts in the collection that were not included in MAC calculations.

The labor time needed to manufacture the 98 tubular earflares, crescent pectorals, and ring pendants was estimated at 2,194–2,367 workdays. What is striking is that the amount of time needed to manufacture these few artifacts represents almost 20 percent of the work time that was needed to construct the Acropolis platform (table 7.4). These were important artifact classes, but the time needed to manufacture them does not begin to approximate the effort represented in all of the 2,836 artifacts (see table 6.1) incorporated into ritual deposits in the Iglesia and North Precincts.[32] It is not possible to estimate the total effort required to manufacture the entire lapidary assemblage without more comprehensive experimental data. Nevertheless, it is likely that the amount of time needed to manufacture all the offerings at Salitrón Viejo far exceeded the effort required to construct the Acropolis platform and other civic-ceremonial structures in the Iglesia Precinct. Dedication offerings were vital and just as important for the construction of civic-ceremonial architecture at Salitrón as the structures themselves. The amount of effort residents in the El Cajón region had to engage in to acquire these offerings can be appreciated in part by the amount of artisan time needed to manufacture them.

SUMMARY

The foregoing discussion has sought to situate the evidence of ritual activities at Salitrón Viejo within the broader context of prehispanic cultural development in west-central Honduras. Three features of the ritual economy were important in the integration of its regional chiefdom: ritual feasting, the construction of civic-ceremonial precincts where festivities were held, and the procurement of sacred regalia needed to dedicate the ritual spaces.

The most fundamental of these three features was the practice of collective feasting. Feasting was an integrative mechanism that permeated all levels of society, from celebrating life events within families to building alliances and regulating inter-community relationships at the regional level (Dalton 1977; Drucker and Heizer 1967; Earle 1987, 2021; Hayden 2014; Hirth 2020:60–62). At Salitrón Viejo, all the evidence for feasting during the Early and Late Yunque phases is found in the Iglesia Precinct. During the Early Sulaco phase, feasting spread to the West and South Residential Groups. This suggests two important aspects about the role of feasting in this society. The first is that centralized feasting was an important dimension in the formation and integration of Salitrón Viejo's Late Yunque chiefdom. The second is that feasting could also undermine social integration depending on the social context in which it was carried out. The increase in feasting noted at intermediate levels both in the West and South Residential Groups and at other large sites throughout the region very likely served to weaken Salitrón Viejo's central authority and its monopoly on feasting celebrations.

Feasting was a primary means of mobilizing labor in ethnographic settings around the world (Dietler and Hayden 2001; Heider 1969). Festive labor groups were a common way this was done, and feasting was used in this way in traditional Lenca groups in Honduras. An ethnohistoric account from AD 1598 records a feast for the collection of the first maize harvest that was celebrated by neighborhoods, probably representing lineage groups (Herrera y Tordesillas 1944–1947:6:23). The fact that this feast involved the consumption of large quantities of both food and fermented beverages is made clear where Amtonia de Herrera y Tordesillas states: "They take to drinking with one another, until they are drunk, and their faces swell, and the body, and they go about numb, and out of their minds: and as noon arrives, they get together to eat: for which, eight Days earlier, they have had a great Hunt, and the Women take care to cook it, and prepare it, and take it to the House of the Municipality and give them to drink" (translated by Wells and Davis-Salazar 2008:198).

Feasting was part of Lenca *compostura* celebrations recorded ethnographically by Anne Chapman (1985). *Composturas* were periodic celebrations intended to compensate ancestors for damage done to the environment and to mobilize labor for group or community work projects (Wells and Davis-Salazar 2007:34, 2008:195). *Compostura* celebrations were important for integrating dispersed populations, stimulating household surplus production, and demonstrating the social and political affluence of the elite members of society who directed and sponsored them (Wells and Davis-Salazar 2007:35). Feasting was undoubtedly a key ingredient in mobilizing the labor to construct the Iglesia Precinct and other civic-ceremonial structures both at Salitrón Viejo and in other communities throughout the El Cajón region.

The second feature of the ritual economy was the creation of a special purpose area where people could assemble for communal celebrations. At Salitrón Viejo, this involved the construction of two civic-ceremonial zones during the Late Yunque. The Iglesia Precinct was the most important ritual area at Salitrón Viejo, and the scale of its architectural construction is a testimony to its central role in the region. It is estimated that 22,210 days of labor were involved in the construction of the Iglesia Precinct, most of which occurred during the Late Yunque phase (table 7.4). But there was also the North Precinct, with its large ceremonial plaza and modest mound structures used to receive different groups linked to Salitrón Viejo. The fact that two separate civic-ceremonial spaces were constructed during the Late Yunque phase indicates that the community recognized the importance of regional groups and actively incorporated them in collective celebrations at Salitrón Viejo. It is likely that all of this construction was carried out in the context of *compostura*-like celebrations to mobilize corvée labor.

Third and finally, ritual practice at Salitrón Viejo involved the assembly of high-value offerings to sanctify and dedicate the civic-ceremonial structures in these two precincts. We believe the offerings associated with the Acropolis platform and other civic-ceremonial structures were intended to enliven and animate these human-made structures. More than 60 percent of the wealth goods in these offerings were fragmented, and the analysis of intra-deposit refits (see chapter 6) indicates that they were broken when they were deposited. Greenstone, especially jade, was held in high esteem because its color was associated with life itself. It is possible that the breakage of these materials was intended to release the life force carried within them into the built environment.

This last aspect of ritual behavior implies several things about the belief systems of pre-Columbian groups in west-central Honduras. Chapter 8 discusses this aspect of ritual behavior in greater detail in the hope of expanding our understanding of the spiritual forces and beliefs that produced and guided the ritual economy.

8

Chiefdom societies are diverse in the ways they were organized. Examples can be found of societies that were organized around elite-centered and coercive strategies as well as cases that employed more collective and cooperative forms of social integration.[1] Leaders in these societies integrated groups through a variety of ideological, socio-political, and economic means—whether their populations resided in nucleated communities or isolated households scattered across the landscape (Drennan and Uribe 1987; Earle 1991; Fowler 1989; Helms 1979; Ibarra Rojas 1990; Kirch 1989; Lara-Pinto 1991b). Religious ritual was a strong force in many chiefdom societies that reinforced common identify and provided a framework for the emergence of community and regional leadership. Whether leaders can be identified in the archaeological record depends on how their status was reflected in residential architecture, domestic inventories, and the mortuary practices of their respective societies (Friedman and Rowlands 1978; Hayden 2001b; Sheehy 1996).

This study has examined the organization and development of pre-Columbian society in the El Cajón region through an exploration of ritual economy. Ritual was a primary integrative mechanism for establishing and maintaining the Salitrón chiefdom. Feasts, dances, and other celebrations conducted in prominent civic-ceremonial spaces were important ingredients in building a network of relationships that extended from Salitrón Viejo to its surrounding communities.

Belief and Integration in a Ritual Economy

https://doi.org/10.5876/9781646424757.c008

273

Communal ritual helps develop a shared ideology among participants that incorporates both social and sacred propositions (Rappaport 1971). Ritual is a belief system in motion, whose actions can produce physical remains appropriate for archaeological interpretation. This study has used the perspective of ritual economy to evaluate how it was used to shape the region's social and political landscape. Instrumental in this endeavor has been estimating the economic costs involved in creating the ritual environment in which corporate identity was reinforced.

Ritual reflects the reciprocal relationships groups establish with spiritual entities by offering their time and material goods. This chapter begins by examining how aspects of worldview and social ideology were materialized in the goods consumed in ritual activities. Prominent in this discussion is the relationship among imagery, ritual, and the natural and built environments. The discussion then shifts to the ritual activities found at Salitrón Viejo: feasting, the construction of civic-ceremonial architecture, and the procurement of ritual offerings through long-distance trade. The chapter concludes by examining the factors involved in the development of chiefdom societies in west-central Honduras and how they changed over time.

BELIEF SYSTEMS AND RITUAL

Rituals reinforced the shared spiritual beliefs and experiences of participants at the same time they strengthened the network of social relationships fundamental to unifying chiefdom societies. But what were the spiritual beliefs behind rituals in the El Cajón region? Do they reflect some of the animistic elements of Mesoamerican and Central American religions; if so, how can they be deduced from archaeological evidence? The physical landscape in Mesoamerica was viewed as a living entity often characterized as a reptile or alligator whose scales represented the mountains and valleys of the earth's surface (Nicholson 1971:406).[2] Among the Maya, both rocks and trees were viewed as animate entities that could aid or oppose the people who used them (Thompson 1970:165). This was why the Aztec considered jade to be a living rock that attracted moisture and helped the plants around it to grow (Sahagún 1963:222–223). It was why jade was linked symbolically with maize, water, wind, and the breath of life (Taube 2005:23, 33).

The animistic nature of pre-Columbian belief systems is evident in the imagery portrayed in the El Cajón lapidary assemblage. Pendants display a wide range of zoomorphic images that may reflect the belief that animal spirits could protect individuals from malevolent forces inhabiting the animistic world. The notion of an animal spirit protector and guide is pervasive across many areas of Mesoamerica (Brinton 1894; Gossen 1975; Kaplan 1956; Rojas 1947; Vogt 1965). George Foster (1944:103) distinguished between two animal spirit forces, the *tonal* and the *nagual* (see also Gossen 1975; Vogt 1965). The *tonal* was a companion spirit animal that influenced an individual's fate, while the *nagual* was the spirit companion of shamans. Spiritual forces in an animistic world could be simultaneously beneficial or dangerous, and the *tonal* companion could help an individual navigate between them (Sandstrom 2005:43).

A key element of *nagualism* was the belief that shamans could transform themselves into an animal form through ritual practice. This belief was originally proposed for the Olmec by Peter Furst (1968) based on his comparison of Olmec art to shamanistic practices in South America (see also Gutiérrez and Pye 2010:27). The belief in *nagual* transformation extends across Mesoamerica into Honduras. Daniel Brinton (1894:42) cites an example of a Honduran ruler named Coamizagual who could transform himself into a Thunder Bird through shamanistic practices (Gutiérrez and Pye 2010:39). The legend of Coamizagual is found across western Honduras and El Salvador, where it is presented in the form of a woman with wings (Mejía 1986; Rivas and Gómez 2005). Among the Lenca, the *nagual* could take any animal form in a person's life (Chapman 1985:80, 211–214).

Animistic belief systems are reflected throughout Central America in the animal imagery displayed on pottery, stone benches, jade carvings, and elaborately carved grinding stones. In Honduras, zoomorphic images are depicted on ceramic serving vessels, lapidary goods, and the handles of ceramic jars and Ulúa marble vessels (Joyce 2017; Stone 1938, 1941; Strong, Kidder, and Paul 1938). In the El Cajón lapidary assemblage, animistic themes are represented in all stone types but are especially prominent in artifacts carved from micaceous jade, where only animal images are depicted. Since artisans preferred to use local materials when they could, the replication of animal imagery in multiple mediums suggests that animistic beliefs were widespread. This contrasts with jade carving throughout the Maya region, where zoomorphic imagery is not as strongly represented.

Among the Maya, the emphasis on divine kingship and the role of the ruler in mediating spiritual forces led to an emphasis on human imagery and its association with the maize god, ancestors, and the divine (Schele and Freidel 1990). Human images depicted on head pendants and masks reinforced rank and personified the elevated status of the wearer. The result was a heavier focus of anthropomorphic imagery in Maya lapidary assemblages.

This is reflected in the jade artifacts recovered from the Cenote at Chichen Itzá, where nearly 85 percent of the more than 400 carved images illustrated in the catalog (Proskouriakoff 1974) depict human images (see chapter 5, note 25, this volume). This contrasts with the El Cajón assemblage, where zoomorphic, anthropomorphic, and geometric designs occur in relatively equal proportions (see table 5.6). It is possible that the scrolls and undulating geometric images represented in the collection reflect wind, water, and other seen and unseen forces in the natural world (e.g., see figure 5.46a–b). Whatever the geometric images (30.9%) were meant to represent, the parity between zoomorphic carvings (33.9%) and anthropomorphic images including hunched or hunchback figures (35.2%) suggests that animalistic themes and *tonal* beliefs were important components of the broader ritual system.

RITUAL AND THE BUILT ENVIRONMENT

A unifying principle of an animistic worldview is that all features of the landscape were endowed with spiritual forces. The contemporary Nahua of Veracruz see the earth as alive and requiring "recompense for any human activity that disturbs or injures its physical body" (Sandstrom 2005:42). This includes agricultural and forging activities, as well as the construction of houses, temples, walls, ditches, and other human-made features. Cutting timber and mining stone are landscape disturbances that required ritual mediation. Likewise, the buildings made from these materials had to be endowed with a spirit to remain in harmony with the rest of nature (McGee 1998:41; Thompson 1970:200; Vogt 1998). Evon Vogt (1998) discussed this process when the Maya built individual residential structures.

According to Brian Stross (1998), all products of human manufacture had to be given a soul, brought to life, and nourished if they were to become harmonic parts of the animate world. This would have been especially important for structures intended for civic-ceremonial use (McGee 1998:41–43; Stross 1998:31). It is in this context that the offerings in the Iglesia Precinct are best understood. The Iglesia Precinct was designed as a large civic-ceremonial area with the Central Plaza at its center. It was here that feasts were celebrated, dances were conducted, and ritual performances involving the entire community would have been carried out. The centrality and importance of the Central Plaza was accentuated by the construction of the Acropolis platform, which elevated the plaza surface 2 m above the rest of the community. It is within the construction matrix of the Acropolis platform that the majority of the offerings recovered at Salitrón Viejo were concentrated.[3]

We believe the dedicatory offerings recovered from the Acropolis platform were part of an ensoulment process that imbued it and adjoining structures with life. A total of 1,609 artifacts were recovered from a range of offerings within the construction matrix of the Acropolis platform (see table 6.1). Of these, more than 80 percent were located along the central east–west axis of the Acropolis platform.[4] The positioning of these offerings was important because in Mesoamerican societies, the structure's central axis was seen as its lifeline and the main avenue of communication with spiritual deities (Ashmore 2009; Benson 1981; Pendergast 1968:61; Taube 2003). Fully one-third (33.7%) of the offerings deposited in the Acropolis platform were broken, which was very likely intended to release the life force contained within them into its construction matrix. Positioning jade artifacts along the east–west centerline of the Acropolis was the optimum location for transferring their life force into the body of the platform.

The most frequently broken artifacts within offerings were conical and tubular flares (94.6%), especially those manufactured of apple green jade.[5] There were two possible reasons for this. First, tubular earflares in the El Cajón collection are generally large, ranging from 62.0 mm to 134.0 mm across their face, with an average diameter of 95.3 mm. As such, flares were among the largest items included in offerings. While jade earflares were incorporated into ritual deposits, they were not associated with elite burials, elite structures, or their associated assemblages. Individuals wearing earflares are not a design element found on locally made Sulaco polychrome as they are on some Ulúa polychrome types (Joyce 2017). There is no direct evidence, therefore, that they were regularly worn by elites in the El Cajón region. Nevertheless, their association with individuals of high status in neighboring regions gave them high symbolic value as sacrificial items in the ceremonial life of the community. Perhaps more important, earflares were the regalia of the gods and spirit-beings and are shown on all the hunched and hunchback figures in the collection (see below). Was the high breakage rate of flares a transference or release of these spiritual properties into the structures in which they were deposited? We believe it was. Whatever the reason, their high breakage rates are a consistent pattern in the El Cajón collections regardless of the type and color properties of the raw material used to manufacture them.[6] But color was a contributing factor in breakage rates, since the majority of all the artifacts manufactured of apple green jade (86.5%) were intentionally fragmented. It is likely that artifacts in this hue were believed to have an especially potent life force and were broken to release that force into the Acropolis platform.

While the breakage of earflares was clearly intentional, a range of other artifacts including beads, bead pendants, and some carved pendants was left largely intact. Fully 92.6 percent of the 855 beads included in Acropolis deposits were unbroken. To some degree, this may be due to their robustness, but this does not seem to be the only reason. Rather, there was a degree of intentionality between artifact classes in determining which to sacrifice, since some very fragile artifact classes such as ring pendants and crescent pectorals were often recovered unbroken in cache offerings. While the criteria that determined breakage are not completely clear, it may be that a range of artifacts was left intact so the life force stored within them could continue to animate the construction over time, in the same way a battery holds an electrical charge for future use. This, of course, is speculative, but it would help explain the differential and selective breakage patterns identified in construction deposits. The idea that offerings could provide a perpetual life force to structures parallels the observed pattern that some cache deposits like the famous jade figurine group in Offering 4 at La Venta were remembered and celebrated in the ritual life of the structures in which they were placed (Drucker, Heizer, and Squier et al. 1959:plates 30–32; Kovacevich 2013:100).

The carved imagery in the El Cajón lapidary assemblage also provides insights into local belief systems. If a belief in *tonal* spirits was part of regional religious practice, then it would be reasonable to expect that objects with the carved imagery of animals, plants, and anthropomorphic figures would be handled selectively in ritual deposits. If the *tonal* of carved images could be transferred into the built environment, then carved images of these spirits might be deposited without breakage in offerings so they could continue to provide protection to the structure in which they were deposited. In this sense, *tonal* spirits could protect the sanctity of a civic-ceremonial structure in the same way Nahua groups in the Huastec bring the clothing or a photograph of a person to a curing ceremony so they can participate in it even if they are not physically present (Alan Sandstrom, personal communication, 2020).

The possibility that a carved image had some enduring protective value was evaluated by examining differential breakage rates in the lapidary assemblage. The majority of the artifacts with carved imagery consist of pendants and bead pendants, and these were compared as a group to plain pendants that lacked decoration. Table 8.1 examines breakage rates of these two artifact groups in comparisons (1) from offerings in the construction fill of the Acropolis platform and (2) from other areas of the Iglesia Precinct and across the site. Two things are immediately apparent from this comparison. First, the majority

TABLE 8.1. Breakage patterns of plain and carved pendants at Salitrón Viejo

Location at Salitrón Viejo	Carved Pendants and Bead Pendants						Plain Pendants						Z-score	P-value
	Complete		Fragmented		Total		Complete		Fragmented		Total			
	No.	%	No.	%	No.	%	No.	%	No.	%	No.	%		
Inside Acropolis construction fill	147	88.0	20	12.0	167	100	62	53.9	53	46.1	115	100	5.697	0.00
Other ritual contexts	37	44.0	47	56.0	84	100	64	22.7	218	77.3	282	100	6.172	0.00
Total artifacts	184	73.3	67	26.7	251	100	126	31.7	271	68.3	397	100	11.62	0.00

(88.0%) of carved items recovered from the Acropolis platform (n = 167) were deposited without breakage compared to plain pendants (53.9%). A comparison of means tests revealed that the difference in breakage rates between plain and carved artifacts deposited in the Acropolis platform was highly significant ($z = 5.697$, $p = 0.00$), reflecting a pattern of depositing most carved imagery without breakage. The same pattern was observed for other ritual deposits across Salitrón Viejo ($z = 6.172$, $p = 0.00$). When this pattern is examined for all contexts at Salitrón Viejo, there is a clear preference not to fragment artifacts with carved imagery ($z = 11.623$, $p = 0.00$). We think this reflects a belief that the *tonal* spirits of carved images could provide protective value to the structures in which they were deposited (table 8.1).

RITUAL AND THE NATURAL ENVIRONMENT

Pre-Columbian groups of west-central Honduras also identified mountains, caves, springs, and pools in the natural landscape as sacred and special places (Healy 2007; Moyes and Brady 2012). The result was that locations in the sacred geography were venerated and could be destinations for pilgrimages and the locations where burials with special offerings were interred (Joyce n.d.). Caves were one of these important places in Honduras. During the Formative period, burials were placed in caves at Copán (Gordon 1898a; Rue, Freter, and Ballinger 1989) and Talgua (Brady, Hasemann, and Fogarty 1995; Brady et al. 2000) and along the Rio Aguan at Cuyamel (Healy 1974). Caves in Mesoamerica were perceived as entrances to the underworld, and placement of a burial in a cave helped accelerate the journey of the deceased into the afterlife (Brady 2005). Rock art in the form of paintings and engravings also marked important locales and sacred places in the pre-Columbian Honduran landscape (Figueroa and Scheffler 2021).

Caves were associated with water, moisture, and the residences of deities like the *chacs* or *tlaloque* that brought the rain necessary for agriculture (Nicholson 1971; Thompson 1970). Sources of water such as pools and springs were important ritual sites and were often destination locales of pilgrimages where offerings were made (Ortíz Ceballos and Rodríguez 1997; Wells and Nelson 2007:139). In the pre-Columbian world, the association of a spring with a cave was an especially powerful place in the spiritual landscape. These locations were important secular and spiritual reference points for prehispanic groups and can provide important information on their ritual practices and beliefs (Umberger 2002).

The idea that caves and water sources were venerated places in Honduras is evident from a largely forgotten but important set of excavations carried out at the La Laguna water source located 4 km southeast of Copán. Here, a large quantity of offerings was excavated that had been deposited at the water source in front of a small cave. Explorations in 1955 and 1964 by Jesus Nuñez Chinchilla (1966, 1972) documented the presence of large-scale offerings at this location, which in both size and composition resemble those recovered at Salitrón Viejo. More than 300 items, including 30–40 lbs of fragmented jade and non-jade artifacts, were recovered in front of La Laguna cave. The jade offerings included fragmented earflares, twenty complete beads,[7] and a variety of carved pendants. The fact that these were ritual offerings was confirmed by the type of material recovered, which included marine shell (*Spondylus Princeps*), ceramic censers, red pigment, the residue from copal incense, two incensarios portraying zoomorphic and rain god images, and a rectangular box of white sandstone that could be granular marble (Nuñez Chinchilla 1966:48). These offerings were made at an important locale in the sacred landscape and reflect the animistic nature of Honduran religion. The offerings made to sanctify ritual structures at Salitrón Viejo are parallel practices of this broader animistic worldview.

CONCERNING HUNCHBACKS AND DWARFS

The most frequently occurring image in the El Cajón assemblage is that of a small dwarf or hunched human figure. The consistency with which this figure is portrayed indicates that it was a powerful spiritual entity in Honduran mythology. Forty-two hunched and hunchback figures occur in the collection: thirty-six as carved pendants (see figures 5.25, 5.26, 5.27, 5.28), three as bead pendants (see figure 5.45a, c–d), and three others as three-dimensional effigy carvings (see figure 5.48b–d). These figures are consistently represented with stooped shoulders and in a crouching position, occasionally with a hump protruding behind the head of the figure (see figures 5.26b–c, 5.27b, e–f). Hunched figures were carved in profile, in kneeling or sitting positions, and leaning forward with their hands tucked under their chin. They wear a belt and loincloth visible at the back of the figure. Most figures are shown wearing earflares and often display some sort of cap or head covering.

Hunchback figures and dwarfs were important in pre-Columbian belief traditions across the Americas (Butler 1935:644; Rodríguez, Isaza, and Pachajoa 2012). In Mesoamerican mythology, dwarfs were believed to have special powers. They were often attendants to the gods and are included in some creation stories (Thompson 1970:340–341). In Central Mexican mythology, Quetzalcoatl was attended by a host of hunchbacks and dwarfs on his migration journey to Cholula (McCafferty and McCafferty 2009:202). Among the Maya, dwarfs were occasionally depicted as accompanying the maize god because of their association with rain (Boot 2013:55). The *tlaloque* were dwarfish assistants to the rain god Tlaloc, who resided in caves and assisted in bringing clouds, rain, and lightning (Brady 1988:53; Nicholson 1971:414). Their residence in mountains linked the *tlaloque* to illnesses associated with the cold as well as the ability to heal them (Robelo 1982:571). It may be their association with mountains that explains their incorporation into offerings in the Acropolis platform.

Dwarfs and hunchbacks often served as attendants to rulers because they were viewed as individuals with special abilities who were touched by the gods. They were important members of large royal courts in many Mesoamerican societies. According to Fray Diego Durán (1971:122), "It was one of the glories of the noblemen to be attended by humpbacks and the ladies to be served by humpbacked women." Their role as attendants (Sahagún 1979:30, figure 64) is why they often were sacrificed at the death of a nobleman. Virginia Miller (1985:152) feels that dwarfs were members of royal Maya households, where they fulfilled the role of surrogate children. Sharisse and Geoffrey McCafferty (2009:202) suggest that their diminutive stature made them living, supernatural talismen.

Hunched and hunchback figures in Honduras were probably linked to beliefs about the underworld, death, creation stories, and other spiritual forces, as they were in the Maya region. Among the Tzotzil and Tzetzal Maya, dwarfs and hunchbacks were characterized as mountain deities who were closely associated with death and the underworld (Miller 1985). Death was portrayed as a dwarf or child-size deity known as Larrainzar, who lived in a cave by day and came out at night to attack people (Thompson 1970:323). Similarly, in the Historia de los Xpantzay (Recinos 1957:139), the messenger of death is portrayed as a hunchback.[8] In the Yucatan creation story, it was a hunchback or twisted one (*p'uz*) who with the ancient *zayamuincob* dwarfs built the archaeological ruins (340–341). For Ceclio Robelo (1982:701), the dwarfish *tlaloque* were malevolent spirits known as *tzitzimeme*, associated with the evil spirits of the air (Siméon 1991).

The Honduran folk category that most closely corresponds to hunchback spirit entities involves the *duendes* of the Sierra de La Paz. The term *duende* was adopted from colonial Spain and was used to refer to a range of spirits from Mexico to the Andes (Fontes 2020; López Romero 2019). According to the Lenca, *duendes* are magical spirits who are caretakers of particular places such as mountains, ponds, caves, and the plants and animals around them. They can be either benign or malicious in the way they interact with humans. The *duendes* who inhabit mountains and caves in the Sierra de La Paz are called by various names, including Tacayo, Itacayo, Sisimite, and Sipesipe (Aguilar Paz 1989; Dixon 2008a; Figueroa and Scheffler 2021:40). In the way they are described, these spirit entities appear to be derived from the pre-Columbian mountain-dwelling *tlaloque*. In Honduran myth, they are credited with kidnaping women who they carry off to copulate with in their caves (Aguilar Paz 1989).

Whatever spirit entities the El Cajón hunched and hunchback pendants were meant to represent, they likely had both malevolent and benevolent attributes. The association of hunchbacks and dwarfs with death and the underworld helps explain the unusual way these pendants were shaped and drilled. They are the only pendants in the collection that have their suspension holes placed at the head and feet of the figure so they hung face-down when they were suspended on a cord. A face-down orientation would reinforce their association with death, the earth, and the underworld. Their association with death and the underworld may also be the reason the majority of these pendants (77.1%) were manufactured from gray jade.

Figure 8.1 and table 8.2 show the distribution of hunched and hunchback pendants recovered from known archaeological sites. What is clear is that most of these pendants are from eastern Mesoamerica, with 71 percent of all currently reported examples occurring at Salitrón Viejo. All of the hunchback pendants recovered from Copán, Quirigua, and Kaminaljuyú, as well as most of those from Salitrón Viejo, were manufactured of jade from the Motagua

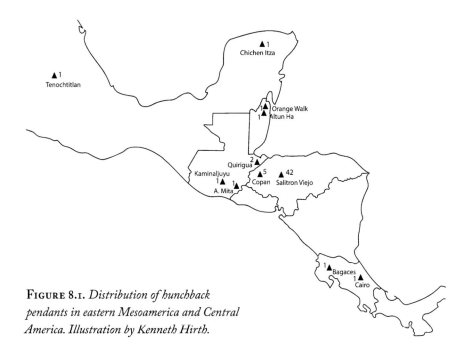

FIGURE 8.1. *Distribution of hunchback pendants in eastern Mesoamerica and Central America. Illustration by Kenneth Hirth.*

TABLE 8.2. Hunchback pendants reported from Mesoamerica and Central America

Location	Number of Pendants	Source
Altun Ha, Belize	3	Pendergast 1979:figures 2:56a, 2:58e, 3:figure 16b
Asunción Mita, Guatemala	1	Ashmore 1980:39
Bagaces, Costa Rica	1	Stone 1977b:figure 78a
Cairo, Línea Vieja, Costa Rica	1	Balser 1961:213
Chichen Itzá, Mexico	1	Proskouriakoff 1974:figure 146
Copán, Honduras	5	Agurcia Fasquelle 2016:figure 12; Ashmore 1980:figure 11a–b; Digby 1972:plates XII and XIII
Kaminaljuyú, Guatemala	1	Kidder, Jennings, and Shook 1946:figure 47
Orange Walk, Belize	1	Digby 1972:plate VIII
Quirigua, Guatemala	2	Ashmore 1980:figure 10
Salitrón Viejo, Honduras	42	This volume
Tenochtitlan	1	
Total	59	

valley (see chapter 5). An interesting aspect of the Salitrón pendants is that some were also manufactured from granular marble and other non-jadeite stone. The presence of similar images in three raw material groups produced by different artesanal communities indicates that the beliefs behind this imagery were shared over a wide area, from eastern Guatemala through Honduras.

ALTARS, SHRINES, AND MONUMENTS

Many civic-ceremonial structures in the El Cajón region are over 2 m tall and fall into one of two architectural categories: conical mounds with square bases and restricted summit areas, and elongated rectangular mounds known as Range structures (Hasemann 1987:90). The function of these structures differed. Range structures are believed to have supported elite residences, while conical mounds had other ritual and celestial functions.[9] While these were the most prominent civic-ceremonial structures, a third class of small structures was identified that appears to be made up of altars or shrines. The two distinguishing features of these structures are their diminutive size and their location in public plazas. Four such structures were identified in the Iglesia Precinct.

Altars were important ritual structures in most Mesoamerican societies. According to Alan Sandstrom (2008:94), every Nahua ritual involved the construction of some type of altar, which was the focal point for all transactions between humans and the spirit entities with whom they negotiated. The same is true of ethnographically documented rituals among the Honduran Lenca (Chapman 1985:110–111; Wells and Davis-Salazar 2008:196). The surface of the altar was the plane of interaction with the spirit world, which conceptually could represent the surface of the earth, a milpa, or the entire cosmos depending on the ritual. In terms of ritual practice, the altar is the place where sacrifices and offerings were made to repay spirits for rain, health, and fertility; to make future petitions; or to repair damages to the world they live in. Altars were central features of ritual among the ancient Maya (Chase and Chase 2012:260; Jones and Satterthwaite 2014; Kappelman 2004), including the site of Copán (Fash 2001). Despite this important function, altars are infrequent occurrences in civic-ceremonial spaces at non-Maya sites across Honduras.[10]

Four altar and shrine features were identified in the Iglesia Precinct: two in Plaza Two and two on the periphery of the Central Plaza.[11] These features were described in chapter 4. The two in Plaza Two were referred to as Altars 1 and 2, while the two in the Central Plaza were Structures 12 and 397. Altar 1 was located in Patio M1 in front of Structure 7 (see figure 4.17). It was composed of three sections of a shaped boulder monument that had been carefully positioned on the floor of the patio. The original boulder sculpture had a cupulate depression carved in its surface; at some point in the past, it was intentionally broken and reassembled as a trefoil arrangement in front of Structure 7 (see figure 4.18). Each of the three stones had a remnant cup-shaped depression positioned on its west side. The largest of these depressions was inverted with its largest diameter facing downward, perhaps symbolizing an emptying or pouring out of its previous significance. The reason for breaking the boulder monument is unclear. But its reassembly and rededication may reflect a cyclical view of time like that found in other areas of Mesoamerica (Elson and Smith 2001; Hassig 2001:3–5; Hirth 1987a; Thompson 1970:173–175).

Whatever the beliefs associated with Altar 1, it was important enough to require a dedication offering that was placed in a subfloor cache when it was reassembled (see figure 4.19). The vessels in this cache were sealed beneath the plaza floor but were left accessible, suggesting that they may have been periodically accessed during rituals in the plaza. Four human teeth were included in this offering (see chapter 4) that may be from elite ancestors or the person or persons involved in making the offerings. If so, they may represent the embodiment of the officiant as a feature of the offering, in the same way photographs of individuals can be included in rituals in contemporary communities (Alan Sandstrom, personal communication, 2020).

A low platform located in the center of Plaza Two between Structures 4 and 8 was identified as Altar 2 (see figures 4.17, 4.20). Seven ground stone artifacts (two manos, five metates) were recovered from Altar 2, which suggests that it was associated with food display as part of communal feasting. Structure 397-subA was a low platform 30 cm high, located along the southeastern periphery of the Central Plaza. The diminutive height of this structure—together with evidence for burning, a fire pit, and concentrations of ceramics, carbon, and food residues on its floor surfaces—suggests that it received offerings or was used to prepare food during the Late Yunque phase.

Structure 12 is a unique and enigmatic construction located at the southwest corner of the Iglesia Precinct. It is identified here as a possible altar or shrine based on its small size and unique architectural construction. Several design features made Structure 12 unique in the Iglesia Precinct. The first was the use of a *talud-tablero* design that has not been reported at other non-Maya sites in Honduras (see figures 4.11, 4.12, 4.13). Second, there was no evidence that a building was constructed on its summit during either construction episode. Finally, although over 2 m tall, the structure did not have a stairway to provide access to its summit. The ritual importance of Structure 12 is underscored by having the largest quantity of both lapidary offerings and broken ceramic censer ware of any structure at Salitrón Viejo other than the Acropolis platform (see figure 6.1). These characteristics suggest that it was a special altar-shine that was used until it was engulfed in the construction of the Acropolis platform.

THE ECONOMY OF RITUAL AT SALITRÓN VIEJO

This study has examined ritual activity at Salitrón Viejo from the perspective of the *economy of ritual* (Watanabe 2007), which seeks to identify the economic costs involved in carrying out ritual performances. In its most complete form, the economy of ritual includes calculating the time, labor, and expense of organizing ritual events—in short, evaluating the effort involved in producing and assembling the material goods used in rituals and how they reinforced the social and political ideologies that held the Salitrón chiefdom together. What has been accomplished here provides only a partial picture of that activity.

The economics of ritual at Salitrón Viejo involved three primary components: the construction of civic-ceremonial architecture, the production and assembly of food and other consumables used in feasts, and the procurement of symbolically meaningful goods used to sanctify and dedicate civic-ceremonial structures in the Iglesia and North Precincts. As at many other sites across Honduras, special structures were constructed in public plazas to celebrate important events both within and between communities. Four important civic-ceremonial areas were identified at Salitrón Viejo that span the full occupation of the site: the Iglesia and North Precincts and monumental structures in the West and South Residential Groups. The construction of this civic-ceremonial architecture involved the mobilization of community labor to assemble and prepare the earth, stone, wood, and thatch to build the mounds and the perishable structures on their summits. Calculating the effort involved in building these structures, while far from easy, is the dimension of a ritual economy that is most amenable to archaeological assessment.

The labor and effort needed to construct civic-ceremonial architecture at Salitrón Viejo was presented and discussed in chapter 7. The Acropolis platform was the most prominent architectural construction at Salitrón Viejo, and energetic analysis was carried out using the parameters proposed by Charles Erasmus (1965) from his experimental study on prehispanic mound building. The analysis concluded that it would have taken approximately 17,084 person-days to construct the Iglesia Precinct, 9,146 of which were needed for the Acropolis platform (see table 7.4). This was a significant amount of work that could have been carried out on an irregular basis over time. The calculations summarized in table 7.3 indicate that the entire Acropolis platform could have been constructed in 37–46 days by a labor force of 200–250 workers. While a significant effort, this level of construction was well within the abilities of the Salitrón Viejo community, especially if some labor was also mobilized from a few other regional communities.

This labor estimate needs to be read with several caveats in mind. First, it is a rock and earth estimate only. No consideration was made for constructing structures on the summits of buildings; building ramps and stairways; preparing clay, cobble, or stucco floors; or assembling special types of building materials such as manufacturing adobe blocks where they were used.[12] To this must be added the effort involved in the feasts that would have accompanied communal work projects. As such, this estimate should be viewed as a rough approximation rather than a precise calculation of the work required for its civic-ceremonial architecture. Second, as important as the Acropolis was, it represents only a partial picture of the effort invested in civic-ceremonial construction. The architectural investment found at Salitrón Viejo needs to be viewed in relation to the growth of its regional chiefdom.

The results of survey and excavation indicate that Salitrón Viejo grew rapidly into the region's largest and dominant regional center during the Late Yunque phase. Coincident with its growth was a large investment in civic-ceremonial constructions. Both the Iglesia and North Precincts were constructed during the Late Yunque phase, and the scale of investment at that time far exceeds that found at other times during the site's occupation. Table 7.4 summarizes the number of structures and provides a volumetric estimate of building activities during different chronological phases. Thirty-two of the forty-nine civic-ceremonial structures at Salitrón Viejo (65.3%) date to the Late Yunque phase. They include all of the structures in the North Precinct and the majority of structures in the Iglesia Precinct. Likewise, the thirty-two Late Yunque structures represent 62.8 percent of the total architectural volume of civic-ceremonial structures constructed at Salitrón Viejo over its 1,400-year occupation. In comparative terms, the level of construction during the Late Yunque is 2.5 times higher than it was during the subsequent Early to Late Sulaco phases. Using Erasmus's (1965) estimate of 1.3 m³ of construction per day, all 22,404 m³ of Late Yunque civic-ceremonial construction would have required 17,234 worker-days to complete. While significant, all of this work could have been completed in as little as 69–87 days by a workforce of 200–250 persons.

Creating civic-ceremonial spaces was clearly a priority during the Late Yunque phase and reflected the role of ritual in providing social cohesion within the Salitrón chiefdom. The construction of two distinct civic-ceremonial precincts during the Late Yunque phase was a result of their different roles within Salitrón Viejo. Whereas the Iglesia Precinct was the central ritual area for the site's resident population, the location and layout of the North Precinct suggest that it was intended to receive groups from outside the community. The fact that construction in the North Precinct was limited to the Late Yunque phase suggests that the role it provided was not long-lived.

There is enough evidence of feasting at Salitrón Viejo to indicate that it was an important component of ritual activity throughout the site's occupation. As in other sites in Honduras, all the evidence for feasting was recovered from civic-ceremonial contexts. It occurs in the Iglesia Precinct as early as the Early Yunque phase, both at Structure 2 and across the surface of Plaza One. Feasting residues that date to the Early and Middle Sulaco phases were recovered from the main plaza of the West Residential Group (see figures 4.1, 7.2), and feasts continued to be sponsored in the Iglesia Precinct up through the end of the site's occupation.

Feasts were integral components of religious celebrations and games across Mesoamerica and Central America (Ibarra Rojas 2014; Mckenzie 2008). One only has to read the *Ancient Calendar* by Fray Diego Durán (1971) to appreciate the continual round of ceremonies in the ritual life of pre-Columbian people. While Durán's work focused on the ritual life in Mexico, a rich pattern of feasts is well documented for Mesoamerica (Hendon 2003; Joyce and Henderson 2007; Tozzer 1941). Ethnohistoric and ethnographic research indicates that feasting was a central component of religious practice across Honduras (Chapman 1985; Herrera y Tordesillas 1944–1947:6:23; Lara-Pinto 1985) and was a central feature of labor mobilization in traditional Lenca society (Wells and Davis-Salazar 2004, 2008).

Anne Chapman (1985:83) argues that the Lenca adopted the 360-day calendar from other groups in Mesoamerica and with it, some of its feast day celebrations. While many were later reorganized into the religious calendar of the Catholic Church, others can be linked to earlier pre-Columbian concerns and practices. Foremost among them were *compostura* ceremonies carried out in domestic and community contexts. They included *composturas* designed to bless agricultural practices and the spirits that brought good harvests as well as to address sickness and mollify bad spirits living in different places. Other *compostura* celebrations commemorated births and deaths, building a new house, engaging in ceramic production, and blessing the water of streams and lagoons (Chapman 1985). Archaeological evidence believed to reflect *compostura*-like ceremonies has been identified at the sites of Copán and El Coyote in Honduras (Wells and Davis-Salazar 2004).

Of broader significance were the reciprocal feasts and *guancasco* celebrations carried out between leaders of different communities. Chapman (1986:134) believes these were pre-Columbian ceremonies intended to maintain peaceful relations between Lenca communities. This type of reciprocal feasting would have provided a framework for establishing linkages between communities within the Salitrón chiefdom. During the Late Yunque phase, Salitrón Viejo was the only community in the region where this type of ritual would have been carried out. But during the Middle and Late Sulaco phases, reciprocal feasting between large communities likely served to build network linkages between lineage heads and community leaders.

While feasts were important, it is impossible to estimate the effort needed to produce and assemble the resources consumed. To a large degree this depended on the number, length, and scale of ritual celebrations, which cannot be estimated with the data at hand. Since ritual was one of the primary ways socio-political networks were formed and held together (e.g., Clark and Blake 1994), it is likely that feasts were large inter-community activities that were held on a regular and recurring schedule.

The third component of ritual economy was the large quantity of high-value goods recovered from the Iglesia and North Precincts. The context of these deposits indicates that they were dedicatory offerings associated with the construction of civic-ceremonial architecture. The predominant materials in these offerings were jade and marble lapidary goods fashioned into earflares, beads, and pendants. Items of personal adornment marked wealth and social status in pre-Columbian societies, so their inclusion in ritual deposits reflected sacrifices on the part of the obligates who made the offerings. While these objects had high social value, they were not included in burials beyond the occasional bead (see also Stone 1941:50). On the whole, wealth goods did not play a prominent role in marking social rank in the El Cajón region throughout its 1,400-year occupation. Instead, the majority of these materials were procured for specific ritual use during the Late Yunque phase.

Calculating the costs involved in procuring wealth goods for ritual use is also a difficult task. It was argued that all the wealth goods represented at Salitrón Viejo were obtained through some form of direct procurement trade exchange. A range of perishable goods was proposed as possible trade goods to obtain them (see table 7.5), but how long it would have taken residents to amass sufficient quantities of items for exchange is unknown. A partial solution for evaluating procurement costs was to estimate the energetic cost of the wealth goods obtained and to assume that items of equivalent value were used to acquire them. Energetic costs of manufacture were calculated for three jade artifact classes: tubular earflares, ring pendants, and crescent pectorals (see table 7.6). The resulting estimates reveal that a large amount of effort was required to produce the jade artifacts recovered in the Salitrón Viejo collection. Unfortunately, not enough experimentation is available for jade and marble lapidary production to provide reliable estimates for the entire collection.

The results revealed that somewhere between 2,194 and 2,367 artisan-days would have been required to produce the 98 tubular earflares, ring pendants, and crescent pectorals represented in the collection. In terms of workdays, the time to manufacture these few artifacts was more than all the time needed to construct the nineteen structures in the North Precinct and as much as 25 percent of the Acropolis platform (see table 7.4). A total of 2,836 complete and fragmented artifacts were recovered from the Iglesia and North Precincts. While this number is large, the number of items imported for ritual purposes was undoubtedly very much larger, since the project did not excavate all of the areas known to have contained ritual deposits. In artisan workdays, the time needed to manufacture the 98 artifacts represents nearly 14 percent of *all the effort* needed to construct civic-ceremonial structures in the Iglesia Precinct.[13]

The implications of this comparison are provocative. If the time needed to manufacture only 98 artifacts represented one-seventh of the effort to construct the Iglesia Precinct, how much more time would have been required to produce all of the lapidary artifacts in the collection? In relative terms, the amount of labor represented in the offerings appears to far exceed the effort needed to construct all of the civic-ceremonial architecture in Salitrón Viejo. Whether residents of Salitrón Viejo had to invest the same amount of labor to obtain the goods to procure these offerings is another question entirely. But the only way objects would have been obtained was through some form of balanced exchange, where the value of the goods received was held to be equivalent to the goods provided. The quantity of items used as a medium of exchange—whether cacao, brightly colored feathers, animal pelts, cotton clothes, or any of the other items (see table 7.5)—must have been high and must have involved considerable effort on the part of the Salitrón Viejo community to assemble.

Analyzing the economics of ritual involves calculating the costs in time and material for different activities. Estimating the cost of constructing civic-ceremonial architecture is a straightforward procedure, while the effort involved in conducting ritual feasts is somewhat nebulous without specific parameters for the number, scale, and duration of these activities. Likewise, the amount of work involved in procuring ritual offerings is difficult to calculate beyond the indirect means used here. But if anything can be inferred from these estimates, it is that the work involved in manufacturing the dedication offerings greatly exceeded the amount of labor used to build the structures in which they were deposited. Furthermore, while the construction of civic-ceremonial structures occurred periodically, feasts commemorating planting, harvesting, and other celebrations conducted on a ritual calendar would have been recurrent activities throughout the year. When these three activities are taken together, the amount of effort needed to maintain the ritual economy appears to have been very high and would have involved a considerable time investment by households to support it.

LONG-DISTANCE TRADE AND ASSEMBLAGE DIVERSITY

Three alternative procurement models were discussed in chapter 7 for obtaining the high-value goods used in ritual offerings: on-site production, down-the-line exchange, and direct procurement trade. The available evidence indicates that direct procurement trade was the way jade, marble, and the other wealth items were obtained. There was no evidence of on-site lapidary work, and wealth goods did not move regularly enough through interregional trade networks to accumulate the quantity of high-value items recovered at Salitrón Viejo. No other contemporary sites in west-central Honduras have been identified that have even a fraction of these materials. Until such time that alternative explanations are possible, direct procurement—where individuals traveled from Salitrón Viejo to distant areas where high-value goods were available and could be obtained through trade—is the best explanation for how they were procured.

The direct procurement model has several implications for how chiefdoms in west-central Honduras should be viewed. The first is about how communities like Salitrón Viejo operated to fulfill their ritual needs. The quantity of jade and marble goods at Salitrón stands out as an anomaly for non-Maya sites in eastern Mesoamerica. It even surpasses what is found in most Maya sites. These wealth goods have two important features. They were assembled over a very short period during the Late Yunque phase, and they were used specifically for the sanctification of civic-ceremonial architecture instrumental in the organization of the Salitrón chiefdom. The procurement of wealth goods was not continuous over time. This is clear from the decrease in wealth goods after the Late Yunque phase and their general absence from other social contexts throughout the remainder of the site's occupation.

The Late Yunque phase was a period of considerable interregional interaction, with Usulután ceramics moving over long distances between regions. Recent INAA analyses have shown that Usulután ceramics were manufactured in multiple areas across Honduras and were traded over distances of up to 150–200 km.[14] This included the Usulután ceramics manufactured in the El Cajón region that reached the Ulúa and Comayagua valleys as well as Copán (Goralski 2008). Ceramic exchange in west-central Honduras is often characterized as taking place through a series of short-distance relays and gift exchanges between members of different households (Dixon 1989b:269; Goralski 2008:272; Hendon, Joyce, and Sheptak 2009:9; Joyce 2021:302). While this accurately characterizes the structure of interregional exchange networks operating across a good deal of Honduras, it does not account for the quantity of high-value lapidary goods that reached the El Cajón region. Although a few lapidary items have been recovered from Late Formative contexts at Los Naranjos and in the Ulúa valley (Baudez and Becquelin 1973:386–389; Gordon 1898b; Robinson 1989:189; Wonderley 1985:5), these goods did not circulate in large quantities through interregional trade.

Members of the Salitrón Viejo community apparently took an active role in procuring the wealth goods they needed for installing their civic-ceremonial architecture. They were entrepreneurial in meeting these needs and very likely used existing interregional trade connections to locate and travel to the areas where wealth goods could be procured in significant quantities. Members of the Salitrón Viejo community most likely operated as intermittent merchants for short periods of time to obtain the items they needed for their ritual offerings. In effect, they were target marketers. The focus of their mercantile endeavors is clear from the goods they procured. All of the items included in the Late Yunque offerings were non-local goods manufactured from some form of precious and semi-precious stone (e.g., jade, marble, obsidian, chalcedony, slate). Ceramic vessels and other items including figurines, censors, and candeleros were *not* included in Yunque or Early Sulaco phase ritual deposits unless they were associated with burials like those identified in Structure 3 (see figures 4.6–4.8).[15] The durability of these goods, together with their symbolic value derived from properties of color, carved imagery, and associated social significance, made them essential items of ritual use. In this regard, members of Salitrón Viejo functioned as part-time freelance traders, as Robert Sharer (1984:83) proposed for interactions between the Maya and groups in lower Central America.

The destinations these intermittent merchants visited are unclear, although it appears they traveled considerable distances. The different material types and carving styles represented in the assemblage suggest that they went to multiple different locations to obtain finished goods. A large percentage of the collection was fashioned from the Motagua valley jade whose source was located 180 km west of the El Cajón region (see table 5.1). To get these materials, intermittent merchants visited either towns in the regions where artisans resided or nearby communities that had access to finished goods (Rochette 2009a, 2009b; Walters 1982, 1989). While the source location of granular marble is unknown, the most likely area is the Montaña de Comayagua 60 km south of Salitrón Viejo (Fakundiny 1970:166, 190). The source locations for micaceous jade and many of the other non-jadeite materials in the collection remain unknown, although Christopher Begley (1999) has reported a location for greenstone talc along the Tulito River in northeastern Honduras.

One of the most important aspects of these materials is the stylistic variability and the diversity of artisanal *techné* represented in the El Cajón assemblage. The items carved in Olmec and Maya style are the easiest to identify. The clam shell plaques in Olmec style (see figure 5.38) are likely legacy pieces from the Middle Formative period (Andrews 1987; Healy and Awe 2001). Several pendants were carved in a clear Maya style (see figures 5.30b, 5.32), although the number of these items is considerably less than might be anticipated given the importance and proximity of Copán and other Maya sites to the west. Perhaps this is a result of the way many fine pieces of Maya jade were fashioned, with their final carving carried out in the courts of the lords who used them (Andrieu, Rodas, and Luin 2014:160; Widmer 2009).

Hunchback and anthropomorphic pendants in curvilinear style have been characterized as part of an early Maya jade carving tradition (Digby 1972; Rands 1965). Unfortunately, this characterization is based on items with limited stratigraphic context or knowledge about the date of the workshops that produced them (but see Garber 1983; Garber et al. 1993; Guderjan 1998 for stratigraphic contexts). The distribution of known hunched and hunchback pendants is displayed in figure 8.1. This distribution suggests that beliefs about these spiritual entities were primarily distributed along the eastern periphery of Mesoamerica rather than throughout the lowland Maya heartland. Two other very different lapidary styles are also represented by the triangle face pendants and the micaceous jade bead pendants in the collection. The former is widely distributed across the highlands of Guatemala in small stone *camahuile* carvings, while the latter has not been previously reported from Mesoamerica. Archaeological excavations at the Proto-Classic site of La Lagunita in highland Guatemala have uncovered a multitude of stone *camahuiles* in association with a burial tomb (Ichon and Arnauld 1985). While stylistically distinct from the El Cajón hunched figure carvings, they may be similar entities since they are believed to represent supernatural guardians of caves and the deceased (Ichon 1989; Ichon and Arnauld 1985:42).

Finally, there are the conical and tubular flares that were manufactured using two distinctly different technologies. Conical flares were heavy and massive and were fashioned using a technology involving flaking, pecking, and grinding in much the same way ground stone axes were manufactured. Their size and weight made it likely that they were intended as regalia worn on belts rather than suspended from the ear. Tubular earflares, by comparison, were much lighter and were manufactured using sawing and drilling techniques. While the two types of flares resemble each other in general form, they come from communities of practice that followed two very different manufacturing traditions.

INTERREGIONAL INTERACTION AND TEOTIHUACAN

Intermittent merchants from Salitrón Viejo undoubtedly traveled hundreds of kilometers to procure lapidary goods in the areas where they were produced or from communities where they could be obtained through trade. But somewhere in their trade ventures, they also came into contact with some of the broader Teotihuacan influences that were moving through Mesoamerica during the Late Yunque phase. This was not direct contact with the city or its merchants, but it is reflected in several ways at Salitrón Viejo. Teotihuacan influence was felt in a number of Maya sites in eastern Mesoamerica, stretching from coastal Guatemala and Kaminaljuyú (Arroyo 2020:451; Bove and Medrano Busto 2004; Braswell 2004b; Kidder, Jennings, and Shook 1946) to Belize and the Guatemala lowlands (Canuto, Auld-Thomas, and Arredondo 2020; Pendergast 1971; Spence 1996). The closest point of contact for Salitrón merchants would probably have been Copán, where evidence of Teotihuacan contact occurs in textual references, *talud-tablero* architecture, ceramic imports, and their imitations.[16]

One result of this influence was the construction of Structure 12, whose *talud-tablero* design is reminiscent of platform architecture at Teotihuacan and other sites in the Mexican highlands. The *talud* to *tablero* proportions of Structure 12 are 2.2:1 compared to Teotihuacan, where the ratio of *talud* to *tablero* ranges from 1:1.6 to 1:2.5—the result of using a low *talud* and a higher *tablero* (Braswell 2004c:121). At Kaminaljuyú, this ratio is closer to 1:1 (Arroyo 2020; Cheek 1997:133). But the length to height ratios of the *talud* and *tablero* vary across Mesoamerica, and in this case the proportions of these construction elements may have been strongly influenced by having to use river cobbles set in a clay matrix rather than cut stone. In any event, no *talud-tablero* architecture has been reported elsewhere in Honduras outside of Copán (Ashmore

2015:220; Sharer 2004:figure 5.2). We believe its use at Salitrón Viejo was stimulated by its prestigious, if vague, association with Teotihuacan and perhaps Kaminaljuyú. It is not hard to imagine that Structure 12 served as a small shrine for those intrepid individuals who made the long journeys to obtain the wealth goods used in ritual dedications in the Iglesia and North Precincts.

Other evidence for Teotihuacan influence is found in the jade assemblage at Salitrón Viejo. Several of the jade artifacts share stylistic similarities with artifacts associated with Teotihuacan culture. The ring pendants recovered (see figure 5.19) strongly resemble the jade ring disks associated with Teotihuacan and related sites, including Copán (Ashmore 2015:220; Evans 2010:15; Sharer 2004:figure 5.5). Likewise, the crescent pectoral carved with stylized jaguar imagery (see figure 5.37a) strongly resembles the Banda de Tlaloc nose elements from Teotihuacan (see figure 5.37b). It is possible that all the crescent pectorals were nose ornaments and jade versions of the iconic *narigueras de mariposa* associated with Teotihuacan culture (Angulo 1969) (see figures 5.34–5.37).

If there is one trade item that is unquestionably associated with Teotihuacan interaction, it is green obsidian from the Sierra de las Navajas obsidian source. Two large sinuous eccentric bifaces or silhouette figures were recovered (see figure 5.51a) that were manufactured from Sierra de las Navajas obsidian. The fact that these bifaces were manufactured using transverse-parallel pressure flaking indicates that they were trade pieces from Central Mexico, possibly even from Teotihuacan itself since this technique is not found on Mayan bifacial eccentrics (Pastrana and Hruby n.d.; Spence 1996). Four other Sierra de las Navajas obsidian pressure blades were recovered at Salitrón Viejo, reflecting additional indirect contact with the source. Finally, there are several very good local imitations of Thin Orange vessels in Sulaco Orange ware that fire to an even orange color when completely oxidized.[17] Particularly diagnostic in Sulaco Orange are sub-hemispherical ring-base bowls and vase forms with round and slab supports (Hirth, Kennedy, and Cliff 1989).

All of the Teotihuacan-related evidence is limited, and none of it suggests direct contact with Central Mexico. Furthermore, it does not align exactly with the dating of Teotihuacan-related materials in other sites in eastern Mesoamerica. At Copán, both ceramic and architectural materials associated with Teotihuacan date to AD 400/425–450 (Sharer 2004). The *talud-tablero*–style architecture found at Structure 12, together with associated jade and obsidian materials recovered from the Iglesia Precinct, is earlier and dates to AD 238–352 (see table 4.1:PSU6406, PSU7058) based on AMS radiocarbon dating. These dates align better with Aurora phase material at Kaminaljuyú, where *talud-tablero* architecture also occurs during the later

Esperanza (Braswell 2004a:99–100). In this regard, a good deal of the architecture and offerings from the Iglesia Precinct align better with some sites in the Pacific Coast region and Belize, where evidence of Teotihuacan interaction predates AD 400 (e.g., Bove and Medrano Busto 2004; Braswell 2004a:100; García-Des Lauriers 2020; Pendergast 1971, 2004). Nevertheless, the appearance of locally made Thin Orange ceramic imitations as both ring-base and vase forms is slightly later, dating to the Early Sulaco phase (AD 400–600). This evidence indicates that the importance of Teotihuacan resonated and was felt through indirect contacts made by its merchants even as far away as Salitrón Viejo.

THE DEVELOPMENT OF CHIEFDOM SOCIETIES
IN WEST-CENTRAL HONDURAS

Chiefdoms are socially and politically centralized societies that were integrated through a variety of ideological and economic means (Creamer and Haas 1985; Earle 1991). They were organized into social hierarchies, with leaders who provided service and solved problems for the communities they served (Hirth 2020:76–94). How they were integrated varied greatly from society to society. In the El Cajón region, ritual was a primary mechanism used to create social cohesion and the bonds linking populations in outlying communities into a social web centered on Salitrón Viejo. In this regard, the authority of the elites at Salitrón Viejo did not reside in the power or wealth they wielded, even though it was by far the largest community in the region. Instead, authority resided in the fact that elites lived at the center of their sacred landscape, where they supervised the important rituals that integrated society and reinforced their leadership position. It is not surprising, therefore, that considerable effort was invested in building and expanding the Iglesia Precinct into the central religious feature in the El Cajón region.

Societies identified as chiefdoms were present in Honduras by the beginning of the Middle Formative period (around 800 BC). Differential social status is evident in mortuary assemblages at a few sites at this time that included Copán (Fash and Davis-Salazar 2008:143–144), sites in the Ulúa valley (Joyce and Henderson 2001, 2010; Popenoe 1934), and the Cuyamel caves along the Rio Aguan (Healy 1974). An important feature of early chiefdoms in Honduras was the investment in large ritual constructions. The two best examples are Los Naranjos at Lake Yojoa and Yarumela in the Comayagua valley, where large-scale civic-ceremonial architecture was constructed that mobilized a considerable amount of human labor. An important component of the most important ritual centers during the Formative period was the presence of carved stone monuments that conveyed ideological information and reinforced beliefs fundamental to these early chiefdoms. Sumptuary mortuary offerings associated with a few burials placed in large civic-ceremonial structures attest to the social status and wealth of early leaders in these societies.

While chiefdoms flourished with population growth during the Late Classic period, the conditions of ritual practice appear to have changed. Civic-ceremonial precincts increased in number, although the overall scale of monumental constructions within them was reduced. Similarly, elaborate burials were no longer found, suggesting that the power of leaders had either declined or changed in nature. Likewise, few stone sculptures were produced for display in ceremonial precincts that reinforced leadership roles and the ideologies intrinsic to their social structure. One significant innovation during the Classic period was the construction of ballcourts and the spread of the Mesoamerican ball game as an important component of ritual interaction (Begley 1999:9; Fox 1996; Gillespie 1991; Hendon, Joyce, and Sheptak 2009) (see table 2.6). Despite these changes, there was one fundamental continuity in ritual practice between the Formative and Late Classic periods. Ritual feasting remained a central feature in integrating social segments and building bonds between different communities (Joyce and Henderson 2007). The importance of feasting can account for the interregional trade in Usulután resist ceramics during the Late Formative as well as in Cópador, Ulúa, and Sulaco polychromes during the Classic period (Beaudry-Corbett 1987; Goralski 2008:283; Henderson and Beaudry-Corbett 1993b; Joyce 2017).

But what accounts for the changes in the morphology of sites and their civic-ceremonial architecture between the Formative and Classic periods? Were they the result of changes in the ritual practice and organization of Honduran chiefdoms or a simple function of population growth? The authors of this volume believe these changes reflect chiefly cycling and the changes that can occur in the growth cycles of chiefdom societies (Anderson 1996; Flannery 1999; Menzies and Haller 2012). The changes observed in the El Cajón region are a microcosm of broader socio-political processes found elsewhere throughout Honduras during the Formative and Classic periods. The fundamental role of ritual in integrating community and regional populations remained the same. What changed was the effectiveness of ritual to create large, integrated regional chiefdoms like those organized around the primary centers of Yarumela and Los Naranjos during the Late Formative period.

Salitrón Viejo was the central ritual community in the El Cajón region, and its development paralleled that of other primary centers during the Late

Formative period. As discussed above, the Late Yunque phase was the period when the Salitrón chiefdom grew, and small outlying communities were incorporated in it through ritual celebrations in the Iglesia and North Precincts. Over time, however, the centrality of Salitrón Viejo and the functionality of these two precincts declined. While the Iglesia Precinct remained the central feature at Salitrón Viejo, more civic-ceremonial activity was carried on in the central plazas of the South and West Residential Groups from the Early Sulaco phase onward. It was here that large Range structures were constructed for the elite and feasts were conducted for members of their group. The result was a gradual weakening in the centrality of elite leadership in Salitrón Viejo.

Complex settlement hierarchies are often associated with tightly integrated social systems and are cited as a characteristic of complex societies, including chiefdoms (Lightfoot 1987; Peebles and Kus 1977; Spencer 1987:371–372). Population growth, increases in community size, and the development of complex settlement hierarchies are characteristics documented in regions across Honduras during the Late Classic period (Dixon 1989b; Joyce and Sheptak 1983; Robinson 1989; Schortman and Urban 1987b; Urban 1986; Wells and Davis-Salazar 2008:201). But this did not mean that chiefdom societies were more tightly integrated during the Late Classic than they were during preceding periods. In fact, they likely were not.

Population growth in the El Cajón region appears to have produced increased competition between elites that led to a decrease in regional integration. This same process was at work in other regions of Honduras. Monumental Range structures began to be constructed at other large sites in the El Cajón region at the beginning of the Middle Sulaco period, around AD 600. This trend marked the appearance of new elites and increased feasting at large communities outside Salitrón Viejo. Increased ritual activity at the regional level may have increased social tensions, which may explain the high residential densities found at larger sites (Hirth n.d.). Whatever the reason, the trend could only have weakened the centralized integration of the Salitrón chiefdom. By the end of the Sulaco period, the sites of Intendencia (see figure 3.9) and Guarabuquí (see figure 3.17) had grown into large communities that may well have challenged the leaders of Salitrón Viejo in both prestige and authority. Ritual was still the foundation for social integration, but the presence of more elites in outlying communities who sponsored feasts and celebrations had the effect of weakening the authority of Salitrón Viejo throughout the region.

CONCLUDING OBSERVATIONS

Honduras is an excellent place to study the growth and integration of ranked societies like those described for the El Cajón region. The richness and diversity of their material assemblages provides ample opportunity to examine the emergence of social inequality over time and space (Joyce 2021). Long-distance trade and the presence of craft production in small-scale workshops in the Ulúa valley (Joyce n.d.; Urban et al. 2013; Wells and Davis-Salazar 2008) provide an opportunity to examine the role and importance of artisanship in the development of inequality. But at the core of Honduran societies was the role of ritual in creating a collective spiritual identity among participants and unifying groups through shared beliefs and experiences (Urban and Schortman 2013).

This volume has used the perspective of ritual economy to describe and analyze pre-Columbian society in the El Cajón region. As discussed in the book's introduction, ritual economy can be explored from two different perspectives. The first of these is the *ritual of economy*, which attempts to understand the array of beliefs and preconditioned behaviors that structured every aspect of work and social interaction in a spiritually animated pre-Columbian world (McAnany 2010; McAnany and Wells 2008). This certainly was the case in Honduras, as Chapman (1978, 1985, 1986) has richly documented with ethnographic work among the Lenca. But how ritual factored into *all* of the everyday activities of pre-Columbian people is largely inaccessible to archaeological investigation. For that reason, the focus here has been on the economy of ritual, which is more amenable to archaeological study.

The *economy of ritual* (Watanabe 2007) is concerned with the economics of producing and carrying out ritual performances. Material evidence of ritual activity can be identified in the archaeological record in the form of feasts, civic-ceremonial architecture, and their associated ritual offerings. This approach attempts to identify and quantify the consumption of symbolically significant materials and goods as well as the permanent features used in ritual contexts (Davis-Salazar 2007:197). While not providing a complete assessment of the ritual economy, the economy of ritual perspective is a starting point for investigators interested in exploring the importance of ritual in shaping social and political ideologies.

An examination of ritual economy fits very well into the broader field of behavioral economics because it recognizes that decisions are made based on a range of social, cultural, emotional, and even spiritual criteria rather than on strict material provisioning (Thaler 2015, 2016). It acknowledges that the basis for many economic choices is enculturated and dictated by the social principles people learn. Behavioral economics is the psychology of economic decision making. It recognizes that ritual behavior has transactional utility—that is, the greater the investment in ritual activity, the higher the expected return from the effort. Likewise, ritual behaviors are sunk costs that make sacred propositions and associated constructions durable in the minds of their practioners. The tendency for people to only remember the successful outcomes of ritual events is referred to as hindsight bias, which together with the sunk costs of carrying them out helps endow them with special significance and reinforce tradition (the endowment effect). In short, the willingness to invest considerable effort in ritual activities is based to a large degree on the psychology and belief about what one will get out of doing so. As a framework, behavioral economics provides a theoretical perspective that is especially well suited to examine how and why ritual investments were made by pre-Columbian societies.

This study has explored the economy of ritual at Salitrón Viejo and what it informs about how ritual served to integrate pre-Columbian communities in the El Cajón region. The evidence suggests two things. First, although Salitrón Viejo was a small community, its residents invested a great deal of time and effort in different types of ritual behavior. The most prominent of these was their willingness to construct large-scale ritual architecture and to engage in long-distance trade to obtain the high-value goods used in the buildings' dedication. In this regard, the residents resemble members of chiefdom societies in central Panama and elsewhere who engaged in long-distance trade as a means to acquire sacred esoteric knowledge that reinforced social status and leadership authority (Helms 1979, 1988). Unlike the Panamanian situation, however, the acquisition of high-value goods was intended to animate and dedicate their ritual precincts, not to reinforce the authority of elite leaders. The result was a broader involvement by residents of Salitrón Viejo and most likely their affiliated communities in traveling to distant places to obtain the sacred goods.

Second, the available information underscores the overwhelming importance ritual played in integrating communities along the lower Sulaco River into a chiefdom centered on Salitrón Viejo. The highwater mark of the Salitrón chiefdom was during the Late Yunque phase. This was the time when the bulk of civic-ceremonial architecture was constructed and massive offerings of wealth goods were assembled. Salitrón Viejo was large enough to have accomplished both of these tasks on its own, acting as patron for the entire region. While this would have elevated the status of the Salitrón elite, it would have minimized the level of buy-in by the regional population they sought to incorporate under their authority. For this reason, it is likely that both the construction of ritual architecture and the assembly of associated offerings would probably have involved some participation by outlying groups. Evidence of multiple collaborators in these efforts can be found in the variation in the construction materials used in architecture (adobe, river cobbles) and the compositional diversity of offering groups used in the dedication of the buildings.

Over time, the strength and position of Salitrón Viejo gradually declined. Elites in several other centers throughout the region intensified ritual activities during the Middle and Late Sulaco phases that competed with those at Salitrón Viejo. While these processes have been framed in terms of data from the El Cajón region, they reflect the process of chiefly cycling and ritual-based development found in many neighboring regions of Honduras during the Late Formative and Classic periods.

Ritual was the spiritual and socio-political glue that integrated the multitude of regional chiefdoms that thrived, survived, and eventually declined across west-central Honduras. What the information from Salitrón Viejo tells us is that Honduran chiefdoms could make huge investments in ritual activities beyond the construction of civic-ceremonial structures. At Salitrón Viejo, a great deal of effort was involved in procuring jade and other wealth goods for offerings in the Iglesia and North Precincts. While the scale of these offerings has not been identified in other contemporary sites, they are emblematic of the importance of ritual activities in all west-central Honduran societies. Mesoamerican archaeologists often point to the grandeur and large-scale civic-ceremonial architecture of Maya societies at Copán, Quirigua, and other sites further to the west. While significant, we are more impressed by the level of effort a small community like Salitrón Viejo invested in ritual activities. Future work needs to look beyond the size and number of a site's civic-ceremonial structures or ritual monuments and consider ritual effort in relation to the size of the participating population that produced it. Only then will we be able to accurately evaluate the relative importance of ritual as an integrative focus in the pre-Columbian societies of Honduras and lower Central America.

Sample	Analysis Type	Site	Location	Context	^{14}C yr (BP) ± 1σ	cal BC–AD (2σ) Oxcal 4.4 (IntCal20)
PSU 7688	AMS	PC109	Str. 8	D-2-C	1195 ±15	774–855 AD
PSU 7695	AMS	PC15	Str. 7	K-1-b	1210 ± 15	783–880 AD
PSU 7696	AMS	PC15	Str. 78	L-8-c	1220 ± 15	783–880 AD
PSU 7065	AMS	PC1	Str. 118	CX-50-i	1260 ± 15	676–778 AD
PSU 7692	AMS	PC13	Str. 46	J-19-b	1260 ± 15	676–778 AD
PSU 7693	AMS	PC13	Ritual Plaza	N-3-c	1260 ± 15	676–778 AD
PSU 7061	AMS	PC1	Iglesia, Str. 9-subA	AL-1-e	1265 ± 20	672–777 AD
PSU 7056	AMS	PC1	Iglesia, Str. 1	1984-R15	130 ± 15	1682–1937 AD
PSU 7694	AMS	PC15	Str. 10	J-5-n	1300 ± 15	663–775 AD
SMU 1867	C14	PC1	Str. 118	CX-50-i	1300 ± 30	660–774 AD
SMU 2299	C14	PC109	Str. 8	D-6-e	1300 ± 60	645–880 AD
PSU 7687	AMS	PC109	Str. 58	DD-4-E	1325 ± 15	656–774 AD
PSU 7697	AMS	PC15	Str. 79	N-3-f	1390 ± 15	609–664 AD
PSU 7689	AMS	PC1	Str. 120	AE-2-ae	1395 ± 15	607–663 AD
SMU 2300	C14	PC109	Str. 117	R-25-a	1410 ± 50	549–678 AD
PSU 6410	AMS	PC1	Str. 121	N-22-d	1425 ± 20	601–654 AD
PSU 6403	AMS	PC1	Str. 66	B-5-q	1445 ± 20	586–650 AD
SMU 1933	C14	PC1	Iglesia, Str. 9-subA	AL-1-d	1445 ± 60	436–679 AD
PSU 7062	AMS	PC1	Str. 114	CB-1-k	1490 ± 20	549–638 AD
PSU 7063	AMS	PC1	Str. 226	CQ-1-c	1540 ± 20	436–595 AD

continued on next page

Sample	Analysis Type	Site	Location	Context	¹⁴C yr (BP) ± 1σ	cal BC–AD (2σ) Oxcal 4.4 (IntCal20)
PSU 6411	AMS	PC1	Iglesia, Plaza 2, hearth	M-41-b	1585 ± 20	425–545 AD
SMU 2295	C14	PC1	Iglesia, Plaza 2, hearth	M-41-b	1590 ± 50	384–593 AD

CHAPTER 1: INTRODUCING
RITUAL ECONOMY

1. The term *chiefdom* has a checkered past and has been criticized by some investigators because of its use as a specific typological category (see Feinman and Neitzel 1984; Skalnik 2004:78). The term *chiefdom* is used here as a matter of descriptive convenience because these polities are multiscalar entities with leaders who have different levels of authority. Chiefdom has wide usage by archaeologists working across Central America. Some scholars prefer to refer to these polities as middle-range ranked societies instead of chiefdoms (Duffy 2015; Spielmann 1998; Upham 1987).

2. Examples of sumptuous goods include jade artifacts and elaborate caved metates from Costa Rica (e.g., Aguilar 2003; Hoopes 2007; Hoopes, Mora-Marín, and Kovacevich 2021; McEwan and Hoopes 2021a:74–237; Stone 1977b, 1993) as well as the elaborate gold work found across Central America (e.g., Erickson and Fenton 2021; Fernádez Esquivel 2021; Mayo Torné, Mayo Torné, and Guinea Bueno 2001; McEwan and Hoopes 2021a:262–277; Uribe Villegas, Martinón-Torres, and Quintero Guzmán 2021).

3. The strongest evidence for wealth inequality in societies in west-central Honduras occurs during the Early and Middle Formative periods, where a few prominent burials are found with sumptuous burial offerings. The nature of these materials is discussed in chapter 2.

4. For a broader discussion of how extra-household production can be organized to meet public or civic-ceremonial needs, including those of formal institutions, see Hirth (1996b, 2016, 2020).

5. The concept of ritual mode of production has been applied both for the production of specific goods used in socially designated rituals and as a general framework for organizing work in domestic contexts.

6. The sponsor of the celebration can just as easily be a clan or a community, as seen in the case of the Northwest Coast Potlatch (Codere 1966; Drucker and Heizer 1967), which is an individual aggrandizer.

7. Richard Thaler (2015:4–5) characterized the difference between actual and assumed neoclassical behavior as the product of what humans do as opposed to what the mythical individuals do, which he refers to Econs (*homo economicus*).

8. Thaler (2015:65) calls the neoclassical assumption that previous expenditures do not affect human behavior the *sunk cost fallacy*.

9. Ruben Reina and Richard Hill (1978:258–262) discuss an interesting case in highland Guatemala where a highly skilled and innovative woman potter who made figurines for the tourist market was unable to marry until she returned to making traditional water jars in the community where she lived. Innovation was held in check by traditional social norms and *costumbre* in her Chinautla community.

10. Specific spirits that govern the desired outcomes of individual petitioners are targeted by cutting paper images of that spirit's image and laying it on the community altar along with associated offerings (Sandstrom and Sandstrom 1986). The ritual is held as a collective action for the community as a whole while still enabling individual negotiation with individual spirits by petitioners.

CHAPTER 2: CHIEFDOM SOCIETIES IN WEST-CENTRAL HONDURAS

1. Peter Skalník (2004) argues that when warlordships, political parties, trade unions, and business entities are examined in terms of their composition, organizational structures, and modes of operation, they actually compare quite well to the classic descriptions of a chiefdom society.

2. Examples of archaeologists who use the term *chiefdom* to describe cultural development in Honduras and Central America include Begley (1999), Creamer and Haas (1985), Dixon (1989b), Drennan and Uribe (1987), Goralski (2008), Hasemann (1987), Healy (1974), Hendon, Joyce, and Lopiparo (2013), Hirth (1996a), Joesink-Mandeville (1987), Joyce (n.d.), and Robinson (1989), to name a few. The term *chiefdom* has also been applied to describe the *cacicazgo* societies throughout Honduras at the time of the Spanish Conquest (Chapman 1978; Gómez Zúñiga 2021; Helms 1979; Lara-Pinto 1980, 1991a, 1991b, 2020, 2021; Weeks, Black, and Speaker 1987).

3. The discussion draws heavily on areas where research has been more extensive such as the Ulúa and Naco valleys, the Lake Yojoa region, the Comayagua valley, central Santa Bárbara, and the La Entrada region.

4. Good surface visibility at Yarumela made it possible to identify Formative period domestic debris over 30 ha (Dixon 1989a:259). Likewise, it was clear that some domestic structures at Yarumela were constructed on low mounds under 1 m in height.

5. A large defensive ditch was constructed during the Jaral phase to protect the site; it was 1,300 m long, 15–20 m wide, and 6.5 m deep. A second defensive ditch was constructed during the Late Formative Eden phase that was 3 km long and several m deep (Baudez and Becqueline 1973:51–53, 66–68, 75; Urban, Schortman, and Ausic 2002:147).

6. Excavations revealed that Structure 101 supported a large residential or ceremonial building on its summit. This was a pole and thatch building that was 32 m long (N–S) and 14 m wide (E–W), with a covered drain to remove rainwater off its summit (Dixon et al. 1994:77).

7. Of these six sculptures, four are still accessible and have been described and illustrated by Rosemary Joyce and John Henderson (2002).

8. The two anthropomorphic sculptures are monuments 4 and 5, which were recovered in the foundation platforms of stelae 4 and 5, which have long count dates of AD 452 and 523, respectively.

9. Jade, shell, and marble artifacts all appear in burial and architectural cache offerings at Puerto Escondido by 1100 BC (Joyce and Henderson 2002:5).

10. Wendy Ashmore (1987:34) reports an Olmec-style mask, presumably of jade, in a local collection that was reportedly obtained from an undisclosed site in central Santa Bárbara.

11. Percussion flaking dominated Jaral phase obsidian assemblages at Los Naranjos, with communities in west-central Honduras relying on the obsidian sources of San Luis (Aoyama, Tashiro, and Glascock 1999:237; Joyce et al. 2004) in Santa Bárbara and the La Esperanza source in southern Honduras (Sorensen and Hirth 1984).

12. Considerable variation can be found in the locations where blades occur throughout the Formative period in relation to percussion flaking, with main centers receiving more obsidian blades while smaller rural sites relied more heavily on percussion flaking for their cutting tool needs (Pope and Robinson 1987:112). At Los Naranjos, blades constitute 25 percent of the Eden I obsidian assemblage, increasing to 47 percent during Eden II. In the Late Formative contexts in the Ulúa valley, obsidian blades represent 39 percent of the assemblage at Río Pelo and between 57 percent and 87 percent of the obsidian assemblage at La Guacamaya (Pope and Robinson 1987:110).

13. At Yarumela, most cutting tools were manufactured from obsidian instead of chert, with obsidian representing between 69 percent and 76 percent of the flaked stone artifacts recovered from Early through Late Formative (Yarumela I–III) deposits. Obsidian pressure blades increased over time, rising from 15 percent of assemblages during the Early Formative to 39 percent–41 percent during the Middle and Late Formative periods (Elder 1984:table 3).

14. Some of these Classic period polychrome traditions include the ceramic types referred to as Babilonia, Ulúa, Sulaco, Las Flores, Tenampua, La Vegas, and Bold Geometric polychromes (Baudez 1966; Baudez and Becquelin 1973:99–358; Beaudry-Corbett et al. 1993; Glass 1966; Henderson and Beaudry-Corbett 1993b; Hirth, Kennedy, and Cliff 1993; Joyce 1993; Robinson 1989; Urban 1993a, 1993b, 1993c; Viel 1977, 1983).

15. Sites in the upper two levels of the site hierarchy usually have at least one plaza area 50 m or more in size that is bounded by rectilinear Range structures that are larger and taller than normal domestic structures. These large buildings are often characterized as "monumental" structures if they are over 2 m in size (Hasemann 1985; Joyce 2014:66) and may employ construction materials (e.g., cut stone, plaster floors and building surfaces) not commonly found in small domestic structures. These larger buildings are believed to have served special civic-ceremonial functions that included elite residences and temple ritual.

16. Jeanne Lopiparo (2006; Hendon, Joyce, and Lopiparo 2013:77–79) has used thiessen polygons and nearest neighbor distances to propose territories of twelve Late Classic chiefdoms in the lower Ulúa valley. While theoretically attractive, these territory polygons are drawn around sites of very different sizes and scales. While they imply something about social interaction within a few kilometers around these sites, they do not provide an accurate reconstruction of a political hierarchy since the site of Campo Dos (CR-132), a small village community, was handled the same way as the primary center of Travesía (Hendon, Joyce, and Lopiparo 2013:figure 5.1).

17. Terminal Classic period centers located on defensible hilltops include the sites of Tenampua, in the Comayagua valley; Tulian, on the Caribbean Coast west of the Ulúa valley; and Cerro Palenque in the Ulúa valley (Dixon 1989b:264; Joyce 2014:38).

18. As a rule, residential house mounds are less than 1 m in height. We consider population estimates based on house mound counts to be minimal estimates, since it cannot be assumed that all domestic structures were built on mounds. It is likely that some residential structures were built directly on ground surface without a basal mound during both the Late Formative and Postclassic periods.

19. Population is estimated using mound counts as a proxy measurement for total domestic residences. Given that a residence may employ more than a single structure, a range estimate of three–five persons per structure was used to estimate population (Hasemann and Lara-Pinto n.d.; Hirth n.d.). This is a conservative estimate compared to William Loker's (1986:385) estimate of 5.4 persons per structure in the El Cajón region, Dennis Puleston's (1974:309) similar estimate of 5.4 persons for the Maya region, and Rosemary Joyce's (1985:123) estimate of 5.6 persons per structure at Cerro Palenque.

20. The Comayagua valley covers 550 km² and contains a large amount of high-quality land for prehispanic agricultural groups. Intensive survey registered a Late Classic settlement pattern of sites with 25–100 mounds under 1 m in height (Dixon

1989b:262). This is markedly different from other regions that had larger on-site populations in primary and secondary centers (see table 2.4).

21. Julia Hendon and Rosemary Joyce estimate that there were 250 structures at Travesía based on a study of aerial photographs and pedestrian survey done in the 1980s (Hendon, Joyce, and Lopiparo 2013:8; Joyce and Sheptak 1983). However, excavations and mapping at Travesía by James Sheehy (1977, 1978) in 1976 indicate that the land at Travesía had been cleared in a 1–2 km radius around the central mounds, leveling and obliterating most of the mounds in this area. The only structure remains visible in leveled areas outside the main group at Travesía are locations where concentrations of calcareous rocks suggest prior building materials. Doris Stone (1941) believed there were about 1,000 structures at the site, but this seems to have been a gloss for saying there were many structures there.

22. Cerro Palenque was carefully mapped by Rosemary Joyce (1985, 2014). Since the site has a light occupation during the Late Classic, we use her estimate of 500 or more structures for the Terminal Classic population. Dorothy Hughes Popenoe (1935) engaged in early work at Tenampua and estimated that there were 500 mounds within its defensive perimeter. Tenampua was subsequently mapped by Boyd Dixon (1987), who counted over 400 mounds still within its defensive walls.

23. Eugenia Robinson (1989:189) notes the presence of other uncarved stelae in the Ulúa valley at Currusté, Amaya, La Mora, La Guacamaya, Travesía, YR-124, and Calabazas.

24. The stela was actually recovered at the site of El Cedral (PC205), which was not a residential community. The closest residential community may be underneath the modern community of Meambar. Nevertheless, a Late Classic date for this monument is reinforced by carving elements that resemble glyphic features for the day 17 Caban from the Maya calendar (Thompson 1971:figure 10).

25. Joyce (n.d.) notes that in the Cataguana valley, ballcourts can be found in small village communities.

26. Sites where ballcourts were incorporated into elite residence areas include Travesía, La Sierra, and Palmerejo (Stone 1941:figure 48; Wells and Davis-Salazar 2008:202). While they occur in sites of different sizes, ballcourts have also been used as a diagnostic feature of towns with regional influence (Lopiparo 2006; Hendon, Joyce, and Sheptak 2009:figure 5.1).

27. Not all ethnographically documented ball games in Mesoamerica were played on a court with two flanking architectural mounds. The games could also be played on an open flat field, as documented by Ted Leyenaar (1978).

28. David Abbott (2010) has noted that ball game events were also important among the Hohokam in the southwestern United States because they drew people together for regional marketplaces held at the same time, which were important for

domestic provisioning. The same practice could also have occurred in communities hosting ball games in west-central Honduras.

29. The phosphorous contained in organic debris forms phosphates, which are highly stable and remain fixed in the soil for long periods of time and are good indicators of a range of human activities, especially organic pollution (Eidt 1977; Terry et al. 2000).

30. Specialized craft production emphasizes the orientation of the artisan to produce items for exchange. This is distinct from ad hoc production that goes on in every household, where residents make tools that they use in work and social interaction during the normal course of their lives. The distinction between specialized crafting and ad hoc production rests on the quantity of items produced and whether all the goods produced could be consumed within the household or unit of production where they were made. Ad hoc production can include the manufacture of small amounts of goods used in gift exchange outside the household.

31. The 123 obsidian artifacts analyzed from the El Cajón region were drawn from the sites of Salitrón Viejo, La Ceiba, and Guarabuquí. Analysis was conducted using particle-induced X-ray emission (PIXE). Guinope obsidian was only recovered as nodules used to produce percussion flakes, while the other sources of La Esperanza, Ixtepeque, and El Chayal occurred as both percussion flakes and prismatic pressure blades. The separation of flake and blade industries is important because the later implies the presence of specialists while the former does not (Hirth and Cyphers 2020).

32. La Esperanza was the dominant source represented in analysis at the site of Salitrón Viejo, Guinope was the most frequent source identified at La Ceiba, and Ixtepeque was the primary source recovered and identified at Guarabuquí (Hirth 1987b:cuadro 3).

33. Ulúa polychromes were highly esteemed, and this is reflected in the imitation of their vase form in the manufacture of marble vases (Joyce n.d.:21).

34. A chemical analysis of ceramic pastes from the El Cajón and Ulúa valleys using INAA established that ceramics of the Sulaco paste group were manufactured at Salitrón Viejo and traded north into the Ulúa valley (Beaudry et al. 1989).

CHAPTER 3: PRE-COLUMBIAN SOCIETY AND ECOLOGY IN THE EL CAJÓN REGION

1. The El Cajón Archaeological Project, or Proyecto Arqueológico El Cajón (PAEC), was initiated by the Instituto Hondureño de Antropología e Historia between 1980 and 1989 as a research project of national importance. Funding for the research came from a variety of national and international sources, with the government of Honduras contributing over 75 percent of the financial resources to conduct the research. Contributing national agencies included the Empresa Nacional de Energia Electrica (ENEE), the Instituto Hondureño de Antropología e Historia (IHAH),

and the National Congress of Honduras. International contributors included the National Science Foundation, the University of Kentucky, the American Philosophical Society, the United States Information Service, and the Fulbright-Hays research program. The El Cajón Archaeological Project was directed by Kenneth Hirth, Gloria Lara-Pinto, and George Hasemann.

2. The average elevation of the upland plain is 1,000 m MSL near the modern town of Las Lajas. The highest elevations in the project zone are found at the Montaña de El Indio, southwest of Valle Bonito (1,513 m MSL), and at Cerro Negro, northwest of the modern town of La Libertad (1,733 m MSL) (Hirth and Cosgren 1989:19–23).

3. Flooding within the reservoir impact zone was expected to inundate all areas along the Sulaco and Humuya Rivers between 110 m MSL at the dam site to 300 m MSL within the reservoir catchment area.

4. The archeobotanical remains recovered by PAEC indicate that many of the same species found today were also represented in the archaeological assemblages of prehispanic sites (see Lentz 1989a).

5. The exception to this pattern in vega size is the large vega located at the intersection of the Sulaco and Yunque Rivers where the site of Salitrón Viejo is found. The vega at this location is 1.5 km² in size and is the largest area of good alluvial land for agriculture on the valley floor (Hirth and Cosgren 1989:23).

6. This contrasts with agriculture in the piedmont slopes, where two–three years of continuous cultivation required four–five years of fallow and produced a yield only two-thirds that of vega land (Loker 1986:252).

7. The productivity of the uplands is roughly 27 percent–37 percent less than yields from vega lands, with much longer fallow cycles. While William Loker's (1986:245, 250) informants told him that some vega fields had up to forty years of continuous use without fallow, he could not confirm this assertion with any degree of confidence. He calculated that sustainable cultivation on vega lands could be maintained with a 10:5 crop-to-fallow cycle, while cultivation in piedmont areas would need a crop-to-fallow cycle of 4:5 and steep slopes would require a crop-to-fallow cycle of 2:5 (Loker 1989b:159).

8. Farmers who plant the *postrera* normally leave cut vegetation in the field without burning to better retain the moisture that falls from precipitation during the remainder of the rainy season. They also plant a quick-growing variety of maize known locally as maize ligero that matures in seventy-five–eighty days. Cultivation of the *postrera* has decreased over time because of labor opportunities for people to work in the coffee harvest and because of increased use of the land for grazing animals (Loker 1989a:53–55).

9. Examination of gastropod specimens in the collection suggests that two separate species (smooth and corrugated shell) were exploited and consumed in the El Cajón region (Larry Feldman, personal communication, 1982).

10. The recovery of coyol from a series of three-stone fire hearths or ovens in Plaza One at Salitrón Viejo (F-5-ar) indicates that it was cooked or prepared to extract the usable oil.

11. Coyol wine is sweet when it is fresh, and the volume of alcohol increases as it ferments.

12. Chert outcrops occur as nodules up to 60 cm in size in two areas in the study region. Nine outcrops were identified along the Sulaco River between the sites of Salitrón Viejo (PC1) and La Ceiba (PC13). Three outcrops were identified on the Humuya River: two at the intersection wth the Yure River and one other along the upper reaches of the Quebrado El Chamo (Hirth and Cosgren 1989:figure 1.3; Lara-Pinto and Hasemann 1982:map insert).

13. All ceramics were classified first by paste and then by surface finish (slipping, burnishing) and techniques of decoration (painting, incising, plastic application). The attributes used to classify paste included the color of the oxidized clay, texture, and paste composition. This permitted the establishment of six primary paste groups that comprised the majority of paste variability within the El Cajón region. Adopting this approach enabled us to examine ceramics as products of manufacturing traditions using different paste sources and recipes, which is congruent with a communities of practice analytical approach (Costin 2016; Sassaman and Rudolphi 2001; Wendrich 2012; Wenger 1998). This approach revealed how different types and decorative modes typically used in type-variety classification systems cut across and were imitated by groups using different clay resources. Vessel forms did not define taxa but were identified and studied within each ceramic type.

14. Seventeen of the twenty-four sites tested in the regional testing program were located on the Sulaco River. These included two major sites (PC59, PC71), four intermediate sites (PC4, PC7, PC12, PC37), and eleven small sites (PC2, PC5, PC6, PC8, PC9, PC22, PC33, PC38, PC41, PC42, PC72). Stratigraphic probes at these sites consisted of more than 4,000 shovel tests and 69 stratigraphic pits in plaza areas and platform structures (Hasemann 1998:135–136).

15. Initial mapping in 1980 identified 394 architectural features (Hirth 1981; Robinson, O'Mack, and Loper 1985), which increased to 410 as the project proceeded and clearing continued to locate additional small structures and walls.

16. Recycling of house mound fill was identified at Structure 261 (Op O). It had begun by removing material from the north side of the house mound, eating into its center but leaving much of its south side relatively unaffected.

17. The organization of residential structures into small patio groups at the large sites was identified in a few cases at Intendencia, Guarabuquí, and La Ceiba in the El Cajón region (Benyo and O'Mack 1985; Lara-Pinto and Sheptak 1985; Messenger 1982).

18. All three ramps were surfaced with river cobbles. The two ramps that provided access leading into the central plaza of the South Group were Structures 265 and 266.

19. Two structures along the Sulaco valley were under 2 m in height but were classified as monumental because their foundation walls were unexcavated, extended below the surface, and in all other regards conformed to the definition of civic-ceremonial structures. They are the ritual structure at PC3 that was 1.95 m tall and Structure AF13 at La Ceiba (PC13) that was located in the site's public plaza area and was 1.8 m in height (Benyo 1986).

20. Large-scale excavations on the Humuya River were conducted at the large site of Intendencia (PC109), with regional testing at the sites of PC101, PC105, PC116, PC 117, PC 118, PC121, PC131, and PC138.

21. The two Yunque phase house mounds that survived were Structures 75 and 76. Their preservation may be due to their location on the far western margins of the site.

22. The sites along the Humuya River that have a Late Yunque occupation are PC105, PC109, PC117, PC131, and PC138.

23. Tamaro Incised occurs in a variety of forms, including straight-neck and collared jars with tubular spouts, neckless jars, and shouldered, inflected, and vertical-wall bowls. Incised decoration during this phase includes zig-zag or false rocker stamping and cross-hatching arranged in triangular or rectangular panels.

24. Stratigraphic excavations were carried out in eleven of the twenty-two structures located within the North Precinct. The structures tested included Structures 37, 38, and 40 and the lineal platform features of Structures 29, 30, 32–34, 36, 44, and 45. Archaeological testing was also carried out across the floor of the North Plaza.

25. Both of these sets of platforms were low earthen constructions that averaged about 2 m wide and ranged from 20 cm to 60 cm in height over their greater length. Sections of these low platforms were constructed simply as earthen alignments without cobble retention walls that have eroded over time. We do not believe they ever exceeded 50–60 cm in height anywhere over their greater extent.

26. Structures 34 and 35 are small platforms that flank either side of the opening through the longer platforms formed by Structures 33 and 244. A second opening between platform Structures 29 and 30 aligns with that of Structures 34 and 35 and appears to be another entrance through a possible palisade.

27. The six low linear feature structures where a small amount of midden was identified were Structures 29, 30, 32, 34, 44, and 45. While dismantled households could be completely invisible, they often leave behind traces of some construction debris (*bajareque*, rock alignments), none of which were visible across the open expanse of the North Group.

28. Four large Range structures (Structures 210, 211, 212, and 213) were tested in the South Group, with axial trenching that transected the center of each mound. A fifth

(Structure 209) was excavated using test pits and perimeter shovel tests. Three large Range structures were excavated, with axial trenching and large-scale perimeter testing in the West Group (Structures 118, 119, and 120).

29. Excavations in Structure 6 indicate that the substructure of this Range platform dates to the Late Yunque phase, and the location probably already served as the residence for Salitrón's highest-ranking elite family during the Early Yunque phase.

CHAPTER 4: THE IGLESIA PRECINCT: CONSTRUCTING A RITUAL LANDSCAPE AT SALITRÓN VIEJO

1. The Acropolis platform at Salitrón Viejo represents a total volume of 13,116 m^3 of construction fill as presented in chapter 7.

2. Our limited understanding of the Terminal Formative and Early Classic periods is a result of two problems in Honduran archaeology. The first is the need for finer-grain ceramic chronologies reinforced by high-precision radiocarbon dating that can isolate these occupations from the preceding Late Formative period. The second problem stems from the large increase in population during the Late Classic period and the practice of expanding or recycling earlier platform mounds into later constructions, effectively removing constructions from this time period from the archaeological record.

3. Structures 2-subA and 3-subA were constructed along with Structure 21-subA during the first occupation episode (Stage 1) of the Iglesia Precinct. Structures 1 and 3 in Plaza One were the tallest platform mounds in the precinct.

4. The buried structures that lined and defined the perimeter of the original Central Plaza, from west to east, were Structures 3-subA, 12-subA, 395, 6-subA, 398, 7-subA, 8-subA, and 21-subA.

5. The irregular configuration of the northwest side of the Acropolis platform may also be the product of recycling portions of its cobble retention facade into some of the last monumental constructions in the South and West Residential Groups.

6. The structures sampled and exposed in addition to the Acropolis platform include Structures 1–10, 12, 21–22, 395, and 397–398 and Altars 1 and 2.

7. Domestic settlement during this period was most heavily concentrated in the West Residential Group.

8. The hard-packed earthen floor (Feature 84-R81) was identified in the pre-architectural layer underneath the southeast corner of Structure 1. An additional basal support wall and associated activity surface 4.5 m in length and 4–8 cm in thickness was identified on the northwest side of Structure 1 (Features 81-R38 and 81-R39, respectively).

9. Excavations have confirmed that all household platforms in the El Cajón region were constructed using cobble retention walls.

10. A 13 m long section of the western exterior wall of the structure was buried and covered by an expansion of the structure during Stage 6 that preserved portions of the delicate adobe facade up to the structure's full height.

11. Three elements define Floor 3-subC1 and its associated floor zone on the summit of Structure 3-subC. A layer of lightly burnt clay 5–10 cm thick was used as floor preparation on which the hard-packed and partially fired red clay surface of Floor 3-subC1 was prepared. The floor ranged from 2 cm to 3 cm in thickness and was covered by a thick concentration of ash that appears related to the structure's use.

12. The nine ceramic vessels consisted of three bowls with resist decoration, one tetrapod bowl with resist decoration covered with stucco, and five jars and in-curving bowls with incised decoration. While the wood of the two stuccoed vessels in this offering had long since decomposed, their shape could be partially reconstructed from their painted interior and exterior stucco layers.

13. The construction and use of these hearths or roasting pits fired the ground surface between them, resulting in a highly distinctive signature that was only identified in Plaza One.

14. The consumption of fermented beverages is a basic feature of collective work parties in indigenous Lenca communities, and coyol was reportedly used for fermented beverages in several areas of southeastern Mesoamerica (Conzemius 1932; Roys 1931; Williams 1981:249–250).

15. The difficulty in defining the lateral extent of early structures was a combination of limited time and resources, together with the fact that a number of early structures were partially dismantled or difficult to trace within the Acropolis platform, where lines and layers of cobbles were used for both fill and exterior structure walls. This was complicated by the dislocations from the roots of large tropical trees that grew up over the Iglesia Precinct after the site was abandoned. For illustration purposes, the sizes of substructures that were not completely excavated were estimated by scaling down the structures' final dimensions.

16. It is possible to imagine that construction within some stages was carried out as back-to-back labor projects during the dry season of consecutive years. Interior retainment walls were identified as internal features within the Acropolis platform that may represent short periods of sequential construction.

17. The retainment wall of Feature 84-R50 was considered the product of sequential construction within Stage 3, for two reasons. First, the cobble pavement across the summit of the Acropolis platform was constructed as a continual surface from north to south, suggesting a single construction episode. Second, the 84-R50 retainment wall is oriented N-S and intersects the middle of Structure 7-subA at a 90 degree angle to its western side. This would have been an unusual architectural arrangement if it was left that way for any prolonged period of time.

18. The preserved adobe wall reveals that the second tier of the structure was situated 1.8 m back from the edge of the platform's lower level. The lower level of the structure from the previous stage was 15.00 m (N–S) and 8.25 m (E–W). If this distance was maintained around the entire structure, then its upper summit was 11.40 m long (N–S) by 4.65 m wide (E–W).

19. This suggests that Structure 2 was in periodic use from Stage 1 into Stage 6 of the Iglesia Precinct construction sequence. Ceramic refuse associated with Stage 1 and later use of this structure is spread out over an area of approximately 200 m² within Plaza One.

20. The east wall of Structure 395 could not be defined and may have been destroyed or incorporated into the later expansion of the Acropolis platform. The dimensions provided here are approximations based on remnant wall alignments.

21. The fill consisted of large cobbles 25–40 cm in diameter set in a sandy clay mortar. The combination of adobe walls with cobble fill used in the construction of Structure 1-subA is a signature of Late Yunque phase construction in the Iglesia Precinct.

22. Excavations revealed that the east side of Structure 21 had been partially dismantled and the fill carried off for use elsewhere. It is likely that this occurred in Stage 5 or 6, when Structure 21 no longer played an important role within the Iglesia Precinct.

23. The wall of the second tier was set 1.8–2.0 m back from the edge of the lower platform, which would have created a summit area of the second level that was approximately 13.0 m long (N–S) and 10.0 m wide (E–W).

24. Fourteen of these caches were located on the northeast side of Structure 1 while the other was located on its northwest side. An additional eighteen carved artifacts were recovered in slope wash on the lower sides of Structure 1 that appear to have eroded out of these and possibly other caches.

25. Structure 398 was not considered to be a substructure of Structure 9, for three reasons. It was not located directly underneath it, no interfacing construction linked it with Structure 9, and it had an orientation of N10W, which was different from the true north orientation of Structure 9.

26. The unconsolidated nature of this deposit suggests that it was intended solely to erect a small open-sided structure that was used to prepare food for feasting or to initiate construction of Structure 9. A circular stone hearth located directly on the cobble pavement of Plaza Two was identified as Feature 81AL-R2. A layer of mixed ash, charcoal, and carbonized food remains was distributed across the pavement adjacent to the hearth that included burnt bone, jutes, coyol, carbon, and burnt daub. Not only does this deposit resemble Structure 2 in Plaza One, but the layer of soil would have been necessary to support the poles of a temporary cooking structure that was later incorporated into the fill of Structure 9.

27. Structure 10 was identified as having a small frontal platform during initial mapping of the Iglesia Precinct, which was not confirmed by archaeological testing.

28. The east end of the Iglesia Precinct was limited by the bluff line leading down the Rio Yunque. The identification of two badly eroded ramps (Structures 394a, 394b) traversing that bluff line and leading into the East Courtyard indicates that the precinct's eastern margin was geologically stable.

29. The two censorware ceramic types are Masaguara Spiked Striated and Lajas Plain Textured. These vessels range from 18 cm to 40 cm in diameter at the mouth.

CHAPTER 5: THE JADE, MARBLE, AND RITUAL OFFERINGS

1. Nephrite is an amphibole mineral of calcium magnesium silicate in monoclinic crystalline form. The chemical formula for nephrite is $Ca_2(Mg, Fe)_5Si_8O_{22}(OH)_2$. Jadeite is a green monoclinic mineral of the pyroxene group that is a silicate of sodium and aluminum. The chemical formulas for jadeite are $NaAlSi_2O_6$ and $Na(Al,Fe+++)Si_2O_6$.

2. Willilam Foshag (1957:2) points out that the term *jade* was first used by Europeans to refer to greenstone from the New World before Chinese jade and nephrite were known. Fray Alonso de Molina (1977:74) translates *yjade* as "part of the body" and "sickness," referring to the stone's presumed curative properties for curing kidney and other bodily ailments. Early Spanish sources often referred to jade simply as emerald, conflating it with that well-known gemstone from Colombia. Our term for jade appears to come from the French phrasing of *pierre l'ejade* (Foshag 1957:7–9).

3. While classified as anthropomorphic, it is possible that these images could also be abstract forms of non-human primates and other animal species.

4. Earflares can be fragmented into multiple segments depending on the thinness of their front-facing disks. The difficulty was in matching the edge of the thin disk pieces with the earflare stem when the intervening connecting fragments could not be identified.

5. While the stem is a highly diagnostic feature of the earflare that is unique from artifact to artifact, other features are also diagnostic for obtaining minimum artifact counts (MAC). They include flare profile, disk width, thickness, and edge type along with tubular shape, length, and diameter.

6. One pound (lb) equals 453.6 g, and it is unlikely that a weight that heavy could be supported by the thin membrane of an earlobe. The world record for weight lifted from the ear was set by Rakesh Kumar, who lifted 82.6 kg with one ear using a clamp covering the whole ear. How much weight the earlobe would support by itself remains unclear (https://www.guinnessworldrecords.com).

7. The overall width of the front face of tubular flares was computed by the equation TW+2DW, where TW equals the width of the central tubular drilling and DW represents the width of the disk from the tubular drilling to its outer edge. DW needs to be multiplied by 2 so that both sides of the flare are considered.

8. Stylistic variation in crescent pectorals led to the creation of four subtypes to capture the stylistic variation in decoration.

9. Ring pendants occur as pairs in cached clusters 6, 24, 65, 492, 1,326, and 1,423.

10. The circular carved design on pendant 2,134 (figure 5.19d) may have been an attempt to imitate a cartouche. In another instance (2,324), lines were organized to possibly imitate a foot or shell design (figure 5.19b). Some of the more abstract associations of geometric elements can be difficult to interpret.

11. In mineralogical terms, the materials resemble Alaskite in appearance, which is a leucocratic granite of medium or fine grain composed primarily of quartz and alkali feldspars that give the stone a sparkling appearance.

12. Isotopic research by Christina Luke and colleagues (2006) identified two marble sources in the Ulúa valley (Santa Rita, El Cutuco) as likely sources for manufacturing marble vessels. A third source at Baracoa has some isotopic similarities with Ulúa marble vases, but the source material is very coarse and not an ideal material to work with.

13. Robert Fakundiny (1970:33–34) reports several siliceous marble outcrops among the towns of El Roblito, Loma de Cordero, and Cacaguapa.

14. Many granular marble artifacts recovered from shallow subsurface deposits were in poor condition as a result of tropical rain and the way acid soils accelerated the destructive process. Some of the first artifacts recovered were located in shallow deposits on the west side of Structure 12 (see chapter 6) and were so poorly preserved that their original form could not be detected. When extremely eroded, they may not even resemble manmade artifacts.

15. Preliminary identifications of lithic material types were made by the geologist Charles Norville (1986) as a component of his geo-archaeological research.

16. Although beads were abundant in the El Cajón lapidary assemblage, this was the only case where it was clear that they were deposited as an articulated necklace.

17. The three cluster caches in which chalcedony nodules and flakes were incorporated within the Acropolis platform are clusters 185, 325, and 471.

18. Collections from the Cenote at Chichen Itzá (Coggins and Shane 1984; Proskouriakoff 1974) are the largest collections of finished jade artifacts from a single context in eastern Mesoamerica. While providing a great deal of material for stylistic comparisons, there is no direct dating that can be associated with any of the artifacts recovered. The site of Blackwater Eddy (Guderjan 1998) also provides a large sample of jade from a single tomb deposit that is slightly later in time (AD 500).

19. The average weight of the twenty-one complete conical flares in the collection was 311.9 g.

20. Tapered flares are a larger and heavier subtype of tubular flares. The two complete examples in the collection are 305.9 and 354.2 g in weight, respectively. Linda

Schele and Mary Miller (1986:67) consider small versions of this type of flare to be headdress ornaments through which the frontal lock of hair was pulled (Schele and Miller 1986:plate 7).

21. One of the interesting aspects of hunched and hunchback representations in the collection is that they occur in all major raw material categories except micaceous jade.

22. It is noteworthy that the carvings identified as dwarf and hunchback figures throughout eastern Mesoamerica are always characterized as males. Why this is the case is unclear, since there is no difference in the occurrence of dwarfism in human biological populations.

23. Earflares were the only artifact class that does not occur in non-jade materials in the collection.

24. All of the granular marble pendants in the collection have short anterior stems, which we believe is the result of having narrow layers of marble to work with as raw material.

25. A total of 342 human images can be found in the catalog compared to 61 zoomorphic images. Fourteen of the human images are dated to the Toltec era on the basis of style; when these are removed from consideration, the frequency of anthropomorphic images remains high, at 84.3 percent for human portraiture (n = 328) compared to 15.7 percent for zoomorphic representations.

CHAPTER 6: THE PATTERNING OF RITUAL DEPOSITS AT SALITRÓN VIEJO

1. Salitrón Viejo had a total of 330 house mounds at the height of its Middle to Late Sulaco development. However, the population during the Late Yunque phase did not cover the entire site and appears to have been concentrated in the West Group, with a smaller scattering of houses in the South Group. The estimate of 175–250 households is a reasonable but conservative estimate for the Late Yunque phase.

2. The fifteen artifact clusters from the Stage 5 construction of Structure 1 were numbers 1300 (n = 6), 1302 (n = 11), 1309 (n = 10), 1319 (n = 10), 1320 (n = 9), 1326 (n = 10), 1349 (n = 6), 1360 (n = 16), 1383 (n = 34), 1394 (n = 23), 1416 (n = 12), 1419 (n = 9), 1423 (n = 13), 1433 (n = 8), and NS 2315 (n = 6).

3. The slate disk was recovered from cluster 1360 on the northeast side of Structure 1.

4. The eleven artifact clusters located on the east side of Structure 3 are cluster numbers 2117 (n = 3), 2205 (n = 4), 10041 (n = 3), 10049 (n = 2), 10051 (n = 8), 10064 (n = 4), 10067 (n = 2), 10070 (n = 3), 10073 (n = 7), 10090 (n = 3), and 10093 (n = 2).

5. The ten artifact clusters in the pedestrian surface on the west side of Structure 12 include numbers 1 (n = 14), 6 (n = 15), 23 (n = 7), 24 (n = 16), 65 (n = 29), 103 (n = 13), 111 (n = 10), 116 (n = 17), 155 (n = 9), and 171 (n = 5).

6. The granular marble artifacts were very poorly preserved because they were only 10–15 cm below the original ground surface. The twenty-two artifacts reported here were so badly eroded that it was difficult to determine their overall size and whether they were plain or carved. For that reason, they should be considered minimum counts for the number of marble artifacts represented.

7. The reason more excavations were carried out in the western Iglesia Precinct than in the east had to do with the early identification and recovery of large ritual deposits around Structure 12 and along the centerline of the Western Acropolis platform. Excavations were oriented to understand the contexts in which these deposits occurred.

8. It is likely that the twenty-two artifacts scattered throughout the cobble fill were originally incorporated into the eleven clusters that contained the majority of the artifacts in this area. The reason is that the cobble fill of the Acropolis platform is unstable in the face of tree growth and root action that may have dislocated individual beads and other small fragments from their original contexts within clusters. The two largest clusters recovered alongside Structure 12 (1128, 1180) had twenty-four and sixteen artifacts, respectively.

9. These eleven clusters are numbers 1091 (n = 3), 1128 (n = 24), 1131 (n = 6), 1159 (n = 2), 1165 (n = 8), 1166 (n = 8), 1180 (n = 16), 1202 (n = 3), 1205 (n = 5), 1210 (n = 5), and 1216 (n = 2).

10. The five unbroken artifacts in this deposit included two beads, two anthropomorphic pendants, and one zoomorphic pendant.

11. All 1,304 artifacts in this offering were placed along the east–west centerline within 1.5 m of the eastern exterior Stage 4 wall of the Western Acropolis platform.

12. The forty artifact cluster numbers in this huge deposit as they were excavated from top to bottom are 185 (n = 201), 215 (n = 31), 252 (n = 18), 274 (n = 47), 323 (n = 9), 325 (n = 19), 329 (n = 7), 346 (n = 3), 368 (n = 103), 471 (n = 19), 492 (n = 42), 533 (n = 112), 850 (n = 12), 860 (n = 12), 875 (n = 2), 883 (n = 56), 970 (n = 9), 1226 (n = 2), 1230 (n = 5), 1235 (n = 11), 1252 (n = 2), 1255 (n = 20), 1270 (n = 122), 1597 (n = 18), 1615 (n = 7), 1626 (n = 24), 1655 (n = 36), 1693 (n = 12), 1720 (n = 4), 1732 (n = 7), 1744 (n = 31), 1764 (n = 5), 1771 (n = 9), 1792 (n = 32), 1818 (n = 4), 1825 (n = 58), 1900 (n = 43), 1935 (n = 2), 1953 (n = 6), and 12379 (n = 3).

13. Final salvage operations were conducted in 1984 by Dr. George Hasemann using heavy machinery as the reservoir flood was under way.

14. Although jade beads were common in offerings at Salitrón Viejo, this necklace manufactured of non-jadeite materials was the only case where we could be certain that the beads were strung together. Three bits of evidence reinforced this conclusion. The beads are unusually small in the Salitrón Collection, they provide a matched set manufactured from the same raw material, and a number of adjacent beads were stuck

together and articulated with one another, as would be expected if they were deposited as a complete string.

15. The offerings in the subfloor cache were registered as cluster 2083. The human teeth were intentionally placed in the vessel offering and consisted of one incisor, two premolars, and one molar.

16. Nearly half of all the pendants recovered were carved (n = 57), which is unusual in that most pendants in the collection are plain. Two-thirds of these (68.4%) are manufactured from granular marble, the majority of which (71.8%) have geometric designs. In contrast, most plain pendants (82.3%) were jade.

17. The practice appears to have been to dig a small hole down to the level of sterile hardpan underlying the plaza surface, where artifacts were deposited. The level of the original North Precinct plaza surface was identified from the base of Structures 37, 38, and 40.

18. The five adjacent house mounds were Structures 112, 114, 115, 138, and 396.

19. The five adjacent house mounds were Structures 302, 306, 361, 365, and 369. The single beads from Structures 306 and 365 were recovered from preconstruction surfaces below the level of the house mounds and may be from an earlier occupation.

20. Reassembly of complete or near complete artifacts that were intentionally fragmented, however, is rare. Only 7.1 percent of the artifacts broken when placed in their depositional contexts were complete enough to register all physical dimensions.

21. The 2,376 items recovered from the Iglesia Precinct, 1,242 were complete and 1,134 were fragmented. This contrasts with the North Precinct, where 73 of the 349 items recovered were complete and 276 were fragmented when deposited.

22. Jade beads and bead pendants are resistant to breakage because of their small robust profiles. Higher fragmentation rates for earflares and pendants are easier to explain, although conical flares (see figures 5.13a–d, 5.14, 5.15) are robust through their midsection and difficult to break.

23. The four sites where lapidary artifacts were recovered were PC12 (n = 1), PC13 (n = 6), PC15 (n = 4), and PC109 (n = 12).

24. The refitting study was not a separate study because of the limitations of space in our field laboratory and the need to maintain security in the Instituto Hondureño de Antropología e Historia in Tegucigalpa. Instead, refitting was conducted alongside the analysis and coding of the collection. We believe a separate dedicated study of refitting would expand the results presented here. Although we are confident that all close matches of artifacts broken and deposited in contexts in close proximity to one another were identified, it is likely that some cross-site matches were missed.

25. The five artifacts that had conjoining pieces on either side of the east wall of the West Acropolis platform included parts of four earflares: three conical flares and one tubular earflare.

26. One of the pendants (#2609) recovered from the fill of Structure 38 was carved in the form of a zoomorphic image. The other pendant (#2609) was part of cluster cache 2604 buried alongside and below the base of Structure 38. Its carving displayed an anthropomorphic image.

27. Single-ritual events involving large-scale offerings of jade artifacts are not unknown from eastern Mesoamerica. Over a thousand pieces of jade were incorporated into a cache associated with a single Middle Classic mortuary interment at the site of Blue Creek in northwestern Belize (Guderjan 1998).

28. This necklace is composed of 109 matched beads and a central pendant that presumedly entered Salitrón Viejo in its assembled form. When it is handled as a single item instead of a count of 110 individual items, the total number of lapidary items drops to 89, with non-jadeite materials representing 22.5 percent of the assemblage.

29. Two hundred twenty of the 2,072 artifacts fashioned from Motagua valley jade were weak green in color.

CHAPTER 7: THE WHAT, HOW, AND WHY OF RITUAL ACTIVITY IN THE SALITRÓN CHIEFDOM

1. This was likely a function of scale, since the residues from feasts conducted in individual households would be difficult to distinguish from normal domestic refuse, while community-level feasting deposits would be notable in both size and their location in public contexts.

2. Wyllys Andrews (1976) was one of the first to note the widespread distribution of Usulután ceramics, which he called the Uapala ceramic sphere characterized by fine paste and resist decoration.

3. The communities in figure 3.14 are only those with a Late Yunque occupation confirmed by excavation. It is likely that a number of the large but untested communities upriver from PC59 were also incorporated into the Salitrón chiefdom at this time.

4. Estimating site size during the Late Yunque phase relied on the identification of ceramic remains recovered from preconstruction surfaces underneath later house mound constructions. Using this approach, domestic occupation was identified across the greater extent of the West Residential Group as well as along the east flank of the South Residential Group, covering an area 4–5 ha in size. The use of recorded structure densities at Salitrón Viejo produces an on-site population estimate for this period of 700–1,000 individuals. Population was calculated using a combination of the area occupied together with an estimate of the number of structures in that area.

5. Test excavations conducted across the West Plaza recovered Late Yunque materials but without indications that they were associated with earlier and dismantled domestic structures. Furthermore, Late Yunque materials were identified in higher

concentrations from the preconstruction surfaces underlying the Range structures on the periphery of the plazas in both the South and West Groups.

6. The heavy tropical vegetation reduced visibility, and sites were identified on the basis of low house mound constructions and/or retention walls. Ceramics and lithics were not usually able to be identified on the surface of sites, which meant that the temporal identification relied on test excavations conducted by the regional testing program. Because of limited time and resources, sites along the Sulaco River were only tested as far upriver as the site of Cueva Grande (PC59). We believe other communities as far east as La Pimienta (PC75, PC85) and possibly beyond were also part of the Salitrón chiefdom.

7. Like the population estimates calculated at Salitrón Viejo, the estimates at regional sites during this period were calculated from the distribution materials recovered from preconstruction surfaces and extrapolated to the level of the entire site. Population is estimated at four persons per household. The actual level of population in the region may have been somewhat larger than projected in table 7.1.

8. The ten grinding stones consisted of seven metates and three manos. What is notable is that all ten grinding stones were recovered from a single trench that only sampled about 15 percent of the structure's interior deposits. This is one of the highest concentrations of food preparation equipment recovered anywhere at Salitrón Viejo. More would have been recovered had excavations been expanded.

9. An AMS radiocarbon date (PSU 6409) from one of these pit hearths dates their use to 2δcal 110 BC–AD 21 (see table 4.1).

10. A large concentration of broken ceramics was associated with Structure 22, and a large number of grinding stones used for food production were recovered from the East Courtyard.

11. A total of 124 m² was excavated in the West Plaza, which represents 5.6 percent of the 2,200 m² plaza surface. Six percent is used as a rough estimate of the amount excavated because the size of the plaza changed over time as structures were added to its periphery.

12. One of these three features dates to the Late Yunque phase, while the other two are Early Sulaco in age (82CY-R5, 82CY-R6, 82CY-R7). One of the Early Sulaco pit ovens (82CY-R5) is located 10 m southwest of the large 82CY-R1 midden and has two manos, four metates, and a burnt floor area associated with it.

13. Platform mounds whose external retention walls were constructed of adobe include Structures 1, 3, 8-subA, and 21 (see chapter 4 for discussion). Adobe was also used in the Stage 3 retention wall of the Eastern Acropolis platform, where a double course of adobe was set on a cobble base (84-R12). Even here, however, there is no indication that adobe was used along the entire extent of the wall.

14. The experiments were conducted in the towns of Las Bocas, Sonora, and Tikul, Guatemala, in 1964 (Erasmus 1965).

15. Using North American students, Scott Hammerstedt (2005) found that 2 m³ of earth could be mined with stone hoes in a seven-hour day. Niels Andersen (1988) used a figure of 2 m³ of earth as the average productivity rate for the construction of the earthworks at Sarup, Scandinavia.

16. The structures engulfed and covered by the construction of the Acropolis platform include Structures 3, 6–8, 12, 395, and 397–398.

17. Stage 3 adjustments to the Acropolis volume include the 432 m³ of Structure 6, 80 m³ of Structure 7, 104 m³ of Structure 8, and 294 m³ of Structure 398. Stage 4 adjustments to the Acropolis volume include the 90 m³ of Structure 3 and 32 m³ of Structure 12. Stage 5 adjustments to the Acropolis volume include 32 m³ of Structure 12 and 194 m³ of Structure 395.

18. Charles Erasmus (1965) indicated that the person excavating soil filled the buckets the transporter was carrying. We have no idea if he worked continuously or periodically over the course of the five hours used in the experiment. Hammerstedt (2005) points out that in his experiment, soil could be excavated more rapidly if a vertical wall could be mined and the builders at Salitrón Viejo could do that by working off cut bank exposures of the Yunque River.

19. The reason cobbles were incorporated so readily into the fill of the Acropolis platform, in addition to providing architectural stability, is that they could be easily and rapidly collected from the Yunque River. One individual with a pry bar could easily keep three–four individuals busy transporting cobbles from the river channel up onto the Iglesia building site.

20. The basis for positing that Stages 4 and 5 of the Acropolis were completed close to one another is based on two lines of inference. The first is the identical AMS dates obtained from samples off of the preconstruction surfaces underneath the Stage 4 and 5 construction episodes of the Acropolis platform around Structure 12. The second line of inference is the refits identified among five jade artifacts behind the Stage 4 retention wall with those from the Stage 5 ritual offering placed alongside the wall at the completion of the Acropolis platform.

21. The construction histories of civic-ceremonial structures are grouped into three phases instead of the five ceramic phases established for the El Cajón region. The reason is that excavations were often not extensive enough to date and separate construction episodes into the five ceramic phases. For that reason, it was decided to use the three-phase grouping to capture the main construction trends in Salitrón Viejo.

22. Additional activities that used labor from outlying communities could have included obtaining large logs and beams for the buildings located on civic-ceremonial structures as well as procuring roofing materials and the specialists who might have been used to prepare them (von Hagen 1943).

23. Burials were only recovered in two other civic-ceremonial structures at Salitrón Viejo. They included an adult female burial (1-50) in Structure 9 and a child burial (1-34) at Structure 118 in the West Group. Both burials lacked offerings.

24. We are aware that separating the natural world in terms of animate (wood, thatch) and inanimate objects (earth, stone, mud) makes a distinction that prehispanic people did not make. We do so to make it easier to conceptualize that in the prehispanic worldview, both trees and rocks had animated spirits that had to be taken into consideration when they were removed from their natural setting and used in creating a built environment.

25. In operational terms, it is often difficult to distinguish whether an offering was a termination or a dedicatory ritual. A number of artifacts were encountered in the Stage 4 fill of the Acropolis platform that covered Structure 12. Were these objects termination offerings associated with burying Structure 12, or were they dedicatory items included in the construction of the Acropolis platform? Either could have occurred at the same time, so it is useful not to be categorically constrained in the way offerings are viewed and classified.

26. The ratio was calculated by comparing the 8 nodules and the 1 percussion flake to the 2,881 finished lapidary items recovered at Salitrón Viejo (see table 5.1). This is a low-precision measure, but it provides a useful contrast with workshop sites where lapidary goods were produced.

27. The reference to merchants here includes both full-time merchants and the operation of ethnic merchants moving between trade partners, as documented in some chiefdom and tribal societies elsewhere around the world (Harding 1967; Hirth 2020:204–206).

28. A good deal of the experimentation on Alpine axes involved percussion, pecking, and grinding. Nevertheless, Pétrequin and colleagues (2012:275) experimented with a variety of materials and demonstrated that it took only ten–twelve hours to saw through and split a 30 cm × 10 cm block of serpentine using an oak plank and crushed quartzite. Since the majority of the lapidary goods in the El Cajón collection are jade, this less arduous time estimate is only suitable for estimating production for non-jadeite materials.

29. The manufacture of even a plain tubular earflare involved a considerable amount of work as well as the manufacturing process following the steps illustrated by Andrieu and colleagues (2014:figure 7). Tubular earflares range from 62.0 mm to 134.0 mm in diameter, with an average diameter of 95.3 mm. Based on Pétrequin and colleagues (2012:278), it would take 40 hours to cut the face of the earflare and another 53 hours to make the eight cuts necessary to roughly shape the round tubular spout (Andrieu, Rodas, and Luin 2014:figure 7). The central hole is estimated to take 13.4 hours using

the cutting rate of 2.4 mm/hour. Shaping the perimeter of the earflare, final shaping of the tubular stem using pecking, and the final finishing and polishing of the entire artifact are estimated at 30 hours. Given these calculations, the total working time to produce a tubular jade earflare is estimated at 130–140 hours of artisan time.

30. Ring pendants are plain and well-polished artifacts that range from 68.0 mm to 127.0 mm in diameter. Their average diameter is 94.3 mm and their average thickness is 7.7 mm. Two parallel cuts were used to prepare a preform to shape these circular pendants; 37 hours were estimated to make each of these cuts. The time to drill the large central hole and the two small suspension holes was estimated at 9.6 hours. Shaping the circular edge of the pendant together with finishing and polishing was estimated to require 12 hours. Given these figures, the total working time for an average-size ring pendant in the El Cajón collections was estimated at 90–95 hours of crafting time.

31. Crescent pectorals were shaped from a thinly sawn piece of jade that was shaped and decorated with a variety of drilling and sawing activities. Crescent pectorals average 126.7 mm wide, 63.75 mm high, and 11.65 mm thick. It is estimated that it took 53 hours to make the two parallel cuts and create a preform 63.75 mm in height. Crescent pectorals are straight across the top, and an additional 12.9 hours would have been needed to make this cut and to shape the curved lower portion of the pendant. Drilling was used to create the central crescent on the top of the pectoral and its associated suspension holes: 14.7 hours are estimated for this work at a perforation rate of 2.4 mm/hour. The surface of most crescent pectorals was decorated with designs created with a tubular drill, incisions, or both. Four hours were added for these decorative elements and an additional 2.0 hours for finishing and polishing. Given these estimates, the working time for the average crescent pectoral is estimated at 80.0–90.0 hours.

32. The 98 MAC estimated for tubular earflares, crescent pectorals, and ring pendants were derived from 264 artifact fragments. The MAC very likely underestimate the original number of these artifacts.

CHAPTER 8: BELIEF AND INTEGRATION IN A RITUAL ECONOMY

1. Many scholarly works discuss the different forms of organization in emerging complex society. Some of the most important of these are Blanton and Fargher 2008; Blanton et al. 1996; DeMarrais, Castillo, and Earle 1996; Earle 1997; Friedman and Rowlands 1978; and Stanish 2017, to name a few.

2. Among the contemporary Nahua of northern Veracruz, the earth was seen as alive and existing in human form, where the "soil is its flesh, rocks are its bones, and water is its blood" (Sandstrom 2005:42).

3. A total of 1,609 of the 2,881 artifacts and artifact fragments excavated at Salitrón Viejo were recovered from offering and fill deposits in the three stages of construction of the Acropolis platform (see tables 5.1, 6.1).

4. The 1,317 lapidary items were recovered along the centerline from five excavation units in Operation G. These included (1) 13 artifacts as part of the Stage 4 offering behind the exterior wall of the West Acropolis platform in units G165 and G175, and (2) the principal and final Stage 5 offering of 1,304 items recovered in units G44, G46, and G47.

5. Fully 99.1 percent of the earflare artifacts recovered from the Acropolis that were manufactured of apple green jade were fragments.

6. Of the 343 earflares recovered from deposits in the matrix of the Acropolis platform, 218 were manufactured of bright apple green jade.

7. Nuñez Chinchilla (1966:44) reports that one of the complete jade beads was 10 cm in diameter, similar to two of the large complete beads recovered from ritual deposits in the Acropolis platform at Salitrón Viejo.

8. A hunchback is the messenger of death in the Historia de los Xpantzay of 1524, when he is sent to inform a man's wife that her husband had died (Recinos 1957:139).

9. While some conical mounds had burials in them, their upper summits are too small to have supported a residential structure.

10. Mesoamerican archaeologists are accustomed to using the term *altar* for a range of low stone blocks, platforms, and boulders set before stelae or in open plazas. George Kubler pointed out that the term *altar* was a misleading transfer from European usage, where it was a table of sacrifice. Among the Maya, Kubler (1984:248) thought the same structure could be a pedestal of rank for rulers.

11. Several other structures may also have had this function in the North Precinct at Salitrón Viejo, but only those in the Iglesia Precinct are discussed here.

12. Adobe walls were used in the construction of Structures 1, 3, and 21 as well as in portions of the Acropolis platform, as both fill and retention walls. The time to prepare adobe blocks can vary, but modern estimates suggest that a crew of three workers can lay approximately 250 adobe bricks into a wall in an eight-hour day (https://findanyanswer.com/how-long-does-it-take-to-build-a–ADobe-house).

13. This estimate was calculated by taking the total volumetic estimate for the Iglesia Precinct (22,210 m^3 in table 7.4) and dividing it by 1.3 m^3 per worker, as estimated by Erasmus (1965), to obtain 17,084 worker days to build the Acropolis. The 2,367 artisan days needed to manufacture the 98 tubular earflares, ring pendants, and crescent pectorals were then divided by 17,084 worker days to obtain 13.9 percent.

14. INAA analysis sampled 327 Usulután ceramic sherds from twelve areas of Honduras and El Salvador (Goralski 2008). Thirteen different paste groups were identified in this sample, three of which matched pastes used to make Usulután-style ceramics at Salitrón Viejo and throughout the El Cajón region.

15. Ceramic vessels were associated with Burials 1-16 and 1-17 in Structure 3. The only other ceramic items recovered from a ritual deposit in the Iglesia Precinct were

the four vessels associated with Altar 1 in Plaza Two, which was a Middle to Late Sulaco phase offering.

16. Links to Teotihuacan have been proposed for the founder of the Copán dynasty on Altar Q and the Papagayo step inscription (Fash 2001:84, 88). *Talud-tablero* architecture was noted on Structure 10L-26 (96). Thin Orange and Teotihuacan stucco vase ceramics have also been recovered at Copán (94, figure 47).

17. One of the features of the Sulaco Orange paste group, also referred to as Bold Geometric, is that it fires to an orange to light orange (5yr 6–7/6–8) or red-orange (2.5yr 6/6–8) when it is completely oxidized, providing a good surface color reminiscent of Thin Orange.

ABBREVIATIONS

AP3A: Archaeological Papers of the American Anthropological Association

BAR: British Archaeological Reports

CEMCA: Centre d'études mexicaines et centraméricaines

CIW: Carnegie Institution of Washington

DORLC: Dumbarton Oaks Research Library and Collection

FAMSI: Foundation for the Advancement of Mesoamerican Studies, Inc.

HMAI: *Handbook of Middle American Indians*

IHAH: Instituto Hondureño de Antropología e Historia

INAH: Instituto Nacional de Antropología e Historia

MARI: Middle American Research Institute

SMA: Sociedad Mexicana de Antropología

UNAM: Universidad Nacional Autónoma de México

Abbott, David. 2010. "The Rise and Demise of Marketplace Exchange among the Prehistoric Hohokam of Arizona." In *Archaeological Approaches to Market Exchange in Pre-Capitalistic Societies*, ed. C. Garraty and B. Stark, 61–83. University Press of Colorado, Boulder.

Abell, Natalie. 2020. "Rethinking Household-Based Production at Ayia Irini, Kea: An Examination of Technology and Organization in a Bronze Age Community of Practice." *American Journal of Archaeology* 124:381–416.

https://doi.org/10.5876/9781646424757.c010

Abrams, Elliot. 1994. *How the Maya Built Their World: Energetics and Ancient Architecture.* University of Texas Press, Austin.

Abrutyn, Seth, and Kirk Lawrence. 2010. "From Chiefdom to State: Toward an Integrative Theory of the Evolution of Polity." *Sociological Perspectives* 53:419–442.

Adams, William. 2005. *Religion and Adaptation.* CSLI Publications, Stanford, CA.

Aguilar, Carlos. 2003. *El jade y el chamán.* Editorial Tecnológico de Costa Rica, Cartago.

Aguilar Paz, Jesús. 1989. "Tradiciones y leyendas de Honduras." Museo del Hombre Hondureño, Tegucigalpa.

Agurcia Fasquelle, Ricardo. 2016. "La estructura Oropéndola en la Acrópolis de Copán." *Revista Ciencias Espaciales* 9:73–106.

Andersen, Niels. 1988. "Sarup: Two Neolithic Enclosures in South-West Funen." *Journal of Danish Archaeology* 7:93–114.

Anderson, David. 1996. "Chiefly Cycling and Large-Scale Abandonments as Viewed from the Savannah River Basin." In *Political Structure and Change in the Prehistoric Southeastern United States,* ed. J. Scarry, 150–191. University Press of Florida, Ganesville.

Anderson, Heath, and Kenneth Hirth. 2009. "Obsidian Blade Production for Craft Consumption at Kaminaljuyu." *Ancient Mesoamerica* 20:163–172.

Anderson, Patricia, Jacques Chabot, and Annelou Van Gijn. 2004. "The Functional Riddle of 'Glossy' Canaanean Blades and the Near Eastern Threshing Sledge." *Journal of Mediterranean Archaeology* 17:87–130.

Andrews, Wyllys. 1976. *The Archaeology of Quelepa, El Salvador.* MARI Publication 42. Tulane University, New Orleans.

Andrews, Wyllys. 1977. "The Southeast Periphery of Mesoamerica: A View from El Salvador." In *Social Process in Maya Prehistory: Studies in Honour of Sir Eric Thompson,* ed. N. Hammond, 113–134. Academic Press, New York.

Andrews, Wyllys. 1987. "A Cache of Early Jades from Chacsinkin, Yucatan." *Mexicon* 9:78–85.

Andrieu, Chloé, Edna Rodas, and Luis Luin. 2014. "The Values of Classic Maya Jade: A Reanalysis of Cancuen's Jade Workshop." *Ancient Mesoamerica* 25:141–164.

Angulo, Jorge. 1969. "Banda labial de Tlaloc." *Boletín del INAH* 38:45–50.

Aoyama, Kazuo, Toshiharu Tashiro, and Michael Glascock. 1999. "A Pre-Columbian Obsidian Source in San Luis, Honduras: Implications for the Relationship between Late Classic Maya Political Boundaries and the Boundaries of Obsidian Exchange Networks." *Ancient Mesoamerica* 10:237–249.

Arroyo, Barbara. 2020. "Teotihuacan, Kaminaljuyu, and the Maya Highlands." In *Teotihuacan: The World beyond the City*, ed. K. Hirth, D. Carballo, and B. Arroyo, 435–461. DORLC, Washington, DC.

Ashmore, Wendy. 1980. "Discovering Early Classic Quirigua." *Expedition* 23:35–44.

Ashmore, Wendy. 1987. "Cobble Crossroads: Gualjoquito Architecture and External Elite Ties." In *Interaction on the Southeast Mesoamerican Frontier: Prehistoric and Historic Honduras and El Salvador*, ed. E. Robinson, 1:28–48. BAR, Oxford, England.

Ashmore, Wendy. 2009. "Mesoamerican Landscape Archaeologies." *Ancient Mesoamerica* 20:183–187.

Ashmore, Wendy. 2015. "Contingent Acts of Remembrance: Royal Ancestors of Classic Maya Copan and Quirigua." *Ancient Mesoamerica* 26:213–231.

Balser, Carlos. 1961. "Some Costa Rican Jade Motifs." In *Essays in Pre-Columbian Art and Archaeology*, ed. S. Lothrop, 210–217. Harvard University Press, Cambridge, MA.

Barber, Sarah, and Arthur Joyce. 2007. "Negotiating Political Centralization through Ritual in the Lower Rio Verde Valley, Oaxaca." In *Mesoamerican Ritual Economy: Archaeological and Ethnological Perspectives*, ed. C. Wells and K. Davis-Salazar, 221–244. University Press of Colorado, Boulder.

Baudez, Claude. 1966. "Niveaux céramiques au Honduras: Une reconsidération de l'évolution culturelle." *Journal de la Société des Américanistes* 55:299–341.

Baudez, Claude. 1977. "Arqueologia de la frontera sur de Mesoamerica." In *Las fronteras de Mesoamerica, XXII Mesa Redonda de Antropología*, 1:133–141. SMA, Mexico City.

Baudez, Claude. 1986. "Southeast Mesoamerican Periphery Summary Comments." In *The Southeast Maya Periphery*, ed. P. Urban and E. Schortman, 333–337. University of Texas Press, Austin.

Baudez, Claude, and Pierre Becquelin. 1973. *Archéologie de Los Naranjos, Honduras*. Etudes Mésoaméricaines Mexico 2, Mission Archeologique et Ethnologique Francaise au Mexique, Mexico City.

Beaudry, Marilyn, Ronald Bishop, John Henderson, and Kenneth Hirth. 1989. "Determining Ceramic Production: A View from Honduras." In *Ceramic Ecology Revisited*, ed. C. Kolb, 97–116. BAR, Oxford, England.

Beaudry-Corbett, Marilyn. 1987. "Interregional Exchange, Social Status, and Painted Ceramics: The Copan Valley Case." In *Interaction on the Southeast Mesoamerican Frontier: Prehistoric and Historic Honduras and El Salvador*, ed. E. Robinson, 1:227–246. BAR, Oxford, England.

Beaudry-Corbett, Marilyn. 1993. "Lake Yojoa Region." In *Pottery of Prehistoric Honduras: Regional Classification and Analysis*, ed. J. Henderson and M. Beaudry-Corbett, 180–193. UCLA Institute of Archaeology, Los Angeles.

Beaudry-Corbett, Marilyn, Pauline Caputi, John Henderson, Rosemary Joyce, Eugenia Robinson, and Anthony Wonderley. 1993. "Lower Ulúa Region." In *Pottery of Prehistoric Honduras: Regional Classification and Analysis*, ed. J. Henderson and M. Beaudry-Corbett, 64–135. UCLA Institute of Archaeology, Los Angeles.

Begley, Christopher. 1999. "Elite Power Strategies and External Connections in Ancient Eastern Honduras." PhD dissertation, University of Chicago, Chicago.

Benson, Elizabeth, ed. 1981. *Mesoamerican Sites and World-Views: A Conference at Dumbarton Oaks, October 16th and 17th, 1976*. DORLC, Washington, DC.

Benyo, Julie. 1986. "An Archaeological Investigation of Intra-Community Social Organizations at La Ceiba, Comayagua, Honduras." PhD dissertation, State University of New York, Albany.

Benyo, Julie, and Thomas Melchionne. 1987. "Settlement Patterns in the Tencoa Valley, Honduras: An Application of the Coevolutionary Systems Model." In *Interaction on the Southeast Mesoamerican Frontier: Prehistoric and Historic Honduras and El Salvador*, ed. E. Robinson, 1:49–64. BAR, Oxford, England.

Benyo, Julie, and Scott O'Mack. 1985. "Investigaciones sobre las unidades domésticas del sitio de La Ceiba, Depto de Comayagua." *Yaxkin* 8:59–65.

Benyo, Julie, Rebecca Storey, and Kenneth Hirth. n.d. "The El Cajon Human Mortuary Catalog." In "Investigaciones arqueológicas en la región de El Cajón," tomo 2: "Bioantropología, práticas mortuorias, y patrones comunitarios" / "Archaeological Research in the El Cajón Region," volume 2: "Bioanthropology, Mortuary Practices, and Community Patterning," ed. K. Hirth, G. Lara-Pinto, and G. Hasemann (manuscript).

Berdan, Frances. 1992. "Appendix B: Annual Tribute in the Codex Mendoza Part 2." In *The Codex Mendoza*, ed. F. Berdan and P. Anawalt, 1:154–156. University of California Press, Berkeley.

Berdan, Frances. 2007. "Material Dimensions of Aztec Religion and Ritual." In *Mesoamerican Ritual Economy: Archaeological and Ethnological Perspectives*, ed. C. Wells and K. Davis-Salazar, 245–266. University Press of Colorado, Boulder.

Berdan, Frances, and Patricia Rief Anawalt. 1997. *The Essential Codex Mendoza*. University of California Press, Berkeley.

Berrey, Adam. 2015. "Inequality, Demography, and Variability among Early Complex Societies in Central Pacific Panama." *Journal of Anthropological Archaeology* 40:196–212.

Berrey, Adam, Robert Drennan, and Christian Peterson. 2021. "Local Economies and Household Spacing in Early Chiefdom Communities." *Plos One* 6:e0252532.

Bishop, Ronald, Edward Sayre, and Joan Mishara. 1993. "Compositional and Structural Characterization of Maya and Costa Rican Jadeites." In *Jade and Ritual in Mesoamerica*, ed. F. Lange, 30–60. University of Utah Press, Provo.

Bishop, Ronald, Edward Sayre, and Lamburtus van Zelst. 1986. "The Characterization of Mesoamerican Jade." In *Applications of Science in Examination of Works of Art*, ed. P. England and L. van Zelst, 151–156. Research Laboratory, Museum of Fine Arts, Boston.

Blanton, Richard, and Lane Fargher. 2008. *Collective Action in the Formation of Pre-Modern States*. Springer, New York.

Blanton, Richard, Gary Feinman, Stephen Kowalewski, and Peter Peregrine. 1996. "A Dual-Processual Theory for the Evolution of Mesoamerican Civilization." *Current Anthropology* 37:1–14.

Bloch, Maurice. 1978. "The Disconnection between Power and Rank as a Process: An Outline of the Development of Kingdoms in Central Madagascar." In *The Evolution of Social Systems*, ed. J. Friedman and M. Rowlands, 303–340. University of Pittsburgh Press, Pittsburgh, PA.

Boone, Elizabeth. 1985. "The Color of Mesoamerican Architecture and Sculpture." In *Painted Architecture and Polychrome Monumental Sculpture in Mesoamerica*, ed. E. Boone, 173–186. DORLC, Washington, DC.

Boot, Erik. 2013. "Mesoamerican Maize God Mythology: The 'Enano De Uxmal' Folktale." In *The Maya in a Mesoamerican Context: Comparative Approaches to Maya Studies*, ed. J. Nielsen and C. Helmke, 51–68. Proceedings of the 16th European Maya Conference, December 5–10, 2011. Verlag Anton Saurwein, Copenhagen.

Boteler Mock, Shirley, ed. 1998. *The Sowing and the Dawning: Termination, Dedication, and Transformation in the Archaeological and Ethnographic Record of Mesoamerica*. University of New Mexico Press, Albuquerque.

Bove, Frederick, and Sonia Medrano Busto. 2004. "Teotihuacan, Militarism, and Pacific Guatemala." In *The Maya and Teotihuacan: Reinterpreting Early Classic Interaction*, ed. G. Braswell, 45–79. University of Texas Press, Austin.

Brady, James. 1988. "The Sexual Connotation of Caves in Mesoamerican Ideology." *Mexicon* 10:51–55.

Brady, James. 2005. *In the Maw of the Earth Monster: Mesoamerican Ritual Cave Use*. University of Texas Press, Austin.

Brady, James, Christopher Begley, John Fogarty, Donald Stierman, Barbara Luke, and Ann Scott. 2000. "Talgua Archaeological Project: A Preliminary Assessment." *Mexicon* 22:111–118.

Brady, James, George Hasemann, and John Fogarty. 1995. "Harvest of Skulls and Bones." *Archaeology* 48:36–40.

Braswell, Geoffrey. 2004a. "Dating Early Classic Interaction between Kaminaljuyu and Central Mexico." In *The Maya and Teotihuacan: Reinterpreting Early Classic Interaction*, ed. G. Braswell, 81–104. University of Texas Press, Austin.

Braswell, Geoffrey, ed. 2004b. *The Maya and Teotihuacan: Reinterpreting Early Classic Interaction*. University of Texas Press, Austin.

Braswell, Geoffrey. 2004c. "Understanding Early Classic Interaction between Kaminaljuyu and Central Mexico." In *The Maya and Teotihuacan: Reinterpreting Early Classic Interaction*, ed. G. Braswell, 105–142. University of Texas Press, Austin.

Brinton, Daniel. 1894. "Nagualism, a Study in Native American Folk-Lore and History." *Proceedings of the American Philosophical Society* 33:11–73.

Brown, Linda. 2001. "Feasting on the Periphery: The Production of Ritual Feasting and Village Festivals at the Ceren Site, El Salvador." In *Feasts: Archaeological and Ethnographic Perspectives on Food, Politics, and Power*, ed. M. Dietler and B. Hayden, 368–390. Smithsonian Institution Press, Washington, DC.

Brumfiel, Elizabeth. 1992. "Distinguished Lecture in Archeology: Breaking and Entering the Ecosystem—Gender, Class, and Faction Steal the Show." *American Anthropologist* 94:551–567.

Brumfiel, Elizabeth. 2008. "Aztec Craft Specialists." In *Craft and Social Identity*, ed. C. Costin and R. Wright, 145–152. Archaeological Papers of the American Anthropological Association 8. American Anthropological Association, Arlington, VA.

Brumfiel, Elizabeth, and Timothy Earle, eds. 1987a. *Specialization, Exchange, and Complex Societies*. Cambridge University Press, Cambridge.

Brumfiel, Elizabeth, and Timothy Earle. 1987b. "Specialization, Exchange, and Complex Societies: An Introduction." In *Specialization, Exchange, and Complex Societies*, ed. E. Brumfiel and T. Earle, 1–9. Cambridge University Press, Cambridge.

Butler, Mary. 1935. "A Study of Maya Mouldmade Figurines." *American Anthropologist* 37:636–672.

Cahen, Daniel. 1987. "Refitting Stone Artifacts: Why Bother?" In *The Human Uses of Flint and Chert*, ed. G. Sievekind and M. Newcomer, 1–10. Cambridge University Press, Cambridge.

Canby, Joel. 1949. "Excavations at Yarumela, Spanish Honduras: Recovery, Description, and Interpretation of a Long Ceramic Sequence." PhD dissertation, Harvard University, Cambridge, MA.

Canouts, Veletta, and Juan Vicente Guerrero. 1988. "Vallejo and Jicote Ceramic Codes: The Case for Stylistic Analogy in the Late Polychrome Period." In *Costa Rican Art and Archaeology: Essays in Honor of Frederick R. Mayer*, ed. F. Lange, 215–259. University Press of Colorado, Boulder.

Canuto, Marcello. 2004. "The Rural Settlement of Copan: Changes through the Early Classic." In *Understanding Early Classic Copan*, ed. E. Bell, M. Canuto, and R. Sharer, 29–53. University of Pennsylvania Museum of Archaeology and Anthropology, Philadelphia.

Canuto, Marcello, Luke Auld-Thomas, and Ernesto Arredondo. 2020. "Teotihuacan and Lowland Maya Interpretations: Characterizing a Mesoamerican Hegemony." In *Teotihuacan: The World beyond the City*, ed. K. Hirth, D. Carballo, and B. Arroyo, 371–408. DORLC, Washington, DC.

Canuto, Marcello, and Ellen Bell. 2008. "The Ties That Bind: Administrative Strategies in the El Paraíso Valley, Department of Copan, Honduras." *Mexicon* 30:10–20.

Canuto, Marcello, and Ellen Bell. 2013. "Archaeological Investigations in the El Paraíso Valley: The Role of Secondary Centers in the Multiethnic Landscape of Classic Period Copan." *Ancient Mesoamerica* 24:1–24.

Carballo, David, ed. 2013. *Cooperation and Collective Action: Archaeological Perspectives*. University Press of Colorado, Boulder.

Carías de López, Ana María. 1996. "El patrimonio cultural de Honduras, conservación de piezas de una ofrenda-cerámica de la zona arqueológica El Cajón." *Yaxkin* 14:96–105.

Carr, Archie. 1950. "Outline for a Classification of Animal Habitats in Honduras." *Bulletin of the American Museum of Natural History* 94:563–594.

Cartwright, Edward. 2018. *Behavioral Economics*. Routledge, London.

Chapman, Anne. 1978. *Los Lencas de Honduras en el siglo XVI*. Estudios anthropologios e historicos 2. IHAH, Tegucigalpa.

Chapman, Anne. 1985. *Los hijos del copal y la candela: Ritos agrarios y tradición oral de los lencas de Honduras*, volume 1. UNAM, Mexico City.

Chapman, Anne. 1986. *Los hijos del copal y la candela: Ritos agrarios y tradición oral de los lencas de Honduras*, volume 2. UNAM, Mexico City.

Chase, Arlen, and Diane Chase. 2012. "Complex Societies in the Southern Maya Lowlands." In *The Oxford Handbook of Mesoamerican Archaeology*, ed. D. Nichols and C. Pool, 255–267. Oxford University Press, Oxford.

Cheek, Charles. 1977. "Excavations at the Palangana and the Acropolis, Kaminaljuyu, Guatemala." In *Teotihuacan and Kaminaljuyu*, ed. W. Sanders and J. Michels, 1–204. Pennsylvania State University Press, University Park.

Ciudad Ruiz, Andrés. 1986. "El culto de los caseríos del área quiché: Los camagüiles." In *Los mayas de los tiempos tardíos*, ed. M. Rivera Dorado and A. Ciudad Ruiz, 63–82. Sociedad Española de Estudios Mayas, Instituto de Cooperación Iberoamericana, Toledo, Spain.

Clark, John. 1986. "From Mountains to Molehills: A Critical Review of Teotihuacan's Obsidian Industry." In *Research in Economic Anthropology, Supplement 2*, ed. B. Isaac, 23–74. JAI, Greenwich, CT.

Clark, John. 1987. "Politics, Prismatic Blades, and Mesoamerican Civilization." In *The Organization of Core Technology*, ed. J. Johnson and C. Morrow, 259–285. Westview, Boulder.

Clark, John. 1990. "Fifteen Fallacies in Lithic Workshop Interpretation: An Experimental and Ethnoarchaeological Perspective." In *Etnoarqueología: Primer coloquio Bosch-Gimpera*, ed. Y. Sugiura and M. C. Serra Puche, 497–512. UNAM, Mexico City.

Clark, John, and Michael Blake. 1994. "The Power of Prestige: Competitive Generosity and the Emergence of Rank Societies in Lowland Mesoamerica." In *Factional Competition and Political Development in the New World*, ed. E. Brumfiel and J. Fox, 17–30. Cambridge University Press, Cambridge.

Clark, John, and William Parry. 1990. "Craft Specialization and Cultural Complexity." In *Research in Economic Anthropology*, ed. B. Isaac, 12:289–346. JAI, Greenwich, CT.

Cliff, Maynard. 1990a. "The Guarabuqui Ceramic Analysis." Unpublished Manuscript.

Cliff, Maynard. 1990b. "The Intendencia Ceramic Analysis." Unpublished Manuscript.

Codere, Helen. 1966. *Fighting with Property: A Study of Kwakiutl Potlatching and Warfare, 1792–1930*. University of Washington Press, Seattle.

Coggins, Clemency, and Orrin Shane. 1984. *Cenote of Sacrifice: Maya Treasures from the Sacred Well at Chichen Itza*. University of Texas Press, Austin.

Conzemius, Eduard. 1932. *Ethnographical Survey of the Miskito and Sumu Indians*. Bureau of American Ethnology Bulletin 106. Smithsonian Institution, Washington, DC.

Costin, Cathy, ed. 2016. *Making Value, Making Meaning: Techné in the Pre-Columbian World*. DORLC, Washington, DC.

Creamer, Winifred, and Jonathan Haas. 1985. "Tribe versus Chiefdom in Lower Central America." *American Antiquity* 50:738–754.

Crumley, Carol. 1995. "Heterarchy and the Analysis of Complex Societies." In *Heterarchy and the Analysis of Complex Societies*, ed. R. Ehrenreich, C. Crumley, and J. Levy, 1–6. Wiley, Hoboken, NJ.

Dalton, George. 1977. "Aboriginal Economies in Stateless Societies." In *Exchange Systems in Prehistory*, ed. T. Earle and J. Ericson, 191–212. Academic Press, New York.

Davis-Salazar, Karla. 2007. "Ritual Consumption and the Origins of Social Inequality in Early Formative Copan, Honduras." In *Mesoamerican Ritual Economy:*

Archaeological and Ethnological Perspectives, ed. C. Wells and K. Davis-Salazar, 197–220. University Press of Colorado, Boulder.

De Borhegyi, Stephan. 1980. *The Pre-Columbian Ballgames: A Pan-Mesoamerican Tradition*. Milwaukee Public Museum, Milwaukee.

Demarest, Arthur. 1986. *The Archaeology of Santa Leticia and the Rise of Maya Civilization*. MARI Publication 52. Tulane University, New Orleans.

Demarest, Arthur, and Robert Sharer. 1982. "The Origins and Evolution of Usulután Ceramics." *American Antiquity* 47:810–822.

Demarest, Arthur, and Robert Sharer. 1986. "Late Preclassic Ceramic Spheres, Culture Areas, and Cultural Evolution in the Southeastern Highlands of Mesoamerica." In *The Southeast Maya Periphery*, ed. P. Urban and E. Schortman, 194–223. University of Texas Press, Austin.

DeMarrais, Elizabeth, Luis Jaime Castillo, and Timothy Earle. 1996. "Ideology, Materialization, and Power Strategies." *Current Anthropology* 37:15–31.

Dietler, Michael. 2001. "Theorizing the Feast: Rituals of Consumption, Commensal Politics, and Power in African Contexts." In *Feasts: Archaeological and Ethnographic Perspectives on Food, Politics, and Power*, ed. M. Dietler and B. Hayden, 65–114. Smithsonian Institution Press, Washington, DC.

Dietler, Michael, and Brian Hayden, eds. 2001. *Feasts: Archaeological and Ethnographic Perspectives on Food, Politics, and Power*. Smithsonian Institution Press, Washington, DC.

Dietler, Michael, and Ingrid Herbich. 2001. "Feasts and Labor Mobilization: Dissecting a Fundamental Economic Practice." In *Feasts: Archaeological and Ethnographic Perspectives on Food, Politics, and Power*, ed. M. Dietler and B. Hayden, 240–264. Smithsonian Institution Press, Washington, DC.

Digby, Adrian. 1972. *Maya Jades*. British Museum Publications, London.

Dixon, Boyd. 1987. "Conflict along the Southeast Mesoamerican Periphery: A Defensive Wall System at the Site of Tenampua." In *Interaction on the Southeast Mesoamerican Frontier: Prehistoric and Historic Honduras and El Salvador*, ed. E. Robinson, 1:142–153. BAR, Oxford, England.

Dixon, Boyd. 1989a. "Prehistoric Settlement Patterns on a Cultural Corridor: The Comayagua Valley, Honduras." PhD dissertation, University of Connecticut, Storrs.

Dixon, Boyd. 1989b. "A Preliminary Settlement Pattern Study of a Prehistoric Cultural Corridor: The Comayagua Valley, Honduras." *Journal of Field Archaeology* 16:257–271.

Dixon, Boyd. 2008a. "Los orígenes del sipesipe en las leyendas hondureñas." *Yaxkin* 24:148–163.

Dixon, Boyd. 2008b. "Yarumela: Revalorizando un sitio arqueológico en el sitio y su lugar en la prehistoria Hondureña." *Yaxkin* 24:199–210.

Dixon, Boyd, Leroy Joesink-Mandeville, Nobukatsu Hasebe, Michael Mucio, William Vincent, David James, and Kenneth Petersen. 1994. "Formative-Period Architecture at the Site of Yarumela, Central Honduras." *Latin American Antiquity* 5:70–87.

Douglas, Mary, and Baron Isherwood. 1979. *The World of Goods*. W. W. Norton, London.

Drennan, Robert. 1987. "Regional Demography in Chiefdoms." In *Chiefdoms in the Americas*, ed. R. Drennan and C. Uribe, 307–323. University Press of America, Lanham, MD.

Drennan, Robert, and Christian Peterson. 2006. "Patterned Variation in Prehistoric Chiefdoms." *Proceedings of the National Academy of Sciences* 103:3960–3967.

Drennan, Robert, and Christian Peterson. 2008. "Centralized Communities, Population, and Social Complexity after Sedentarization." In *The Neolithic Demographic Transition and Its Consequences*, ed. J. P. Bocquet-Appel and O. Bar-Yosef, 359–386. Springer, New York.

Drennan, Richard, and Carlos Uribe, eds. 1987. *Chiefdoms in the Americas*. University Press of America, Lanham, MD.

Drucker, Philip. 1955. *The Cerro de las Mesas Offering of Jade and Other Materials*, volume 157. US Government Printing Office, Washington, DC.

Drucker, Philip, and Robert Heizer. 1967. *To Make My Name Good: A Reexamination of the Southern Kwakiutl Potlatch*. University of California Press, Berkeley.

Drucker, Philip, Robert Heizer, and Robert Squier. 1959. *Excavations at La Venta Tabasco, 1955*. Bulletin 170. Smithsonian Institution, Washington, DC.

Duffy, Paul. 2015. "Site Size Hierarchy in Middle-Range Societies." *Journal of Anthropological Archaeology* 37:85–99.

Duncan, Earle. 1992. "Authority, Social Conflict, and the Rise of Protestantism: Religious Conversion in a Mayan Village." *Social Compass* 39:377–388.

Dupey García, Élodie. 2015. "The Materiality of Color in the Body Ornamentation of Aztec Gods." *RES: Anthropology and Aesthetics* 65:72–88.

Durán, Fray Diego. 1971. *Book of the Gods and Rites and the Ancient Calendar*, trans. F. Horcasitas and D. Heyden. University of Oklahoma Press, Norman.

Durrenberger, Paul. 2008. "The Political Ecology of Ritual Feasting." In *Dimensions of Ritual Economy*, ed. P. McAnany and C. Wells, 73–89. Research in Economic Anthropology 27. JAI, Bingley, UK.

Earle, Duncan. 1992. "Authority, Social Conflict, and the Rise of Protestantism: Religious Conversion in a Mayan Village." *Social Compass* 39:377–388.

Earle, Timothy. 1987. "Chiefdoms in Archaeological and Ethnohistorical Perspective." *Annual Review of Anthropology* 16:279–308.

Earle, Timothy, ed. 1991. *Chiefdoms: Power, Economy, and Ideology.* Cambridge University Press, Cambridge.

Earle, Timothy. 1997. *How Chiefs Come to Power: The Political Economy in Prehistory.* Stanford University Press, Stanford, CA.

Earle, Timothy. 2021. *A Primer on Chiefs and Chiefdoms.* Eliot Werner, Clinton Corners, NY.

Easby, Elizabeth. 1961. "The Squier Jades from Tonina, Chiapas." In *Essays in Pre-Columbian Art and Archaeology*, ed. S. Lothrop, 66–79. Harvard University Press, Cambridge, MA.

Easby, Elizabeth. 1992. "The Beginnings of Classic Maya Jade Carving in the Southeast." In *Jade and Ritual in Mesoamerica*, ed. F. Lange, 133–140. University of Utah Press, Provo.

Eckert, Penelope. 2006. "Communities of Practice." *Encyclopedia of Language and Linguistics* 2:683–685.

Ehrenreich, Robert, Carole Crumley, and Janet Levy, eds. 1995. *Heterarchy and the Analysis of Complex Societies.* Wiley, Hoboken, NJ.

Eidt, Robert. 1977. "Detection and Examination of Anthrosols by Phosphate Analysis." *Science* 197:1327–1333.

Elder, David. 1984. "The Stone Tools of Yarumela and the Early Formative Period of Mesoamerica." MA thesis, California State University, Fullerton.

Elson, Christina, and Michael Smith. 2001. "Archaeological Deposits from the Aztec New Fire Ceremony." *Ancient Mesoamerica* 12:157–174.

ENEE. 1978. *El Cajon Project Ecology.* Motor-Columbus, Inc., Baden, Switzerland.

Erasmus, Charles. 1956. "Culture Structure and Process: The Occurrence and Disappearance of Reciprocal Farm Labor." *Southwestern Journal of Anthropology* 12:444–469.

Erasmus, Charles. 1965. "Monument Building: Some Field Experiments." *Southwestern Journal of Anthropology* 21:277–301.

Erickson, Clark, and Monica Fenton. 2021. "Who Is the Chief? The Central People of Burial 11, Sitio Conte." In *Pre-Columbian Central America, Colombia, and Ecuador: Toward an Integrated Approach*, ed. C. McEwan and J. Hoopes, 197–233. DORLC, Washington, DC.

Evans, Susan Toby. 2010. "Pair of Jadeite Disks [B.133a and b]." In *Ancient Mexican Art at Dumbarton Oaks: Central Highlands, Southwestern Highlands, Gulf Lowlands*, ed. S. Evans, 15–17. DORLC, Washington, DC.

Fakundiny, Robert. 1970. "Geology of the El Rosario Quadrangle, Honduras, Central America." PhD dissertation, University of Texas, Austin.

Fash, William. 2001. *Scribes, Warriors, and Kings: The City of Copán and the Ancient Maya.* Thames and Hudson, London.

Fash, William, and Karla Davis-Salazar. 2008. "Intercambio interregional e ideología del horizonte temprano en el valle de Copán, Honduras." In *Ideología política y sociedad en el período Formativo: Ensayos en homenaje al doctor David C. Grove*, ed. A. Cyphers and K. Hirth, 127–151. UNAM, Mexico City.

Feinman, Gary. 1996. "Chiefdoms and Nonindustrial States." In *Encyclopedia of Cultural Anthropology*, ed. D. Levinson and M. Ember, 185–191. Henry Holt, New York.

Feinman, Gary, and Jill Neitzel. 1984. "Too Many Types: An Overview of Sedentary Prestate Societies in the Americas." In *Advances in Archaeological Method and Theory*, ed. B. Schiffer, 39–102. Academic Press, New York.

Fernandez, Eric. 1987. "Avances del análisis de la paleofauna de la zona de embalse de El Cajón, Honduras." *Yaxkin* 10:1:1–27.

Fernández Esquivel, Patricia. 2021. "Metallurgy in Costa Rica." In *Pre-Columbian Art from Central America and Colombia at Dumbarton Oaks*, ed. C. McEwan and J. Hoopes, 239–247. DORLC, Washington, DC.

Figueroa, Alejandro, and Timothy Scheffler. 2021. "Integrating the Prehistoric Natural and Social Landscapes of the Highlands of Southwest Honduras: A Deep History." In *Southeastern Mesoamerica: Indigenous Interaction, Resilience, and Change*, ed. W. Goodwin, E. Johnson, and A. Figueroa, 27–53. University Press of Colorado, Louisville.

Fischer, Ronald, Rohan Callander, Paul Reddish, and Joseph Bulbulia. 2013. "How Do Rituals Affect Cooperation?" *Human Nature* 24:115–125.

Flannery, Kent. 1972. "The Cultural Evolution of Civilizations." *Annual Review of Ecology and Systematics* 3:399–426.

Flannery, Kent. 1999. "Process and Agency in Early State Formation." *Cambridge Archaeological Journal* 9:3–21.

Flannery, Kent, and Joyce Marcus. 2012. *The Creation of Inequality.* Harvard University Press, Cambridge, MA.

Foias, Antonia. 2007. "Ritual, Politics, and Pottery Economies in the Classic Maya Southern Lowlands." In *Mesoamerican Ritual Economy: Archaeological and Ethnological Perspectives*, ed. C. Wells and K. Davis-Salazar, 167–194. University Press of Colorado, Boulder.

Fontes, Cristina. 2020. "Encuentros con dueños, duendes y diablos: Intersubjetividad, movimiento y paisaje en los caminos de las Quebrada de Humahuaca." *Ciencias Sociales y Religión / Ciências Sociais e Religião* 22:1–25.

Foshag, William. 1957. *Mineralogical Studies on Guatemalan Jade.* Smithsonian Miscellaneous Collections, volume 135. Smithsonian Institution, Washington, DC.

Foster, George. 1944. "Nagualism in Mexico and Guatemala." *Acta Americana* 2:85–103.

Fowler, William. 1989. *The Evolution of Ancient Nahua Civilizations: The Pipil-Nicarao of Central America.* University of Oklahoma Press, Norman.

Fowler, William, ed. 1991. *The Formation of Complex Society in Southeastern Mesoamerica.* CRC Press, Boca Raton, FL.

Fox, John. 1996. "Playing with Power: Ballcourts and Political Ritual in Southern Mesoamerica." *Current Anthropology* 37:483–509.

Frankenstein, Susan, and Michael Rowlands. 1978. "The Internal Structure and Regional Context of Early Iron Age Society in South-Western Germany." *Bulletin of the Institute of Archaeology London* 15:73–112.

Franklin, Jay, and Jan Simek. 2008. "Core Refitting and the Accuracy of Aggregate Lithic Analysis Techniques: The Case of 3rd Unnamed Cave, Tennessee." *Southeastern Archaeology* 27:108–121.

Freidel, David. 1998. "Sacred Work: Dedication and Termination in Mesoamerica." In *The Sowing and the Dawning: Termination, Dedication, and Transformation in the Archaeological and Ethnographic Record of Mesoamerica,* ed. S. Boteler Mock, 189–193. University of New Mexico Press, Albuquerque.

Freidel, David, Marilyn Masson, and Michelle Rich. 2017. "Imagining a Complex Maya Political Economy: Counting Tokens and Currencies in Image, Text, and the Archaeological Record." *Cambridge Archaeological Journal* 27:29–54.

Friedman, Jonathan. 1975. "Religion as Economy and Economy as Religion." *Ethnos* 40:46–63.

Friedman, Jonathan. 1982. "Catastrophe and Continuity in Social Evolution." In *Theory and Explanation in Archaeology,* ed. C. Renfrew, M. Rowlands, and B. Abbott Segraves, 175–196. Academic Press, New York.

Friedman, Jonathan, and Michael Rowlands. 1978. "Notes towards an Epigenetic Model of the Evolution of Civilization." In *The Evolution of Social Systems,* ed. J. Friedman and M. Rowlands, 201–276. University of Pittsburgh Press, Pittsburgh, PA.

Furst, Peter. 1968. "The Olmec Were-Jaguar Motif in the Light of Ethnographic Reality." In *Dumbarton Oaks Conference on the Olmec,* ed. E. Benson, 143–174. DORLC, Washington, DC.

Furst, Peter. 1972. "Symbolism and Psychopharmacology: The Toad as Earth Mother in Indian America." In *Religion in Mesoamerica,* 61–68. XII Mesa Redonda, SMA, Mexico City.

Garber, James. 1983. "Patterns of Jade Consumption and Disposal at Cerros, Northern Belize." *American Antiquity* 48:800–807.

Garber, James, David Grove, Kenneth Hirth, and John Hoopes. 1993. "Jade Use in Portions of Mexico and Central America." In *Precolumbian Jade: New Geological and Cultural Interpretations*, ed. F. Lange, 211–231. University of Utah Press, Salt Lake City.

García-Des Lauriers, Claudia. 2020. "Gods, Cacao, and Obsidian: Multidirectional Interactions between Teotihuacan and the Southeastern Pacific Coast of Mesoamerica." In *Teotihuacan: The World beyond the City*, ed. K. Hirth, D. Carballo, and B. Arroyo, 409–433. DORLC, Washington, DC.

Gazzola, Julie. 2007. "La producción de cuentas en piedras verdes en los talleres lapidarios de La Ventilla, Teotihuacan." *Arqueología* 36:52–70.

Gifford, James. 1960. "The Type-Variety Method of Ceramic Classification as an Indicator of Cultural Phenomena." *American Antiquity* 25:341–347.

Gilissen, Tijn. 2003. "A Revision and Application of Rowlands and Frankenstein's Prestige-Goods Economy Model and a Consideration of Other Options." SOJA 2002 Luc Amkreutz Een 'shortcut'naar Paleolithische kunst Yannick Henk and Floris van Oosterhout Bronstijdsmeden in Nederland: rondreizende allochtonen, nederzettingsgebonden autoch, 18–45.

Gillespie, Susan. 1991. "Ballgames and Boundaries." In *The Mesoamerican Ballgame*, ed. V. Scarborough and D. Wilcox, 317–345. University of Arizona Press, Tucson.

Gilman, Antonio. 1995. "Prehistoric European Chiefdoms." In *Foundations of Social Inequality*, ed. D. Price and G. Feinman, 235–251. Springer, Boston.

Glass, John. 1966. "Archaeological Survey of Western Honduras." In *Handbook of Middle American Indians*, ed. G. Ekholm and G. Willey, 4:157–179. University of Texas Press, Austin.

Goldman, Charles. 1973. "Consideraciones biológicas." In *Proyecto El Cajon, estudio de factibilidad*, volume 5: *Ecologia*. Empresa Nacional de Energia Elétrica, Tegucigalpa.

Goldschmidt, Walter. 2006. *The Bridge to Humanity: How Affect Hunger Trumps the Selfish Gene*. Oxford University Press, Oxford.

Goldstein, Lynne. 1981. "One-Dimensional Archaeology and Multi-Dimensional People: Spatial Organization and Mortuary Analysis." In *The Archaeology of Death*, ed. R. Chapman, I. Kinnes, and K. Randsborg, 53–69. Cambridge University Press, London.

Golitko, Mark, and Gary Feinman. 2015. "Procurement and Distribution of Pre-Hispanic Mesoamerican Obsidian 900 BC–AD 1520: A Social Network Analysis." *Journal of Archaeological Method and Theory* 22:206–247.

Golitko, Mark, James Meierhoff, Gary Feinman, and Patrick Williams. 2012. "Complexities of Collapse: The Evidence of Maya Obsidian as Revealed by Social Network Graphical Analysis." *Antiquity* 86:507–523.

Gómez Zúñiga, Pastor Rodolfo. 2021. "Honduran Lenca Chiefdoms of the Contact Period (1502–1550)." In *Southeastern Mesoamerica: Indigenous Interaction, Resilience, and Change*, ed. W. Goodwin, E. Johnson, and A. Figueroa, 258–279. University Press of Colorado, Louisville.

Goralski, Craig. 2008. "An Examination of the Uapala-Usulután Ceramic Sphere Using Instrumental Neutron Activation Analysis." PhD dissertation, Penn State University, University Park.

Gordon, George Byron. 1898a. *Caverns of Copan, Honduras*. Peabody Museum of Archaeology and Ethnology Memoirs 1, no. 5. Harvard University, Cambridge, MA.

Gordon, George Byron. 1898b. *Researches in the Uloa Valley, Honduras: Report on Explorations by the Museum, 1896–97*. Peabody Museum of Archaeology and Ethnology Memoirs 1, no. 4. Harvard University, Cambridge, MA.

Gordon, George Byron. 1921. "The Ulúa Marble Vases." *Museum Journal* 12:53–74.

Gossen, Gary. 1975. "Animal Souls and Human Destiny in Chamula." *Man* 10:448–461.

Gran Diccionario Náhuatl. 2012. UNAM, Mexico City. http://www.gdn.unam.mx.

Guderjan, Thomas. 1998. "The Blue Creek Jade Cache: Early Classic Ritual in Northwestern Belize." In *The Sowing and the Dawning: Termination, Dedication, and Transformation in the Archaeological and Ethnographic Record of Mesoamerica*, ed. S. Boteler Mock, 101–111. University of New Mexico Press, Albuquerque.

Gutiérrez, Gerardo. 2013. "Negotiating Aztec Tributary Demands in the Tribute Record of Tlapa." In *Merchants, Markets, and Exchange in the Pre-Columbian World*, ed. K. Hirth and J. Pillsbury, 141–167. DORLC, Washington, DC.

Gutiérrez, Gerardo, and Mary Pye. 2010. "Iconography of the Nahual: Human-Animal Transformations in Preclassic Guerrero and Morelos." In *The Place of Stone Monuments: Context, Use, and Meaning in Mesoamerica's Preclassic Transition*, ed. J. Guernsey, J. Clark, and B. Arroyo, 27–54. Harvard University Press, Cambridge, MA.

Håkansson, Thomas, and Mats Widgren. 2007. "Labour and Landscapes: The Political Economy of Landesque Capital in Nineteenth Century Tanganyika." *Geografiska Annaler: Series B, Human Geography* 89:233–248.

Håkansson, Thomas, and Mats Widgren, eds. 2014. *Landesque Capital: The Historical Ecology of Enduring Landscape Modifications*. Left Coast Press, Walnut Creek, CA.

Halstead, Paul. 1989. "The Economy Has No Surplus: Economic Stability and Social Change among Early Farming Communities of Thessaly, Greece." In *Bad Year Economics*, ed. P. Halstead and J. O'Shea, 68–80. Cambridge University Press, Cambridge.

Halstead, Paul, and John O'Shea, eds. 1989. *Bad Year Economics*. Cambridge University Press, Cambridge.

Hammerstedt, Scott. 2005. "Mississippian Construction, Labor, and Social Organization in Western Kentucky." PhD dissertation, Penn State University, University Park.

Hammond, Norman, Duncan Pring, Richard Wilk, Sara Donaghey, Frank Saul, Elizabeth Wing, Arlene Miller, and Lawrence Feldman. 1979. "The Earliest Lowland Maya? Definition of the Swasey Phase." *American Antiquity* 44:92–110.

Hanson, Donald. 1982. "Distribution of the Quetzal in Honduras." *Ornithology* 99:385.

Harding, Thomas. 1967. *Voyagers of the Vitiaz Strait*. University of Washington Press, Seattle.

Hasemann, George. 1983. "Recorrido de las tierras altas en la región de estudio." In *Proyecto arqueológico El Cajón IV informe trimestral, Octubre–Deciembre*, ed. K. Hirth, G. Lara-Pinto, and G. Hasemann, 1–6. IHAH, Tegucigalpa.

Hasemann, George. 1985. "Desarrollo de los asentamientos Clásicos Tardíos a lo largo del Río Sulaco." *Yaxkin* 8:25–45.

Hasemann, George. 1987. "Late Classic Settlement on the Sulaco River, Central Honduras." In *Chiefdoms in the Americas*, ed. R. Drennan and C. Uribe, 85–102. University Press of America, Lanham, MD.

Hasemann, George. 1998. "Regional Settlement History on the Lower Sulaco River, West Central Honduras: Rural Settlement Theory and Ancient Settlement Pattern in the Honduran Highlands." PhD dissertation, University of Kentucky, Lexington.

Hasemann, George, Boyd Dixon, and John Yonk. 1982. "El rescate arqueológico en la zona de embalse de El Cajón: Reconocimiento general y regional, 1980–1981." *Yaxkin* 5:22–36.

Hasemann, George, and Gloria Lara-Pinto. n.d. "An Overview of Household Size and Archaeological Population Estimates in Southern Mesoamerica: The Problems and a Cautious Proposal for the El Cajón Region in the Highlands of West Central Honduras." In "Investigaciones arqueológicas en la región de El Cajón," tomo 2: "Bioantropología, práticas mortuorias, y patrones comunitarios" / "Archaeological Research in the El Cajón Region," volume 2: "Bioanthropology, Mortuary Practices, and Community Patterning," ed. K. Hirth, G. Lara-Pinto, and G. Hasemann (manuscript).

Hasemann-Lara, Ana, and Gloria Lara-Pinto. 2014. "Un Paisaje Cultural Sagrado: La Gruta de Intibucá, Occidente de Honduras." III Coloquio Internacional Repensar América Latina desde sus Categorías Culturales. Paper presented at

Centro de Investigación en Identidad y Cultura Latinoamericana (CIICLA). October 15–17, Universidad de Costa Rica, San José.

Hassig, Ross. 2001. *Time, History, and Belief in Aztec and Colonial Mexico.* University of Texas Press, Austin.

Hayden, Brian. 2001a. "Fabulous Feasts: A Prolegomenon to the Importance of Feasting." In *Feasts: Archaeological and Ethnographic Perspectives on Food, Politics, and Power*, ed. M. Dietler and B. Hayden, 23–64. Smithsonian Institution Press, Washington, DC.

Hayden, Brian. 2001b. "Richman, Poorman, Beggarman, Chief: The Dynamics of Social Inequality." In *Archaeology at the Millennium: A Sourcebook*, ed. G. Feinman and D. Price, 231–272. Kluwer Academic, New York.

Hayden, Brian. 2014. *The Power of Feasts from Prehistory to the Present.* Cambridge University Press, Cambridge.

Healy, Paul. 1974. "The Cuyamel Caves: Preclassic Sites in Northeast Honduras." *American Antiquity* 39:435–447.

Healy, Paul. 1992. "Ancient Honduras: Power, Wealth, and Rank in Early Chiefdoms." In *Wealth and Hierarchy in the Intermediate Area*, ed. F. Lange, 85–108. DORLC, Washington, DC.

Healy, Paul. 2007. "The Anthropology of Mesoamerican Caves." *Reviews in Anthropology* 36:245–278.

Healy, Paul, and Jaime Awe. 2001. "Middle Preclassic Jade Spoon from Belize." *Mexicon* 23:61–64.

Heider, Karl. 1969. "Visiting Trade Institutions." *American Anthropologist* 71:462–471.

Helms, Mary. 1979. *Ancient Panama: Chiefs in Search of Power.* University of Texas Press, Austin.

Helms, Mary. 1987. "Art Styles and Interaction Spheres in Central America and the Caribbean: Polished Black Wood in the Greater Antilles." In *Chiefdoms in the Americas*, ed. R. Drennan and C. Uribe, 67–83. University Press of America, Lanham, MD.

Helms, Mary. 1988. *Ulysses' Sail: An Ethnographic Odyssey of Power, Knowledge, and Geographical Distance.* Princeton University Press, Princeton, NJ.

Henderson, John, and Marilyn Beaudry-Corbett. 1993a. "Introduction to Regional Summaries." In *Pottery of Prehistoric Honduras: Regional Classification and Analysis*, ed. J. Henderson and M. Beaudry-Corbett, 7–10. UCLA Institute of Archaeology, Los Angeles.

Henderson, John, and Marilyn Beaudry-Corbett, eds. 1993b. *Pottery of Prehistoric Honduras: Regional Classification and Analysis.* UCLA Institute of Archaeology, Los Angeles.

Henderson, John, Ilene Sterns, Anthony Wonderley, and Patricia Urban. 1979. "Archaeological Investigations in the Valle de Naco, Northwestern Honduras: A Preliminary Report." *Journal of Field Archaeology* 6:169–192.

Hendon, Julia. 2003. "Feasting at Home: Community and House Solidarity among the Maya of Southeastern Mesoamerica." In *The Archaeology and Politics of Food and Feasting in Early States and Empires*, ed. T. Bray, 203–233. Kluwer Academic, New York.

Hendon, Julia, and Traci Ardren. 2020. "Cuisine and Feasting in the Copán and Lower Ulúa Valleys in Honduras." In *Her Cup for Sweet Cacao: Food in Ancient Maya Society*, ed. T. Ardren, 219–242. University of Texas Press, Austin.

Hendon, Julia, Rosemary Joyce, and Jeanne Lopiparo. 2013. *Material Relations: The Marriage Figurines of Prehispanic Honduras.* University Press of Colorado, Louisville.

Hendon, Julia, Rosemary Joyce, and Russell Sheptak. 2009. "Heterarchy as Complexity: Archaeology in Yoro, Honduras." *The Cupola.* http://cupola.gettysburg.edu/anthfac/15.

Hernández Reyes, Carlos. 1974. "Una banda labial en serpentina del dios Tlaloc." *Notas Antropológicas de la UNAM* 1:121–129.

Herrera y Tordesillas, Antonia de. 1944–1947. *Historia general de los hechos de los castellanos, en las islas, y tierra-firme de el mar océano.* 10 volumes. Editorial Guarania, Asunción del Paraguay, Paraguay.

Hirth, Kenneth. 1981. "Excavaciones en Salitrón Viejo." *Yaxkin* 5:51–66.

Hirth, Kenneth. 1985. "Comercio prehispánico y intercambio inter-regional en el área de El Cajón: Resultados preliminares de los análisis técnicos." *Yaxkin* 8:3–11.

Hirth, Kenneth. 1987a. "La diversidad arquitectónica y la interacción social en la región de El Cajón: La perspectiva desde Salitrón Viejo." Paper presented at the fourth Seminario de Arqueologia Hondureña. June 22–26, La Ceiba, Honduras.

Hirth, Kenneth. 1987b. "La subsistencia y comercio prehispánico en la región de El Cajón." *Yaxkin* 10:39–50.

Hirth, Kenneth. 1988. "Beyond the Maya Frontier: Cultural Interaction and Syncretism along the Central Honduran Corridor." In *The Southeastern Maya Periphery*, ed. E. Boone and G. Willey, 297–334. DORLC, Washington, DC.

Hirth, Kenneth. 1989a. "The El Cajon Archaeological Project: An Introduction." In *Archaeological Research in the El Cajon Region*, volume 1: *Prehistoric Cultural Ecology*, ed. K. Hirth, G. Lara-Pinto, and G. Hasemann, 1–17. University of Pittsburgh and IHAH, Pittsburgh, PA, and Tegucigalpa.

Hirth, Kenneth. 1989b. "Observation about Ecological Relationships and Cultural Evolution in a Prehistoric Tropical Subsistence System." In *Archaeological*

Research in the El Cajon Region, volume 1: *Prehistoric Cultural Ecology*, ed. K. Hirth, G. Lara-Pinto, and G. Hasemann, 233–252. University of Pittsburgh and IHAH, Pittsburgh, PA, and Tegucigalpa.

Hirth, Kenneth. 1996a. "Community and Society in a Central Honduran Chiefdom: Inferences from the Built Environment." In *Arqueologia Mesoamericana: Homenaje a William T. Sanders*, ed. A. G. Mastache, J. Parsons, R. Santley, and M. C. Serra, 2:169–191. UNAM, Mexico City.

Hirth, Kenneth. 1996b. "Political Economy and Archaeology: Perspectives on Exchange and Production." *Journal of Archaeological Research* 4:203–239.

Hirth, Kenneth. 1998. "The Distributional Approach: A New Way to Identify Market Behavior Using Archaeological Data." *Current Anthropology* 39:451–476.

Hirth, Kenneth, ed. 2006. *Obsidian Craft Production in Ancient Central Mexico*. University of Utah Press, Salt Lake City.

Hirth, Kenneth. 2008. "The Economy of Supply: Modeling Obsidian Procurement and Craft Provisioning at a Central Mexican Urban Center." *Latin American Antiquity* 19:435–457.

Hirth, Kenneth, ed. 2009a. *Housework: Craft Production and Domestic Economy in Ancient Mesoamerica*. AP3A 19, Wiley Periodicals, Malden, MA.

Hirth, Kenneth. 2009b. "Intermittent Domestic Lapidary Production during the Late Formative Period at Nativitas, Tlaxcala, Mexico." In *Housework: Craft Production and Domestic Economy in Ancient Mesoamerica*, ed. K. Hirth, 157–173. AP3A 19, Wiley Periodicals, Malden, MA.

Hirth, Kenneth. 2010. "Finding the Mark in the Marketplace: The Organization, Development, and Archaeological Identification of Market Systems." In *Archaeological Approaches to Market Exchange in Pre-Capitalistic Societies*, ed. C. Garraty and B. Stark, 227–247. University Press of Colorado, Boulder.

Hirth, Kenneth. 2016. *The Aztec Economic World: Merchants and Markets in Ancient Mesoamerica*. Cambridge University Press, Cambridge.

Hirth, Kenneth. 2020. *The Organization of Ancient Economies: A Global Perspective*. Cambridge University Press, Cambridge.

Hirth, Kenneth. 2023. *Once upon a Time in Archaeology: A Research Diary from Central Honduras*. Occasional Papers in Anthropology 34. Penn State University, University Park. https://journals.psu/edu/opa/issue/archive.

Hirth, Kenneth. n.d. "Population Fertility, Residential Nucleation, and Community Health in the El Cajon Region." In "Investigaciones arqueológicas en la región de El Cajón," tomo 2: "Bioantropología, práticas mortuorias, y patrones comunitarios" / "Archaeological Research in the El Cajon Region," volume 2:

"Bioanthropology, Mortuary Practices, and Community Patterning," ed. K. Hirth, G. Lara-Pinto, and G. Hasemann (manuscript).

Hirth, Kenneth, and Dennis Cosgren. 1989. "Geography, Geology, and Natural Resource Availability." In *Archaeological Research in the El Cajon Region*, volume 1: *Prehistoric Cultural Ecology*, ed. K. Hirth, G. Lara-Pinto, and G. Hasemann, 19–40. University of Pittsburgh and IHAH, Pittsburgh, PA, and Tegucigalpa.

Hirth, Kenneth, and Ann Cyphers. 2020. *Olmec Lithic Economy at San Lorenzo Tenochtitlan.* University Press of Colorado, Boulder.

Hirth, Kenneth, Ann Cyphers, Robert Cobean, Jason De Leon, and Michael Glascock. 2013. "Early Olmec Obsidian Trade and Economic Organization at San Lorenzo." *Journal of Archaeological Science* 40:2784–2798.

Hirth, Kenneth, and Susan Hirth. 1993. "Ancient Currency: The Style and Use of Jade and Marble Carvings in Central Honduras." In *Precolumbian Jade: New Geological and Cultural Interpretations*, ed. F. Lange, 173–190. University of Utah Press, Provo.

Hirth, Kenneth, Susan Hirth, George Hasemann, and Gloria Lara-Pinto. 2023. *The Pre-Columbian Lapidary Art of Salitrón Viejo, Honduras.* Occasional Papers in Anthropology 35. Penn State University, University Park. https://journals.psu.edu/opa/issue/archive.

Hirth, Kenneth, Nedenia Kennedy, and Maynard Cliff. 1989. "Chronology and Ceramic Variability within the El Cajon Region." In *Archaeological Research in the El Cajon Region*, volume 1: *Prehistoric Cultural Ecology*, ed. K. Hirth, G. Lara-Pinto, and G. Hasemann, 207–232. University of Pittsburgh and IHAH, Pittsburgh, PA, and Tegucigalpa.

Hirth, Kenneth, Nedenia Kennedy, and Maynard Cliff. 1993. "El Cajón Region." In *Pottery of Prehistoric Honduras: Regional Classification and Analysis*, ed. J. Henderson and M. Beaudry-Corbett, 214–232. UCLA Institute of Archaeology, Los Angeles.

Hirth, Kenneth, Gloria Lara-Pinto, and George Hasemann. 1984. *Proyecto arqueológico El Cajon II informe trimestral Abril–Junio 1984.* IHAH, Tegucigalpa.

Hirth, Kenneth, Gloria Lara-Pinto, and George Hasemann. 1989. "Investigaciones arqueológicas en la región de El Cajon," tomo 1: "Ecología cultural precolombina/Archaeological Research in the El Cajon Region," volume 1: "Prehistoric Cultural Ecology." University of Pittsburgh and IHAH, Pittsburgh, PA, and Tegucigalpa.

Hirth, Kenneth, Gloria Lara-Pinto, and George Hasemann. 1990. *Ventanas al pasado: Proyecto de Investigación y Salvamento Arqueológico El Cajon.* INAH, Tegucipalpa.

Hirth, Kenneth, Gloria Lara-Pinto, and George Hasemann. n.d. "Investigaciones arqueológicas en la región de El Cajón," tomo 2: "Bioantropología, práticas mortuorias, y patrones comunitarios" / "Archaeological Research in the El Cajón

Region," volume 2: "Bioanthropology, Mortuary Practices, and Community Patterning" (manuscript).

Hirth, Kenneth, Patricia Urban, George Hasemann, and Vito Véliz. 1981. "Patrones regionales de asentamiento en la region de El Cajon: Departmentos de Comayagua y Yoro, Honduras." *Yaxkin* 4:33–55.

Hodge, Mary, Hector Neff, James Blackman, and Leah Minc. 1993. "Black-on-Orange Ceramic Production in the Aztec Empire's Heartland." *Latin American Antiquity* 4:130–157.

Hoopes, John. 2007. "Sorcery and the Taking of Trophy Heads in Ancient Costa Rica." In *The Taking and Displaying of Human Body Parts as Trophies by Amerindians*, ed. R. Chacon and D. Dye, 444–480. Springer, Boston.

Hoopes, John, David Mora-Marín, and Brigitte Kovacevich. 2021. "Jadeworking." In *Pre-Columbian Art from Central America and Colombia at Dumbarton Oaks*, ed. C. McEwan and J. Hoopes, 29–46. DORLC, Washington, DC.

Hurtado de Mendoza, Luis, and Elena Troy Vargas. 2007–2008. "Simbología de poder en Guayabo de Turrialba." *Cuadernos de Antropología* 17–18:23–65.

Ibarra Rojas, Eugenia. 1990. *Las sociedades cacicales de Costa Rica, siglo XVI*. Editorial de la Universidad de Costa Rica, San José.

Ibarra Rojas, Eugenia. 2014. *Entre el dominio y la Resistencia: Los pueblos indígenas del Pacífico de Nicaragua y Nicoya en el siglo XVI*. Editorial Universidad de Costa Rica, San José.

Iceland, Harry. 2013. "Refining Paleo-Indian Lithic Technology at Shawnee-Minisink via an Artifact Refitting Study." *North American Archaeologist* 34:237–267.

Ichon, Alain. 1989. "Les camahuiles, statuettes protoclassiques du Quiché, Méridional." In *Enquêtes sur L'Amérique Moyenne: Mélanges offerts à Guy Stresser-Péan*, ed. D. Michelet, 93–103. CEMCA-INAH, Mexico City.

Ichon, Alain, and Marie Charlotte Arnauld. 1985. *Le Protoclassique á La Lagunita El Quiché, Guatemala*. Centre National de la Recherche Scientifique, Paris.

Inizan, Marie-Louise, Michèle Reduron-Ballinger, Hélèn Roche, and Jacques Tixier. 1999. *Technology and Terminology of Knapped Stone*. Préhistoire de la Pierre Taillée, volume 5. Cercle de Recherches et d'Etudes Préhistoriques, Nanterre, France.

Inomata, Takeshi, and Stephen Houston, eds. 2001. *Royal Courts of the Ancient Maya*, volume 1: *Theory, Comparison, and Synthesis*. Westview, Boulder.

Joesink-Mandeville, Leroy. 1987. "Yarumela, Honduras: Formative Period Cultural Conservatism and Diffusion." In *Interaction on the Southeast Mesoamerican Frontier: Prehistoric and Historic Honduras and El Salvador*, ed. E. Robinson, 1:196–214. BAR, Oxford, England.

Jones, Christopher, and Linton Satterthwaite. 2014. "Tikal Stelae and Stela/ Altar Pairs." In *The Monuments and Inscriptions of Tikal—the Carved Monuments*, ed. C. Jones and L. Satterthwaite, 9–77. University of Pennsylvania Press, Philadelphia.

Joyce, Rosemary. 1983. "Travesia (CR-35): Archaeological Investigations, 1983." Informe submitted to INAH, Tegucigalpa.

Joyce, Rosemary. 1985. "Cerro Palenque, Valle del Ulúa, Honduras: Terminal Classic Interaction on the Southern Mesoamerican Periphery." PhD dissertation, University of Illinois, Urbana-Champaign.

Joyce, Rosemary. 1993. "Key to Ulúa Polychromes." In *Pottery of Prehistoric Honduras: Regional Classification and Analysis*, ed. J. Henderson and M. Beaudry-Corbett, 257–278. UCLA Institute of Archaeology, Los Angeles.

Joyce, Rosemary. 1999. "Social Dimensions of Pre-Classic Burials." In *Social Patterns in Pre-Classic Mesoamerica*, ed. D. Grove and R. Joyce, 15–47. DORLC, Washington, DC.

Joyce, Rosemary. 2014. *Cerro Palenque: Power and Identity on the Maya Periphery*. University of Texas Press, Austin.

Joyce, Rosemary. 2017. *Painted Pottery of Honduras: Object Lives and Itineraries*. Koninklijke Brill, Leiden.

Joyce, Rosemary. 2021. "An Alternative Framework for Honduran Archaeology." In *Southeastern Mesoamerica: Indigenous Interaction, Resilience, and Change*, ed. W. Goodwin, E. Johnson, and A. Figueroa, 295–316. University Press of Colorado, Louisville.

Joyce, Rosemary. n.d. "Is Extreme Inequality Inevitable? What Archaeology Can Tell Us about the 99 Percent." Manuscript in the author's possession.

Joyce, Rosemary, and John Henderson. 2001. "Beginnings of Village Life in Eastern Mesoamerica." *Latin American Antiquity* 12:5–23.

Joyce, Rosemary, and John Henderson. 2002. "La arqueología del periodo Formativo en Honduras: Nuevos datos sobre el 'estilo olmeca' en la zona Maya." *Mayab* 15:5–17.

Joyce, Rosemary, and John Henderson. 2007. "From Feasting to Cuisine: Implications of Archaeological Research in an Early Honduran Village." *American Anthropologist* 109:642–653.

Joyce, Rosemary, and John Henderson. 2010. "Being 'Olmec' in Early Formative Period Honduras." *Ancient Mesoamerica* 21:187–200.

Joyce, Rosemary, and John Henderson. n.d. "Visual Imagery and Material Practices in Formative Period Honduras: Monumental Stone Sculpture of Los Naranjos and Puerto Escondido." Unpublished manuscript on file, Central American Archaeology Laboratory, Department of Anthropology, University of California, Berkeley.

Joyce, Rosemary, Julia Hendon, and Russell Sheptak. 2008. "Una nueva evaluación de Playa de los Muertos: Exploraciones en el periodo Formativo Medio en Honduras." In *Ideología política y sociedad en el período Formativo: Ensayos en homenaje al doctor David C. Grove*, ed. A. Cyphers and K. Hirth, 283–310. UNAM, Mexico City.

Joyce, Rosemary, Steven Shackley, Kenneth McCandless, and Russell Sheptak. 2004. "Resultados preliminares de una investigación con EDXRF de obsidiana de Puerto Escondido." In *Memoria, VII seminario de antropología de Honduras "Dr. George Hasemann,"* ed. R. Joyce, S. Shackley, K. McCandless, R. Sheptak, and K. Rubén Avalos, 115–130. IHAH, Tegucigalpa.

Joyce, Rosemary, and Russell Sheptak. 1983. *Settlement in the Southwest Hills and Central Alluvium, Valle de Ulúa*. Report submitted to Proyecto Arqueológico Sula, IHAH, Tegucigalpa.

Joyce, Rosemary, Russell Sheptak, Julia Hendon, Christopher Fung, and John Gerry. 1989. "Settlement Patterns in Yoro, Honduras." Paper presented at the 88th Annual Meeting of the American Anthropological Association. November 15–19, Washington, DC.

Junker, Laura Lee. 1993. "Craft Goods Specialization and Prestige Goods Exchange in Philippine Chiefdoms of the Fifteenth and Sixteenth Centuries." *Asian Perspectives* 32:1–35.

Kaplan, Lucille. 1956. "Tonal and Nagual in Coastal Oaxaca, Mexico." *Journal of American Folklore* 69:363–368.

Kappelman, Julia Guernsey. 2004. "Demystifying the Late Preclassic Izapan-Style Stela-Altar 'Cult.'" *RES: Anthropology and Aesthetics* 45:99–122.

Kate, Emily, and Kenneth Hirth. n.d. "Mortuary Patterns in the El Cajon Region." In "Archaeological Research in the El Cajon Region," volume 2: "Bioanthropology, Population, and Settlement," ed. K. Hirth, G. Lara-Pinto, and G. Hasemann (manuscript).

Kennedy, Nedenia. 1981. "The Formative Period Ceramic Sequence from Playa de los Muertos, Honduras." PhD dissertation, University of Illinois, Urbana-Champaign.

Kennedy, Nedenia. 1986. "The Periphery Problem and Playa de los Muertos: A Test Case." In *The Southeast Maya Periphery*, ed. P. Urban and E. Schortman, 179–193. University of Texas Press, Austin.

Kennedy, Nedenia. 1987. "La chronología cerámica de Salitrón Viejo, region de El Cajon Honduras." *Yaxkin* 10:1:51–57.

Kennedy, Nedenia, Phyllis Messenger, and John Yonk. 1982. "A Preliminary Ceramic Sequence from Salitrón, Honduras." Report submitted to the El Proyecto Arqueologico El Cajon, IHAH, Tegucigalpa.

Kennett, Douglas, and Timothy Beach. 2013. "Archeological and Environmental Lessons for the Anthropocene from the Classic Maya Collapse." *Anthropocene* 4:88–100.

Kidder, Alfred, Jesse Jennings, and Edwin Shook. 1946. *Excavations at Kaminaljuyu, Guatemala.* CIW Publication 561, Washington, DC.

Kirch, Patrick. 1989. *The Evolution of the Polynesian Chiefdoms.* Cambridge University Press, Cambridge.

Knapp, Bernard. 2009. "Monumental Architecture, Identity, and Memory." In *Proceedings of the Symposium Bronze Age Architectural Traditions in the East Mediterranean: Diffusion and Diversity*, 47–59. Verein zur Förderung der Aufarbeitung der Hellenischen Geschichte, Weilheim.

Knowlton, Timothy. 2021. "Theology and Economy in the *Popl Wuj* and *Theologia Indorum*." *Ancient Mesoamerica* 32:1–13.

Kopytoff, Igor. 1987. *The African Frontier: The Reproduction of Traditional African Societies.* Indiana University Press, Bloomington.

Kovacevich, Brigitte. 2006. "Reconstructing Classic Maya Economic Systems: Production and Exchange at Cancuen, Guatemala." PhD dissertation, Vanderbilt University, Nashville, TN.

Kovacevich, Brigitte. 2007. "Ritual, Crafting, and Agency at the Classic Maya Kingdom of Cancuen." In *Mesoamerican Ritual Economy: Archaeological and Ethnological Perspectives*, ed. C. Wells and K. Davis-Salazar, 67–114. University Press of Colorado, Boulder.

Kovacevich, Brigitte. 2013. "The Inalienability of Jades in Mesoamerica." In *The Inalienable in the Archaeology of Mesoamerica*, ed. B. Kovacevich and M. Callaghan, 95–111. AP3A 23, Wiley Periodicals, Malden, MA.

Kovacevich, Brigitte. 2015. "La tecnología del jade: Explotación, técnicas de manufactura, talleres especializados." *Arqueología Mexicana* 23:42–47.

Kovacevich, Brigitte, and Michael Callaghan. 2019. "Fifty Shades of Green: Interpreting Maya Jade Production, Circulation, Consumption, and Value." *Ancient Mesoamerica* 30:457–472.

Kowalewski, Stephen, Gary Feinman, Laura Finsten, and Richard Blanton. 1991. "Pre-Hispanic Ballcourts from the Valley of Oaxaca, Mexico." In *The Mesoamerican Ballgame*, ed. V. Scarborough and D. Wilcox, 25–44. University of Arizona Press, Tucson.

Kubler, George. 1984. *The Art and Architecture of Ancient America: The Mexican, Maya, and Ancient Andean Peoples.* Penguin Books, New York.

Kurin, Richard. 1983. "Indigenous Agronomics and Agricultural Development in the Indus Basin." *Human Organization* 42:283–294.

Kyriakidis, Evangelos. 2007. *The Archaeology of Ritual.* Cotsen Institute of Archaeology, University of California, Los Angeles.

Lange, Frederick. 1993. "Introduction." In *Precolumbian Jade: New Geological and Cultural Interpretations*, ed. F. Lange, 1–8. University of Utah Press, Salt Lake City.

Langley, James, and Janet Berlo. 1992. "Teotihuacan Sign Clusters: Emblem or Articulation." In *Art, Ideology, and the City of Teotihuacan*, ed. J. Berlo, 247–280. DORLC, Washington, DC.

Lara-Pinto, Gloria. 1980. "Beiträge zur indianischen Ethnographie von Honduras in der 1: Hälfte des 16, Jahrhunderts, unter besonderer Berücksichtigung der Historischen Demographie." PhD dissertation, University of Hamburg, Hamburg, Germany.

Lara-Pinto, Gloria. 1985. *Organización sociopolítica de las tierras centrales de Honduras al tiempo de la conquista*. Editorial Guaymuras, Tegucigalpa.

Lara-Pinto, Gloria. 1991a. "Change for Survival: The Case of Sixteenth-Century Indigenous Populations of Northeast and Mideast Honduras." In *Columbian Consequences*, volume 3: *The Spanish Borderlands in Pan-American Perspective*, ed. D. Hurst Thomas, 227–243. Smithsonian Institution Press, Washington, DC.

Lara-Pinto, Gloria. 1991b. "Sociopolitical Organization in Central Honduras at the Time of the Conquest: A Model for the Formation of Complex Society." In *The Formation of Complex Society in Southeastern Mesoamerica*, ed. W. Fowler, 215–235. CRC Press, Boca Raton.

Lara-Pinto, Gloria. 2011. "Producción Artesanal con Fibras Vegetales en Honduras: Del Pasado Remoto al Siglo XXI." VIII Congreso Centroamericano de Antropología. Paper presented at Los Retos de la Antropología en Centroamérica: Identidades, Diversidad Cultural y Procesos Políticos. February 21–25, Tegucigalpa, Honduras.

Lara-Pinto, Gloria. 2015. "De las Rutas Prehispánicas de Intercambio a las Rutas Coloniales en Honduras, Siglos XVI al XVIII: Mesa Antes y Después: Aportes de la Arqueología y la Etnohistoria a una Re-Lectura del Pasado." Paper presented at X Congreso Centroamericano de Antropología Universidad Nacional Autónoma de México, March 23–27, 1995. Mérida, Yucatán.

Lara-Pinto, Gloria. 2019. "Cantería y tallado en piedra de los Antiguales del Nororiente de Honduras: discontinuidad de una comunidad de práctica." *Revista de Ciencias Sociales UNAH* 5:55–71.

Lara-Pinto, Gloria. 2020. "Geopolítica de la identidad étnica y lingüística del Istmo centroamericano: Una propuesta desde el territorio ancestral lenca." In *La profunda huella histórica de los pueblos del istmo centroamericano*, ed. A. Jiménez and S. Carmen y Salgado, 36–58. Centro de Investigaciones Antropológicas, Universidad de Costa Rica, San José.

Lara-Pinto, Gloria. 2021. "The Politics of Ethnic Identity in the Context of the 'Frontier': Ethnohistory of the Lenca, Chorti, and Nahua Peoples of Honduras." In *Southeastern Mesoamerica: Indigenous Interaction, Resilience, and Change*, ed. W. Goodwin, E. Johnson, and A. Figueroa, 230–257. University Press of Colorado, Louisville.

Lara-Pinto, Gloria, and George Hasemann. 1982. "El salvamento arqueológico en la region de El Cajón, Honduras." *Mexicon* 4:42–45.

Lara-Pinto, Gloria, and Russell Sheptak. 1985. "Excavaciones en el sitio de Intendencia, Rio Humuya: Primeros resultados." *Yaxkin* 8:13–23.

LeCount, Lisa. 2001. "Like Water for Chocolate: Feasting and Political Ritual among the Late Classic Maya at Xunantunich, Belize." *American Anthropologist* 103:935–953.

Lentz, David. 1982. "Descripción preliminar de las zonas de vegatación en los sistemas fluviales del Bajo Rio Sulaco y Humuya, departamentos de Comayagua, Yoro y Cortés." *Yaxkin* 5:73–80.

Lentz, David. 1984. "A Description of the Plant Communities and Archaeoethnobotany of the Lower Sulaco and Humuya River Valleys, Honduras." PhD dissertation, University of Alabama, Tuscalosa.

Lentz, David. 1986. "Ethnobotany of the Jicaque of Honduras." *Economic Botany* 40:210–219.

Lentz, David. 1987. "Etnobotánica de los Jicaques de Honduras." *Yaxkin* 10:2:29–48.

Lentz, David. 1989a. "Botanical Remains from the El Cajon Area: Insights into a Prehistoric Dietary Pattern." In *Archaeological Research in the El Cajon Region*, volume 1: *Prehistoric Cultural Ecology*, ed. K. Hirth, G. Lara-Pinto, and G. Hasemann, 187–206. University of Pittsburgh and IHAH, Pittsburgh, PA, and Tegucigalpa.

Lentz, David. 1989b. "Contemporary Plant Communities in the El Cajon Region." In *Archaeological Research in the El Cajon Region*, volume 1: *Prehistoric Cultural Ecology*, ed. K. Hirth, G. Lara-Pinto, and G. Hasemann, 95–133. University of Pittsburgh and IHAH, Pittsburgh, PA, and Tegucigalpa.

Lentz, David. 1993. "Medicinal and Other Economic Plants of the Paya of Honduras." *Economic Botany* 47:358–370.

Lentz, David, and Rani Alexander. 1986. "Prehistoric Environment and Subsistence in the Lower Sulaco and Humuya River Valleys, Honduras." Paper presented at the 85th Annual Meeting of the American Anthroological Association. December 3–7, Philadelphia.

Lentz, David, Jason Yaeger, Cynthia Robin, and Wendy Ashmore. 2005. "Pine, Prestige, and Politics of the Late Classic Maya at Xunantunich, Belize." *Antiquity* 79:573–585.

Leyenaar, Ted. 1978. *Ulama: The Perpetuation in Mexico of the Pre-Spanish Ball Game Ullamaliztli*, trans. I. Seeger. Mededelingen van het Rijksmuseum voor Volkenkunde 23. E. J. Brill, Leiden.

Lightfoot, Kent. 1987. "A Consideration of Complex Prehistoric Societies in the US Southwest." In *Chiefdoms in the Americas*, ed. R. Drennan and C. Uribe, 43–66. University Press of America, Lanham, MD.

Loker, William. 1986. "Agricultural Ecology and Prehistoric Settlement in the El Cajon Region of Honduras." PhD dissertation, University of Colorado, Boulder.

Loker, William. 1989a. "Climate and Agriculture in the El Cajon Region." In *Archaeological Research in the El Cajon Region*, volume 1: *Prehistoric Cultural Ecology*, ed. K. Hirth, G. Lara-Pinto, and G. Hasemann, 41–58. University of Pittsburgh and IHAH, Pittsburgh, PA, and Tegucigalpa.

Loker, William. 1989b. "Contemporary Land Use and Prehistoric Settlement: An Ethnoarchaeological Approach." In *Archaeological Research in the El Cajon Region*, volume 1: *Prehistoric Cultural Ecology*, ed. K. Hirth, G. Lara-Pinto, and G. Hasemann, 135–186. University of Pittsburgh and IHAH, Pittsburgh, PA, and Tegucigalpa.

López Austin, Alfredo. 1988. *The Human Body and Ideology: Concepts of the Ancient Nahuas*, trans. T. Ortiz de Montellano and B. Ortiz de Montellano. University of Utah Press, Salt Lake City.

López Lujan, Leonardo. 2005. *The Offerings of the Templo Mayor of Tenochtitlan*. University of New Mexico Press, Albuquerque.

López-Ortega, Esther, Xosé Pedro Rodríguez, and Manuel Vaquero. 2011. "Lithic Refitting and Movement Connections: The NW Area of Level TD10–1 at the Gran Dolina Site (Sierra de Atapuerca, Burgos, Spain)." *Journal of Archaeological Science* 38:3112–3121.

López Romero, Laura Elena. 2019. *Cosmovisión, cuerpo y enfermedad: El espanto entre los nahuas de Tlacotepec de Díaz, Puebla*. INAH, Mexico City.

Lopiparo, Jeanne. 2006. "Producing Social Landscapes in the Terminal Classic Ulúa Valley, Honduras." Paper presented at the 52nd Congreso Internacional de Americanists. July 17–23, Seville, Spain.

Lothrop, Samuel. 1921. "The Stone Statues of Nicaragua." *American Anthropologist* 23:311–319.

Lucero, Lisa. 2002. "The Collapse of the Classic Maya: A Case for the Role of Water Control." *American Anthropologist* 104:814–826.

Luke, Christina. 2003. *Ulúa-Style Marble Vase Project: Dissemination of Results*. Final report to FAMSI. http://www.famsi.org/reports/02081/index.html.

Luke, Christina, Rosemary Joyce, John Henderson, and Robert Tykot. 2003. "Marble Carving Traditions in Honduras: Formative through Terminal Classic." In *ASMOSIA 6, Interdisciplinary Studies on Ancient Stone: Proceedings of the Sixth International Conference of the Association for the Study of Marble and Other Stones in Antiquity*, ed. Lorenzo Lazzarini, 485–496. Bottega d'Erasmo, Padova, Italy.

Luke, Christina, and Robert Tykot. 2007. "Celebrating Place through Luxury Craft Production: Travesìa and Ulúa Style Marble Vases." *Ancient Mesoamerica* 18:315–328.

Luke, Christina, Robert Tykot, and Robert Scott. 2006. "Petrographic and Stable Isotope Analyses of Late Classic Ulúa Marble Vases and Potential Sources." *Archaeometry* 48:13–29.

Lupo, Alessandro. 1995. *La tierra nos eschuca: La cosmología de los nahuas a través de las súplicas rituales*. Instituto Nacional Indigenista, Mexico City.

MacNeish, Richard, Antoinette Nelken-Terner, and Irmgard Weitlaner de Johnson, eds. 1967. *The Prehistory of the Tehuacan Valley*, volume 2: *Non-Ceramic Artifacts*. University of Texas Press, Austin.

Maffie, James. 2014. *Aztec Philosophy: Understanding a World in Motion*. University Press of Colorado, Boulder.

Mauss, Marcel. 1990. *The Gift*. Routledge, London.

Mayo Torné, Julia, Carlos Mayo Torné, and Mercedes Guinea Bueno. 2021. "Funerary Rituals among the Elite of the Río Grande Chiefdom, Panama." In *Pre-Columbian Art from Central America and Colombia at Dumbarton Oaks*, ed. C. McEwan and J. Hoopes, 331–361. DORLC, Washington, DC.

McAnany, Patricia. 2008. "Shaping Social Difference: Political and Ritual Economy of Classic Maya Royal Courts." In *Dimensions of Ritual Economy*, ed. P. McAnany and C. Wells, 219–247. Research in Economic Anthropology 27. JAI Press, Bingley, UK.

McAnany, Patricia. 2010. *Ancestral Maya Economies in Archaeological Perspective*. Cambridge University Press, Cambridge.

McAnany, Patricia, and Christian Wells. 2008. "Toward a Theory of Ritual Economy." In *Dimensions of Ritual Economy*, ed. P. McAnany and C. Wells, 1–16. Research in Economic Anthropology 27. JAI Press, Bingley, UK.

McCafferty, Sharisse, and Geoffrey McCafferty. 2009. "Alternative and Ambiguous Gender Identities in Postclassic Central Mexico." In *Que(e)rying Archeology: Proceeding of the 37th Annual Chacmool Conference*, ed. S. Terendy, N. Lyons, and M. Janse-Smekal, 196–206. Chacmool Archaeological Association of the University of Calgary, Calgary, AB.

McEwan, Colin, and John Hoopes, eds. 2021a. *Pre-Columbian Art from Central America and Colombia at Dumbarton Oaks*. DORLC, Washington, DC.

McEwan, Colin, and John Hoopes, eds. 2021b. *Pre-Columbian Central America, Colombia, and Ecuador: Toward an Integrated Approach*. DORLC, Washington, DC.

McGee, Jon. 1998. "The Lacandon Incense Burner Renewal Ceremony." In *The Sowing and the Dawning: Termination, Dedication, and Transformation in the Archaeological and Ethnographic Record of Mesoamerica*, ed. S. Boteler Mock, 41–46. University of New Mexico Press, Albuquerque.

McGuire, Randall. 1983. "Breaking down Cultural Complexity: Inequality and Heterogeneity." In *Advances in Archaeological Method and Theory*, ed. B. Schiffer, 91–142. Academic Press, New York.

Mckenzie, Jessome. 2008. "An Examination on the Balsería and the Nature of Overproduction in Central Panamanian Chiefly Societies." Master's thesis, St. Francis Xavier College, St. Louis, MO.

McMahon, Augusta. 2013. "Space, Sound, and Light: Toward a Sensory Experience of Ancient Monumental Architecture." *American Journal of Archaeology* 117:163–179.

Mejía, Medardo. 1986. *Comizahual: Leyendas, tradiciones y relatos de Honduras*. Editorial Universidad Nacional Autónoma de Honduras, Tegucigalpa.

Melgar, Emiliano, Emiliano Gallaga, and Reyna Solís. 2014. "La pirita y su manufactura: Análisis de cuatro contextos Mesoamericanos." *Estudios de Cultura Maya* 43:41–68.

Menzies, Adam, and Mikael Haller. 2012. "A Macroregional Perspective on Chiefly Cycling in the Central Region of Panama during the Late Ceramic II Period (AD 700–1522)." *Latin American Antiquity* 23:449–466.

Messenger, Lewis. 1982. "El antiguo Guarabuquí: Informe preliminar de las excavaciones en PC-15." *Yaxkin* 5:1:67–72.

Messenger, Lewis. 1984. "Excavations at Guarabuquí, El Cajon, Honduras: Frontiers, Culture Areas, and the Southern Mesoamerican Periphery." PhD dissertation, University of Minnesota, Minneapolis.

Miller, Arthur. 1973. *The Mural Painting of Teotihuacan*. DORLC, Washington, DC.

Miller, Virginia. 1985. "The Dwarf Motif in Classic Maya Art." In *The Fourth Palenque Round Table, 1980*, ed. E. Benson, 141–153. Pre-Columbian Art Research Institute, Palenque, Mexico.

Molina, Fray Alonso de. 1977. *Vocabulario en lengua Castellana y Mexicana y Mexicana y Castellana*. Editorial Porrua, Mexico City.

Monaghan, John. 1996. "Fiesta Finance in Mesoamerica and the Origins of a Gift Exchange System." *Journal of the Royal Anthropological Institute* 2:499–516.

Monaghan, John. 1998. "Dedication: Ritual or Production?" In *The Sowing and the Dawning: Termination, Dedication, and Transformation in the Archaeological and*

Ethnographic Record of Mesoamerica, ed. S. Boteler Mock, 47–52. University of New Mexico Press, Albuquerque.

Monroe, Burt. 1965. *A Distributional Survey of the Birds of Honduras*. Louisiana State University and the Agricultural and Mechanical College, Baton Rouge.

Morehart, Christopher, David Lentz, and Keith Prufer. 2005. "Wood of the Gods: The Ritual Use of Pine (*Pinus* spp.) by the Ancient Lowland Maya." *Latin American Antiquity* 16:255–274.

Morrow, Toby. 1996. "Lithic Refitting and Archaeological Site Formation Processes." In *Stone Tools*, ed. G. Odell, 345–373. Springer, Boston.

Moyes, Holley, and James Brady. 2012. "Caves as Sacred Space in Mesoamerica." In *Sacred Darkness: A Global Perspective on the Ritual Use of Caves*, ed. H. Moyes, 151–170. University Press of Colorado, Louisville.

Neff, Hector, Jeffrey Blomster, Michael Glascock, Ronald Bishop, James Blackman, Michael Coe, George Cowgill, Richard Diehl, Stephen Houston, Arthur Joyce, Carl Lipo, Barbara Stark, and Marcus Winter. 2006. "Methodological Issues in the Provenance Investigation of Early Formative Mesoamerican Ceramics." *Latin American Antiquity* 17:54–76.

Nicholson, Henry. 1971. "Religion in Pre-Hispanic Central Mexico." In *HMAI*, ed. Gordon Ekholm and Ignacio Bernal, 10:395–446. University of Texas Press, Austin.

Norville, Charles. 1986. "Geoarchaeological Investigations of the Cajon Archaeological Project, Districts of Comayagua, Yoro, and Cortes, Honduras, C.A." MA thesis, University of Kentucky, Lexington.

Norville, Charles, and Michael Collins. 1989. "Geoarchaeology in the El Cajon Area." In *Archaeological Research in the El Cajon Region*, volume 1: *Prehistoric Cultural Ecology*, ed. K. Hirth, G. Lara-Pinto, and G. Hasemann, 95–133. University of Pittsburgh and IHAH, Pittsburgh, PA, and Tegucigalpa.

Nuñez Chinchilla, Jesus. 1966. "Informe preliminar de la exploración de una cueva votiva en la zona arqueológica de las Ruinas de Copán." *Revista de la Sociedad de Geográfica e Historia de Honduras* 18:43–48.

Nuñez Chinchilla, Jesus. 1972. "Reconocimiento y exploración de una cueva votiva en la zona arqueológica de las Ruinas de Copán." *Anales de la Sociedad de Geográfica e Historia de Honduras* 45:102–105.

Orellana, Sandra. 1981. "Idols and Idolatry in Highland Guatemala." *Ethnohistory* 28:157–177.

Ortíz, Víctor Manuel. 1991. "Algunos antecedentes sobre el uso del color en el México indígena." *Relaciones: Estudios de Historia y Sociedad* 12:105–114.

Ortíz Ceballos, Ponciano, and María del Carmen Rodríguez. 1997. *Las investigaciones arqueológicos en el cerro sagrado Manatí, Veracruz, México.* Universidad Veracruzana, Jalapa.

Parsons, Lee. 1967–1969. *Bilbao, Guatemala: An Archaeological Study of the Pacific Coast Cotzumalhuapa Region.* Publications in Anthropology 11–12. Milwaukee Public Museum, Milwaukee, WI.

Pastrana, Alejandro, and Zachary Hruby. n.d. "Eccentric or Silhouette: A Preliminary Typology of Ceremonial Chipped-Stones from Sierra de las Navajas and Teotihuacan." In *Crafting Celestial Fire in Classic Mesoamerica,* ed. Z. Hruby. University Press of Colorado, Denver.

Peebles, Christopher, and Susan Kus. 1977. "Some Archaeological Correlates of Ranked Societies." *American Antiquity* 42:421–448.

Pendergast, David. 1968. *Altun Ha, British Honduras (Belize): The Sun God's Tomb,* volume 19. Royal Ontario Museum, Toronto.

Pendergast, David. 1971. "Evidence of Early Teotihuacan–Lowland Maya Contact at Altun Ha." *American Antiquity* 36:455–460.

Pendergast, David. 1979. *Excavations at Altun Ha, Belize, 1964–1970.* 3 volumes. Royal Ontario Museum, Toronto.

Pendergast, David. 2004. "Teotihuacan at Altun Ha: Did It Make a Difference." In *The Maya and Teotihuacan: Reinterpreting Early Classic Interaction,* ed. G. Braswell, 235–247. University of Texas Press, Austin.

Pétrequin, Pierre, Christophe Bontemps, Daniel Buthod-Ruffier, and Nicolas Le Maux. 2012. "Approche expérimentale de la production des haches alpines." In *Jade: Grandes haches alpines du Néolithique européen: Ve et IVe millénaires av. J.C. tome 1,* ed. P. Pétrequin, S. Cassen, M. Errera, L. Klassen, A. Sheridan, and A.-M. Pétrequin, 258–291. Presses Universitaries de Franche–Comté, Besançon.

Plourde, Aimée. 2009. "Prestige Goods and the Formation of Political Hierarchy." In *Pattern and Process in Cultural Evolution,* ed. S. Shennan, 265–276. Cambridge University Press, Cambridge.

Pope, Kevin, and Eugenia Robinson. 1987. "The Ecology and Economy of the Formative-Classic Transition along the Ulúa River, Honduras." In *Interaction on the Southeast Mesoamerican Frontier: Prehistoric and Historic Honduras and El Salvador,* ed. E. Robinson, 1:95–128. BAR, Oxford, England.

Popenoe, Dorothy Hughes. 1934. "Some Excavations at Playa de Los Muertos Ulúa River, Honduras." *Maya Research* 1:62–86.

Popenoe, Dorothy Hughes. 1935. *The Ruins of Tenampua, Honduras.* Annual Report 3375. Smithsonian Institution, Washington, DC.

Proskouriakoff, Tatiana. 1974. *Jades from the Cenote of Sacrifice, Chichen Itza, Yucatan.* Peabody Museum of Archaeology and Ethnology, Harvard University, Cambridge, MA.

Puleston, Dennis. 1974. "Intersite Areas in the Vicinity of Tikal and Uaxactun." In *Mesoamerican Archaeology: New Approaches,* ed. N. Hammond, 303–312. University of Texas Press, Austin.

RAE (Real Academia Española). 2021. *Diccionario de la lengua Española.* https://dle .rae.es/ijada.

Ramírez Hernández, Blanca, Julia Zañudo Hernández, Javier García de Alba Verduzco, John Delano Frier, Enrique Pimienta Barios, and Miguel Angel García Martínez. 2013. "Importancia agroecológica del Coyul (*Acrocomia mexicana* Karw. ex Mart.)." *Estudios Sociales* 21:96–113.

Rands, Robert. 1965. "Jades of the Maya Lowlands." In *HMAI,* ed. Gordon Willey, 3:561–580. University of Texas Press, Austin.

Rapoport, Amos. 1969. *House Form and Culture.* Prentice-Hall, Englewood Cliffs, NJ.

Rappaport, Roy. 1968. *Pigs for the Ancestors: Ritual in the Ecology of a New Guinea People.* Yale University Press, New Haven, CT.

Rappaport, Roy. 1971. "The Sacred in Human Evolution." *Annual Review of Ecology and Systematics* 2:23–44.

Rappaport, Roy. 1979. "Ecology, Adaptation, and the Ills of Functionalism." In *Ecology, Meaning, and Region,* ed. R. Rapport, 43–95. North Atlantic Books, Richmond, CA.

Rappaport, Roy. 1999. *Ritual and Religion in the Making of Humanity.* Cambridge University Press, Cambridge.

Rathje, William. 1972. "Praise the Gods and Pass the Metates: A Hypothesis of the Development of Lowland Rainforest Civilizations in Mesoamerica." In *Contemporary Archaeology: A Guide to Theory and Contributions,* ed. M. Leone, 365–392. Southern Illinois University Press, Carbondale.

Rattray, Evelyn. 1991. "New Findings on the Origins of Thin Orange Ceramics." *Ancient Mesoamerica* 1:181–195.

Recinos, Adrian. 1957. *Crónicas indígenas de Guatemala.* Editorial Universitaria, Guatemala City.

Reents-Budet, Dorie. 1998. "Elite Maya Pottery and Artisans as Social Indicators." In *Craft and Social Identity,* ed. C. Costin and R. Wright, 71–89. AP3A 8, Wiley Periodicals, Malden, MA.

Reina, Ruben. 1963. "The Potter and the Farmer: The Fate of Two Innovators in a Maya Village." *Expedition* 5:4:18–30.

Reina, Ruben, and Robert Hill. 1978. *The Traditional Pottery of Guatemala*. University of Texas Press, Austin.

Renfrew, Colin. 1974. "Beyond a Subsistence Economy: The Evolution of Social Organization in Prehistoric Europe." *Bulletin of the American Schools of Oriental Research* 20:69–95.

Renfrew, Colin. 1975. "Trade as Action at a Distance: Questions of Integration and Communication." In *Ancient Civilization and Trade*, ed. J. Sabroff and C. C. Lamberg-Karlovsky, 3–59. University of New Mexico Press, Albuquerque.

Reyes Mazzoni, Roberto. 1976. *Introducción a la Arqueología de Honduras*. Editorial Nuevo Continente, Tegucigalpa.

Richardson, Francis. 1977. "Non-Maya Monumental Sculpture of Central America." In *The Maya and Their Neighbors*, ed. C. Hay, R. Linton, S. Lothrop, H. Shapiro, and G. Vaillant, 395–416. Dover, New York.

Rivas, Ramón, and Esteban Gómez. 2005. *Antropología y arqueología de la isla Conchagüita en el Golfo de Fonseca*. Universidad Tecnológica de El Salvador, San Salvador.

Robelo, Ceclio. 1982. *Diccionario de mitología Nahoa*. Editorial Porrúa, Mexico City.

Robinson, Eugenia. 1989. "The Prehistoric Communities of the Sula Valley, Honduras: Regional Interaction on the Southeast Mesoamerican Frontier." PhD dissertation, Tulane University, New Orleans.

Robinson, Kenneth, Scott O'Mack, and William Loker. 1985. "Excavaciones en la plaza principal del conjunto residential oeste de Salitrón Viejo (PC1)." *Yaxkin* 8:47–57.

Rochette, Erick. 2009a. "Jade in Full: Prehispanic Domestic Production of Wealth Goods in the Middle Motagua Valley, Guatemala." In *Housework: Craft Production and Domestic Economy in Ancient Mesoamerica*, ed. K. Hirth, 205–224. AP3A 19, Wiley Periodicals, Malden, MA.

Rochette, Erick. 2009b. "The Late Classic Organization of Jade Artifact Production in the Middle Motagua Valley, Zacapa, Guatemala." PhD dissertation, Penn State University, University Park.

Rodríguez, Carlos, Carolina Isaza, and Harry Pachajoa. 2012. "Achondroplasia among Ancient Populations of Mesoamerica and South America: Iconographic and Archaeological Evidence." *Colombia Médica* 43:212–215.

Rojas, Alfonso Villa. 1947. "Kinship and Nagualism in a Tzeltal Community, Southeastern Mexico." *American Anthropologist* 49:578–587.

Rojas Rabiela, Teresa. 1979. "La organización del trabajo para las obras públicas: El coatequitl y las cuadrillas de trabajadores." In *El trabajo y los trabajadores en la historia de México / Labor and Laborers through Mexican History*, ed. C. Frost, M.

Meyer, J. Zoraida Vázquez, and L. Díaz, 41–66. El Colegio de México and University of Arizona Press, Mexico City and Tucson.

Roys, Ralph. 1931. *The Ethnobotany of the Maya*. Institute for the Study of Human Issues, Philadelphia.

Rue, David, AnnCorinne Freter, and Diane Ballinger. 1989. "The Caverns of Copan Revisited: Preclassic Sites in the Sesesmil River Valley, Copan, Honduras." *Journal of Field Archaeology* 16:395–404.

Sabloff, Jeremy. 2008. "Considerations of Ritual Economy." In *Dimensions of Ritual Economy*, ed. P. McAnany and C. Wells, 269–277. Research in Economic Anthropology 27. JAI Press, Bingley, UK.

Sahagún, Fray Bernardino de. 1963. *Florentine Codex*, Book 11: *Earthly Things*, ed. and trans. C. Dibble and A. Anderson. University of Utah Press, Salt Lake City.

Sahagún, Fray Bernardino de. 1979. *Florentine Codex*, Book 8: *Kings and Lords*, ed. and trans. A. Anderson and C. Dibble. University of Utah Press, Salt Lake City.

Sanders, William, ed. 1986. *Proyecto arqueológico Copán segunda fase: Excavaciones en el área urbana de Copán*, tomo I. IHAH, Tegucigalpa.

Sandstrom, Alan. 2005. "The Cave-Pyramid Complex among the Contemporary Nahua of Northern Veracruz." In *The Maw of the Earth Monster: Mesoamerican Ritual Cave Use*, ed. J. Brady and K. Prufer, 35–68. University of Texas Press, Austin.

Sandstrom, Alan. 2008. "Ritual Economy among the Nahua of Northern Veracruz, Mexico." In *Dimensions of Ritual Economy*, ed. P. McAnany and C. Wells, 93–119. Research in Economic Anthropology 27. JAI Press, Bingley, UK.

Sandstrom, Alan, and Pamela Effrein Sandstrom. 1986. *Traditional Papermaking and Paper Cult Figures of Mexico*. University of Oklahoma Press, Norman.

Sandstrom, Alan, and Pamela Effrein Sandstrom. 2017. "The Behavioral Economics of Contemporary Nahua Religion and Ritual." In *Rethinking the Aztec Economy*, ed. D. Nichols, F. Berdan, and M. Smith, 105–129. University of Arizona Press, Tucson.

Santley, Robert, Michael Berman, and Rani Alexander. 1991. "The Politicization of the Mesoamerican Ballgame and Its Implications for the Interpretation of the Distribution of Ballcourts in Central Mexico." In *The Mesoamerican Ballgame*, ed. V. Scarborough and D. Wilcox, 3–24. University of Arizona Press, Tucson.

Sassaman, Kenneth, and Wictoria Rudolphi. 2001. "Communities of Practice in the Early Pottery Traditions of the American Southeast." *Journal of Anthropological Research* 57:407–425.

Scarborough, Vernon, and David Wilcox. 1991. *The Mesoamerican Ballgame*. University of Arizona Press, Tucson.

Schele, Linda, and David A. Freidel. 1990. *A Forest of Kings: The Untold Story of the Ancient Maya*. William Morrow, New York.

Schele, Linda, and Peter Mathews. 1999. *The Code of Kings: The Language of Seven Sacred Maya Temples and Tombs*. Simon and Schuster, New York.

Schele, Linda, and Mary Miller. 1986. *The Blood of Kings: Dynasty and Ritual in Maya Art*. Kimbell Art Museum, Fort Worth, TX.

Schortman, Edward, and Patricia Urban. 1987a. "Modeling Interregional Interaction in Prehistory." In *Advances in Archaeological Method and Theory*, ed. B. Schiffer, 11:37–95. Academic Press, New York.

Schortman, Edward, and Patricia Urban. 1987b. "Survey within the Gualjoquito Hinterland: An Introduction to the Investigations of the Santa Barbara Archaeological Project." In *Interaction on the Southeast Mesoamerican Frontier: Prehistoric and Historic Honduras and El Salvador*, ed. Eugenia Robinson, 1:5–27. BAR, Oxford, England.

Schortman, Edward, and Patricia Urban. 1994. "Living on the Edge: Core/Periphery Relations in Ancient Southeastern Mesoamerica." *Current Anthropology* 35:401–430.

Schortman, Edward, and Patricia Urban. 2021. "Sociopolitical Dynamism, Fluidity, and Fragmentation in Southeast Mesoamerica." In *Southeastern Mesoamerica: Indigenous Interaction, Resilience, and Change*, ed. W. Goodwin, E. Johnson, and A. Figueroa, 317–334. University Press of Colorado, Louisville.

Schortman, Edward, Patricia Urban, Wendy Ashmore, and Julie Benyo. 1986. "Interregional Interaction in the SE Maya Periphery: The Santa Barbara Archaeological Project 1983–1984 Seasons." *Journal of Field Archaeology* 13:259–272.

Selsor Walker, Debra. 1998. "Smashed Pots and Shattered Dreams: The Material Evidence for an Early Classic Maya Site Termination at Cerros, Belize." In *The Sowing and the Dawning: Termination, Dedication, and Transformation in the Archaeological and Ethnographic Record of Mesoamerica*, ed. S. Boteler Mock, 81–99. University of New Mexico Press, Albuquerque.

Sejourne, Laurette. 1962. "Interpretación de un jeroglifo Teotihuacan." *Cuadernos Americanos* 124:137–158.

Serra Puche, Mari Carmen, and Felipe Solís Olguín. 1994. *Cristales y obsidiana prehispánicos*. Siglo Veintiuno, Mexico City.

Service, Elman. 1962. *Primitive Social Organization: An Evolutionary Perspective*. Random House, New York.

Service, Elman. 1978. "Classification and Modern Theories of the Origins of Government." In *Origins of the State: The Anthropology of Political Evolution*, ed. R. Cohen and E. Service, 21–34. Institute for the Study of Human Issues, Philadelphia.

Sharer, Robert, ed. 1978. *The Prehistory of Chalchuapa, El Salvador*. 3 volumes. University of Pennsylvania Press, Philadelphia.

Sharer, Robert. 1984. "Lower Central America as Seen from Mesoamerica." In *The Archaeology of Lower Central America*, ed. F. Lange and D. Stone, 65–86. University of New Mexico Press, Albuquerque.

Sharer, Robert. 2004. "Founding Events and Teotihuacan Connections at Copán, Honduras." In *The Maya and Teotihuacan: Reinterpreting Early Classic Interaction*, ed. G. Braswell, 143–166. University of Texas Press, Austin.

Sheehy, James. 1977. "1976 Excavations at Travesia: A Preliminary Report." Paper presented at the forty-second annual meeting of the Society for American Archaeology. April 28–30, New Orleans, LA.

Sheehy, James. 1978. "Informe preliminar sobre las excavaciones en Travesía en 1976." *Yaxkin* 2:175–201.

Sheehy, James. 1996. "Ethnographic Analogy and the Royal Household in Eighth Century Copan." In *Arqueología Mesoamericana: Homenaje a William T. Sanders*, ed. A. G. Mastache, J. Parsons, R. Santley, and M. C. Serra Puche, 2:253–276. INAH, Mexico City.

Sheets, Payson, Kenneth Hirth, Frederick Lange, and Fred Stross. 1990. "Obsidian Sources and Elemental Analyses of Artifacts in Southern Mesoamerica and the Northern Intermediate Area." *American Antiquity* 55:144–158.

Siméon, Rémi. 1991. *Diccionario de la lengua Náhuatl o Mexicana*. Siglo Veintiuno, Mexico City.

Skalník, Peter. 2004. "Chiefdom: A Universal Political Formation?" *Focaal—European Journal of Anthropology* 43:77–98.

Smith, Ledyard, and Alfred Kidder. 1943. *Explorations in the Motagua Valley, Guatemala*. CIW Publication 546, Washington, DC.

Smith, Ledyard, and Alfred Kidder. 1951. *Excavations at Nebaj, Guatemala*. CIW Publication 594, Washington, DC.

Smith, Michael, and Arthur Demarest. 2001. "Climatic Change and the Classic Maya Collapse: The Return of Catastrophism." *Latin American Antiquity* 12:105–107.

Smith, Robert, Gordon Willey, and James Gifford. 1960. "The Type-Variety Concept as a Basis for the Analysis of Maya Pottery." *American Antiquity* 25:330–340.

Sorensen, Jerrel, and Kenneth Hirth. 1984. "Minas precolombinas y talleres de obsidiana en La Esperanza, Departamento de Intibuca." *Yaxkin* 7:31–45.

Spence, Michael. 1996. "Commodity or Gift: Teotihuacan Obsidian in the Maya Region." *Latin American Antiquity* 7:21–39.

Spencer, Charles. 1987. "Rethinking the Chiefdom." In *Chiefdoms in the Americas*, ed. R. Drennan and C. Uribe, 369–390. University Press of America, Lanham, MD.

Spielmann, Katherine. 1998. "Ritual Craft Specialists in Middle Range Societies." In *Craft and Social Identify*, ed. C. Costin, 153–159. AP3A 8, Wiley Periodicals, Malden, MA.

Spielmann, Katherine. 2002. "Feasting, Craft Specialization, and the Ritual Mode of Production in Small-Scale Societies." *American Anthropologist* 104:195–207.

Spielmann, Katherine. 2008. "Crafting the Sacred: Ritual Places and Paraphernalia in Small-Scale Societies." In *Dimensions of Ritual Economy*, ed. P. McAnany and C. Wells, 37–72. Research in Economic Anthropology 27. JAI Press, Bingley, UK.

Squier, Ephraim. 1855. *Note on Central America, Particularly the States of Honduras and San Salvador*. Harper and Brothers, New York.

Stanish, Charles. 2017. *The Evolution of Human Co-Operation*. Cambridge University Press, Cambridge.

Stark, Barbara, Matthew Boxt, Janine Gasco, Rebecca González Lauck, Jessica Hedgepeth Balkin, Arthur Joyce, Stacie King, Charles Knight, Robert Kruger, Marc Levine, Richard Lesure, Rebecca Mendelsohn, Marx Navarro-Castillo, Hector Neff, Michael Ohnersorgen, Christopher Pool, Mark Raab, Robert Rosenswig, Marcie Venter, Barbara Voorhies, David Williams, and Andrew Workinger. 2016. "Economic Growth in Mesoamerica: Obsidian Consumption in the Coastal Lowlands." *Journal of Anthropological Archaeology* 41:263–282.

Steponaitis, Vincas. 1981. "Settlement Hierarchies and Political Complexity in Nonmarket Societies: The Formative Period in the Valley of Mexico." *American Anthropologist* 83:320–363.

Stone, Doris. 1938. *Masters in Marble*. Middle American Research Monograph Series 8. Middle American Research, New Orleans.

Stone, Doris. 1941. *Archaeology of the North Coast of Honduras*. Peabody Museum of Archaeology and Ethnology Memoirs 9, no. 1. Harvard University, Cambridge, MA.

Stone, Doris. 1957. *The Archaeology of Central and Southern Honduras*. Papers of the Peabody Museum of Archaeology and Ethnology 49, no. 3. Harvard University, Cambridge, MA.

Stone, Doris. 1977a. *Pre-Columbian Man Finds Central America*. Peabody Museum, Cambridge, MA.

Stone, Doris. 1977b. *Pre-Columbian Man Finds Costa Rica*. Peabody Museum, Cambridge, MA.

Stone, Doris. 1993. "Jade and Jade Objects in Precolumbian Costa Rica." In *Precolumbian Jade: New Geological and Cultural Interpretations*, ed. F. Lange, 141–148. University of Utah Press, Salt Lake City.

Strong, William Duncan. 1935. *Archaeological Investigations in the Bay Islands, Spanish Honduras.* Smithsonian Miscellaneous Collections, Washington, DC.

Strong, William Duncan, Alfred Kidder, and A. Drexel Paul. 1938. *Preliminary Report on the Smithsonian Institution–Harvard University Expedition to Northwest Honduras, 1936.* Smithsonian Institution, Washington, DC.

Stross, Brian. 1998. "Seven Ingredients in Mesoamerican Ensoulment: Dedication and Termination in Tenejapa." In *The Sowing and the Dawning: Termination, Dedication, and Transformation in the Archaeological and Ethnographic Record of Mesoamerica,* ed. S. Boteler Mock, 31–39. University of New Mexico Press, Albuquerque.

Taube, Karl. 1983. "The Classic Maya Maize God: A Reappraisal." In *Fifth Palenque Round Table,* ed. K. Taube, V. Fields, and M. Robertson, 171–181. University of Texas Press, Austin.

Taube, Karl. 2003. "Ancient and Contemporary Maya Conceptions about Field and Forest." In *The Lowland Maya Area: Three Millennia at the Human-Wildland Interface,* ed. A. Gómez-Pompa, M. Allen, S. Fedick, and J. Jiménez-Osornio, 461–492. Haworth, New York.

Taube, Karl. 2005. "The Symbolism of Jade in Classic Maya Religion." *Ancient Mesoamerica* 16:23–50.

Taube, Karl, and Reiko Ishihara-Brito. 2012. "From Stone to Jewel: Jade in Ancient Maya Religion and Rulership." In *Ancient Maya Art at Dumbarton Oaks,* ed. J. Pillsbury, M. Doutriaux, R. Ishihara-Brito, and A. Tokovinine, 135–153. DORLC, Washington, DC.

Terry, Richard, Sheldon Nelson, Jared Carr, Jacob Parnell, Perry Hardin, Mark Jackson, and Stephen Houston. 2000. "Quantitative Phosphorus Measurement: A Field Test Procedure for Archaeological Site Analysis at Piedras Negras, Guatemala." *Geoarchaeology* 15:151–166.

Thaler, Richard. 2015. *Misbehaving: The Making of Behavioral Economics.* W. W. Norton, New York.

Thaler, Richard. 2016. "Behavioral Economics: Past, Present, and Future." *American Economic Review* 106:1577–1600.

Thompson, Eric. 1970. *Maya History and Religion.* University of Oklahoma Press, Norman.

Thompson, Eric. 1971. *Maya Hieroglyphic Writing: An Introduction.* University of Oklahoma Press, Norman.

Tozzer, Alfred. 1941. *Landa's relación de las cosas de Yucatan.* Papers of the Peabody Museum of American Archaeology and Ethnology 18. Harvard University, Cambridge, MA.

Tremain, Cara. 2014. "Pre-Columbian 'Jade': Towards an Improved Identification of Green-Colored Stone in Mesoamerica." *Lithic Technology* 39:137–150.

Trigger, Bruce. 1990. "Monumental Architecture: A Thermodynamic Explanation of Symbolic Behaviour." *World Archaeology* 22:119–132.

Turner, Billie Lee, and Peter Harrison. 1978. "Implications from Agriculture for Maya Prehistory." In *Pre-Hispanic Maya Agriculture*, ed. P. Harrison and B. L. Turner, 337–373. University of New Mexico Press, Albuquerque.

Umberger, Emily. 2002. "Imperial Inscriptions in the Aztec Landscape." In *Inscribed Landscapes: Marking and Making Place*, ed. D. Bruno and M. Wilson, 187–199. University of Hawaii Press, Honolulu.

Upham, Steadman. 1987. "A Theoretical Consideration of Middle Range Societies." In *Chiefdoms in the Americas*, ed. R. Drennan and C. Uribe, 345–367. University Press of America, Lanham, MD.

Urban, Patricia. 1986. "Precolumbian Settlement in the Naco Valley, Northwestern Honduras." In *The Southeast Maya Periphery*, ed. P. Urban and E. Schortman, 275–295. University of Texas Press, Austin.

Urban, Patricia. 1993a. "Central Santa Bárbara Region." In *Pottery of Prehistoric Honduras: Regional Classification and Analysis*, ed. J. Henderson and M. Beaudry-Corbett, 136–170. UCLA Institute of Archaeology, Los Angeles.

Urban, Patricia. 1993b. "Naco Valley." In *Pottery of Prehistoric Honduras: Regional Classification and Analysis*, ed. J. Henderson and M. Beaudry-Corbett, 30–63. UCLA Institute of Archaeology, Los Angeles.

Urban, Patricia. 1993c. "Southwestern Honduras." In *Pottery of Prehistoric Honduras: Regional Classification and Analysis*, ed. J. Henderson and M. Beaudry-Corbett, 172–179. UCLA Institute of Archaeology, Los Angeles.

Urban, Patricia, and Edward Schortman. 2013. "Monumentality, Territoriality, and Networks during the Middle Preclassic in Northwest Honduras." In *Territoriality in Archaeology*, ed. P. VanValkenburgh and J. Osborne, 87–106. AP3A 22, Wiley Periodicals, Malden, MA.

Urban, Patricia, Edward Schortman, and Marne Ausec. 2002. "Power without Bounds? Middle Preclassic Political Developments in the Naco Valley, Honduras." *Latin American Antiquity* 13:131–152.

Urban, Patricia, Aaron Shugar, Laura Richardson, Edward Schortman, and Scott Simmons. 2013. "The Production of Copper at El Coyote, Honduras: Processing, Dating, and Political Economy." In *Archaeometallurgy in Mesoamerica: Current Approaches and New Perspectives*, ed. A. Shugar and S. Simmons, 77–112. University Press of Colorado, Boulder.

Uribe Villegas, María Alicia, Marcos Martinón-Torres, and Juan Pablo Quintero Guzmán. 2021. "The Muisca Raft: Context, Materiality, and Technology." In *Pre-Columbian Central America, Colombia, and Ecuador: Toward an Integrated Approach*, ed. C. McEwan and J. Hoopes, 275–303. DORLC, Washington, DC.

Vaquero, Manuel, Francesca Romagnoli, Amèlia Bargalló, M. Gema Chacón, Bruno Gómez de Soler, Andrea Picin, and Eudald Carbonell. 2019. "Lithic Refitting and Intrasite Artifact Transport: A View from the Middle Paleolithic." *Archaeological and Anthropological Sciences* 11:4491–4513.

Viel, René. 1978. "Etude de la céramique Ulúa-Yojoa polychrome (Nord-ouest du Honduras), essai d'analyse stylistique du Babilonia." PhD dissertation, Université René Descartes, Paris.

Viel, René. 1983. "Evolución de la cerámica de Copán: Resultados preliminares." In *Introducción de la arqueología de Copán, Honduras*, ed. C. Baudez, 1:472–549. Secretaría de Cultura y Turismo, Tegucipalpa.

Vogt, Evon. 1965. "Zacateco 'Souls.'" *Man* 65:33–35.

Vogt, Evon. 1969. *Zinacantan: A Maya Community in the Highlands of Chiapas*. Harvard University Press, Cambridge, MA.

Vogt, Evon. 1998. "Zinacanteco Dedication and Termination Rituals." In *The Sowing and the Dawning: Termination, Dedication, and Transformation in the Archaeological and Ethnographic Record of Mesoamerica*, ed. S. Boteler Mock, 21–30. University of New Mexico Press, Albuquerque.

von Hagen, Wolfgang. 1943. *The Jicaque (Torrupan) Indians of Honduras*. Museum of the American Indian, Heye Foundation, New York.

Wallace, Anthony. 1956. "Revitalization Movements." *American Anthropologist* 58:264–281.

Walters, Gary. 1982. "The Pre-Columbian Jade Processing Industry of the Middle Motagua Valley of East-Central Guatemala." PhD dissertation, University of Missouri, Columbia.

Walters, Gary. 1989. "Un taller de jade en Guaytan, Guatemala." In *La obsidiana en Mesoamérica*, ed. M. Gaxiola and J. Clark, 253–262. Colección Científica 176. IHAH, Mexico City.

Watanabe, John. 2007. "Ritual and Political Economies." In *Mesoamerican Ritual Economy: Archaeological and Ethnological Perspectives*, ed. C. Wells and K. Davis-Salazar, 301–322. University Press of Colorado, Boulder.

Wauchope, Robert. 1948. *Excavations at Zacualpa, Guatemala*. MARI Publication 14. Tulane University, New Orleans.

Webster, David. 2002. *The Fall of the Ancient Maya*. Thames and Hudson, London.

Webster, Gary. 1990. "Labor Control and Emergent Stratification in Prehistoric Europe." *Current Anthropology* 31:337–366.

Weeks, John, Nancy Black, and Stuart Speaker. 1987. "From Prehistory to History in Western Honduras: The Care Lenca in the Colonial Province of Tencoa." In *Interaction on the Southeast Mesoamerican Frontier: Prehistoric and Historic Honduras and El Salvador*, ed. E. Robinson, 1:65–94. BAR, Oxford, England.

Wells, Christian. 2006. "Recent Trends in Theorizing Prehispanic Mesoamerican Economy." *Journal of Archaeological Research* 14:265–312.

Wells, Christian. 2007. "Faenas, Ferias, and Fiestas: Ritual Finance in Ancient and Modern Honduras." In *Mesoamerican Ritual Economy: Archaeological and Ethnological Perspectives*, ed. C. Wells and K. Davis-Salazar, 29–65. University Press of Colorado, Boulder.

Wells, Christian, and Karla Davis-Salazar. 2004. *Situational Sacredness: Temporary Ritual Space and Authority in Ancient and Modern Honduras*. Research Report Cuaderno 1. Latin American and Caribbean Studies, University of South Florida, Tampa.

Wells, Christian, and Karla Davis-Salazar. 2007. "Mesoamerican Ritual Economy: Materialization as Ritual and Economic Process." In *Mesoamerican Ritual Economy: Archaeological and Ethnological Perspectives*, ed. C. Wells and K. Davis-Salazar, 1–26. University Press of Colorado, Boulder.

Wells, Christian, and Karla Davis-Salazar. 2008. "Environmental Worldview and Ritual Economy among the Honduran Lenca." In *Dimensions of Ritual Economy*, ed. P. McAnany and C. Wells, 189–217. Research in Economic Anthropology 27. JAI Press, Bingley, UK.

Wells, Christian, and Ben Nelson. 2007. "Ritual Pilgrimage and Material Transfers in Prehispanic Northwest Mexico." In *Mesoamerican Ritual Economy: Archaeological and Ethnological Perspectives*, ed. C. Wells and K. Davis-Salazar, 137–165. University Press of Colorado, Boulder.

Wendrich, Willeke. 2012. *Archaeology and Apprenticeship: Body Knowledge, Identity, and Communities of Practice*. University of Arizona Press, Tucson.

Wenger, Etienne. 1998. *Communities of Practice: Learning, Meaning, and Identity*. Cambridge University Press, Cambridge.

Wenger, Etienne. 2011. *Communities of Practice: A Brief Introduction*. https://scholarsbank.uoregon.edu/xmlui/bitstream/handle/1794/11736/A%20brief%20introduction%20to%20CoP.pdf.

Widmer, Randolf. 2009. "Elite Household Multicrafting Specialization at 9N8, Patio H, Copan." In *Housework: Craft Production and Domestic Economy in Ancient Mesoamerica*, ed. K. Hirth, 174–204. AP3A 19, Wiley Periodicals, Malden, MA.

Williams, Howel, and Alexander McBirney. 1969. *Volcanic History of Honduras*. University of California Press, Berkeley.

Williams, Louis. 1981. "The Useful Plants of Central America." *Ceiba* 24:1–342.

Wolf, Eric. 1966. *Peasants*. Prentice-Hall, Englewood Cliffs, NJ.

Wonderley, Anthony. 1985. "Late Preclassic Occupation at Rio Pelo, Yoro, Honduras." Paper presented at the Tercer Seminario de Arqueología Hondureña. June 24–28, Tela, Honduras.

Wonderley, Anthony, and Pauline Caputi. 1984. "Archaeological Investigations at Rio Pelo (YR125), Sula Plain, Northwestern Honduras." Information prepared for IHAH, Tegucigalpa.

Yde, Jens. 1938. *An Archaeological Reconnaissance of Northwestern Honduras: A Report of the Work of the Tulane University–Danish National Museum Expedition to Central America 1935*. Levin and Munksgaard, Copenhagen.

Zavala, Silvio. 1984–1989. *El servicio personal de los indios en la Nueva España*. 4 volumes. El Colegio de Mexico, Mexico City.

Zorita, Alonso de. 1994. *Life and Labor in Ancient Mexico*. University of Oklahoma Press, Norman.

Uapala ceramic sphere, 263
Ulúa marble vassels, 45, 143, 190, 197, 275
Ulúa polychrome, 46, 49, 63, 84, 88–89, 246, 277
Ulúa valley, 25–26, 33–34, 39, 41, 46, 62, 90, 92, 143, 190, 204, 245–46, 263, 292, 296, 299
Usulután ceramics, 35–37, 46, 50, 77, 79, 246, 263, 265, 267, 291, 297

Vogt, Evon, 260, 276

Watanabe, John, 6
wattle-and-daub, 61, 67, 69, 98, 116, 119, 126
Wells, Christian, 9
West Residential Group. *See* Salitrón Viejo
Wolf, Eric, 8

Yarumela site, 4, 26, 28–29, 33, 35, 39, 41, 49, 51, 93, 95, 244–45, 296–97
    marble vessels at, 35
    public architecture, 28
    sculpted monuments, 33